Key

─────── Kingdom of Denmark

─ ─ ─ ─ Arab possessions

Kingdom of France

Byzantine possessions

Holy Roman Empire possessions

⊙ Monasteries

✚ Archbishoprics

✖ Rome–Pope
   Constantinople–Patriarch

✚ Kiev

Black Sea

Dyrrhachium

Constantinople

Thessaloniki • Nicaea

Kastoria • Caesarea

• Iconium

• Antioch

Beirut • Damascus

• Jerusalem

The Far-Farers

Also by Victoria Clark

WHY ANGELS FALL

THE FAR-FARERS

*A Journey from Viking Iceland
to Crusader Jerusalem*

VICTORIA CLARK

MACMILLAN

First published 2003 by Macmillan
an imprint of Pan Macmillan Ltd
Pan Macmillan, 20 New Wharf Road, London N1 9RR
Basingstoke and Oxford
Associated companies throughout the world
www.panmacmillan.com

ISBN 0 333 90219 X

A CIP catalogue record for this book is available from
the British Library.

Typeset by SetSystems Ltd, Saffron Walden, Essex
Printed and bound in Great Britain by
Mackays of Chatham plc, Chatham, Kent

For my dear twenty-first-century nephews, nieces and godchildren
  Anna, Gabriel, Ellie and Crispin Clark
  Francesca and Isabel Clark
  Hebe Field
  Mungo Russell
  Ella Mutler-Marculescu

CONTENTS

LIST OF ILLUSTRATIONS

ACKNOWLEDGEMENTS

My first and most heartfelt thanks go to all those I encountered along my way from Iceland to Jerusalem. Without their willingness to speak to me, and even invite me into their homes I would have had no book to write.

My debt to historians of the eleventh century – especially to Richard Southern, H. E. J. Cowdrey, Christopher Brooke and Sir Steven Runciman – is equally enormous. But any errors and misjudgements I have made are entirely my own.

Various people – David Willie and Judy Harris, Fares Kallas, Anna Maria Boura, Bruce Clark, Phil and Mandy Reeves, Nick Blandford, the Risi-Carellis – eased my progress between Iceland and Jerusalem with either practical assistance, vital contacts or timely hospitality. Andrew Sparke provided constant stern encouragement as well as a holiday. Dr Paolo Ferrante helped with Italian translation. My father, Noel Clark, was translating archaic German and Polish texts for me until serious illness landed him in hospital for six months. I am extremely grateful to Mr Mark Palazzo and dozens of nurses in Charing Cross Hospital's Intensive Care Unit for saving his life.

Other members of my family helped in various ways. Ben and Nicola Clark fetched and carried me from airports at antisocial hours. Ben put me in contact with Taizé. Nicola designed and painted the cover illustration. My mother, Marianne Clark, who shares my interest in medieval history, read each chapter as I wrote them.

ACKNOWLEDGEMENTS

My agent David Godwin maintained his high enthusiasm for the book throughout and Macmillan backed it generously, in the marked absence of a coherent proposal. A heartfelt thanks goes to my editor, Georgina Morley, to her assistant Stefanie Bierwerth and to Josine Meijer who hunted down the illustrations.

Europe in
the year 1099

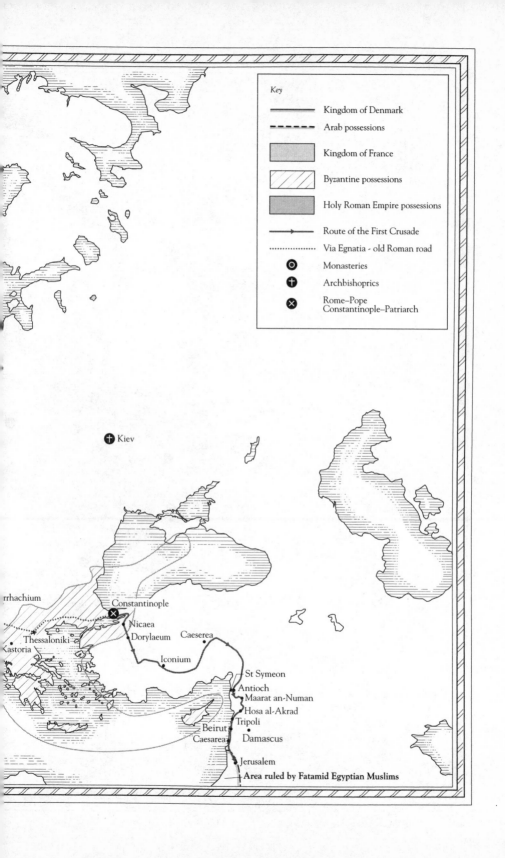

Key

Kingdom of Denmark

Arab possessions

Kingdom of France

Byzantine possessions

Holy Roman Empire possessions

Route of the First Crusade

Via Egnatia - old Roman road

Monasteries

Archbishoprics

Rome–Pope
Constantinople–Patriarch

Kiev

rrhachium

Constantinople

Nicaea

Dorylaeum   Caeserea

Thessaloniki

Kastoria

Iconium

St Symeon

Antioch
Maarat an-Numan

Hosa al-Akrad

Tripoli

Beirut

Caesarea   Damascus

Jerusalem

Area ruled by Fatamid Egyptian Muslims

Europe in
the year 1000

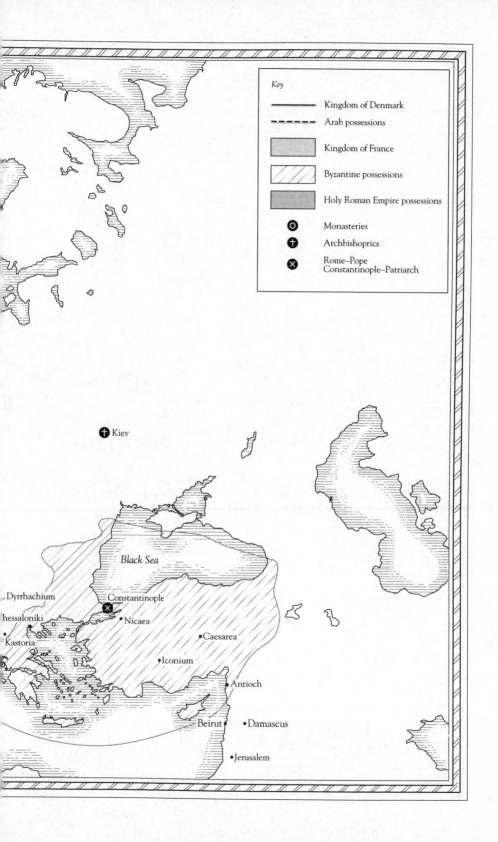

Key

Kingdom of Denmark

Arab possessions

Kingdom of France

Byzantine possessions

Holy Roman Empire possessions

⊙ Monasteries

✚ Archbishoprics

✖ Rome–Pope
Constantinople–Patriarch

✚ Kiev

Black Sea

Dyrrhachium

hessaloniki

Kastoria

✖ Constantinople

•Nicaea

•Caesarea

•Iconium

•Antioch

Beirut•

•Damascus

•Jerusalem

The author's journey in 2000–2001

PREFACE

Religion in the West was long ago privatized under the dual pressures of Protestantism and the Enlightenment. The separation of Church and State, achieved with much violence and hatred, has long been viewed as a necessary step in the forward march of human progress.

But the West is now embarking on its third millennium in a state of shock at discovering that for a very large part of the world religion remains a factor shaping the cultures and fates of nations, that there is no agreement that Church and State must be separated. Instead, there is much dismay, in the West as well as elsewhere, at where secularism has led us. After decades of favouring economic explanations above all others, Western historians, journalists and teachers are now having to accord religion the crucial attention it clearly demands.

I started writing this book about western Europe a thousand years ago in the hope and belief that if we in the West could recall a time in our own history when religion informed every corner of life we might be better positioned to understand the outlook of much of the rest of the world. The more closely I researched the eleventh century the clearer it seemed to me that Western Christendom underwent crucial changes during that hundred years. It might be argued that the ten hundreds laid the essential groundwork for the rest of the second millennium with its eventual removal of religion from its central place.

I discovered that the century had begun promisingly. A German emperor and a pope were peacefully co-operating in the task of building a federal Europe, united in the name of Christ. Halfway through the century the Roman Church launched a fundamentalist reform programme, designed to extend and expand the papal control over all Western Christendom, rulers as well as ruled. To achieve this ambitious end the Roman popes needed armies, and they got them. By the end of the century Pope Urban II was despatching the soldiery of Western Christendom to the East, to recapture the holy places from the Infidel. The Crusader states, first western colonies, were created. Growing intolerance of Eastern Byzantine Christianity, intense anti-Semitism, the growth of secularism in the West in reaction to the power of the Church, and the demonizing of Islam were all side effects of this ultimately doomed fundamentalist project.

The fallout from each of these phenomena is still with us today.

PART ONE

'a white mantle of churches'
980–1048

A world still unborn, or already long dead.

Under a wide blue sky, empty of anything but dazzling light, nothing moves. Neither human life nor time counts here.

A mind revolts and battles to find life where there is none. Iceland's black mountains, lined with snow, become worn and wrinkled skin, its ice-clogged streams fat-clogged arteries. Tussocky clumps of dead grass are bleached blond hair, a hillock an ear or a nose. Where is the human in this world? Without it, I am at sea. Improbable as the accelerated swirling of a satellite forecast, the weather is constantly changing now, from bright sunshine to fog in a valley, through a light snowfall on a mountain and on to lashing rain and wind or heavy sleet. My rented silver Volvo on this ribbon of black road is only virtually real.

I have to reach for the past and people to steady me.

A thousand years ago, the descendants of the dozen or so tax-dodging Norwegians who had sailed west to settle this inhospitable island in the 870s were doing the same. Through long winter nights on isolated farmsteads, during long sea voyages as far as North America, they spun their family histories into sagas. Driving through this unearthly landscape I am beginning to see those first histories of ordinary Icelanders and their ruinous wrangles over land and women as brave protests against this overpoweringly hostile natural world of theirs, as trusty weapons to wield against an existential terror.

I am embarked on this voyage from Iceland to Jerusalem to tell another saga, to register another protest and confront another terror – at sailing onward into the fearful unknown of a third millennium without any useful understanding of the second.

A suspicion that vital keys to our present lie buried in the first hundred years of the last millennium has been hardening into a firm conviction. Now, after months of immersion in eleventh-century history, I am satisfied that what happened to Western Christendom between the year 1000 and 1099 set the western world's course for the rest of that millennium. As I make my slow way down through Iceland and across the North Sea, down western Europe, across the Alps and the length of Italy, over the Adriatic and through the northern Balkans, across half of Turkey and on, down the eastern coast of the Mediterranean, I will follow the lead of medieval Iceland's storytellers. My saga, and the test of my thesis, will be about thoughts and deeds of people – eleventh and twenty-first-century people.

Just before the turn of the second millennium, an Icelandic Viking, the hero of a short saga called *Thorvald the Far-farer*, set off on the same journey from Iceland to the enlarged golden heart of all medieval world maps, Jerusalem. In this ocean of emptied land-scape I am about to begin, on the north-west coast of Iceland at the fjord-side farm of Stora Giljá, where Thorvald the Far-farer was born towards the end of the tenth century.

The younger son of the son of one of the first Norwegian settlers of Iceland, Thorvald had a miserable early childhood. Cinderella-like, he was sadly neglected in favour of his older brother until a local priestess called Thordis took pity on him and offered to take charge of his upbringing. The saga says that Thorvald's father, Kodran, offered the woman 'a fat purse full of silver'[i] to be rid of his younger son. Away from Stora Giljá, Thorvald thrived under Thordis's tutelage, growing into a strapping young Viking who sailed away to Denmark to seek his fortune in the early 980s. There he entered the service of the Danish king Swein Forkbeard, father of England's King Canute, and 'spent several summers raiding with him'.[ii] Although he was still a pagan, Thorvald's innate virtue –

presumably nurtured by the pagan priestess – was already evident, for all the 'booty he obtained by raiding he gave to the needy, and for the release of prisoners, and he helped many who were in distress.'[iii]

After some particularly heroic and self-sacrificing activities in Wales, King Swein was reportedly so entranced by his Icelander that, seated at dinner with a couple of fellow kings one night, he boasted, 'I can find you a foreign farmer's son who, in any true judgement, has in his own person no less dignity and nobility than we three kings together'. Ho, ho, they laughed in disbelief, and who might that be? 'The man I am speaking of,' he said, 'is as wise as a wise king ought to be, as strong and bold as the fiercest berserk, as well bred and well mannered as the noblest sage'[iv] – Thorvald.

Raiding was not our virtuous Viking's true vocation for next he 'took the true faith'. The announcement is abrupt and unexplained. What could have fired his fancy for Christ? From an Icelandic point of view the Christian doctrine of non-violence was thoroughly impractical. 'Love one another as I have loved you', 'love your enemies' and 'turn the other cheek' was what the Lord Jesus Christ, who had lived and lost his life far from Thorvald's often frozen but occasionally explosive home in the Atlantic Ocean, had commanded. The Icelanders' originally Germanic tribal code of honour, more akin to the Old Testament's 'an eye for an eye, a tooth for a tooth', functioned well. And, since there was no Icelandic monarch or aristocracy, only an admirably democratic meritocracy of *gothar* – chieftains who doubled as priests for as long as they merited the allegiance of their followers – the idea of the meek and lowly one day inheriting the earth can have had little meaning or appeal. Any Icelander had an even chance of inheriting the earth by his own efforts.

Somewhere on his travels had Thorvald been impressed by the peaceful haven of a well run monastery, or fallen in pious love with some saintly hermit? Travellers' tales of miracles in the shape of silenced frogs, banished snakes, healed cripples, enemies vanquished by saints who walked on water, visions of Christ himself, or angels or a cross, perhaps just the news of plagues, floods and famines averted by holy relics might have persuaded Thorvald to become a Christian. Perhaps the imminent completion of the first millennium since the birth of Christ impressed him. Perhaps he had heard that Constantinople, capital of the Byzantine Empire and the richest city in the known world, was Christian. But then he might also have heard tell of fabulous Moslem Cordova in southern Spain or Baghdad . . .

There is no knowing now. Whatever it was that won him over to the service of the supreme Lord Jesus Christ, Thorvald renounced his raiding ways and persuaded a German bishop called Frederick to return to Iceland with him on a mission to convert his people. Kodran, enchanted by his son now that Thorvald had won fame and approval as a doughty raider, welcomed him home to Giljà. And, 'without delay Thorvald began preaching God's message to his kinsmen and to all who came to see him',ᵛ for Bishop Frederick spoke not a word of Icelandic.

A little more than a thousand years later the old family seat at Stora Giljá stands alone in the shadow of a low black mountain rising on the right-hand side of the road. On the edge of a slight incline falling gently down towards the hummocky beige valley are some farm buildings, a hillock of hay rolls wrapped in white plastic and the river beyond, shining blueish silver in the afternoon sunlight. The homestead is no longer a turf-covered complex of outbuildings around a long, low feasting hall. A three-storey building of no great beauty with a single frail fir tree beside it, it has a withered wreath affixed to the front door and a line of shiny four-wheel-drive pick-ups in front of it. I parked behind the pick-ups and abandoned the cosy warmth of my Volvo for the freezing, lashing wind, to ring the farmhouse's doorbell.

Oddly, in a country where English is almost as readily spoken as Icelandic, the farmer spoke no more English than Bishop Frederick had spoken Icelandic. But, shivering in her T-shirt at the opened door, the farmer's pale young daughter-in-law knew a little. Inside the house, gazing intently behind my shoulder, she searched shyly for the words she needed to confess that she had never heard of Thorvald the Far-farer, let alone read his saga. Her eyes widened in wonder at the news that I had travelled all the way from England on account of this ancient nonentity. The farmer, a stocky taciturn sort with bleary blue eyes, admitted he had heard of Thorvald but had nothing to say about him. He was more comfortable with prosaic facts about his forty-kilometre-square sheep farm and the fact that the members of the local choir, whose vehicles were obstructing his driveway, had left by bus that morning for a rare engagement in Reykjavik. But at last he relented and took me outside again into the pitiless wind to point into the distance where he assured me I would find the new monument marking the spot where the Christian god had trumped and trounced Kodran's pagan one.

Kodran had resisted conversion to his son's new religion at first, but gradually he found himself more and more attracted to the candlelit confidence surrounding the worship of the Christian god and more and more suspicious of the way his own spiritual protector, whom he claimed lived in a 'large and imposing stone' not far from the farmstead, seemed to fear and shun any light at all. Before long Bishop Frederick judged the time right to see off the pagan opposition and Kodran agreed to a curious contest between the old and new faiths. Every day for three days the bishop conducted a forced baptism of the old god by deluging the stone and its lurking inhabitant in boiling water. On the third night, the saga says, the skulking old deity appeared to Kodran in a dream and launched a 'whining complaint with a snivelling voice'. He told Kodran that 'this evil deceiver, this bishop of the Christians, has deprived me of all my possessions. He has ruined my home, poured boiling water over me, soaked my clothes, wrecked and destroyed them entirely, and inflicted incurable burns on me and my household . . .'[vi]

As I trudged dutifully through that hummocky grass, head lowered against the whipping wind, in the direction indicated by the farmer, I knew I wanted nothing to do with new monuments. Aside from the land itself, the oldest things in Iceland are the sagas, not any building or monument. But I found the bare stone memorial the farmer had spoken of, took a photograph and trudged back to the Volvo. Driving off into the mid-afternoon sunshine, I resumed Thorvald's saga.

With Kodran safely converted, the unlikely pair of missionaries embarked on a testing four-year-long preaching tour of Iceland. Once, a couple of determinedly heathen Viking berserks both called Hauka challenged Bishop Frederick to walk barefoot the length of the fires burning in a line down the middle of a feasting hall. While the bishop was still making ready, donning his episcopal regalia and blessing the fires with sprinkled holy water, the Hauka brothers burst in, howling like wild animals, with drawn swords in their hands. As berserks, renowned for the way they approached conflict by working themselves into a terrifying frenzy, they were 'biting the rims of their shields' the saga says. Approaching the fires and Frederick too fast for safety, they tripped and plunged head first into the flames. This turn of events should have cancelled the horrendous challenge but there must have been others gathered in that feasting hall just as much in need of convincing about the power of the Christian god as the Hauka boys had been. Setting out to win them over, Bishop Frederick walked into the fires and the flames parted 'as though blown by the wind'. He emerged unscathed, none of his robes even slightly singed. A miracle – a *kraftawerk* – but not sufficient to ensure wholesale conversion of the Icelanders.

The pair were luckier in Thorvald's remote northern home region than in the more populated south-west of the island, but the going was generally hard. The Icelanders were not yet minded to give up on their favourite Viking gods – Thor, Odin and Freyr. Thorvald composed an angry little verse to commemorate his patchy progress and the stubborn hostility of a pagan priestess.

> I went with the precious word;
> no man listened to me;
> . . . From her heathen altar

> The old woman yelled
> senseless words at this poet;
> May God punish the witch![vii]

Opposition to their mission from the *gothar*, Iceland's chieftain priests, mounted as Thorvald's converts started defaulting on their temple taxes. Trouble was brewing.

A brief sprinkle of snow, so light that I mistook it for a pristine Nordic dust at first, fell from a clear sky. I drove on for miles in search of Haukagil, a ridge from which the corpses of the beastly berserk brothers had been hurled, and Laekjamot, which Thorvald and Bishop Frederick were said to have used as their base for a couple of years. Neither place was a village as the signposts to them seemed to suggest. Isolated and utterly unremarkable farmsteads made up of modern one-or two-storey white buildings with red roofs, they were surrounded by melting snow, untidy farm machinery, dead grass and hillocks of plastic-covered hay rolls. Glancing at the guidebook, I resisted an urge to drive on into the swiftly descending twilight and empty land, to a farmstead named after a certain Authun (Horse Penis), whose descendants include the British royal family.

Travelling back down south again the next day, buffeted by flurries of snow out of an iron-grey sky, the Tolkien landscape was neither awe-inspiring nor grand. At this uneasy time of the year, which Iceland's Nobel prize-winning novelist Halldór Laxness has identified as 'the uncertain season between hay and grass',[viii] it looked scruffy. But Thorvald and his bishop were travelling in June, when the grass would have been green again, the sun warm on their backs, the wide skies blue all day and white all night. I could easily imagine the young Viking and his spiritual father trussed up in leathers and coarsely woven cloaks at the head of a small entourage. I could picture them on a pair of the sturdy little Icelandic ponies I was seeing to left and right of the road. The bishop might have been clutching a cross, perhaps just ahead of a packhorse heavy laden with his episcopal paraphernalia. Maybe half of Thorvald, the

9

youthfully ardent and impatient half, would have yearned to gallop on ahead, but the other half would have wanted to show proper respect for the man of God. They would probably have opted for the moderate running walk peculiar to the *equus scandinavicus* – faster than a trot but not quite a canter.

The route south led over some very high ground where the snow still lay thick on the ground and there were a few Icelanders out to enjoy it that Sunday afternoon. Some had harnessed smart trailers mounted with gleaming snowmobiles to their four-wheel-drive jeeps. I passed long lines of them snaking along the high plateau and up and down the hills. From a distance, with their headlights glittering in the greyish twilight, those lines could easily have been medieval torch-lit processions. From time to time one of the vehicles would swerve off the road, its driver stop, climb out, unload his snowmobile, jump aboard and rev his engine, before roaring off alone at top speed across country.

Undeterred by ominous signs that their mission was failing, the pious young Viking and his friend were heading slowly south to a place situated a few miles to the east of modern Reykjavik known as Thingvellir. This was where the Icelanders of a thousand years ago used to hold their annual alfresco parliaments, their Althings, at which dozens of *gothar* would converge on Thingvellir from all quarters of the island each June to decide the island's business. If Thorvald could only win the hearts and souls of these people at the 986 Althing, he could consider his work for the Lord Jesus done.

Thingvellir, when I reached it, was deserted, its hotel and church locked up, off-season. Standing in the wet snow and wind a while, I watched three tourists toiling up a harsh cliff face towards a naked flagpole and struggled to imagine Thorvald and the bishop preaching to the unconverted members of the 986 Althing about the 'many true and wonderful signs of Almighty God'[ix] . The reception given them by the *gothar* had been frankly hostile. Thorvald and Frederick were stoned. Worse still – because it constituted a more violent assault on Thorvald's precious honour – two heathen poets composed a savage lampoon against them.

The bishop has borne
nine children
Thorvald is the father
of them all[x]

Their outlandish double act had excited suspicion. The bishop's lacy robes, his generally un-warlike demeanour and, presumably, his immunity to female charms had conspired to raise the Icelanders' eyebrows and signal homosexuality. This and the non-payment of temple taxes by converts to Christianity damaged the pair's cause irreparably. Iceland's conversion to Christianity would not happen for more than another decade, not until the year 1000.

Not long after his public pounding at the Althing Thorvald happened to chance upon the two authors of the scurrilous ditty. Rediscovering his Viking pride and anger, he seized his battleaxe or sword and despatched them with a few vicious blows. The saga tells us that Bishop Frederick meanwhile was some distance away calmly reading a book when he noticed a couple of drops of 'sword's-dew' – blood – on the page. The sign filled him with foreboding. When Thorvald returned the bishop said to him, ' "Either you have killed someone or else you have it in mind to do so . . ." ' Thorvald confessed that the deed was done. ' "I could not bear that they called us effeminate . . ." ' he said. Frederick must have shaken his head in sorrow before delivering his wittily word-playing little sermon. ' "Their lying to say that you had children was no great provocation," ' he said, ' "but you have put a worse gloss on their words. If you happened to have any children I could easily carry them. A Christian should not seek to avenge himself, however loathsomely he is maligned; he should sooner suffer reproach and offences for God's sake." '[xi] Christianity's trump card, that sweet and surprising doctrine of non-violence, was worth something in western Europe in the year 1000. It was to be terribly devalued over the following hundred years and rendered all but worthless by the century's end.

The members of the Althing punished Thorvald for his double

murder by outlawing him. Confined within the boundaries of his own lands he was powerless and friendless so he fled with the bishop to Norway. But it was not long before Frederick learned that his delinquent disciple had sinned again. Chancing upon one of his enemies chopping wood, Thorvald had murdered him. The bishop's patience was exhausted. Frederick berated Thorvald saying, ' "because of this killing we must part company, since you will be slow to give up slaying." '[xii] Packing his saddlebags he returned home to Germany. Thorvald, bereft of his spiritual father and filled at last with Christian remorse, calculated that as long as he was anywhere near his own country 'it was not certain that he would be able to tolerate the opposition and offences of his countrymen as he ought to for the sake of God.'[xiii] Thorvald had concluded that the Viking code of honour and Christianity's turn-the-other-cheek forgiveness were utterly incompatible.

The virtuous Viking vowed never to return to Iceland and set off south from Norway on a pilgrimage of penance – and presumably a marvellous adventure – all the way to Jerusalem and the holy places, earning himself the epithet, Far-farer. In Constantinople – Mikligarthr, as he would have called it – he was splendidly received by the Byzantine emperor of the day who, the saga tells us, 'gave him many excellent gifts of friendship, because God's grace was close about him.'[xiv]

~

Arni Bergmann chuckled into his Solzhenitsyn beard and his blue eyes twinkled merrily as he poured me a glass of lager.

'That's what Icelanders are like and you can see from that saga that we've never been any different. We're asked to believe that Thorvald was treated like visiting royalty by the Byzantine emperor for goodness' sake! There are only two hundred and ninety thousand of us in a country about the size of your England, but as soon as one of us goes abroad he is always received with great honour and rejoicing – red carpets, gold, elevated to a high and responsible position and so forth. He's a great hero back home, of course. You should have seen the fuss made just the other day when our downhill skiing champion managed to come thirty-second in the world championship. If an Icelandic footballer scores a goal, or even just helps someone else to score a goal, there is no end to our joy!'

I was in Reykjavik, in a flat with a shiny parquet floor, white-linen-upholstered pale pine furniture and a fine, wide view through wall-to-wall windows out towards the port and the grey sea. Arni is one of Iceland's best-known contemporary novelists. He is also a highly respected journalist and commentator, critic, lecturer in Russian at Reykjavik University and husband of the elegant Lena, who had fixed us a tasty dish of steamed salmon and boiled potatoes sprinkled with dill in her native Russian manner. She was now trying to stop Arni talking for long enough to eat some of it.

Arni had won some sort of fame and honour for his country abroad by being the first student from western Europe to be allowed to study Russian in the Soviet Union, in 1954. Hence Lena, and hence his interest in Thorvald the Far-farer who, another saga ludicrously claims, ended up governing Russia for the Byzantine emperor.

We were only meeting like this thanks to his country's miserable early spring weather. Wandering out into the sleet and wind on my first evening in Iceland, I had soon sought refuge in Reykjavik's biggest bookshop, where I had asked an assistant for help with finding something in English. The assistant and I had then fallen into conversation and soon I was explaining my presence in Iceland and my particular interest in Thorvald the Far-farer.

'Oh, but there's a new historical novel of that title – very good I've heard,' she had informed me, and immediately located a copy of Arni's book on a long top shelf filled with novels in Icelandic. 'You could meet him; his daughter works here – you see that woman with blonde hair sitting with her back to us?'

I went and introduced myself to her and, the next day, had called her father at the hour she suggested to arrange a meeting. 'How will I recognize you?' I had asked him. 'I wear a beret because my head is bald. I have a beard but no moustache. If you see a fool such as that looking around you will know it is I,' he answered. We had met in the bookshop's upstairs café and talked. 'When you return from Stora Giljå you must come and have dinner with my wife and me,' he had said.

Now that the dinner plates were cleared off the blue check tablecloth and coffee and cakes on the way I wanted to know how Arni had come to write his novel about Thorvald's adventures in exile.

'Well, you know,' he began shyly, twisting his beer glass to left and right, 'I liked this Thorvald because he was just an individual. Apparently no one ordered him on his Christian mission and it seems to me that after he left Iceland he set out on a real spiritual quest to find out how to become a true Christian, like people go alone now to find themselves, so to speak, outside the rigid institutions of the churches.'

'He ended up as a monk, didn't he – after going through Germany, perhaps into Poland and then down the great Russian rivers all the way to the Black Sea and Constantinople and then Jerusalem?'

'Perhaps, even probably, but I have him all over the place – you know how they travelled in those times – as a hermit in Bosnia at one point beset by medieval demons; with Bishop Frederick of course, whom I present as a homosexual; in a castle in Germany; fighting many battles everywhere in the Varangian Guard – you know, those elite Scandinavian mercenaries of the Byzantine emperors. At one point he's carousing in a merchant's home in Kiev. Kievan Rus, effectively Russia, had just converted to Christianity of course in 988. Anyway, that's where he meets a merchant's wife whom he learns to love very well with a pure Christian love. In Kiev with her he becomes a sort of spiritual father to crowds of people who come to consult him—'

'Your Thorvald doesn't go on a pilgrimage to Jerusalem then?'

'No, no! It's a historical novel, after all.'

Arni had not set out to unearth any definitive historical truth.

Like me, he had been mining the dawning eleventh century for parallels with this dawning twenty-first. He had sent his hero out into a brightening world blessed with a single rich Christian tradition, before the widening crack between the twin centres of Rome and Constantinople turned into a division, before the First Crusade turned that division into a schism which hardened into the most durable fault line in Europe.

'You know,' he told me, rid of his writerly reticence now and enjoying the chance to talk about his work, while Lena poured coffee and piled our plates with slices of three different kinds of cake, 'I think it very possible that the first kind of Christianity that ever came to Iceland – even before Thorvald and that Saxon German bishop arrived – came from the east, Constantinople rather than Rome, brought home by the Viking traders who used the route down the Russian rivers from the Baltic Sea to the Black Sea to reach Constantinople. At one stage in the story I have Thorvald sitting in on one of the great Church councils which was trying to solve the differences between Rome and Constantinople in the early ten hundreds. I have him – a mere nobody of an Icelander, you see – come up with the ideal solution to one of the thorniest doctrinal problems of the day, the *Filioque*, which was all about whether the Holy Spirit proceeds from God the Father and the Son or just from God the Father. Naturally, because he's an Icelander, nobody pays a blind bit of attention to the ingenious compromise he dreams up: all about how an apple is able to "proceed" at the same time from both a tree and a branch. I wanted my Icelandic readers to laugh at the ridiculous notion that one of their countrymen almost prevented the schism between Eastern and Western Christianity, and so might even have helped to prevent the murderous religious nationalism we are seeing in the Balkans these days.'*

At the mention of Balkan conflict we were back in the present. 'This has been rather traumatic for us. When NATO forces

* The south-eastern border between Eastern and Western Christianity, between the Catholic Croats and Orthodox Serbs, runs through former Yugoslavia.

intervened in Kosovo last year, Iceland found itself at war for the very first time in its history. We didn't like it much. We are used to fighting ice and fire, not people.'

The Icelanders' love of their island independence runs deep. I wondered if it extended to a distrust of European unity.

'I confess,' said Arni, sipping pensively at his black coffee, 'that I am against Iceland joining the European Union, but as a nation we are more or less evenly split on the subject. Younger people think there is money to be squeezed out of Brussels for research and so forth, but older people worry about having to surrender the fishing rights we gained and which have made us so prosperous since we won our Cod War with you British in the 1970s. My own objections to joining the EU are less material; I'm a nationalist for aesthetic reasons. This global village could be bloody boring, couldn't it?' he said, with one of his chuckles. 'I'm against homogenization. It's better *dlya dushi* – for the soul, as the Russians would say – to be a little eccentric.'

~

Fleeing the wind and the rain as usual, I slid into a back pew of Reykjavik's early twentieth-century Roman Catholic cathedral the following Sunday morning. The place was almost full but there was nothing there to feast the eye on. It would have taken a soul more accustomed than mine to the austere simplicity of Protestant churches to appreciate the plain squares of pale yellow, blue and pink stained glass in those high windows and the spare elegance of a pulpit draped in Lenten purple. The service began, in Icelandic of course, and soon my mind was wandering, wondering if those turn of the first millennium Icelanders had feared a similar homogenization with the coming of Christianity.

Thorvald's two-man mission to convert his fellow countrymen had failed, but by the very late 990s the Icelanders had little choice in the matter of their conversion. If they did not jettison their old gods they could be sure that the king of Norway, an ardent new convert to Christianity, would kill the handful of Icelanders he was holding hostage in a dungeon and send an army to impose his will. Invasion by Norwegians not global homogenization was what they had feared back then. King Olaf's patience with Iceland was exhausted. Apostle Thorvald had been followed by Olaf's emmissary, Stefnir Thorgilsson, but Stefnir had soon got himself outlawed like Thorvald and his ship foundered in a storm, a sign which only reinforced the Icelanders' allegiance to their old gods. The Norwegian king's next Christian missionary to Iceland was a thieving thug, a man tough enough to withstand any Icelandic insults physical or verbal, but even he retired defeated after a couple of years, having slaughtered another couple of those composers of verses for slandering him and having seen his horse swallowed up by a sudden hole in the ground. He had reported back to King Olaf that the Icelanders were beyond help, hopelessly heathen stubborn sorcerers.

As late as 999 Iceland's Christian minority was still being persecuted. One Christian was outlawed for composing the following pithy poison about the Icelanders' fertility god.

> I do not wish to blaspheme the gods
> But I think Freya is a bitch[xv]

Just before the midsummer Althing of the year 1000 the pagans and Christians – the Christian faction led by two Icelanders who had just arrived from Norway having been allowed by the king one last chance to convert their compatriots – ranged themselves for battle near Thingvellir and declared themselves out of law with each other. Without consensus on the validity of a single code of law the situation was pregnant with disaster. Iceland was divided against itself and civil war imminent. It fell to the lawspeaker, the island's top judge, whose job included learning by heart a third of Iceland's unwritten legal code for recital at every Althing, to find a solution. Fortunately, the lawspeaker was the right man for such a delicate task. Although a pagan *gothi*, he hailed from a farmstead in Thorvald's native northern quarter of the island, the stronghold of Iceland's small Christian community at the time, and so had strong ties to the Christian faction. Furthermore, he had held his post for fifteen years. He was wise, highly practised in the art of conflict resolution and quite possibly endowed with the gift of *skyggni* – second sight.

He rose to the extraordinary challenge by announcing to the anxious assembled chieftains that he did not want to be disturbed for twenty-four hours while he retired to his tent and bundled himself from head to toe in his cloak. This was not an Icelandic version of burying one's head in the sand. A modern Icelandic historian, Jón Hnefill Athalsteinsson, has made a useful study of the meaning and origins of the custom. First he writes, one has to appreciate that a medieval man's woollen cloak, almost as much as his sword or his battleaxe, was an extremely valuable and therefore lucky article of clothing. Second, a knowledgeable student of northern European folklore would be familiar with the phrase '*þylja i feld sinn*', meaning to murmur or mutter into one's cloak, because Icelandic, Lapp, shaman and druid lore contains instances of this activity. Muttering into one's cloak, in a darkness and solitude akin to death, was a recognized way of removing oneself into another world, a trusted aid to soothsaying and inspiration.

The lawspeaker completed his retreat and emerged to tell his expectant people: ' "We should not allow those to prevail who are eager for conflict, but we should seek a middle course that would allow both sides to have something of their case, and we should all have one law and one faith, because if we sunder the law, we shall also sunder the peace." '[xvi]

Both sides – pagans and Christians – forthwith agreed to accept any law their wise lawspeaker chose to impose on them. He chose Christianity but his tactful compromises met with general approval. Everyone was to be baptised forthwith but the eating of horse meat, a feature of pagan rituals of that era, and the exposure of unwanted infants were not forbidden. Opposition thereafter was confined to petty matters such as whether a mass baptism should be performed in the icy River Oxara or in some more appealing hot springs, and to the real significance of a volcano's sudden eruption. A *gothi* whose farmstead it was endangering grumbled, ' "It's not surprising that the gods are angry at all this blasphemous talk." ' Another sensibly retorted, ' "And at what were the gods angry when all the lava on which we are now standing burned?" '[xvii] There was nothing impassioned about Iceland's decision to follow Christ.

Jesus became the Icelanders' perfect and mighty Viking, the 'faultless lord of monks', 'Rome's mighty king' and the 'mighty Christ who created the whole world and built the hall of Rome'.[xviii] A nicely material notion, that a *gothi* was guaranteed places in heaven for as many of his followers who could stand in a church he had built, gained currency. Many of the *gothar* turned themselves into priests of the new religion. The infant Icelandic Church was entrusted to the care of the powerful north German archdiocese of Hamburg-Bremen in the 1050s, but if one German monk's understanding of the country is anything to go by, the archbishop can have exerted little control over his distant new domain.

> On this island the ice of the sea catches fire the moment it is broken up and, when it has taken fire, blazes like wood. Here also are good Christians, but on account of the excessive cold they dare not leave their underground hollows in the wintertime. For if they go out, they are burned by the cold, which is so extreme that like lepers they lose their colour as the swelling gradually spreads. Also, if they happen to wipe their noses, the whole nose pulls off with the mucous itself and, having come off, they throw it away.[xix]

By the time Norway annexed Iceland at the end of the thirteenth century, the church was stronger, indeed so strong that the island's old and efficient democracy had broken down. The *gothar* turned priests had gradually begun making their lands over to the Church as was common elsewhere in Europe. By the sixteenth-century Protestant Reformation Iceland had been transferred to Danish rule. Like Denmark, Iceland turned Lutheran.

Hence the rareness and bareness of this Catholic church I was loitering in. Unable to follow a word of the sermon, a little bored and aware that I had strayed far from the Icelandic cultural mainstream, I was just deciding to swaddle myself in my scarf and anorak again and venture back out into the wind, when a single voice sang out, 'Credo in unum Deum.' 'Patrem omnipotentem,' affirmed the rest of the choir. Up and down the scale of plainchant went the fourth-century declaration of Christian faith in Latin, clear and firm; up a whole run of notes to describe how Jesus Christ 'ascendit in caelum' in triumph, and then down again to leave him seated safely to the right of his father. On and on, up and down, past the thorny matter of the Holy Spirit's procession from both God the Father and Jesus Christ, and on to the tiny dramatic pause before my favourite phrase, 'Et unam sanctam catholicam et apostolicam ecclesiam', with each rhyming Latin word-ending accented to stress the rock-solid unchanging character of the Christian God's 'one holy catholic and apostolic Church'.

How sad that by the end of the eleventh century there was no longer one great holy catholic and apostolic church. There were two: the Latin and the Greek halves of the old whole, Rome and Constantinople, drifting further and further apart. With the sixteenth-century Reformation, the western Latin half would divide again. One of the two would become two more, and then three, and more, and more.

It was odd to be so preoccupied with religion again. I had spent the previous couple of years meeting and speaking to Orthodox Christian monks in monasteries located in places as distant from each other as Siberia, Kosovo and Cyprus. But here I was wading in deeper still, contemplating months, years, of immersion in a period of Western history entirely governed by the Christian faith. In a long-lapsed Catholic, such a fixation with religion was surely unseemly, embarrassing even. At the very least it betrayed a pining for the high holy drama of the quest for eternal salvation. But there was nothing for it. If the eleventh century was all important to the second millennium and my quest to understand the present, then religion was a *sine qua non* for comprehending the eleventh century.

I had to imagine myself back in a world in which churchmen – especially Western Christian ones – controlled all the means of communication via their virtual monopoly on reading and writing. The exercise of the law was in their hands too, theirs the sole right to judge and sentence miscreants. The entertainments industry of the time equally belonged to them. Church processions, festivals and services – blazing with candlelight, gold and precious stones, rich in pathos and magic – provided the only glamour in a still dark and dirty world. Finally, via its control of the sacraments of baptism, confession, holy communion and the last rites, the Church enjoyed a monopoly over the Christian world's most valuable commodity which was not oil, land, microchips, futures or even gold, but salvation. At the start of the second millennium the Church of Rome lacked only armies to command and it would have even those by the end of the eleventh century.

Perhaps Thorvald had been seduced by the spectacle of all this power when he took the True Faith to his own heart and then to Iceland. Could simple love for a brokenly crucified man who – a thousand years earlier, in a parched place thousands of miles to the south – advanced a claim to be the son of God have been the only cause of Thorvald's conversion to Christianity? For lack of the faith my imagination was failing me . . .

~

Blinking, flickering, whirring deep inside its mysterious interior, Solveig Olafsdóttir's computer was working its dark magic. A bright-eyed, cheerful woman of about my own age, the friend of a friend, I had contacted her at her workplace, DeCode, on my second morning in Reykjavik. She had immediately suggested I pay her a visit there.

DeCode has positioned itself at the super-modern cutting edge of the millennial boom in genetic research, competing with the world's biggest pharmaceutical companies in the race to build a heaven on Earth by using genomics to conquer death and disease. Solveig's Herculean task, to trace the antecedents and descendants and medical history of every single Icelander who ever lived and then feed all the information into her computer, is only a small part of the company's activities; DeCode's scientists do the bulk of the work. Icelanders' traditional preoccupation with their origins and family trees and the fact that the small national gene pool makes their DNA codes relatively simple to read, are of great help to scientists trying to isolate the genes responsible for disease. Thousands of Icelanders have donated samples of their DNA to the company but about as many are anxious about the sinister uses – cloning, eugenics, insurance-weighting – the information could be put to. It struck me that the Christian Thorvald the Far-farer would have been a loud dissenting voice. I could imagine the virtuous Viking's pale eyes lighting up with anger and his hands reaching for his double-bladed axe as he demanded to know how these people dared to dream they might improve on the arrangements of the greatest Lord Jesus Christ, who sat in the golden feasting hall of his heaven, seeing all, knowing all.

Thorvald was on Solveig's mind too, as she gazed at a screen filling up with dots and curves.

'OK, here we are. Let's see now. Your Thorvald didn't have any children – at least not here in Iceland – but his brother had a couple of wives and two daughters, which means that almost everyone today is related to them. See here; it says there are twenty-nine generations between me and Thorvald's brother.'

Only twenty-nine people separate Solveig from the early eleventh century! I felt a sudden surge of confidence that it would not be so difficult to visit that distant world. The oddly temporary aspect of most of Reykjavik's buildings, with their pretty yellow, blue, rust-red and green painted iron roofs, the atmosphere of a prosperity suddenly built on cod fishing, of new wealth immediately invested in shiny four-wheel-drive cars, and the similarly provisional look of a landscape that was still being formed and rearranged by seismic shiftings, volcanoes and glaciers was already narrowing the yawning gap between the Europe I was trying to recall and the one I was living in. But this discovery of Solveig's seemed miraculous, and she glowed pink with pride at my surprise.

'Now, who else did you want to know about? Arni Bergmann? Wait a minute. Yes . . . Arni Bergmann and I are related to each other five generations back through our mothers.'

Everyone knows almost everyone in a country as sparsely inhabited as Iceland. Solveig knows more than most. Arni was her much respected schoolteacher for a time and she likes Lena very much. By an extraordinary coincidence she even knew the present owners of Thorvald's farm at Stora Giljá, the taciturn farmer and his son. She remembered that when she met him the farmer had just turned fifty, 'He seemed to be speaking in rhymes. I think he'd been drunk for weeks, both before and after his birthday. Probably he still had a hangover when you met him twenty years later!' She laughed, rocking back in her swivel chair and knocking over a stack of books.

Solveig's work station was crazily fenced about with sets of beautifully bound volumes containing photographs and short biographies of everyone who has ever been a doctor in Iceland, for example. A gilt-lettered set lists all the blacksmiths, another calf-bound series details all the pilots, or teachers, or builders. These books – economically viable for the publishers, she assured me, because everyone is guaranteed to buy the volume in which they feature – and the sagas, some censuses and the chronicles contain the data she feeds her computer. If she is lucky, she can supplement its diet from the photocopied booklets filled with photographs, family trees and dates which Icelanders lovingly compile to mark their family reunions.

'I never know what I'm going to find,' Solveig told me. 'The other day I discovered that my parents were related to each other a mere five generations back, as well as to the priest who married them!'

In the next-door office, which we passed on our way out, the rest of the department's staff were busy cooing over a new-born baby boy. 'The latest addition to my database!' said Solveig with a merry laugh.

~

While strolling aimlessly down Reykjavik's main shopping street that sleety afternoon, I saw a signpost to what I thought was the Icelandic Philatelogical Museum. On a second reading, I turned off down a little alleyway into a courtyard in search of the Icelandic Phallological Museum. Inside, beautifully presented in formaldehyde-filled glass cylinders of varying lengths, or flattened and tanned, salted, hollowed out and impressively mounted on carved wooden plaques, was the finest, fullest collection of animal penises the world has seen. Sixteen different species of whales' pizzles, six varieties of seal phalluses and the penises of every mammal ranging from polar bear and goat to mink and mouse had all found their home in what I had no trouble recognizing as a modern shrine to one of the Vikings' favourite pagan gods, Freyr. Lord of sunshine and rain, of birth and death, of the peaceful and pleasant propagation of plants, animals and men, Freyr with his outsize penis came second only to the hammer-wielding Thor in the affections of pre-Christian Icelanders. Beloved of the Swedish Vikings too, his cult was a fine excuse for the orgies of sex and sacrifice which so disgusted the German archbishops of Hamburg and Bremen on their rare visits to Scandinavia.

The shrine's only visitor at that late hour of the day, I had the undivided attention of its latter-day *gothi*, a rotund silver-bearded man with a square face and a ready smile who turned out to be Solveig's former history teacher. Sigurthur Hjartarson was very anxious that I inspect his prize exhibit, a fancy framed document pledging the post-mortem donation to the museum of one human *penis et scrotum*.

'And here, have a look at this,' he continued. 'It's a sperm whale's penis skin, the only part of the animal soft enough to use as leather. You could make a lovely bow tie out of that! Now, you see the lampshades in here? They're all made from bull scrota. I scrape the fat from the inside but I don't like to shave them because the hair pattern is very pretty. I wash them, of course, and then – using a balloon and a hand pump – I leave them to dry into shape. Very effective, don't you think?'

Uncomfortably reminded of Nazis fashioning lampshades from human skin, I could not help laughing but told him I had never seen anything less attractive. He grinned happily and continued the tour.

'Now, over here is my folkloric section. That's a petrified troll's penis. That's a merman's.'

'Marvellous!' I murmured appreciatively, peering closely at a tiny phial containing nothing I could identify.

Up at the desk, whose lamp stand, cash box, ashtray, telephone, kitchen-roll holder, visiting-card box and pen were all carved wooden phalluses, we fell into conversation.

'There are people who think I'm a crazy pervert, but I'm incredibly normal,' he told me. 'I was teaching at the same school for thirty years, but you know how badly paid teachers are and I had to start thinking about my pension. I've been building this collection for years. Recently, I tried to squeeze a business start-up grant out of the Althing for the museum but no luck. Everything today is money, money, money . . .' He sighed.

We talked about his far-faring days, in Scotland, Sweden and Mexico. I found that I liked him and his passion for penises. Not so much Arni Bergmann, but he and Solveig reminded me of the Irish. There was something quick and merry, a little sly but lively about many of these Icelanders, whose country is so dark for most of the year that they are forced to spend long hours inside writing books – one in ten Icelanders is an author – or collecting penises, or sitting in their tiny capital's cosily candlelit cafés, talking and smoking and laughing.

With Arni Bergmann's kind assistance I made the acquaintance of Jörmündur Ingi Hansen, who is Iceland's leading latter-day *gothi**. We met at the elegant Café de Paris, a stone's throw from the modern Althing building which is a nineteenth-century grey stone edifice the size of a country railway station.

'You'll recognize me by my curling moustaches. Anyway, everyone knows me in there; I practically live at the Café de Paris,' he had assured me on the telephone.

Seated at a large round table near the window, his moustaches at least as luxuriantly curling as he had promised, I had no trouble spotting him with his pagan-looking medallion nestling between his blue striped shirt and tie. His table companions were a foxy young man with a straggling red beard who turned out to be a genius at deciphering old black magic spells written in illegible handwriting, and a plump, middle-aged Lutheran priest. The latter happened to know more about eleventh-century Church history than anyone else I had come across in Iceland.

'Please don't be offended by this question,' I began, 'but what is a Lutheran priest doing sitting down to drink coffee with a pagan *gothi*? Or a *gothi* doing in the company of an expert on black magic. Even the pagans outlawed black magic, didn't they?'

'Ho, ho, ho,' they laughed.

'The first thing you need to understand,' began the ponderous Lutheran minister, removing his glasses and swinging them by one of their arms, 'is that all the schisms between pagans and Christians, between Eastern Orthodox and Roman Catholic, between Roman Catholics and Lutherans, never found their way here—'

'Actually, the most important thing to know is that we were never really christened at all; we just accepted one law in the year 1000, that's all,' interrupted the foxy young man.

'That's it,' confirmed the *gothi*, whose title, he told me, translates as Lord of Hosts. 'Christianity never put down proper roots here. People simply came to an agreement in the year 1000. The old

---

* Ingi Hansen had been elected *gothi* by fellow devotees of pagan religion. A rough equivalent would be a Druid society in the UK.

Icelandic texts don't say anything about a conversion. It was a classic Icelandic compromise of the sort we had been skilled at forging for a century or more. Actually, our entire legal system was based on compromise so that the main work of a law court in those times was to get both parties to consent to the verdict. There was no idea of winning or losing a case. In the year 1000, thanks to the lawspeaker's wise judgement, people just agreed to accept the Christian god but to keep the old rules, which were basically excellent. We had our pagan version of the Christian rule, "Do as you would be done by." Ours was, "Do to others as they do to you", which worked much better. Christians are too forgiving, too much of a soft touch. After all, how can you bring up a child properly if you go around forgiving everything they do wrong?'

'True, true . . .' I could not help nodding my understanding of such an ancient and clear-sighted acceptance of the brutal reality about human nature while the elderly man continued in his excellent English.

'The church chronicles all boast that Iceland experienced one hundred and fifty years of peace after the arrival of Christianity. Of course they don't mention that we had already managed a hundred and fifty years of peace under paganism!' The *gothi's* oddly expressionless blue eyes gazed out across the square towards the Althing, deep into a lost Viking distance.

'And that's not all the Catholic Church chronicles have been dishonest about,' weighed in the Lutheran, removing his spectacles to swing them again. 'The Catholic Church and our Lutheran one too have always claimed that Iceland received Christianity from Rome via Germany. But there are all sorts of reasons to believe that it first reached us from Byzantine Constantinople, via the Russian Varangian route—'

'What are those reasons?' I asked eagerly, remembering Arni Bergmann's conjectures about Christianity having reached pre-Thorvald Iceland that way.

'Did you know, for example, that until the early twentieth

century Icelanders used to make the sign of the cross in the Eastern Christian manner – left shoulder to right shoulder – instead of right shoulder to left? That's one important proof.'

I had not known that, nor had I known that the three mysterious 'Armenian bishops', who crop up in a saga or two at the time when the tension between Rome and Constantinople was coming to a head in the mid-eleventh century, were probably missionaries from Byzantium intent on preventing the Icelanders from falling decisively under the Roman yoke. The Althing had scotched their activities by voting to forbid any mission unauthorized by the Roman Church.

The *gothi* was bored by all the churchy talk. He liked expounding his theories on old pagan law and about how one can find strong traces of that superior Icelandic tradition in the way the Mafia operates in southern Italy and Sicily today.

'The Mafia is a Nordic institution and what is so surprising about that,' he asked me, with a puff on his cigar, ' when you think that Vikings, or Normans as you call them, were running everything in that part of the world back in the eleventh and twelfth centuries? Take the old system of the Sicilian Mafia and compare it with the Icelandic Commonwealth and you'll see that it works in exactly the same way. Down there I would be called the *capo di tutti capi*, like a Mafia boss, wouldn't I? Ho, ho!'

We had lingered for three hours over our coffees and it seemed to me suddenly, as I emerged from the café into Althing square, that I had loitered long enough among the Icelanders. I noticed some young ones lolling in the sunshine, stripped down to T-shirts and sunglasses.

At last, a pale spring sun was shining and I was ready to be away far-faring down south.

~

Under a night sky alight with stars, with the snow-topped mountains glowing white behind her, the *Bruarfoss* was a glamorous sea god –

the equal of any medieval Icelanders' *knörr* or modern cruise liner. Lights, like loosely strung pearls, adorned each of her white tower's seven decks. The crashing music of her loading and fuelling filled the otherwise empty port.

Thorvald the Far-farer might have been dismayed at having to leave his homeland in disgrace but if I could feel excited anticipation at the prospect of departing by ship in spite of learning that there had been savage storms off Iceland's south-east coast for the past fortnight, then surely so could he. I wondered if he had reckoned on seeing out the rest of his days in Norway or just on serving his statutory five years as an outlaw before returning home to Stora Giljá. He might already have been hatching his grander scheme. After stealing two lives from his great Lord in heaven, his soul was gravely sick and in need of saving. Only a pilgrimage to Jerusalem, to that centre of the known world where his Lord God had lived and died, could expunge the stain of sin on his conscience. He might have been planning to winter in Norway before setting off again south. Whatever his intentions on leaving Iceland, his killing of a third enemy in that Norwegian wood and subsequent abandonment by Bishop Frederick can only have strengthened the case for a pilgrimage.

I stood on deck watching the preparations and keeping an eye on the gangway, curious to see who my fellow passengers would be. At last the steps were raised and my suspicions confirmed. There would be no other passengers. For the next four days I would be sailing the stormy North Sea with fourteen Icelandic sailors and a friendly cleaning woman called Julia.

'You don't want to eat all alone in the passengers' dining room, do you? I mean, what's the point?' said Julia, as she showed me to my brown Formica-lined, strip-lit cabin on the fifth deck. 'You might as well mess with the sailors. You don't mind? Breakfast at eight, lunch at twelve, dinner at six.'

'Fine,' I told her. And it was, because she and the ship's engineer made it their business to see that I was never bored or lonely. From the very first morning they were my friends on that Polish-built vessel with its dismal lighting and few concessions to comfort. While the others crowded into meals, helped themselves to whatever unappetizing food the cook had produced, ate in silence and then returned to their duties, Julia and Ingi were usually on hand for a chat and a joke.

'How did you sleep?' asked Julia that first morning.

'Not too well,' I admitted. 'There was a bit of a storm, wasn't there?'

I had spent the night in an agony of terror that the ship was about to capsize and send me, everyone else and the cargo to the kind of deep watery grave I had always feared more than any other. The ghastly, gorge-heaving, stomach-churning sensation was something like appalling flight turbulence magnified a hundredfold and foully unrelenting. Wakeful in the small dark hours I knew – like the Vikings knew – that only a strong but stupid bully of a sea being like the giant worm Mithgarthsomur could have exerted himself to create all that pointless disturbance. As the ship rocked and bucked its way through a breaking grey dawn I yearned for dry land and sunshine. Shaken and horribly nauseous I was astonished that none of the sailors mentioned the storm over their full English breakfasts the next morning.

'You think there was a storm?' asked Julia. 'I don't think so. Wait, I'll ask. Ingi, did we have a storm last night?'

'No. In fact you're lucky with the weather,' said the engineer, languidly helping himself to another coffee from the machine. 'The last few trips have been terrible. After twenty-five years of this work, even I was seasick. Any passenger who sails with us in the middle of winter has to be a masochist, but now the spring is starting . . .'

'I thought I was a masochist last night,' I admitted sheepishly.

'That little massage?' He laughed at me.

The weather improved. I spent hours on the bridge of the ship, warmed by a shy spring sun, whipped by a stiff sea breeze. The view seven decks below me, extending ahead for the length of a short London street, was motionless but mesmerizing: a brightly coloured patchwork of metal containers filled with fresh fish and anything else that needed transporting between Iceland, Hamburg and a string of Scandinavian ports. Above it all towered two butter-yellow cranes. From time to time a sailor, toy-like and tiny in his blue overalls and yellow hard hat, appeared for a breath of fresh air, his white coffee cup a tiny dot moving between the railing and his hat.

Arni Bergmann had recounted how Icelandic sailors had honed and preserved their saga-telling skills during centuries of sailing these waters, how those tales of their proud origins and brave deeds had comforted them during their long perilous sea voyages. 'But I don't suppose you'll find any sailors telling stories these days,' he had warned. 'I suppose they'll all be watching dirty videos. There's no sense of adventure any more, no more dicing with death and the gods!'

A thousand years ago Iceland led the world in sea adventuring – in navigating by the sun, the currents, the winds and the stars to seek out the wherewithal to survive on their dangerously explosive and barely inhabitable stronghold in the middle of the ocean. Supplies of timber, metals, flour, wine, honey and linen were all a sea journey away. When Thorvald set sail into exile from Iceland in 986, some of his fellow countrymen were only fourteen years away from an astonishing discovery. In the same year Iceland converted to Christianity and almost five hundred years before Christopher Columbus, a family of Icelanders who had colonized Greenland sailed on west and happened upon what was probably Newfoundland. Others found Markland – probably South Labrador – and a useful supply of timber. Still others reached what was probably the coast of New England, which they called Vinland after the vines they found growing there. 'There was never any frost all winter and the grass hardly withered at all,' the *Greenland Saga* tells us about Vinland. 'The weather was fine. There was dew on the grass, and the first thing they did was to get some of it on their hands and put it to their lips . . .'[xx] The dew-drinking, lumberjacking, grape-picking idyll only soured when some 'small and evil-looking' natives of the new land, who had an uncontrollable lust for weapons and for any material dyed red, attacked the Vikings' makeshift encampment.

Their long-range catapults were terrifying for Norsemen accustomed to hand-to-hand combat.

By 1010 a Viking who had dreamed of permanent settlement was losing heart. He 'realized that although the land was excellent they could never live there in safety or freedom from fear, because of the native inhabitants'.[xxi] He and his family returned home. The saga notes that his widow took the veil and three of his descendants became bishops, but I was more impressed by his own sensibly humane decision not to try and subdue the natives. His predilection for a life lived in 'freedom from fear' seemed to me most admirable.

The Icelanders sailed eastward too, of course – to Norway, to Gotland and down the deep Russian rivers of the Varangian route all the way to the Black Sea and Constantinople – comfortably speaking their own Scandinavian tongue to settlers of their kind on the way. But that was only one of the routes they pioneered down to Jerusalem from their northern fastness. Some sailed for seven weeks at a stretch all the way south-west around the Iberian peninsula to winter there, before proceeding on into the Mediterranean and eastward. Their ships, equipped with three sets of oars each, could accommodate horses, weaponry and stocks of their staple dried fish, salted butter and tubs of sour milk. Not slaves – Iceland outlawed slavery in the year 1000 – but volunteers, often the adventurous sons of *gothar*, manned the oars. The sale of their mighty craft during the return journey, sometimes in Byzantium which particularly prized Scandinavian boat building, would amply reimburse expenses incurred on the outward journey.

The ship's engineer agreed that life as a modern Icelandic sailor had lost all that kind of glamour, even since the days when he first started working on ships. Container ports are uninteresting and usually located so far from the centres of towns that going ashore often seems more trouble than it is worth. The *Bruarfoss's* unchanging route to the Faroes, Hamburg and a string of Scandinavian ports had long ago become tedious and routinely mechanical.

'In Communist times we used to sail to Poland. That was

exciting because we were as rich as kings there, but even on board we used to talk more or play cards in the evenings. Now everyone has their own cabin and their own TV and video. We all record films at home and watch them alone.'

In the hope that he would invite me to join him for a companionable evening's viewing, I enquired into the contents of his private video collection. 'I've got Iceland's very first porn movie,' he suggested with a twinkle in his eye, but thought I might prefer a home video, one made while on holiday with his extended family in the north of Iceland the previous summer.

Here was an aspect of modern Iceland that I had missed. The film showed the engineer, his brother-in-law and teenage son, like the eleventh-century action heroes of the sagas, tooling busily about all the white summer nights long in a speedboat, a four-wheel-drive jeep or tractor. There seemed to be a good deal of hard violent work to do. I watched fascinated, horrified, while they culled seals, painting the beach red with their blood, while they smashed gulls' heads, nicked eider down from duck nests and fired at anything that moved. The hectic way the film had been shot suggested that none of these valiant Vikings paused for breath, let alone food or sleep. From time to time the little hand-held camera panned shakily back to the patriarch of the clan – white-bearded and very still in a corner of the summer house's main room – telling sagas for a passing tourist.

The next sunny morning Julia snapped me standing on deck in a traditional Icelandic cardigan she had knitted and generously decided to present to me. 'I thought, because I'm probably related to this Thorvald you're writing about . . .' was how she explained her gift. We talked about her family, about her father who had been a handsome 'real Viking of a man' with wavy red hair. In 1936 he had participated in Hitler's Berlin Olympics – 'He was white and Aryan like Hitler wanted,' said Julia – but he never returned home. Her mother was left back in Iceland to bring up six children alone. He had worked in a travelling circus and sired six more. 'I have a half-brother in Norway, another in Germany . . .' Julia told me.

'Any in England?' I asked, leaning over the rail, squinting off into the hazy distance right where I guessed the British Isles must be by then.

'No, are you feeling homesick?' she enquired kindly.

No. I was not sorry to be bypassing my homeland.

Mainland Europe was rid of its tenth-century invaders by the year 1000, but not England. Danish Vikings, the young Thorvald perhaps among them, had been raiding there intermittently since 980 but Thorvald was already well away to the south, in Constantinople or Jerusalem, when in 991 they had launched a full invasion with ninety-three ships and been paid off with a tribute of ten thousand pounds of silver. Sixteen thousand pounds by 994, twenty-four thousand by 1002, the humiliating price of temporary freedom from fear had risen to forty-eight thousand pounds by 1012. Swein Forkbeard of Denmark, whose service Thorvald had first entered in the early 980s, conquered England in 1013 and was succeeded by his son Canute a year later. King Aethelred the Unready was forced into exile.* The English also had Aethelred to thank for giving the Normans an excuse to conquer their country some fifty years later. He had yoked the English throne to the Norman duchy in 1002 by marrying Emma, sister of the then duke of Normandy.

But it seems that mid-eleventh-century Englishmen were ready for some of the civilization those originally Viking Normans had acquired in the two hundred years since they had started settling around Rouen. A chronicler monk who prided himself on his impartiality because he was half-Norman, half-English by birth, noted: 'The English at that time wore short garments reaching to their mid-knee; they had their hair cropped, their beards shaven, their arms laden with golden bracelets; their skin adorned with punctured designs. They were accustomed to eat till they became surfeited, and to drink till they were sick.'[xxii]

While examining the causes for English defeat at Hastings, the same historian says nothing about the excellence of the Normans'

---

* Aethelred had ruled England since 978.

warhorses, or about the vulnerability of Englishmen armed only with battleaxes. He omits to mention that they were exhausted, having just defeated an invasion of Norwegian Vikings at Stamford Bridge and marched the two hundred and fifty miles south in only twelve days. Instead, William of Malmesbury blames the English defeat on their addiction to 'the vices attendant on drunkenness which enervate the human mind',[xxiii] endemic alcoholism.

But I was running ahead of myself. The mid-eleventh century and events at least as significant as the Norman conquest of England lay way to the south, in France and Italy. The crane forest of Hamburg's container port was just visible.

~

'*Aber das ist das neue Europa!*' I retorted, gathering up my bags and making for the doors as the underground train slowed into the station.

On a crowded underground S-bahn train bound for Hamburg's railway station, a stout middle-aged man in a suit had settled in the seat beside me and, uninvited, begun inspecting my map. Confirming that I was headed in the right direction, he had struck up a conversation. My plea that I spoke barely a word of German had not deterred him from asking me where I had been staying and opening his heart to me on the subject of immigrants.

'Sadly, we don't get so many English visitors these days, mostly Russians and Poles and Czechs unfortunately. You must have seen all the east European prostitutes on the Reeperbahn near your hotel. (nudge) A young lady like you shouldn't stay in that area. It's not safe.'

I had explained that I was not a tourist but writing a book about the eleventh century, and that he need not concern himself about my safety because I was leaving Hamburg. Beyond being home to the archbishops whose diocese included Iceland from the middle of the eleventh century, his home city played no part in the particular story I was trying to tell.

'Ah! For the eleventh century you must go to Quedlinburg in Saxony, in the former East Germany,' he persisted, 'where our Saxon kings had their capital, and to Poland – to Gnesen where our Holy Roman Kaiser Otto III went on pilgrimage in the year 1000. There you can find the relics of St Adalbert—'

'Yes,' I had said, astonished by his easy familiarity with the subject. 'Actually, I'm on my way now to catch a night train to Quedlinburg. From there I'll be travelling on to Gnesen.* St Adalbert† is one of the most important people in my story.'

'You must be careful on the night train; you should not be alone – there are all sorts of Russians and Albanians travelling at night,' he said, casting a a furtive glance around the carriage.

Sorely missing the vast North Sea and the manly crew of the *Bruarfoss*, I had been irritated by both the stuffy train and this fussy German. My parting shot – that like it or not, this was the new Europe we were all learning to live in – was impatiently delivered, with a borderless eleventh-century Europe in mind.

The night journey east was not comfortable. Swaddled in anything woollen I could find in my bag but still cold, I reclined in my seat and stared out of the window at the trees I had missed so in Iceland and at neat villages racing by in the opposite direction. Later, the immutable distance of a full orange moon in a black sky helped me back a thousand years, to a western Europe struggling to recover from the violent attentions paid it by the previous century's three mighty invasions of heathen Vikings and Magyars and Muslim Saracens, who had descended on the region like biblical plagues from three points of the compass. Under their onslaught central power and the rule of kings had broken down. The glorious apogee of peace and order achieved by Charlemagne around the year 800 had vanished. The land had become planted with the castles of brigand chiefs whose mounted followers sowed terror through the countryside, pillaging and burning, raping and murdering.

* Gniezno in Polish.
† Wojciech in Polish.

But the last decades of the tenth century had also seen the first green shoots of hope that a return to Charlemagne's good order or, still better, to that of the ancient Romans, might be possible. The Viking scourge from the north had abated. Vikings settled in northern France became Normans and acquired the gentler manners of the region's native inhabitants. By the year 1000 only the British Isles were still suffering Viking raids. The Magyars, guerrilla horsemen who had swept out of the east to penetrate as far west as Brittany, had been defeated by the Saxon German Holy Roman Emperor Otto I in 955 and were at last settling peaceably in the area which includes modern Hungary. The Saracens, who had crossed the Mediterranean to sail up the French rivers, were flushed out of their last bandit hideouts in the Alps in 972, after their disgraceful kidnapping of an eminent abbot.

For the churchmen who had closeted themselves in their monasteries and churches, guarding their jewelled church treasures and holy learning from ferocious heathen fanciers of all that glittered or was magic, the approach of a new millennium promised one of two things. Either Western Christendom was about to embark on a blessed golden future in which the Church with its network of bishops and monasteries still intact would reassert itself as the only institution capable of restoring lost order and civilization; or, mankind had sinned so grievously that the world must come to an end and Christ's Last Judgement be nigh. Either way, the mood of the time seems to have been one of heightened energy, much of it religious and markedly emotional. This energy spurred pilgrimages, created an insatiable market for miracle-working relics and motivated stone church building on a scale so grand that a new architectural style – the Romanesque – was born. Christ had to be propitiated with monuments that recalled the last time he had shown favour to his people, during the late Roman Empire. There must be room – in the shape of ambulatories – for pilgrims to process around the tombs and relics of miracle-working saints. In Burgundy, a monk-chronicler eloquently captured the vigorous spirit of the times:

throughout the whole world, but most especially in Italy and Gaul, men began to reconstruct churches, although for the most part the existing ones were properly built and not in the least unworthy. But it seemed as though each Christian community were aiming to surpass all others in the splendour of construction. It was as if the whole world were shaking itself free, shrugging off the burden of the past and cladding itself everywhere in a white mantle of churches.[xiv]

The speed of western Europe's recovery in the eleventh century, the often alarming pace of modernizing change and the passionate desire for peace and order would heap more fuel on the fires of that millennial fervour.

The dawning of this thrilling new world was what Thorvald witnessed as he set off across the continent en route for distant Constantinople and Jerusalem. He probably docked at Hamburg just as I had done and certainly journeyed this way through the lands of the Saxon German Holy Roman Empire, the largest and best-ordered entity in this era of near chaos.

Emperor Otto III would have been six or seven years old at the time. His mother Theophano was ruling the empire as his regent, often from Quedlinburg the hilly stronghold of the Saxon German kings since the beginning of the tenth century. She would have welcomed Thorvald, particularly if she had happened to notice him at prayer crossing himself in the Eastern Christian manner, for she was a Byzantine Christian.

Theophano was more tangible proof that a brighter future might be expected. Relations between Constantinople and Rome were improving by the last quarter of the tenth century. The heinous two-hundred-year-old impertinence of a pope crowning Charlemagne emperor, followed by Charlemagne's unilateral insertion of the *Filioque** into the Creed and another pope's anointing of Theophano's

---

* The Roman Church unilaterally inserted the word *filioque* into the Nicene Creed in the ninth century, thereby amending the fourth-century Nicene Creed. Roman Catholics therefore still hold that the Holy Spirit 'proceeds from the Father *and the Son*', Orthodox Christians that the Holy Spirit 'proceeds from the Father'. Refer also to Arni Bergmann on p.11.

father-in-law Otto I as Holy Roman emperor of the West were not forgotten but fading. When Emperor Otto I had extended an olive branch by requesting the hand of a Byzantine princess for his son Otto II, the Byzantines had obliged.

But the sixteen-year-old Theophano who disembarked at Bari in southern Italy in 972 was not precisely the *porphyrogeneta** they had been promised. She was only the daughter by a first marriage of the emperor's brother-in-law's second wife, a woman who herself happened only to be the great-niece of a former Byzantine emperor. There were two genuine purple-born princesses on the market but the emperor deemed them too valuable to waste on a comparatively barbarian German. Raised at the Byzantine court however, Theophano was anything but shoddy goods. She had been trained for her daunting posting to darkest northern Europe, made fluent in her fiancé's language and conversant with the customs of his land. Her 'conversation was full of attractions'.[xxv] She was vividly comely, glamorous, cultured and – accompanied by a phalanx of Byzantine priests and artists – piously faithful to her Eastern style of Christianity.

For a while Germans muttered curses against the Byzantine Greeks for their *fallatia, invidia et arrogantia* but Theophano's most troublesome enemies seem to have been other women. There was something too sophisticatedly exotic about her for the average early eleventh-century German Frau to stomach. The brilliant confidence bred into her by her ancient and wealthy civilization whose capital city was the most splendid the world had yet seen, irked them. There was scandalized talk of her having *obscoeni negotii* with her confessor John Philagathos, a Greek monk from Byzantine southern Italy who became her son's godfather and tutor. A nun had a dream in which Theophano appeared to her writhing in agony and admitting that she deserved eternal damnation on account of the

---

* Literally born in the purple, a purple marble room in the imperial palace in Constantinople.

splendid garments and fabulous jewellery she had imported from her native Constantinople.

But while her husband lived Theophano's most powerful female foe seems to have been her mother-in-law, the supremely pious and self-denying Adelheid of Burgundy, who had also been left a young widow. What we know about Theophano's relationship with Adelheid is contained in the writings of a saintly Abbot Odilo. He deemed Adelheid the apotheosis of Christian womanhood and slightingly referred to Theophano as *'illa imperatrix greca'*[xxvi] – 'that Greek Empress' dismissing her as a 'friend of dissipation, keen on pleasures' and noting that 'she did not follow the example of her mother-in-law's piety and reserve . . . [Adelheid] knew even if only by silence, how to make the young princess feel her faults and liberties.'[xxvii]

When her husband died far away in southern Italy in 983, Theophano was still in her twenties and Otto III was only three. The imperial succession was in doubt but, always glad of an opportunity to leave her adopted homeland, Theophano lingered south of the Alps overseeing her husband's burial in Rome's St Peter's basilica. In her absence little Otto fell prey to a wicked uncle. Coveting the throne for himself, Uncle Henry the Quarreller kidnapped his nephew and imprisoned him in a monastery. The would-be usurper gained a following and even a crown, but opposition to his rule began to surface. Forgetting their old differences, Adelheid and Theophano took advantage of it.

A summit meeting was scheduled, to be attended by Uncle Henry, little Otto and a powerful female lobby comprising Theophano, her dour mother-in-law and little Otto's Aunt Matilda, who was abbess of Quedlinburg monastery. A heavenly intervention decided its outcome. 'To the astonishment of all present who saw it, a brilliant star shone from the midst of the heavens as the two parties wrangled . . . something unheard of in broad daylight,' a chronicler noted.[xxviii] Uncle Henry admitted defeat and humbled himself before his nephew, promising to serve him loyally. Little Otto's pious kinswomen rejoiced at the victory but forbore from humiliating their errant kinsman, 'for that is the way of charity; not to repay evil with evil but even to return good for evil'.[xxix] Thorvald's Bishop Frederick would have heartily approved of their mercy; impetuous Thorvald might have reached for his battleaxe and despatched the usurper. But he should have been encouraged that a man whose very name – Henry the Quarreller – betrayed the fact that he was uncontrolled and warlike could change his tune and be sweetly forgiven. The mighty was fallen and the succession safe at last. In the same year Otto set off at the head of an army mustered to quell some unruly eastern Slavs. By the time he was seven years old he had proved himself a superior commander-in-chief, a lord of luck whose mere presence could guarantee victory.

At the end of the first millennium the bosky Harz Mountains of Saxon north Germany, towards which my train was speeding, were criss-crossed with trade routes, pocked with valuable silver mines and endowed with powerful monasteries and convents. In these strongholds of the faith Otto's aunts, cousins and three sisters – the vast majority of them either nuns or abbesses – were either politicking efficiently on his behalf, or busily accumulating the empire's spiritual capital, or both. In the grander scheme of a Holy Roman Empire comprising all of modern Germany, Switzerland, Austria, Alsace-Lorraine, Burgundy and most of the Czech Republic as well as the northern half of Italy, this darkly wooded mountainous region was located much too far north and east to be any sort of imperial heartland. But it was young Otto's heartland, his safe house from the unquiet marches still further east and from the troublesome Romans who so resented his overlordship.

The cold war's Iron Curtain – a barrier to far-faring such as my eleventh-century acquaintances never knew – sliced the Harz Mountains and Saxony in half for the latter part of the twentieth century. In today's reunited Germany the region is destined for a quiet prosperity again, as a nature reserve endowed with plentiful modern leisure facilities.

Still bundled in my woollens when the train reached Magdeburg at five o'clock in the morning, I wondered if we had crossed the old Iron Curtain. A glance at the decor of the station buffet and the selection of foods on offer removed any doubt. Instead of the freshly baked and appetizingly shiny range of raisin-stuffed or cin-namon-scented buns nestling in starched gingham cloths in attractive wicker baskets that I had noticed in Hamburg, there was a yellow plastic tray laden with two cupcakes, both past their best and covered with shocking-pink icing. Beside a dusty pot plant was a plastic basket containing some equally crudely coloured plastic Easter eggs. A surly woman offered me a choice of mint tea or tea, no coffee.

Quedlinburg is also just east of the old frontier. As the empty little local train – the first of the day – chugged its way around the foothills of the mountains, through a landscape of green-blue fields blanketed in mist, past a misty lake fringed with weeping willows, past a pair of scruffy houses and a rubbish tip and on through more mist-covered countryside, I sensed the emptiness of modern east Germany. I could find the eleventh century here, I guessed. Staring out at that sunlit, misty, marshy-looking vacancy it was just possible to imagine a continent emptied of over 90 per cent of its inhabi-tants.* There might be the odd lone medieval messenger striding across the marshes on stilts, or using his long spear as a vaulting pole. A solitary monk, carrying a mortuary roll – a parchment announcing the death of a churchman which lengthened with every monastery visited, with every polite message of condolence and request for prayers for their own dead inscribed – would have graced the scene. Could that distant blur be a procession of churchmen 'translating' a casket of holy saints' relics from one church or monas-tery to another in a cloud of incense and chanting . . .?

But eleventh-century Quedlinburg was harder to find than I had hoped. The little town perched among the foothills of the Harz Mountains is an excellently preserved testament to very late medieval craftsmanship and good living. Its rows of half-timbered

---

* The total population of Germany, France, Italy and England at the time of the First Crusade was approximately 20 million. Today it is around 264 million.

pastel-painted houses with their steeply pitched roofs, its pretty market square and grey stone ivy-bearded *Rathaus*, like a cross between a country church and a French vintner's mansion, were very pleasant but also distracting. Where was the solid, dark and awe-inspiring restraint of an eleventh-century Romanesque stone church? All those pretty buildings, some with woodwork exuberantly carved with flowers or fan motifs picked out in colour, were the products of a civilization confidently triumphing over its environment and making itself comfortable.

Eating a Quedlinburg breakfast of brown bread thickly smeared with goose dripping in the sunny market square, I found myself wishing I had checked into the nearby Theophano Hotel. A picture of Otto's Byzantine mother hung in the form of a 'medieval' shop sign over the side entrance to the establishment's wine cellar. Improbably blonde, this Theophano was framed in a circle of vines. She wore a wide-sleeved red robe and headdress and was tipping a glass of ruby-red wine towards her *Mona Lisa* lips. She looked to me slightly tipsy, but was perhaps only welcomingly winking. Theophano had not been forgotten, and nor had her mother-in-law, or even Otto's great-aunt Abbess Matilda. There were serious works of scholarship about each of them in the bookshop opposite the guest house where I was staying.

Young Otto grew up surrounded by his kinswomen including his three sisters, to the eldest of whom, Sophie, he was particularly attached. Indeed, she and Otto were almost inseparable during his adolescence. Although nominally a nun of Gandersheim convent in the northern Harz Mountains, Sophie liked to accompany her little brother on his unceasing rounds of his territories. Theirs was a sort of *perpetuum mobile* of a lifestyle dictated by the medieval world's lack of communications. An emperor was obliged to show himself and his power to his people or risk losing control of the realm. Appearances were all-important if his God-anointed rule was to endure. Processions, magnificent entrances and vast banquets were a *sine qua non* of every visit. Monasteries and convents, usually the only establishments large and wealthy enough to host the emperor and his vast retinue, built imperial guest houses and royal galleries in their churches. Splendid gifts were received in exchange: a silver chalice, a gorgeously jewelled gospel cover, fine wall hangings, an orchard or a village.

Otto relied heavily on his bishops and abbots. With their patchwork of dioceses covering the entire realm and monasteries well situated at crossroads and market centres they were the higher managers in the only kind of civil service his empire could muster. The abbots helped the poor and the sick, farmed the land efficiently and stored up spiritual credit for their royal donors with prayers and fasting. The bishops were at the same time senior judges, and most vitally for the empire, army generals. In effect, they were like pagan Icelandic *gothar* – chieftains who doubled up as religious authorities. The only difference between a bishop and an Icelandic *gothi* was that, rather than enjoying their posts for as long as their followers deemed them worthy, the bishops were appointed by the emperors. But the Roman Church of the mid-eleventh century would not countenance this blurring of functions and allegiances; three quarters of the way through the century the papacy's insistence on its canonical right to appoint German bishops would precipitate war. By asserting papal supremacy, Rome robbed the emperor of his divine ordination and fatally undermined the empire. Some historians argue that when the late eleventh-century popes took the 'holy' out of the Holy Roman Empire they established a pattern of instability and insecurity which hampered the Germans' efforts to organize themselves into a viable nation state until late in the nineteenth century, and the struggle to catch up with France and Britain then fostered an unhealthy determination to surpass and conquer them in two world wars.

The old order was not ideal, of course, even for the emperors who relied on it. The bishops' loyalty to their rulers could only be assured if royal munificence on a gigantic scale was forthcoming. When it was not, when young Emperor Otto was faring too far for too long to reward his prelate managers for their many services, the system could easily collapse. Otto's sister Sophie was the agent of just such a breakdown.

Sophie had grown close to one of Otto's mentors, the Archbishop of Mainz. *Obscoeni negotii* between them were rumoured. In the late 990s she imperiously granted him the honour of presiding over the consecration of her convent's new church, a privilege which belonged to the local Bishop of Hildesheim, another of Otto's tutors. Sophie's high-handed behaviour might not have mattered had the Archbishop of Mainz not suddenly decided to postpone the ceremony by a week, thus throwing the local bishop's nose and diary badly out of joint. The latter determined to preside over the consecration himself after all, on the date originally set. The Gandersheim nuns, with Sophie presumably orchestrating the rebellion, were outraged. A chronicler writes that when the offertory in the mass was reached, the procession of women walked up towards the altar 'furiously and with incredible expressions of anger, throwing down their gifts and uttering wild words of abuse against the bishop'. The poor bishop was 'deeply shaken by this unusual display'. 'With tears streaming down his cheeks', like a persecuted Christ, he suffered the women's 'mad rage' but somehow managed to conclude the mass in the customary fashion.[xxx]

That was not the end of the matter. Otto, hundreds of miles away in Rome at the time, was soon involved in the power struggle provoked by his older sister's predilection for the Archbishop of Mainz. The boy emperor set about soothing the Bishop of Hildesheim's wounded dignity by inviting him to Rome, setting him up in luxurious apartments adjoining his own in the new palace he had built for himself on the Aventine Hill, and even ordering the kitchen to prepare special Saxon dishes in his honour. A synod, presided over by Otto and the pope, soon decided the matter entirely in the bishop's favour. The thing was quite simple: the convent of Gandersheim was in his diocese so the Archbishop of Mainz had no business meddling there. But back in Saxony the troublesome archbishop was having none of the ruling and insulted the pope's emissary who had been sent to restore 'peace, love and concord' in the German Church. He refused to even glance at, let alone read, the pope's letter and had his thugs break into the council chamber where the prelates were gathered to threaten the pope's envoy and the Bishop of Hildesheim. By making off secretly before dawn the next day, the archbishop signalled his contempt for the pope and Otto and all their works. The unspoken agreement requiring mutual back-scratching between emperor and senior prelates was fraying. This unholy battle of the bishops, so needlessly sparked by Sophie, sputtered on into the new millennium and continued after Otto's demise. Given that such fisticuffs were by no means rare in the Latin Church it is perhaps not surprising that so much of the papacy's energy during the eleventh century would be devoted to breaking the unhealthily codependent relationship between rulers and churchmen and to creating a solidly independent Church with a strong chain of command extending out from the pope in Rome to the furthest reaches of Scandinavia and eastern Europe, to southern Italy and northern Spain.

But Otto's reputation seems to have been untarnished by such ugly carryings-on. His gift for passionate friendship may have ensured his popularity in a society which set great store by courtly *familiaritas*. Close relations between sovereign and followers, quite unlike the ritualized grandeur of the Byzantine court, were the norm among the descendants of the Germanic tribes who had settled northern Europe, a norm to which the originally Germanic Vikings also adhered. Otto's relations with his *familiares* were warmer and easier than that of any other monarch of the era. To some he granted special signs of affection. He allowed the wronged Bishop of Hildesheim's brother to wear his clothes and shared a single plate with him at feasts. One of his favourite monk advisers was his beloved '*anima mea*', meaning 'my alter ego'.

For all his youth, his easy debonair ways and delicate good looks, Otto was far from weak. Naturally intelligent and curious he had early on developed an appreciation of his mother's ancient Byzantine heritage. His mentors had been the Greek Orthodox monk Philaga-thos and then, as a sober Latin antidote to all that abstractedly high-minded Greek learning, the Bishop of Hildesheim, followed by the Archbishop of Mainz whom he never much cared for. At the age of seventeen he chose his own mentor in the form of Gerbert of Aurillac, a French cleric who was probably the most intellectually gifted man of his age and a fervent bibliophile. Otto begged Gerbert to cure him of any Saxon *rusticitas* and nurture in him a Greek *subtilitas*. With Gerbert's arrival at court, 'school became almost more important than war and court assemblies became not just functions to attend but dialectical debates to be participated in'.[xxxi]

Excited by ideas, science, by history, logic, the arts and theology, Otto's tutor was hundreds of years ahead of his time. Of humble French peasant stock, Gerbert had received an education at his local monastery where he had managed to impress a pilgrim Catalan duke with his intelligence. The duke had taken him back home with him to Catalonia where Gerbert had been exposed to the dazzling Arabic learning filtering into Christian areas of the largely Arab Iberian peninsula. He is credited with later having introduced into Western Christendom the abacus and the notion if not the practical use of zero.*

A series of lucky accidents had brought him back over the Pyrenees and to the attention of other powerful patrons in the shape of a pope and Otto III's father, to whom he probably taught some mathematics. Lured by a promise that he could pick up the rediscovered secrets of Aristotelian logic at the French cathedral school of Reims, he moved there. Students flocked from all over Europe to sit at his feet and imbibe the ancient classics he was so passionate about reviving. Gerbert dreamed of recreating the Roman Empire of east and west. It was a dream of order, prosperity and high civilization, and he found in young Otto the perfect patron and partner for his project. In a letter accompanying a philosophical treatise on reason which the young emperor had requested, he

* Zero was not generally used in western Europe until the fourteenth century, although Arabic numerals were more convenient.

resorted to rhetoric to fire Otto up with his breathtakingly flattering vision,

> Ours, ours is the Roman Empire. Italy, fertile in fruits, Lorraine and Germany, fertile in men, offer their resources, and even the strong kingdoms of the Slavs are not lacking to us. Our august emperor of the Romans art thou, Caesar, who sprung from the noblest blood of the Greeks, surpass the Greeks in empire and govern the Romans by hereditary right, but both you surpass in genius and eloquence.[xxxii]

Gerbert left Otto in no doubt that the Holy Roman Empire could now boast a ruler to rival Charlemagne two centuries before. *Mirabilia mundi* – the world's miracle – was Otto's nickname.

However, if Professor Heinz Leike is to be believed there might have been no *mirabilia mundi*, perhaps no empire, had it not been for Otto's powerful womenfolk. Otto's women rather than Otto himself, let alone Gerbert, are what fascinate him.

'There was never a time in German history when women had more influence and power – all them were very clever,' the *Herr Doktor* told me over coffee in that market square. 'You know that Theophano was regent. Well, when she died Otto was only twelve so he needed another regent. That was his grandmother, Adelheid. Now she had influenced her husband Otto I to get involved in Italy because she was the one who knew her history. She urged him to get back in touch with ancient Rome by having the pope crown him Holy Roman emperor. Later on, when Otto III was emperor and spending so much of his time in Italy, he left his Aunt Matilda, his father's sister who was abbess here at Quedlinburg, in charge of running the whole empire. He liked his aunt, he was always signing over parcels of land and villages to her . . .'

A morose red-faced man whom I had encountered in the market square's tourist office, *Herr Doktor* Leike was not a historian but a plant biologist who had retired as soon as he saw that the future of his discipline lay with genetics instead of gazing down a microscope.

However, the meagreness of his East German pension had propelled him into guiding tourists around the living museum of his home town. The pocket diary he kept consulting to ensure perfect accuracy was filled with dates and names neatly noted in a spidery scientist's hand. Fortunately he loved history, and I began to understand his regard for the medieval noblewomen of Quedlinburg when he explained that Otto III's great-grandmother had founded the early tenth-century *Stift** up on the hill by the eleventh-century church. Devoted to the education of pious noblewomen 'because those who are well-born can scarcely ever become degenerate,'[xxxiii] the *Stift* grew over the course of almost a thousand years into a significant power in the land. By 1803 the Abbess of Quedlinburg, appointed to her post like all her predecessors by the highest nobility, was the only woman with a seat in the Reichstag. Quedlinburg's Castle Hill, the *Herr Doktor* laboriously joked to me, was an ancient bastion of feminism. He was right. Something of the atmosphere of the early Icelandic sagas in which women enjoyed high status, in which they were prized as priestesses like Thorvald's seeress foster-mother and as respected keepers of the home still hung about the northern Europe of Otto III. Christianity had not extinguished the customs of the old Germanic tribes.

I paid for our coffees and we strolled down a narrow cobbled side street towards the hill with its eleventh-century Romanesque St Servatius church and its museum housed in the fine apartments once used by the abbesses of Quedlinburg. The day had turned out very warm. In his thick pullover and leather jacket *Herr Doktor* Leike looked uncomfortably hot. Like some ghost of the cold war era in that early spring heatwave he emanated the dour melancholy of the inevitably defeated. A German his age would have seen the dismantling of East Germany as another defeat to add to that suffered in 1945. Being elderly and redundant in the new united Germany could not be pleasant, I thought. He averted his eyes from

* A *Stift* is a charitable foundation, in this case a convent.

the sight of a young builder stripped to his vest and whistling at his work on the façade of one of the timbered houses.

'That workman is probably a Pole. They are very good at restoring the wooden carving,' he commented.

Quedlinburg was in the last stages of a makeover aimed at completing its transformation from a shabby eastern German town filthily polluted by its surrounding factories to a sweet oasis of late medieval charm guaranteed to draw coachloads of visitors and ensure a modest living for an ageing population. Puffing his way up the hill beside me, the professor averted his eyes again from some tourists whose discreetly wealthy attire instantly identified them as west Germans.

'*Herr Doktor*, are there things you miss about the old East Germany?'

'Well, (puff, puff) unification had to happen but, you know, because we had so little in the old East Germany family and friend-ship were everything. (puff!) In the West everything is about money and now it's the same here. Our factories have been closed down, our young people are all leaving to find work over there . . .'

That, I thought, would explain why on a working day the town managed to have the empty shut-up atmosphere of a Sunday afternoon, despite all the building works. There were very few young adults and fewer children. The tourists we passed were all elderly. The mournful *Herr Doktor* suited his melancholy, emptied town better than its bright new make-up.

Flicking through my guidebook as we walked, I read about the last time Quedlinburg had strutted the stage of German history. 'As with any chronicle, not every detail is pleasant to read,' the book warned politely. 'In the days of the Third Reich, the National Socialists turned the church into a national shrine . . .'[xxxiv] The creator of the SS, the one-time Bavarian chicken farmer Heinrich Himmler, had fallen in love with the Germany that existed before any Roman pope had started meddling in its business. Himmler believed himself to be the perfect reincarnation of an ancestor of Otto's, the very first tenth-century Saxon German king Heinrich the Fowler, who was buried at Quedlinburg. Much more fervently than Hitler, Himmler believed that Nazism's success depended on its ability to eradicate the value which Christianity placed on meekness and non-violence. Not 'Do as you would be done by' but a virile 'Do to others as they do to you' would be the key to resurrecting Germany, the Nazis believed. It struck me that their thinking in this matter tallied perfectly with that of the luxuriantly moustachioed Icelandic *gothi*, Jormundur Ingi Hansen.

In 1936, on the thousandth anniversary of Heinrich the Fowler's death, Himmler had ordered the eagle on one of the church's twin towers replaced with a Nazi eagle and a grand opening of Heinrich the Fowler's tomb. That summer five hundred top Nazis gathered in the torch-lit church to witness Himmler rising slowly from a trap door in the floor with his arms outstretched in glory and majesty. He was Heinrich the Fowler. While the Third Reich thrived the church was indeed a Nazi shrine. SS officers gathered there to swear allegiance on a sword that Himmler would proffer them, and no Christian service was permitted. In the winter of 1945 the thickly wooded Harz Mountains had almost defeated the American tanks, appropriately rendering the stronghold of the Germans' first Reich one of the last strongholds of their third.

'You should know that your Otto III and Himmler walked just the same way as us,' remarked the *Herr Doktor*.

The fifteen-year-old Otto had spent two weeks here, giving thanks for a victorious campaign against some Slavs, for the veiling of his second sister and for the end of many years of drought and bad winters. The professor paused for thought, before continuing, 'I've been thinking about our wars. You have to remember that Germany has nine different borders. There's never been any question of us living in "splendid isolation" like Britain. Wars are only natural, especially between the Germans and the French because we're really brothers. You know both the eastern and western Franks, Germans and French as they are now, spoke the sort of *Platt Deutsch**

* A German dialect native to the north German seaboard, including Pomerania.

we speak here in northern Germany; French is quite a new invention.'

'Oh, really? But, *Herr Doktor*, what was your experience of the last war?' I asked, fairly confident he was too young to have taken any active part that would prove embarrassing for him to recall.

He was not originally from Quedlinburg; he was a German-speaker from somewhere near the port of Gdansk, or Danzig as it would have been called until the vast surrounding area was lost to Germany after the First World War, acquired again briefly in the Second, and then lost again to become Polish Gdansk.

'In the summer of 1946 the Poles gave my mother, my three sisters and me an hour to leave our home. We couldn't speak Polish so weren't permitted to stay. We went to the Polish port of Stettin where a British ship – actually a German ship commandeered by the British – took us to an island near Lübeck on the coast. There we were in quarantine for two months, trying to contact my father through an aunt living in Berlin. Luckily, her house had survived alone in a street of rubble and my father had written there too, looking for us. He'd ended up in the Russian-administered quarter of the country. We were in the British quarter and they wouldn't let us join him. The British authorities were very arrogant; the French perhaps even more so,' he added politely. 'The Russians and the Americans were fine. Somehow we managed to get ourselves to the border between the Russian and British sections, here in the Harz Mountains. There were thousands of people like us wanting to go east to rejoin their families, waiting at a railway station there for three days in the open air. I remember we were still using Hitler's currency at the time . . .'

'Where did you all sleep? Did you have tents?' I asked him, thinking that his twentieth-century story was more elusively vague than any eleventh-century history.

'I don't know how we managed, and you must remember that I was the head of the family then. One day a kind farmer gave us directions across the border, through a field of rye and a wood. It was two or three kilometres. On the other side we would meet my father. We went.'

'It must have been wonderful to meet up with him again!'

'Meet him? No! There were seven more weeks of quarantine in a camp in the middle of a forest. We had to agree to that if we wanted to qualify for ration cards. There was no other way, but the very moment our second quarantine was completed we set off walking for about nine kilometres. Then we met him with his horse and cart . . . That's how we came to stay in East Germany.'

The *Herr Doktor* had not fared far, only back and forth across the shifting Polish–German border, to and fro across Germany, but it had been in a nominally still Christian Europe at its most over-partitioned and policed, a continent on a horrible cusp between barbaric bloodletting and the tedious bureaucracy of humanitarian aid programmes. To have spent almost four months in quarantine camps when the war was over!

We had a clear view of the hill-top church of St Servatius now, with its dark twin towers symbolizing the gateway to the heavenly Jerusalem. My guidebook told me that Lombard builders from southern Italy had started building it in the 1070s so Otto and his kinswomen could not have seen it. The *Herr Doktor* slipped a ten-Deutschmark note to a bedraggled Russian accordion player at the gateway to Castle Hill.

'No hard feelings towards the Russians, then?' I enquired, recalling the fussy fearfulness of the man on the Hamburg underground.

'No, no . . . that Russian's got a physics degree and I don't know how many children to support.'

In his tone I detected nostalgia for the old comradeship of the socialist eastern European states, the defensive distaste for the opulent west of the country. I thought I could also hear resentment that this ancient heartland of Germany was now such a backwater. Perhaps there was also a trace of a hope that the removal of the capital from Bonn to Berlin, only about a hundred miles east of Quedlinburg, would soon change that sad state of affairs.

The vast church, murkily lit by its narrow Romanesque windows, with its solid pillared arches and run of steps up to a bare, spare altar, was almost empty. Here at last was what I had been missing – that massive, austere solidity. Such a church was the creation of a people firmly convinced of the material truth of the Christian Lord they served as faithfully as they served their earthly king in expectation of their just deserts. Awe, not wonder, was the keynote. The visitors there that morning stood clustered on the left of the entrance, in the first of the three naves and especially around the narrow opening to the treasury with its two-foot-thick stone walls. There lay a part of the treasure that Otto III's second sister, who succeeded as Abbess of Quedlinburg on the death of their Aunt Matilda, began to store up for the dynasty. A charmingly chunky rock crystal and gold reliquary in the form of a fat fish had been donated by Otto and inscribed with the Latin words 'Capills Marie Otto T Impr' – 'Hair of (the Virgin) Mary, Otto Third Emperor'. The cover of Otto's sister's gospel was encrusted with Byzantine ivory reliefs. There were fabulous reliquary boxes in the Byzantine style presumably favoured by Theophano and her retinue housing some of the priceless holy relics amassed for the protection and prosperity of the dynasty and empire: a splinter of Noah's ark and another of the True Cross, a scrap of Christ's swaddling clothes, a few drops of the Virgin Mary's milk and some of the palms waved to welcome Christ into Jerusalem the week before he was crucified. The boxes – inlaid with walrus ivory, with pearls and coral and gems set in gold and bronze – bore all the signs of handiwork performed with heartfelt faith. Solidly haloed figures of the Apostles sat crouched in their long robes, their hands and feet enlarged in a touching way, their heads huge and eyes staring. There was a golden Christ seated in glory as befitted the Lord of Lords, framed by a mandorla of amethysts. But there was also another Christ, hanging slightly askew on his cross, humble and spindly with those enlarged hands and feet. It seemed to me suddenly that Renaissance art with its much vaunted devotion and attention to the human form, had

in no way outclassed this earlier aesthetic in its ability to communicate a deep humanity. I recalled something a French historian of
the period, Georges Duby, has written about the age which produced
such art: 'That is why the greatest and possibly the only sacred art
in [western] Europe was born at this particular point in history, in
the brief interval when man, although he had not shaken off his age-
old dreads, had access to very effective instruments of creativity.'[xxxv]

Like the abbesses of Quedlinburg, the treasury had survived the
upheaval of the Reformation and the frequent wars of the sixteenth
to the early twentieth centuries undisturbed. Only the total war of
the mid-twentieth century almost destroyed it. In 1939 Himmler
had taken the precaution of storing the treasure in a Quedlinburg
bank vault, but Allied bombing in 1943 meant that it had had to
be moved to a cave in the woods south-east of the town. There,
in 1945, it was discovered by an American soldier. Immediately
apprehending the priceless nature of his find, he had secretly shipped
some of it home to Texas. The items were deeply mourned and
assumed lost until the soldier died in the early 1990s and they
began appearing for sale on the international art market. Reunited
Germany demanded their immediate restitution. An acrimonious
legal dispute ensued. Eventually the German government found
some three million dollars to pay for their safe return.

Professor Leike admitted that he was pleased his country was
embarking on the new millennium with its Quedlinburg treasures
safely back home. So was I, but I had a train – or three – to catch:
Quedlinburg to Berlin, Berlin to Poznan, Poznan to Gniezno.

~

That unseasonably warm Good Friday evening the train driver
wished us all a 'herzlich wilkommen' aboard his coolly air-conditioned
Posnania Express from Berlin to Poznan.

My mind was still crammed with images of King Heinrich
Himmler, forest quarantine camps, jewelled reliquaries and a twentieth-century Texan who had seen fit to behave like a tenth-century

Viking. It was time to recall my turn of the second millennium heroes, Thorvald the Far-farer and Otto; this particular journey east is one both men seem to have made.

Thorvald passed this way from Germany into Slav lands, no doubt intending to pick up the Varangian route south down the Russian rivers to the Black Sea, Constantinople and Jerusalem. On his way, at a place on the Baltic coast just across the border into modern Poland, he encountered the Norwegian King Olaf I. Jumne was a large and bustling settlement, glowingly described by one contemporary as 'a most noble city' despite the fact that its inhabitants were 'still blundering about in pagan rites. Otherwise,' he continued in surprise, 'as far as morals and hospitality are concerned, a more honourable or kindlier folk cannot be found. Rich in the wares of all the northern nations, that city lacks nothing that is either pleasing or rare.'[xxxvi] Just as I had learned in Iceland, Christianity was not a requirement for ordered living in the early eleventh century.

One of the Norwegian sagas tells us that Thorvald and Olaf were delighted to make each other's acquaintance. It seems that the news of Thorvald's failed mission had not reached the Norwegian king because 'as each of them had heard a lot about the good sense, renown and glory of the other, they greeted each other as if they knew each other, although they had never seen each other before'.[xxxvii] Thorvald told Olaf all about his passionate allegiance to the great Lord Jesus Christ and, in so doing, might have planted the first seeds of faith in the ferocious man because Olaf became Christian shortly afterwards and went on to bully the Icelanders into converting too in the year 1000.

As youthfully, idealistically energetic as Thorvald, Otto III was as eager as the Viking had been to usher in the new millennium with a change for the better. Thanks to Theophano, Otto was imbued with that beautiful Byzantine notion of an emperor ruling in partnership – *symphonia* – with the head of the Church, with the goal of realizing Christ's vision of peace on earth. Determined to restore the enfeebled papacy, his first act as emperor was to place his twenty-three-year-old cousin Bruno, on the papal throne as Gregory V, while he returned home to fight some more troublesome Slavs on his eastern border. A German surrounded by Romans who resented him as a foreigner, cousin Bruno was soon chased out of his palace and replaced by one of the powerful Roman families with none other than Otto's godfather and childhood tutor, the rumoured lover of Theophano, John Philagathos. Preferring the looser style of Byzantine dominion over southern Italy to any heavy German hand, Rome's Crescenti clan had succeeded in winning Byzantium's backing for their antipope.

Young Otto's wrath at Rome's flouting of his imperial will knew no bounds. Crossing the Alps with an army, he descended on Rome to reinstate his cousin. He must have felt horribly betrayed by Philagathos because the punishment he devised for him was barbaric. Philagathos's nose, ears and hands were hacked off, his tongue sliced away and his eyes popped out of their sockets before he was thrown into a monastery to rot to death. But he did not die and an old Greek hermit called Nilus took up his fellow countryman's cause. A church council was convened in Rome to which the eighty-eight-year-old Nilus travelled from his hermitage in the wilds of Byzantine southern Italy. He entered the church with Otto and Cousin Bruno supporting his faltering steps, and they placed him between them in the seat of honour. Then in came the monstrously mutilated Philagathos, robed in all his antipope's finery, which he was ordered to surrender item by item. Soon he was standing, Christ-like in his naked humiliation, in the middle of the church. Next, Otto commanded a grotesque cavalcade to be formed. The disgraced Philagathos was dressed in a penitent's robe and his head covered with a hairy hide. Seated back to front on a donkey he was led on a tour of the city, the Romans trembling at this barbaric German vengeance.

With tears streaming down his cheeks saintly old Nilus begged the emperor and pope to forgive Philagathos and offered to make himself responsible for the antipope's proper reformation. Unmoved, Cousin Bruno was satisfied that justice was being done, but Emperor

Otto, suddenly overcome with remorse at his abominable flouting of Christ's commandment to forgive and love one's enemies, burst into tears. Such monstrous vengeance would not hasten the arrival of the second millennium that Otto was hoping to see. Philagathos was permitted to live out a quiet retirement in a German monastery, safely removed from any fresh temptation to conspire with Byzantium against the Holy Roman Empire. But this was not Otto's last meeting with Nilus.

Like his mother before him the young emperor was much drawn to the company of solitary, fatherly and palpably holy Eastern Christian hermits like Nilus. Such men had been colonizing the rocky forested wastes of southern Italy in large numbers since Saracen rule had replaced Byzantine control of Sicily in the ninth century. Otto also set great store by an activity of whose value Christians of both the East and West were convinced – pilgrimage, preferably performed barefoot and clothed in a penitent's homespun garb. He believed that long arduous journeys to any of the holy shrines in his empire were as vital and useful a means of safeguarding his realm as waging a war or granting trading privileges to towns or engaging in diplomacy with foreign powers. With his adviser the Bishop of Worms he once set off for a remote cave, barefoot and wearing a hair shirt, to spend a fortnight in prayer, night vigils and strict fasting. It was only natural that he should include old Nilus' hermitage at Gaeta, a rocky outcrop a few miles up the coast from modern Naples, in a round trip taking in the cave shrine to St Michael on Monte Sant' Angelo, and the great Benedictine monastery of Monte Cassino.

Arriving at Gaeta, the young emperor's heart was filled with joy at the rough huts and barren rock of the hermit's place. ' "Here are the tents of Israel, the tabernacle of the Lord among men!" ' he exclaimed. Old Nilus approached his kneeling emperor and, in a gesture of fatherly welcome, hung his long white beard over Otto's head. As he usually did when he scented true piety, Otto wanted to lure Nilus away from his humble hermitage and build him a rich monastery in a more accessible location. ' "Ask of me, as if I was your son, everything you want and I will do it for you," ' he is said to have said to Nilus. At this, the saint to be laid his hand on the emperor's chest and said, ' "I require nothing more of your Majesty than that you think about the health of your soul, because even if you are the sovereign, you must die like everyone else and give an account of your good and bad actions." 'xxxviii Here was a Mediterranean Bishop Frederick gently reprimanding an imperial Thorvald. Once again Otto gave way to bitter tears of repentance at his cruel treatment of Philagathos. Placing his crown in Nilus' hands, he begged for the old man's blessing.

In Otto's soul there was always a painful struggle between his own desire to ensure his eternal salvation and divine assistance for his people by becoming a simple monk or, alternatively, to do his perceived duty by ruling his often unruly empire with a firm hand. Essentially, it was a tension caused by trying to reconcile ancient Germanic mores which, as in Iceland, exalted honour and combat, with a religion which enjoined its followers to turn the other cheek and cultivate humility. Sometimes this strain was too much for him. Otto often talked of abdicating his throne, donning a monk's hairy robe and departing on a pilgrimage to Jerusalem.

Another holy monk was the prime motivation behind Otto's decision to pass this way from German to Polish lands on a long pilgrimage to Gniezno in January 1000. Adalbert was of noble Czech birth but had become a simple monk by the time he and Otto met in Rome, while the latter was still a teenager. Otto seems to have felt great affection and respect for the little man, and Theophano and old Nilus had also loved him for his extraordinary humility, for his sweet charity and his inability to laugh since being consecrated Bishop of Prague. He wore a hair shirt and slept on the ground, cleaned other people's shoes, gathered his own firewood and cooked his own meals. When Theophano gave him some gold to pay for some prayers and cover any expenses he might incur on a planned pilgrimage to Jerusalem, Adalbert donated it straight to the poor of Rome. Otto loved to have Adalbert near him and used to accommodate him in his own bedchamber, where he could be on hand for twenty-four-hour counselling of the spiritual cum political variety commonly practised by Byzantine spiritual fathers. When he was not advising the teenage emperor or beseeching his fellow Czechs to abandon their barbarous ways, outlaw slave trading and follow Christ, Adalbert was a bright beacon of holiness in Rome's monastery of St Alessio and St Boniface and a brave missionary whose beat included the wildest reaches of central and north-eastern Europe.

Adalbert fared very far indeed – through Italy, France and central Europe all the way to the eastern Baltic coast to what is now the Russian enclave of Kaliningrad, managing to represent what was best in both the Byzantine and Western traditions. An active and hard-working bishop and missionary, he was also deeply spiritual, a true ascetic and a miracle-worker. By once stepping on the head of a snake he turned all its fellows to stone for a mile around the spot. He could also silence croaking frogs whose racket disturbed his prayers.

It was either at Otto's suggestion or at the behest of a dream that Adalbert embarked on his final, fatal mission to convert the heathen Prussians. In 997, in the vicinity of modern Gdansk, his mission started badly. Local Prussians were so keen to hear what Adalbert might have to tell them about his sweet Lord Jesus Christ that when he refused to stop singing his psalms they were moved to clobber him with his boat paddle. It took only eight days for the local pagan priests to recognize the threat to their livelihood; Adalbert and his crew were outlawed and escorted back west into Polish territory. But instead of giving up, the doughty holy missionary and his half-brother decided to do some hunting, say a mass and rest a while before making another assault on the pagan souls of the Prussians. They had travelled no more than twenty kilometres back into hostile territory when they were set upon by pagan priests in no mood to give the stubborn Christians a second chance. Adalbert was bludgeoned with axes, lanced by spears and died a horrible death as one of the pagan priests jeered, ' "You ought to rejoice since, to judge from your talk, you desire nothing so much as to die for your Christ." 'xxxix

They decapitated him, hurled his body in a nearby lake and flung his head into a field for wild animals to feast on. But one story relates that the head never landed in that field. Instead, an angel caught it as it flew through the air and transported it to the opposite bank of the lake, where the rest of his body was washed up. Reunited with its head, the corpse rested there in the reeds a while without rotting until some merchants who happened to be sailing past spotted it, recognized the saintly monk, dragged him on board their boat and took him back to the lands of the Poles. Perhaps they dreamed of a tidy profit. They must have calculated that their Polish Duke Boleslaw would be delighted to own the holy, uncorrupted relics of the man who had baptized him. They were right. Boleslaw received them joyfully and paid the merchants handsomely because he knew that a full set of Adalbert's holy relics represented a step on the way to his dream of becoming king of Poland. The sacred remains were laid to rest in a worthy sanctuary in his capital, Gniezno.

Adalbert had been dead three years and Otto was twenty when, in January 1000, he set out on his pilgrimage to revere the remains of his dear friend and spiritual father. Journeying all the way up from Rome, he crossed the Alps and his German dominions, and continued eastward. The north-east German and north-west Polish plains would have been whipped by winds blowing down from the Baltic at that time of year, so his progress at the head of his retinue would have been slow and gruelling, marked by the occasional grand entrance into a town, feasting with the local bishop and long religious services. It was early March before he reached his destination.

It would be near midnight, I calculated, before the Posnania Express reached Poznan. I would have to spend the night there instead of catching the local train on to Gniezno. The border formalities at Frankfurt an der Oder seemed interminable but at last quiet, then a whistle, then lurch . . . lurch . . . lurch, and we were off again, with warm night air blowing through the open windows.

~

The hot air stank of diesel. Poznan railway station was thronged with people heaving huge bags on their shoulders that Good Friday night. Outside, all the chaos of honking taxis, cars backing out of tiny parking spaces, others squeezing into smaller ones, buses revving to leave was alarming after the ordered emptiness of Quedlinburg and my long historical reverie.

A young taxi driver grunted his understanding of my request to be taken to the nearest hotel, jumped into the driving seat, lit a cigarette and proceeded to race his battered Lada too fast over the cobbles of a tree-lined avenue. I was relieved to find myself alone a few minutes later in a plain hotel room a good seven storeys above the street where other motor racers screeched past through the hot night. Polish television would drown out the din. The first channel showed Polish Pope John Paul II, robed in white and purple, at a mournful Good Friday service in Rome. Channel Two had a nun clutching the back seat of a jeep being driven by a moustachioed British army officer. The third channel was airing a timely documentary about safe driving, and BBC World confidently informed its viewers that 'That's what it's all about – selling a car in a competitive marketplace!'

The next button I pressed flashed me back to a close-up of the pope. There I lingered a while, astonished at how aged the Holy Father looked. He was bowed and frail, a fossil of the man he had been back in 1978 when the conclave of cardinals elected him. The staunchly Catholic Poles, whose Church had always been a fortress of opposition to the country's officially atheist Communist regime, were hugely proud that the first non-Italian pope for over four hundred and fifty years was one of them. Their centuries of devotedly upholding the faith there on the north-eastern border of Western Christendom had at last won universal recognition. The joint communiqué issued by the Polish bishops on the occasion of John Paul II's election attributed the triumph to the support of the Holy Spirit and the Virgin Mary and to the 'prayers of the entire Polish people who have received this reward for their faith and the vitality of their religion'.[xl]

No pope in history has ever fared as far and as often as John Paul II in the twenty-two years of his papacy, or striven so effectively to overthrow Communism, or suffered the sort of assassination attempt usually reserved for American presidents. But then few of his modern predecessors have succeeded in arousing so much controversy – by his silencing of dissenters among academic theologians via a committee whose antecedent was the infamous Inquisition and his opposition to contraception for African peoples being decimated by AIDS. But as I studied his ancient stillness from every camera angle offered I could not help liking a man who looked so like my grandmother.

I could have taken the first train on to Gniezno the next morning but instead decided to dawdle awhile in this city the Germans still call Posen. It was already an important bishopric when Otto III passed through on the last leg of his long pilgrimage to Gniezno in 1000. After a wander around the old centre of the town, whose main square was filled with sunburned German tourists photographing each other or quaffing tall glasses of beer at open-air tables, I found myself in a less attractive market square, crowded with winter-pale Poles. Water splashed on mounds of giant radishes, tomatoes and spring onions was keeping the produce fresher and brighter than anything else in sight. I paused for a moment by an old woman displaying her meagre wares in a spot of shade on the pavement. In front of her were pats of pale frozen butter sculpted in the shape of lamb and measuring about four inches long, two and a half inches high. I guessed that no Polish Easter Sunday lunch table could be described as complete without its little butter *Agnus Dei*.

What I was looking for was a pavement café to sit and watch

this world go by from, but there was none in sight. The quietest, coolest spot I could find down a leafily shaded side street was a modern red-brick church in which something out of the ordinary seemed to be going on. Two policemen in grey-blue uniforms came out of the main entrance crossing themselves respectfully, followed by a priest in his shirtsleeves. A police car drove out of the courtyard around the back of the church, through the gates and out into the street. I must have arrived in time for the final minutes of a police-man's funeral, I decided. Inside was a large, mostly kneeling congregation and up on the altar a cardboard structure fashioned to look like a cave, painted grey and adorned with a crazy-paving pattern. Draped with a red and white Polish flag and surrounded by big bunches of red and white flowers, it was guarded by two policemen. As I drew closer, I observed that in the red-lit interior of this bizarre installation lay the naked corpse of their dear departed colleague, his thin ribs clearly visible through wax-pale skin. On still closer inspection – I had slid into the second pew – there could be little doubt that the poor man had met his end violently. A long bleeding wound glistened in his side.

It was a while before I realized that I was not viewing a real corpse at all, but a three-dimensional re-creation of the broken Christ lying in his tomb on the day after crucifixion, prior to his resurrection on Easter Sunday morning. In Germany there had been nothing but the crudely coloured Easter eggs in Magdeburg's railway station buffet to remind me of Easter's proximity. In Poland, butter *Agni Dei* and this lurid life-size Easter crib were more than enough to remind me of the imminence of the most important date in the Christian calendar.

In front of the altar was a coffin draped in a Lenten purple cloth on which was laid a very large cross to which was affixed another gruesomely suffering Christ, and in front of that was a large wooden box marked 'Offerings for Our Lord's tomb in Jerusalem'. Now and again a bowed old woman or a shuffling old man with a plastic bag full of vegetables over his arm would leave their pew to walk up the centre aisle and drop some money in the box. The jangling of coins sounded unnaturally loud in that quiet.

I had been sitting there for some five minutes when the thunder of marching boots disturbed the peace. Two fresh young policemen stamped up to the altar and executed a swift about-turn as the previous guards marched away down the aisle. The points of their fixed bayonets and the toes of their shiny boots gleamed in the gloom.

~

'*Ulica Seminaryjna 2.*'

'The seminary?!'

'Two, Seminary Street,' I repeated firmly.

The taxi driver muttered something but started the car. What business was it of his if a single foreign woman was demanding transportation to Gniezno's Catholic priests' seminary?

My sudden huffiness masked the simple truth: I was nervous at the prospect of staying in a seminary. As I watched a little town of cobbled streets and small, once elegant but now shabby nineteenth-century houses go by in the sunny early afternoon, I told myself that I was lucky to have a seminary to call home for a few days, lucky to have Father Waldemar Szczerbinski awaiting my arrival there. Hadn't he sounded welcoming and helpful on the telephone from Quedlinburg? 'I'll give you my mobile number,' he had said, 'but you can also get me on e-mail. By the way, my American friends call me Wally . . .'

He would have been speaking from the celestial vision which had just appeared at the end of a side road, resplendent behind a pair of high iron gates – the seminary. A new baroque-yellow Italianate palace set near a lake in formal green lawns and flower beds, it was by far the most impressive building we had passed. It outclassed even the fourteenth-century cathedral of the Assumption of the Virgin Mary and St Adalbert, within whose pale green copper roof and rather pedestrian red-brick walls rested the holy relics of

Adalbert. The taxi driver stopped the car at the gates and indicated that I should get out to speak into the intercom panel. A stuttered 'Szczerbinski' won me admission. I collected my bags and slung them over my shoulders, trying hard to picture a travel-soiled Otto III removing his kingly finery and footwear and donning a penitent's rough robe to walk the last part of his way into Gniezno barefoot. Escorted by the Bishop of Poznan, Otto had been led straight to Adalbert's tomb, where he spent a long while weeping and praying. Trudging up the driveway through the gardens, I crossed an empty courtyard and mounted a wide flight of steps towards what seemed to be the building's main entrance. In the cool of a dark hallway a porter telephoned the news of my arrival.

Father Waldemar was much younger than I had expected, probably twenty-eight and no older than thirty. Elegant in a white collarless shirt and black trousers, his black hair was modishly short and his dark eyes behind their fashionable rectangular-framed spectacles scrutinized me with intelligent interest. Explaining that the seminary was almost empty because the students had all gone home for the Easter weekend break, he shepherded me past a larger than life-size statue of the Virgin Mary with a halo of burning light bulbs, up a wide flight of marble stairs, along a shiny parquet-floored corridor and into his apartment, as he called it. Father Waldemar had learned most of his English in Chicago while filling in for priests serving that city's large Polish community.

He sat me down in his comfortable sitting room with a picture of Pope John Paul II on the wall in front of a coffee table laden with plates of creamy cakes and bowls of sweets. Soon we were deeply embroiled in a discussion about how to 'build a new Europe while saving an experience of the transcendent in people's lives'. I mentioned that I believed Otto III had been inspired by the same ideal but Father Waldemar was in no mood for an excursion into the distant past. The problem he was posing was much too urgent to waste any time luxuriating in the year 1000, and he admitted he knew nothing about Otto.

'What I mean is,' he continued, 'how can we teach young people
– children – that reality is not what we can see and touch?'

I liked his passion, which I imagined made him an excellent
teacher here at the seminary, but I also appreciated his occasional
lively illustrations of abstract notions, because he was leaving me
floundering way behind once he progressed to a survey of Plato and
Aristotle, Kant and Hegel. In the manner of a kind teacher, he
returned to rescue me.

'Look,' he said, 'philosophy is like studying a map of London
with a key marking all the places of interest and saying "That's
enough – I don't need to go to London now – I know it." Theology?
Well. Let's imagine you have an uncle, and he organizes a flight
over London for you so that you can see the whole city at once.
That's theology. Do you know the city now? Oh my gosh, I don't
think so! Now mysticism, that's different! With mysticism I travel
into London; I walk around, meet people, spend time there . . .'

We repaired to his balcony and stood there smoking and talking
as the sun went down over the gardens and behind the cathedral.
Our conversation moved on from his vocation, the seeds of which
had been sown by an admirable priest at a Catholic holiday camp
he had visited at the age of eighteen, to his having to resist the
temptation to accept American friends' invitations to emigrate
there.

'Life would be much easier for me in Chicago, of course,' he
said, exhaling into the warm evening air, 'but the archbishop would
never forgive me. He needs me here in Poland. By the way, if you
want to talk about Europe and Otto you should speak to him. He
loves all that history and politics and international affairs. He's a
real politician.'

'I'd love to meet him,' I said, and he kindly offered to arrange it.

'But life is not too bad for you here, is it? A Catholic priest in
Poland still commands respect and love. I've read that twenty-eight
per cent of all Catholic seminarians in 1990 were Polish, that
ninety per cent of Poles describe themselves as Roman Catholic
and seventy-nine per cent answered yes to the question, "Is there a

God who became Man?"* Poland must be easily the best place in Europe to be a Catholic priest and the Polish Church seems to be quite wealthy—'

'Oh my gosh! It's changing! Now we priests are finding that we do not have the authority we used to have. Schoolchildren just tell us to "Fuck off". Only the other day I caught a little boy of about five years old scrawling "Fuck off" on the seminary wall. When I asked him if he knew what it meant, he said he'd heard it on television. Oh my gosh!'

Waldemar explained that for most of the twentieth century, until the end of the Communist era, every Polish mother had dreamed of her son becoming a priest. Many of the nation's very ablest minds and spirits had been dedicated to the service of the Catholic Church, to passively and actively opposing the atheist regime. This was the society that had produced John Paul II, he reminded me. Even in that bleak Communist period the average Polish priest had enjoyed a more than decent standard of living, Waldemar went on. Faithful, grateful congregations would ensure that their men of God owned colour televisions, the latest make of radio and perhaps even a *polski* Fiat.

'What is there to attract us now?' Waldemar continued.

'But you still have young men wanting to join the priesthood?'

'Not as many as we used to, but yes, there are twelve hundred seminarians studying here in Gniezno and that's just one diocese in the country. The others also have big seminaries. This,' he added fervently, 'is what we can give Europe when we join the European Union – our religious vocations!'

Waldemar told me how this question of Poland's special gift to the European Union had come up at a recent meeting here in Gniezno of the central European heads of state. It had been the archbishop's grand inspiration to lure them here for the anniversary celebrations of Otto III's pilgrimage to Gniezno in 1000. By

* Britain 32.9%, USA 69.2%, France 21.8%. Taken from Kloczowski, Jerzy, *A History of Polish Christianity*, Cambridge, Cambridge University Press, 2000, p. 338.

reminding modern Germans of the way their young Otto had vener-
ated St Adalbert and welcomed Poles into his Holy Roman Empire,
of how he had granted them a dignified measure of autonomy and
let them establish their own archdiocese, the present Archbishop
of Gniezno had been hoping to prod them into championing modern
Poland's fast-track entry into the European Union.

'So this is what you mean when you say Archbishop Muszynski's
a politician? I see now . . .' I marvelled, thinking that Gniezno's
archbishop was a much more convincing reincarnation of Poland's
Duke Boleslaw than Heinrich Himmler had ever been of Heinrich
the Fowler. Truly, the eleventh century had been reborn here in
Gniezno.

'Yes, of course,' said Waldemar, continuing with his tale.

In polite deference to their mitred Polish host, the various
politicians had surpassed each other with high-flown sentiments
about Adalbert's legacy and the crucial role western Europe's
Christian heritage would play in the successful unification of the
continent, until it was the turn of the German head of state to
speak. According to Waldemar, President Johannes Rau had brought
the entire occasion back down to earth with a bump by informing
the assembled company that something as prosaic as economics
would be the foundation stone of the new Europe.

'I suppose he had to say something of the sort because Europe
isn't only Christian any more,' I reasoned tentatively.

'But our archbishop was furious. Oh my gosh! He hated it! You
know, he had hired a fancy chef from Poznan. There were all the
finest wines and the most expensive vodka. By the way, he had to
tax the clergy an extra two hundred zlotys to pay for all of that!
Anyway, I can tell you that everyone was very shocked by the
German president's speech,' said Waldemar, 'including myself, actually. Now, I must take you to where you're staying . . .'

'Fine,' I agreed, a little surprised. I had thought I would be
staying in the seminary but was more than happy to leave all such
arrangements in Waldemar's hands.

The doors of the only car in the courtyard, a gleaming new

green Volkswagen Polo, clicked open as we approached. With another click of his key ring the seminary's high metal gates buzzed apart. The streets were quiet that balmy early evening. There was just the odd old man with a plastic shopping bag, a bird-like old lady in black walking a tiny dog, a teenage couple kissing and a tramp with his trousers at half-mast urinating into an empty fountain. It was a very small town but its fine nineteenth-century were buildings in a reasonably good state of repair, especially in the vicinity of the cathedral.

'Well, of course Gniezno is the cradle of the Polish state and the seat of its first archdiocese. Everything looks quite nice in the centre here because a lot of renovation was done for the pope's three visits here in 1979, 1983 and 1997, I think.'

'1997 would have been the anniversary of St Adalbert's death.'

'That's it. That was when the pope said Europe needs re-evangelizing in Christianity with the help of St Adalbert. That's why there's a big slogan on the wall of a building opposite the cathedral, saying "Holy Wojciech,* patron of the new evangelization." It lights up blue at night. Look over there now, the same kind of thing.'

'Oh, yes!' On a red-brick wall were a pair of placards. One was a blue circle containing an outline map of western and central Europe, with a white bishop's crozier and Bible superimposed on it, and Adalbert's dates, in yellow, around the side. I could not decipher the slogan on the second without Waldemar's help.

'With the faith and courage of Holy Wojciech, into the new millennium,' he translated for me, with an embarrassed giggle. Pre-empting my observation that these propaganda placards were strangely reminiscent of the Communist era, he repeated a previous assertion: 'You have to understand that our archbishop is a very political person.'

He stopped the car in a quiet and shady side street, by another securely fenced and gated establishment. It was two storeys high, red brick, and it looked as impressively new as the seminary.

---

* Wojciech is the Polish and Czech name for Adalbert.

'This is a hospice for retired priests of the diocese,' Waldemar explained, 'This is where you'll be staying. It's run by nuns.'

Inside, a sweet-faced Sister Consolata with anxious blue eyes showed me to a light apartment of about the same size as Waldemar's. I managed to thank her with a *'Dziekuje Pani'* and she hugged me in welcome. No sooner had I dropped my bags than Waldemar declared that we were off again. We drove to a house a stone's throw from a large statue of St Adalbert and a church. It was home to Waldemar's friend, Father Christopher, a district army chaplain. There I was also introduced to Waldemar's widowed mother, whose bouts of morbid depression were worrying her son. Apparently recovered from her morning misery she plied us with a variety of cakes and tea before reminding Waldemar that he should stop smoking and arguing with me about whether the new Europe could be founded on human rights instead of Christianity. It was high time he started getting ready.

'Ready for what?' I asked.

'I'm doing the Easter mass at the church next door,' Waldemar explained quickly. 'Father Christopher has asked me because I have a better singing voice. It starts in five minutes,' he said, glancing at his watch, reaching for another cigarette and picking up again where he had left off.

'Look, what are human rights? Human rights have no firm base in anything except the votes of a few people. OK, I know what you're going to say: "That's democracy." But in democracy freedom is the most important value apparently. Well – my gosh, Victoria – didn't Plato warn us that democracy without truth ends in chaos?'

'He may have done, but who decides what the truth is, Waldemar?'

'Good question! Science? No, because it can't answer questions like "What's the meaning of life?" Philosophy? No, because there are too many different philosophies. Religion? YES! And for Europe it must be Christianity because that is our history.'

'But Christianity's curriculum vitae is not altogether excellent,

Waldemar, is it? Crusades, wars, inquisitions, more wars . . . Why should that be our truth?'

'Because the Catholic Church has the truth about how to achieve the salvation of man. The world can't be built on some economic truth or on some truth like human rights which is just about voting. I don't want some court of human rights telling me that homosexual marriage must become legal in my country . . . Oh my gosh – I'm going to be late!'

I was left pondering the fact that John Paul II has expressed the same sort of distrust of the only political doctrine on offer in the new Europe of the third millennium. The Pope has written, 'If there is no ultimate truth to guide political activity, then ideas and convictions can easily be manipulated for reasons of power. As history demonstrates, a democracy without values easily turns into open or thinly disguised totalitarianism.'[xli]

Minutes later Waldemar's mother and I were outside, by a statue of St Adalbert, standing arm in arm among a gathering crowd of churchgoers. I noticed a touchingly reverent family group, father and son in matching pink T-shirts. There was also a stout young nun, frowning and clutching her fat yellow Easter candle like a cosh. Just as the evening sky was turning a luminous shade of apricot and the unseasonal heat of the day relenting a little, a deacon wearing shabby slacks and a pair of scuffed beige lace-ups under his richly embroidered surplice crouched like a playground pyromaniac to set fire to a tiny pile of twigs on the pavement. A few nuns began to sing and some of the congregation joined in. At this signal Waldemar, gloriously handsome in red and gold chasuble emblazoned with a risen Christ motif, appeared. Just as he began to process towards an altar boy holding a giant Easter candle, a couple of young men wearing baseball caps roared by in an open-top Volkswagen. They drowned out the frail thread of the song, distracted the faithful and were followed by a lad riding his bicycle without any hands who shouted something cheery at another altar boy. Too big for his lacy surplice and wearing grubby trainers, the child stared after him longingly. Waldemar stuck five bobbles of red wax – the crucified Christ's five wounds – in the big candle, and the singing picked up again.

Keeping a tight grip on my arm, Waldemar's mother walked me to the front pew of the packed church. The service was emotional and plentifully embellished with special effects, most of them engineered by the exuberant altar boys. During his gospel reading Waldemar vanished behind a thick grey cloud of incense billowing out of a too enthusiastically swung censer. Another boy jangled three bells far too loudly throughout one of the gentler hymns. Waldemar's beautifully delivered sermon was a measured affair. He seemed to be speaking to his suffering mother, but also to the small town's thousands of recently unemployed factory workers; in fact to anyone struggling hard to adapt to the new sort of society being built in the expectation of Poland's speedy inclusion in the European Union. Waldemar was inviting us all to imagine what Christ's apostles must have felt like on the day after his crucifixion. Abandoned, angry, lost, let down . . . Don't we all have the same feelings when someone we love dies, when we lose our jobs, when the world seems to be changing too fast for us to keep up, when we lose hope? We have to believe that there is comfort and hope in Christ's glorious resurrection from the dead was his message. When he consecrated the Holy Communion wafer and wine, Christ's body and blood, a military trumpet blast sounded in triumph. The final hymn was heartfelt, loud and led by Waldemar's mother on my left.

～

Sister Consolata had lovingly laid an Easter Sunday breakfast for me in an empty refectory sparingly adorned with a rubber plant and a reproduction of Christ's face on the Turin Shroud. In pride of place was a butter *Agnus Dei* with a couple of tiny, shiny leaves to mark his tail and mouth, and a fancy red ribbon around his neck. Stuck in a bowl of coloured sugar Easter eggs was a toothpick flying a miniature red banner emblazoned with the single word 'Alleluia!'. Little dishes of ham, sausage, beef, tinned artichokes, fresh radishes, white and brown bread, jam, a pink mousse cake studded with raisins, Thermoses of coffee and tea and a large bar of chocolate completed the spread. Otto and his mighty retinue of a thousand years ago, but also it seemed the political archbishop's posse of presidents only a few weeks ago, had met with a comparable level of hospitality here in Gniezno.

On the earlier occasion, rank upon rank of knights had welcomed the handsome young Holy Roman emperor. Each of them was wearing his finest clothes, 'and this was no cheap spangle of any old stuff', writes a monk chronicler who had an almost feminine eye for quality, colour and price, 'but the most costly things that can be found anywhere on earth'.[xlii] Once the spiritual and political business of the visit had been taken care of there had followed three days of sumptuous feasting. On each of those three days the fine tableware used was replaced with something still finer. By the third day the high table was a gorgeous glitter of gold and silver. At the end of the long celebrations every last drinking horn, beaker, chalice, platter and dish that had been used was collected up and presented to Otto as a gift. As if this were not a staggeringly generous gesture even by the standards of the day, the monk reports that the house servants of Duke Boleslaw's palace were then instructed to gather up all 'cloths, carpets, table-cloths and hand-towels'[xliii] as well, and haul them into Otto's apartments. 'Apart from that,' the prodigious pedant continues, Duke Boleslaw 'donated all other vessels, implements, containers in great number and particularly those in gold and silver of different designs, many coloured cloaks and jewels of rare design, gems . . .'[xliv] 'Not a single servant, among so many, went home without a gift of some sort'[xlv] is the conclusion to this catalogue of material delights.

Emperor Otto was overcome by Duke Boleslaw's munificence. 'By the crown of my empire! What I see far exceeds what I have heard!'[xlvi] he is supposed to have exclaimed in admiration, before protesting to his host that he had come to Gniezno not 'to rob and take, but to give and to pray'.[xlvii] In fact, neither man was in any doubt as to what the true purpose of Otto's visit was.

In the year 1000, Otto was at the height of his powers. He had installed his ex-tutor and great friend Gerbert as Pope Sylvester II. Together, in the harmonious partnership between empire and Church that the Byzantines favoured, Otto III and Sylvester II had conceived a magnificent foreign policy to assist their restoration of the glorious universal Roman Empire, East and West, Rome and Constantinople. Two hundred years before, Charlemagne had dreamed the dream of a *renovatio imperii Romanorum* and so had Theophano's father-in-law Otto I, but it was Otto III who fared furthest on this road.

Twenty-year-old Otto, far from cringing in paralysed terror at dire predictions of the end of the world and Christ's Last Judgement, was marking the start of the second millennium with bold and generous innovations. He wanted to create a loose federation of peoples voluntarily bound together by a common Christian culture. The empire's eastern borders, even in those lands recently conquered by Germans, were to be secured by faith and friendship. Otto, like the Byzantines or today's NATO and European Union, could see the virtue and wisdom in securing one's flanks by means of an inclusive rather than an exclusive policy. It has taken western Europeans almost a thousand years of false starts, brutal hegemonies and heinous religious then national wars to recapture something akin to his vision of a peacefully united continent, albeit one united in the twin 'truths' of market economics and human rights rather than the gospel of Jesus Christ.

Hungarians as well as Poles were to be welcomed into his Christian federation. Pope Sylvester crowned Istvan king of Hungary, thereby removing for ever the dark threat of barbaric Magyars rampaging through Europe causing havoc and bloodshed. The Hungarians gained their own archdiocese at Gran, now Esztergom, a few miles north of Budapest, and with it a welcome measure of independence from German rule. Otto's similar inspiration for Poland was to relieve the Poles of their humiliating tribute-paying status and elevate Duke Boleslaw to a position of dignity within the empire. A new Polish archdiocese at Gniezno would be the Poles' passport to a measure of autonomy equal to that of Hungary. An embassy was briefed to offer the same sort of advantageous terms to Vladimir of Kiev and despatched south-east to the Ukraine. Sadly, it was rebuffed by suspicious Byzantine churchmen who had only recently succeeded in luring Vladimir and his people into the Eastern Christian sphere of influence.

But Otto was also pursuing another avenue in his efforts to improve relations with Byzantium. Negotiations for the hand in marriage of a princess more *porphyrogeneta* than his mother Theophano were in progress. He wooed his unruly Roman subjects too. In the same year that he journeyed to Poland, he sought to pacify them by making their city his capital and by building himself a royal residence, a palace cum fortress, on the salubrious heights of the Aventine Hill. There he instituted every ancient court ritual he could think of, whether ancient Roman, Byzantine or German, and tactfully appointed Italians to top posts in his administration with titles like *Protospatharius, Magister Militiae, Patricius* and *Logothete.* Although he had no good reason to favour the turbulent Romans with his trust and esteem – especially after the Crescenti plot to replace Cousin Bruno with John Philagathos – he gave them the benefit of the doubt. In a manner of speaking, he turned the other cheek.

The Polish plank of his foreign policy, less risky than the Roman one and much easier to achieve, had been carefully laid some time before Otto reached Gniezno. There was a plan to marry one of Otto's nieces to one of Boleslaw's sons and, perhaps most important of all to Otto, the question of the guardianship of holy Adalbert's relics. Otto is said to have requested every last bone of the monk's body in exchange for the wonderful favour he was showing the Poles. Boleslaw found that he could only spare the emperor one of the saint's arms. In an era when such flagrant *lèse majesté* could bring down the wrath of an imperial army, Otto did not insist. Again, he turned the other cheek.

A Polish monk known as the Anonymous Gaul has left us a detailed description of the political transaction between Otto III and Duke Boleslaw and, in so doing, a fine illustration of the way Otto favoured the use of ritual, diplomacy and magnanimity in his dealings with potential enemies. ' "It is not fit that such a man [as you] should be titled a prince or a count, as though he were just a great lord, but he should be elevated with all pomp to a throne and crowned with a crown," ' Otto is reported to have told Duke Boleslaw. In a symbolic gesture of 'union and friendship' he took the crown off his own head and placed it on the duke's. He also presented him with a priceless relic, a nail from the True Cross. The monk-chronicler enthuses that Otto and Boleslaw 'felt such love on that day that the Emperor named him brother and associate of the Empire, and called him the friend and ally of the Roman nation'.[xlviii]

Sister Consolata appeared to wish me happy Easter and check that I was enjoying my breakfast. I had left the sausage and the butter *Agnus Dei* untouched, but she seemed to feel love for me anyway and gave me another hug.

~

Waldemar and I headed out of town for a tour of this oldest region of Poland, Wielkapolska – Great Poland. Relaxed in a pair of jeans and checked shirt, he was proving excellent company. The heatwave was lasting and top of the Polish pops on the car radio was Tom Jones' catchy 'Sex bomb! Sex bomb! You're my sex bomb . . .' Waldemar hummed along happily as we sped through countryside looking mistily, flatly green, past lakes where people picnicked by their cars, and on through a forest where the occupying Soviet soldiers used to have their camp, to the well preserved medieval town of Torun where Waldemar wanted to shop for a pair of smart black sandals to wear under his cassock.

As we approached the outskirts of the town he pointed out to me a nondescript white hotel, famous as the place where, in October 1984, young Father Jerzy Popieluszko was murdered. The handsome young priest had been on his way to Torun to visit a friend and deliver some sermons of the bravely dissenting variety that had already won him a devoted following when his car had been stopped. Three secret policemen had ordered him out, beaten him up and then bundled his mangled body in the boot of their car before driving on to Torun. At the edge of town his abductors panicked at the realization that their cargo wasn't dead, opened the boot and finished him off in much the same way as Adalbert was despatched, with a bout of bludgeoning. His abominable death won the young priest instant martyr status in a society enjoying having a Polish pope in Rome and finding a fresh confidence with which to oppose the Communist authorities. Embarrassed by the outrage and protests, the government had finally claimed that the secret policemen were acting on their own stupid initiative.

'You know how we have a tradition of making a display in our churches of Christ lying in the tomb?' asked Waldemar.

'Yes, I saw a very impressive one in Poznan the other day, actually.'

'Well, perhaps you don't know that there is a competition every year to see which church can do the best display?'

'No, I didn't know that.'

'Well, the Easter after Father Popieluszko's murder – it must have been 1985 – the winning display was one showing Christ lying broken and wounded in a car boot instead of a tomb . . . Oh my gosh, that made the authorities just crazy!'

Simpler, black and white, heroic times. Multicoloured or grey, today's modern Europe cannot breed heroes like that. Great evils breed great heroes.

In Torun we tried a number of shoe shops and, after considering a pair of black and white brogues and some episcopal purple suede boots, found precisely the sort of sandal Waldemar had in mind. Later, while sitting drinking beer in a shady and cobbled town square, he admitted that hearing confessions was one of the toughest aspects of his job.

'For example, what am I supposed to say to a woman who comes to me in tears to confess the sin of having gone on the pill? I know that she has four children; that her husband drinks, beats her up and rapes her. I know that she can't separate from him because of the housing shortage. I also know what the pope says about contraception, but am I going to give her a penance for disobeying him? Oh my gosh, am I crazy? I can't! Forget it!'

The more time I spent with Waldemar the more conscious I was becoming of his unease with his situation. On the one hand he was hearing confessions like this, and on the other the pope, a Polish pope moreover, was refusing to budge on the issue of contraception. Thanks to his frequent visits to the United States, Waldemar had experienced the rebellious avant-garde of the Catholic Church in the form of openly gay Catholic priests handing out free condoms to their gay parishioners. But his heart was here in Poland where, to his mounting alarm, conservative and often anti-Semitic voices in the Church were teaming up with anti-Semitic politicians. From here in Torun a Catholic monk was running a radio station called Radio Maria after the Virgin Mary which pumped out xenophobic bile twenty-four hours a day.

'It's very popular with chronic insomniacs like my mother – older people mostly. The more liberal Church authorities are horrified but they don't want to take action and make a martyr out of him.'

We drove slowly back to Gniezno, past more lakes and through quietly drab little settlements – some only tiny villages – called, in Polish, Venice, Rome and Paris. Here, on the front line between Western and Eastern Christianity, the Poles were displaying their allegiance to the West like bright medieval banners. Now and again we stopped at churches to admire fine examples of Counter-Reformation baroque. Such a concentration of gilt and stucco, red veined marble like raw meat, fleshy cherubs, bleeding scarlet sacred hearts and golden shafts like cartoon lightning instead of haloes around saints' heads left me thirsting for the solid austerity of the Romanesque. Eleventh-century Europeans lived with the sad conviction that their world was a terrible comedown from the glory days of ancient Rome. In every stone of every Romanesque church was a bleak but brave entreaty: might a building with Roman arches be pleasing to God and bring back that ancient ordered heaven on earth? Twenty-first century Poles were still living with the products of a Church which had mounted a dazzlingly unattractive display of its wealth and power in response to the challenge of Protestantism in the seventeenth and eighteenth centuries.

Almost all the churches Waldemar and I visited seemed to be marking the end of the second Christian millennium with curious displays in their pulpits. Plastic dolls of baby Jesus dressed in white, arms in the air and lying on napkins in toy cradles, were propped up for maximum visibility against azure background cloths on which the number 2000 had been printed. In spite of my aversion to baroque art, in one of the churches we visited I could not help delighting in Waldemar's discovery of a large glass-sided coffin containing an almost life-size alabaster figure wearing a gilded mitre, a neat brown beard and fancy white shoes and gloves. His eyes closed and lips slightly opened as if he were in a sweet, deep sleep, he was reclining comfortably on a soft-looking red cushion, with a gilded book in one hand and a golden paddle in the other. The second item enabled Waldemar to identify this baroque dandy.

'It's Adalbert. The paddle's the giveaway,' said Waldemar, 'in memory of his boat trip up the Vistula to where he was killed. By the way, I've arranged a meeting with the archbishop tomorrow. What are you going to speak to him about?'

'Oh, thank you! Something about Otto and Adalbert and uniting Europe . . .'

'That'll be perfect because those are exactly his favourite topics. Did I tell you that as well as the gathering of the central European and German presidents, and another for the central European and German prime ministers which starts on Thursday, he has arranged for a programme of about a hundred events this year, mostly connected to Otto and Adalbert?'

'What sort of events?' I asked, astonished.

'Oh gosh! You know the sort of thing: races along the route that Otto III travelled to Gniezno on foot and by car, stamp exhibitions relating to the anniversary of the canonization of St

Adalbert, symposia about the heritage of St Adalbert and Europe, Rotary Club meetings to discuss a thousand years of Polish – German relations, a play called *Rhapsody about St Adalbert*, some exhibition about Otto III in Poland . . .'

'What do the locals make of all this activity?'

'Well, frankly, most of them are already tired of it. They take no notice and just grumble about all the money being spent. You know, they have their problems. About half the town is unemployed. The food-bottling and clothing factories have closed down in the last two years and now even teachers are being laid off because the birth rate's falling.'

~

Gniezno's archdiocesan headquarters were a flurry of activity on the eve of the political archbishop's second great gathering of the year – of the prime ministers of central Europe and Germany.

Dozens of young priests were dashing back and forth with mobile telephones, taking orders from each other and from a line of young nuns seated at a battery of computers in a room full of ringing telephones. A few laypeople, most of them elderly with plastic shopping bags, loitered in ante-rooms, patiently waiting to be attended to. I felt sincerely grateful that Archbishop Henryk Muszynski was making time to meet me, and a little nervous.

'Now, Waldemar,' I said, 'just fill me in on the archbishop's background, will you?'

'He's very educated. He studied in Rome, Germany and Jeru-salem, which is probably how he got his taste for the finer things in life. Now, don't worry, I think you will charm each other,' were Waldemar's reassuring last words to me at the door of the arch-bishop's office.

As a pale young nun served us doughnuts and coffee from a silver tray and Waldemar failed to relax in a high-backed red velvet-covered chair, I tried very hard to penetrate the eminent churchman's wary defences. He was dignified, cool and every inch the politician as he expounded his vision of how St Adalbert – 'a first real European figure' – could become a rallying point for the creation of a new Christian spirituality to complement Europe's 'growing political and economic links'. Aware that Pope John Paul II – just like Otto III a thousand years ago – dreams of a united Christian Europe greater than the present European Union, one which embraces Eastern Orthodox Christians too, I asked the archbishop whether he thought that not just central and western Europe but East and West – Eastern Christendom and Western Christendom – could be rejoined in the name of Adalbert after a thousand years of often tragic schism.* Had not the pope hinted at such a project way back in 1979 on his first papal visit to Gniezno, when he had made what one writer has described as 'a crucial decision... to ignore the artificial divisions of the Iron Curtain and to remind the world that Christian Europe's historical and geographical limits include the Soviet-controlled parts of eastern and central Europe'?[xlix] Had not this boldly expressed vision helped to sound the death knell for atheist Communism and sent a warm wind of change blowing through the Soviet empire? Poland's renaissance had begun the next year with the formation of Lech Walesa's free trade union, Solidarity. By 1989 President Mikhail Gorbachev was visiting the Vatican. By the end of 1991 the Soviet Union itself had collapsed.

Archbishop Muszynski remembered all that but did not seem too sure that the pope's vision of such a large reunited Christendom could be realized.

'Adalbert used to be revered in the Eastern Church too but as soon as we made him a patron saint of the Polish Church the Russians threw him out of their canon!' he noted testily. 'The Rome – Constantinople schism of 1054 happened for political and cultural reasons. But in the Bible, Peter, the first bishop of Rome, is always mentioned first, and after the Resurrection he *always* spoke in the name of the twelve apostles!' Good politician that he was, the

---

* The split between Orthodox and Catholic Christians is usually dated to 1054.

archbishop stopped himself short and recaptured his careful, neutral tone.

'The big difference today is that we feel the division of the Church is a sin, a tragedy. As long as the Church is divided it is a scandal. The credibility of the Church depends on unity. I spent two years in Jerusalem, you know, the differences are very sharp . . .'

At only one other point did his composure seem to crack again. He was recalling his recent gathering of presidents at Gniezno.

'The German president doubted we could build a new Europe on Christian principles,' he grumbled, 'but President Havel* has recently written that European expansion entails religious and moral questions which are a thousand years old. He says there's *no way* that moral principles can be left out of the new Europe.'

Nor could the archbishop countenance German squeamishness at the Poles' displaying their red and white national flag in churches. 'The word "national" in Germany means National Socialist – Nazi – but here in Poland religion and nationality are so linked that, for example, on the third of May we celebrate the proclamation of the Virgin Mary as Queen of Poland as well as Constitution Day.'

After thirty minutes the archbishop and I had not charmed each other.

A harassed Waldemar bustled me downstairs to meet a historian priest friend of his, Father Czeslaw Pest, the man best qualified to teach me the confused history of Adalbert's precious relics from Gniezno. He told us that when the Czechs invaded Poland a mere thirty-eight years after the happy occasion of Otto's visit, they stole Adalbert's relics. By 1100 some of the saint's remains had been returned but today neither Gniezno nor Prague is quite sure what they have in their cathedrals' gorgeous reliquaries. The Czech Church is agitating for a grand reunion of anything that passes as a relic of Adalbert and the conduct of DNA tests. Only the archbishop's elaborate celebrations to mark the start of this third

* President Vaclav Havel of the Czech Republic.

Christian millennium were putting off the potentially fearful day of reckoning.

The Czechs' theft of Adalbert's relics was not the only mishap subsequent to Otto's joyful pilgrimage to Gniezno. Duke Boleslaw and Otto had decided that Adalbert's memory could best be honoured by completing his abortive mission to the Prussians. In 1001 two Italian monks, Benedict and John, were despatched from a monastery just north of Ravenna to north-east Poland. The project appealed to the pious pair, not least because the marshy wastes around Ravenna were infested by mosquitoes. 'Why should we stay in this swamp and die for nothing? Wouldn't it be better to go someplace where we could live as hermits and die for the gospel?'[l] they had agreed. Brother Benedict seems to have been the brains behind the mission, Brother John of a more practical bent but very devout. 'Smallpox had blinded him in one eye but his appearance was so radiant that he might have had three eyes instead of one,'[li] apparently.

Otto personally supervised all their travel arrangements and they journeyed safely to their distant destination where Duke Boleslaw received them, making over a large tract of land with plenty of wood to them. In order not to antagonize the pagan Prussians they were planning to convert, the two monks applied themselves to learning Polish, grew their hair long and dressed like peasants. But they could not begin their mission in earnest without written authorization from Gerbert, Pope Sylvester, which they were waiting for a German monk to bring them. When it did not arrive, they became as anxious and discouraged as Christ's Apostles must have been during the hiatus between their Lord's death and resurrection. But the worst was yet to come. On the night of 10 November 1003, a band of thugs broke into the little monastery, greedy for some gold they had heard about. Brother John woke up and heard the intruders and whispered something, probably his confession, in Brother Benedict's ear. Just in time, because a ghastly slaughter followed. John was killed with a couple of sword blows. With a single slice the chief thief 'split Benedict's skull, and the jets of blood coloured the walls in the corner where he fell'.[lii] One of the monks' Polish converts, Brother Isaac, yelled 'God help! God help!' and then 'God bless you!' as a sword ran through him. Another Polish convert, Brother Matthew, was stabbed from behind. The monastery's Polish handyman, Christian, was butchered in the chapel.

The murderers found no gold but stole rich Italian vestments, valuable books which Otto had given the monks, and relics. They wrapped them up in oilcloth and then tried to set fire to the monastery. But it would not burn, and as they fled terrified into the woods they were sure they could hear heavenly hymn singing. The Bishop of Poznan, 'an old man rich in good will', was called in to witness the grisly murder scene. He found Benedict, 'the gem, the star, the ornament of them all', lying on his side facing a wall, 'having assumed that position after his happy death, as it were to make himself more comfortable'.[liii]

A furious Duke Boleslaw had his army surround the woods to apprehend the fleeing murderers. It was not difficult. Not one of them had managed to rid himself of his murder weapon because, miraculously, their sword hands had been paralysed. They were sentenced to lifelong enchainment to the tomb of their victims, but in fact spent the rest of their days as monks in the monastery because – again miraculously – their chains had fallen off them as they were being led to the tomb.

Father Czeslaw was still explaining that, as a priest, he was not interested in whether Adalbert's miracle-working relics were real or not: 'We don't pray to old bones. Like every saint, Adalbert is an intercessor and a model to follow. The problem of the relics is merely scientific,' he insisted.

Waldemar and I walked out of his office straight into a crowd of dog-collared seminarians. Noisy and jostling as a pack of hungry hounds, they were en route from their lecture rooms to the refectory for lunch. We escaped outside for a stroll around the seminary grounds. The heatwave had not abated. Bees buzzed among the rows and rows of flowers which a small army of seminarians was planting out in preparation for the next day's political get-together. Paths were being raked, fences painted and woodwork wiped. Suddenly, I felt that I was in the way.

'Waldemar, you've got more than enough to do without me here, what with all those prime ministers showing up tomorrow. I think I'll catch a night train back to Germany.'

Father Christopher, his army chaplain friend, would be happy to take me to Poznan to catch the night train, he said.

Father Christopher's driving through that sensuously warm night, on a scenic route through some verdant countryside filled with white-blossoming cherry trees to the outskirts of Poznan, past brand new superstores lit up as brightly as airports, was as recklessly fast as that of the taxi driver I had encountered on my first night in Poland. 'Sex bomb! Sex bomb! You're my sex bomb!' sang the car radio as we hurtled into the centre of town and screeched to a halt at the station.

Once we had purchased my ticket, we repaired to the station buffet for a Coke. On learning that I was on my long way to Jerusalem, his eyes lit up. It transpired that he had visited the holy city often between 1994 and 1995 while on a much enjoyed tour of UN peacekeeping duty with the Polish contingent on the Israeli – Lebanese border. On a square of thin paper napkin snatched from a dispenser in the middle of the table he sketched me a rough map of the region, shading in the UN buffer zone and reverently marking Jerusalem with a cross. Scrappily drawn in wriggly lines, it looked strangely like the central section of a medieval map of the world.

'Waldemar and I are going to Jerusalem in November. It's good to go in this millennium year because it means a plenary indulgence . . .'

'Perhaps we can meet again there,' I said vaguely. Too preoccupied with sudden worries about how I would cross the UN buffer zone between Lebanon and Israel without having to detour through Jordan or Cyprus and quailing inwardly at the thought of how long and far I still had to journey, I failed to notice his mention of indulgences.

The train pulled in. I found the couchette I was sharing with three young Polish women and went straight to sleep. After a boorish German customs officer had woken us at the border by battering on the door, flicking on the light and barking enquiries about 'Zigaretten' and 'Getränke' it hazily struck me that Otto, travelling back this way with the three hundred Polish knights whom Duke Boleslaw had thoughtfully added to his mountain of other gifts, would have had – at the very least – the priceless relic of Adalbert's arm to declare.

~

A bright early morning in another quiet German medieval market square, not Quedlinburg but Aachen, in the super-civilized heartland of western Europe where Germany, Holland and Belgium meet and almost merge to make up the core of a twenty-first century united western Europe.

I drank my coffee, enjoying the sights and sounds of the city's new day: sun lighting up the house and shop fronts, water filling a stone fountain a few feet away, some hammering on a nearby roof, shining yellow flowers in window boxes and distant church bells. A lone cyclist came bouncing across the cobbles to swerve down a dark alley left of a Rathaus grander than Quedlinburg's, a Rathaus to rival Gniezno's seminary. When a beer lorry rumbled to a stop in front of a restaurant on my left, the wide-awake clatter of its crates filled the square. The Golden Unicorn inn behind me was throwing open its sash windows to let in the day and I could hear the jangle of coins in a till. A sleepy bee settled on the rim of my coffee cup.

After a night in a Gasthaus where the pillows had been plumped to look like bishops' mitres and the proprietress had worn a pearl necklace, ruby-red lipstick and a white linen apron to serve me delectable cold meats and strawberries sprinkled with icing sugar, my spiritual palate tasted better. But if mournful Herr Doktor Leike and anxious Waldemar were a world away, Archbishop Muszynski was still with me. Skim-reading a newspaper containing the usual expressions of concern at how poorly the new European single currency was doing, I happened on a prominent piece about the prime ministers' visit to Gniezno. 'Chancellor Gerhard Schröder of Germany, for one,' it said, 'has announced that he does not intend to discuss [European Union] accession dates for Poland when he meets with Prime Minister Jerzy Buzek for bilateral talks on Thursday in the Polish city of Gniezno.'[liv] The EU would not be expanding to include Poland, the Czech Republic and Hungary by 2002. Sad news for the archbishop.

The square was filling up. An old man and his small grandson sat down at the table beside mine. No sooner had they ordered apple juice spritzers than an elderly acquaintance happened by, to bow and shake hands with grandfather and grandson before sending for his own apple spritzer. Watching the two men clinking their green glasses with a happy 'Prost!' I was remembering the doleful Herr Doktor when a trim elderly woman approached their table to initiate a fresh round of courteous greetings and bows. The grown-ups continued their ritual exchanges about families and the progress of hospital treatments while the boy blinked and swung his legs. 'My greetings to your granny, young man!' called the woman, as she went on her way. The next time I looked up the child was gazing up at the shining sign of the Golden Unicorn and the deep blue sky, lost in wonder.

I had a hazy vision of a four-year-old Otto on the day of his coronation, Christmas Day 983, holding his own Granny Adelheid's hand as he walked up the aisle of the church Charlemagne had built here at Aachen. Instead of an infinite blue sky and a mysterious golden unicorn, Otto would have had all the church's Byzantine gold, its marble pillars, high altar and glittering candles to wonder at. Sixteen years later, a young emperor in Aachen on his way back from Gniezno with the arm of St Adalbert in his luggage and the exalted satisfaction of a job well done in his heart, Otto must have remembered that occasion, and all the stories his Granny Adelheid had told him about the great Charlemagne whose European empire had dazzled and glittered for a high, hopeful moment.

In the year 1000, two hundred years after its construction, Charlemagne's cathedral in Aachen was still the largest and by far the grandest stone building north of the Alps. A pious spell cast in ancient stone and mystical numbers, it had been inspired by churches in Constantinople and Ravenna but built by Italian workmen according to Charlemagne's own grand conception and embellished with ancient marbles transported from Italy. Proportioned in accordance with the ideal new Jerusalem that St John the Theologian had glimpsed and then described in his Book of Revelations, it was a perfect marriage of the ancient and Christian. Inside his heaven on earth Charlemagne had placed some priceless gifts from a patriarch of Jerusalem: the dress the Virgin Mary was wearing the night she gave birth to Christ, the latter's swaddling clothes, the loincloth he wore on the cross and the sheet used to wrap up the executed head of his cousin John the Baptist. Charlemagne's mortal remains, covered with a crimson cloth hung with medallions brought to Aachen by Theophano as part of her dowry, constituted an equally powerful pilgrim magnet.

What Otto III was planning to do in Aachen in the year 1000 – what he did in Charlemagne's church, in Charlemagne's tomb, to Charlemagne – has led many historians to dismiss him as bordering on the insane. Nineteenth-century German nationalists, who deplored the boy emperor's unmanly love of Rome, could easily play down his significance by branding him an effete nobody with a penchant for histrionics and for dressing himself up like a Byzantine emperor in a rich cloak adorned with a bell for every day of the year and shoes embroidered with eagles, lions and dragons. But it struck me, as I sat in that sunny square idly watching a group of Dutch schoolchildren with nylon knapsacks on their backs gather in front of the *Rathaus* and then enter it, that when young Otto had obeyed a dream and secretly entered Charlemagne's church with a small band of trusted followers carrying hammers and shovels, intent on first finding and then opening Charlemagne's grave, he was simply seeking reassurance. Was he, after all, doing God's will by trying to resuscitate the ancient Roman Empire? True, he was peacefully winning Poland and Hungary for Christ and his federal empire, and he was cooperating productively with his pope. But there he was, five years into his rule, with the constant threat of trouble to the north-east from pagan Baltic tribes, with the Romans still kicking against his overlordship and his Saxon followers jealous that corrupt Rome was the centre of his world. Gifted, energetic and inspired as he was, Otto must have wondered if he was overreaching himself. Neither Charlemagne nor his grandfather Otto I had ever tried to make their homes in Rome or dreamed of uniting the holy Christian empires of East and West. Was God on his side? The brutal mutilation of his beloved godfather and tutor Philagathos still burned on his conscience. It seems likely that Otto was working on the theory that if the mortal remains of the great Charlemagne proved intact and sweet-smelling enough to qualify him for saint-hood, some of that holiness would rub off on him.

It took time and a good deal of investigative digging inside the church's octagonal form to locate the exact spot of his hero's grave, but at last Charlemagne was revealed. One of Otto's trusted followers has left us the following startling description of him: 'He was not lying down, as is the manner with the bodies of other dead men, but sat on a certain chair as though he lived. He was crowned with a golden crown, and held a sceptre in his hand, the same being covered with gloves through which the nails had grown and pierced.'

What one witness described as a 'vehement odour' must have been sweet enough to confirm Charlemagne's sanctity because Otto and his companions 'did worship to him forthwith with bended thighs and knees'.[iv] Otto must have been overjoyed to find that Charlemagne's body could be described as uncorrupted, except for the tip of his nose which he immediately had restored in pure gold. He also clipped the corpse's fingernails, re-clothed him in angelic white robes and generally 'made good all that was lacking about him'. Lastly, he helped himself to a couple of souvenir relics – a tooth and a gold cross Charlemagne was wearing around his neck – before resealing the tomb and departing.

Alerted to fresh rebellion in Rome, Otto hastened back to stamp out the fire but dealt leniently with the rebels, unwilling to burden his delicate Christian conscience with fresh sins. His clemency was instantly interpreted as weakness by the Romans and by January 1001 the city was up in arms again and Emperor Otto and Pope Sylvester prisoners in the new palace on the Aventine Hill. Only the news that Otto's ferocious Uncle Henry was heading across the Alps with a German army to rescue his young nephew could sober the volatile Romans. Otto and Pope Sylvester were permitted to leave the palace unharmed. Distraught, bewildered and miserable, Otto addressed what must rank as one of the most touching speeches in history to his Roman subjects. 'Listen to the words of your father, pay attention and contemplate them carefully in your hearts. Aren't you my Romans any more? Because of you I left my homeland, neglected my Saxons, all my Germans, all those of my blood,' he reminded them. 'I adopted you as my children, you have rejected your father.'[lvi] Once again he found it in his heart to forgive them their exasperating trespasses but he and Sylvester abandoned Rome, knowing that only a large and permanent German army of occupation – unthinkable in St Peter's holy city – would serve as a permanent solution.

The pair headed north towards Ravenna, where the third of Otto's favourite spiritual advisers the hermit Romuald resided. There Otto subjected himself to strenuous fasts and pilgrimages, resisted Romuald's command to become a monk and went down with some form of malaria. Nothing daunted, he continued to dream his imperial dreams. He pursued his plan to marry a Byzantine princess called Zoe, made travel arrangements for the two monks he was sending to Poland to complete Adalbert's mission and tried to woo Venice away from its special relationship with Byzantium. He also undertook the construction of a church dedicated to St Adalbert and met young Abbot Odilo of the great Burgundian monastery of Cluny, with whom he discussed theology and philosophy. News of trouble back in Saxony was worrying but he still yearned for Rome and there were problems closer at hand. His vital ally on the other side of the Apennines, Count Hugh of Tuscany, had died. That region turned against Otto and a famine wreaked further havoc. By Christmas 1001 Otto was gravely ill and admitting it to his closest followers. The following month found him humiliatingly barred from re-entering Rome.

At the castle of Paterno, in the shadow of flat-topped Mount Soracte a few miles to the north of his beloved capital, the young emperor lay dying, afflicted by an outbreak of hideous pustules: 'Otto, of whose former beauty none could have their fill, whose fair aspect feasted the eyes of all who saw him, now became an object of loathing and horror.'[lvii] He died on 24 January 1002, aged only twenty-two. His old friend Pope Sylvester was not at his side. All that polymathic genius's hopes, once flatteringly expressed in a letter to Otto, that the young emperor's reign might last as long 'as the last number of the abacus',[lviii] were dashed. Far to the north across the Alps, pious French monks claimed to have spied in the sky a curious portent of Otto's end. Their vision 'had the shape of – or perhaps it simply was – a dragon, and it travelled from north to south shimmering with a great light'.[lix]

Otto had asked to be buried near Charlemagne in Aachen cathedral but northern Italy was in such uproar that the journey was fraught with hazard. It was decided that his demise should be kept secret for the time it would take to get him back over the Alps. Attendants accordingly dressed the dead youth in the sort of purple finery and royal insignia he had always favoured, propped him up on a horse and surrounded him with an impenetrable escort. This sad caravan brought him safely as far as Cologne, in time for Palm Sunday. There he was received as enthusiastically as Christ had been on his entry to Jerusalem. Ferried from one church to the next throughout Holy Week, on Good Friday Otto was taken on the last short leg of his long calvary, from Cologne to Aachen, to his final resting place. Freed from a tragically brief lifetime of far-

faring in body, mind and spirit, he was buried at last on Easter
Sunday to the accompaniment of an Easter antiphon.

> May the angels lead thee into Paradise –
> May the martyrs receive thee at thy coming in –
> And bring thee to the holy city of Jerusalem.[lx]

Informed of Otto's untimely demise the moment her ship docked
at the south Italian port of Bari, his Byzantine bride-to-be re-
embarked and sailed straight back home. There in Constantinople
Zoe waited thirty years until another marriage was deemed politic.
She had lost a handsome young husband and the chance to be an
empress of the Western Christian empire, but she did eventually
occupy the throne of Byzantium and was thrice married after the
age of fifty. By Otto's early death, East and West Christendom lost
more than Zoe had: its best chance of being peacefully united under
one ruler. In his history of Byzantium, John Julius Norwich muses
movingly about one of history's many might-have-beens:

> If she [Zoe] and Otto had had a son, he might in due course have
> inherited not only the Western Empire, but – in the absence of
> any other male heir – the Eastern as well, uniting the two for the
> first time and ruling over a territory extending from the borders
> of France to those of Persia; and the whole subsequent history of
> the world might have been changed.[lxi]

Another historian has observed that it is 'hard not to feel that
Otto III's dream was a great deal more sensible than the national
monarchy which most historians have belaboured him for not
creating'.[lxii] Otto's political vision was larger and more generous than
any nineteenth-century German nationalist, any modern builder of
a united Europe, let alone any start of the last millennium Roman
or Saxon could credit. For all their vaunted Christianity, for all
Otto's efforts, western Europeans were still much too inclined to
reach for the axes instead of turning the other cheek.

The wrecked dream left by Otto's early demise constitutes the first dark milestone on the century-long road destined to end with Crusaders in Jerusalem giving thanks to God and wading up to their knees in the blood of the Jews and Muslims they had slaughtered.

A wander around the boy emperor's final resting place, with its glowing Byzantine gold altarpiece – constructed, it is said, from the gold Otto took from Charlemagne's tomb – and quantities of finely wrought Byzantine objects for which Aachen has Theophano to thank, had brought such thoughts to mind.

I was lending only half an ear to a young Ph.D. student called Heike until she shepherded me towards a bronze memorial plaque to Otto III and began to explain how Napoleonic troops had desecrated Otto's grave in the same way as he had desecrated Charlemagne's. A century later someone else had decided to take a look but, finding only dust, had concluded that Napoleon's soldiers must have stolen the body.

'But then what's so surprising about finding only dust? Remember that Otto's body was conserved in Italy,' said Heike with a shrug. I wondered if she meant that the Italians, far from keen on their German emperor, had deliberately botched the job of embalming him back in 1002, but she went on as we climbed a dimly lit winding staircase, 'The boss of the cathedral treasury here wants to open up Otto's grave again to do some tests – some time over the next couple of years. Since the end of the cold war many German historians have been reassessing Otto and giving him credit for his work with Poland and Hungary and trying to unite Europe peacefully . . .'

This would explain why back in London I had discovered a wealth of new but dauntingly turgid German scholarship about Otto III, none of it translated into English.

'Every generation creates its own history, doesn't it?' she continued in her judiciously neutral way. 'Probably we need our Ottos now to give some depth and history to our EU.'

At the top of the stairs, with a commanding view across a balcony and the glittering church towards the altar, was Charlemagne's plain marble throne with its six steps made from segments of an ancient Roman pillar. On one of the throne's side panels was a curious set of markings. Heike told me that these etchings in the marble, an obscure draughts game of the sort played by bored Roman guards, proved that this particular slab of marble had once been a flagstone somewhere in the eastern half of the Roman Empire. Far-faring stones! If the ancient world was this near, I thought with a sudden surge of happy confidence, the eleventh century must surely be even closer to hand.

Heike and I emerged squinting into the brilliant spring sunshine and went in search of an outdoor café. We were enjoying frothy cappuccinos and warm croissants like good modern Europeans when something she said flattened that surge of optimism about my quest. Rolling up her cardigan sleeves and tilting her pretty face towards the sun, she was accounting for her love of early medieval history.

'Well . . . it's just more interesting than modern history. Our medieval – especially early medieval – ancestors thought as differently from us as a Pakistani or an Afghan would today. We are worlds and worlds apart really, because of that strength of religious faith.'

She was right. That unquestioning belief in the higher reality of the unseen, that confidence in man's special role in the eternal drama of God's universe, all that passionate love for a brokenly crucified man who was also Lord of heaven and earth and blind trust in the judgement he would mete out on the last day are what make the era so distantly mysterious. We voyagers into this twenty-first century seem to have more in common with the stoical humanism of the second-century Roman emperor Marcus Aurelius or with bored Roman soldiers playing draughts than we do with Otto III and his pious peregrinations.

Otto's still vivid idea of one Europe was a safer point of comparison between that distant past and the present, I thought as we sat in the hot noon sun listening to English, German, Dutch and French being spoken all around us.

'You know we live united Europe every day here,' she told me.

'When the supermarkets are closed in the evening it takes only half an hour by car to get to the Dutch ones. They're all open till ten p.m. and they've got better cheeses and delicatessens. Belgium is only ten minutes away. Houses are cheaper over there so plenty of Germans have moved to the border towns and commute back into Germany every day. These days there's a fashion for buying and doing up old farmhouses in Belgium as holiday homes. And then the Dutch have easier building regulations so it's cheaper to build houses there.'

'Sounds wonderful,' I said, thinking that even if Otto could have recognized this borderless patch of his empire, he would have missed a transcendent meaning, a binding spirit to lend point to it all. He would not have known that a twentieth century marred by the mass carnage of two world wars and cold war division had left western Europeans weakened and sobered, wary of emotive ideologies, of unreasoning faiths and utopian visions.

Heike had postponed making a start on the seventy-third page of her three-hundred-page Ph.D. thesis about the public image of one of Charlemagne's sons quite long enough. As we exchanged e-mail addresses she recommended that I head back to the *Rathaus*.

'It's on the site of Charlemagne's old palace,' she told me. 'I was just thinking that if you're interested in modern Europe you've probably heard about the Charlemagne Prize that's awarded in Aachen every year?'

'No?'

'Really? Well, it goes to people who've promoted peace in Europe somehow. There are photographs of all the winners at the *Rathaus*; you'll see them as you go upstairs. I think Clinton won it this year, for authorizing Nato's intervention in Kosovo.'*

'That must have been controversial.'

The McDonald's end of the sunny square had filled up with

* In March 1999, NATO forces attempted to prevent Serbia embarking on a fourth war in eight years in the former Yugoslavia. The wisdom of the intervention was much debated.

school parties of teenagers wearing sweaters knotted around their waists and sunglasses. I trailed a party of French-speakers up the stone flight of steps into the *Rathaus* and inched my way up the grand central staircase, inspecting each of the Charlemagne Prize-winners in turn. In 1989, the year the Berlin Wall and most of the Communist regimes of eastern Europe came tumbling down, a white-robed monk with a neat haircut, outstretched arms and a sweet smile had won it. This was *Frère* Roger, whose Christian community at Taizé I was planning to visit on my way south.

Central European statesmen from the Czech Republic, Hungary and Poland had shared the Charlemagne Prize in the 1990s, presumably in recognition of their tireless efforts to have their countries admitted to the European Union. The acknowledged father of *that* grand idealistic project to unite the continent, the son of a brandy maker, had received the prize in 1953. Portly, long-nosed and slightly balding, the latter-day Europe builder looked as unremarkable as a university lecturer, I thought as I lingered long over his image. The 'father of unification' and the man John F. Kennedy once praised for having had a 'constructive idea' that had done more to unite Europe in twenty years than any number of conquerors in a thousand, Jean Monnet was never elected to any public office but served in ministries of supplies during the world wars and in the doomed League of Nations between them. Lacking in religious belief or much education, not much of a public speaker and already over sixty when he began his life's great work, he apparently loved ocean liners, his daughters and his Italian wife Sylvia, whom he called several times a day. What a character to have succeeded the likes of Charlemagne, Otto III, Napoleon and even Hitler! Perhaps Monnet was the prototype of new European man, prosaic perhaps, but modest, pragmatic, effective.

Writing his memoirs in the late 1970s when he was almost ninety, Monnet indicated the road behind and ahead for a European Community that had expanded to add Britain, Ireland and Denmark to the core which had signed the Treaty of Rome in 1957.* His conception of a union designed to preclude any repeat of the horrendous waste of two world wars in the space of thirty years was neither grand nor visionary.

> The building of Europe is a great transformation, which will take a very long time ... The obstacles will undoubtedly grow in number as we draw closer to our goal ... The only difference is that something is begun, something which can no longer be stopped ... I have never doubted that one day this process will lead us to the United States of Europe, but I see no point in trying to imagine today what political form it will take.[lxiii]

What would Otto have made of such a cautiously colourless statement? He might have wanted to warn his fellow Europe-builder about a danger which Monnet recognized only at the very end of his life. The architect of modern Europe is said to have told someone that if he had the chance to do it all again he would have started by building a cultural union of Europe and only later attended to its economic aspects. Was he belatedly identifying a spiritual vacuum at the heart of his creation? Was he sorry that Europe was becoming all about supermarket opening times, law courts and committees, ranges in delicatessens, bureaucracies, commuting distances, trading regulations and road signs?

Perhaps, like Pope John Paul II, he had guessed that a new creed called human rights would not suffice to feed the spirit and keep the peace. It tallied with the Christian injunction to 'Do as you would be done by' and trumpeted the supreme value of human life, but that was all. It went no further and didn't offer what human beings need: the certainty that their individual lives have meaning and purpose. And without that assurance how could anyone really, truly believe in the value of human life? It was surely the lack of that assurance which had led Nazi-era scientists and

---

* The first European Community comprised West Germany, France, Italy, the Netherlands, Belgium and Luxembourg.

doctors to first sterilize the handicapped, then murder the mentally retarded and finally mass-murder Jews, Gypsies and other undesirables for the higher, common good of the larger community of Aryan Germans. Monnet had seen that abyss and perhaps still feared it at the end of his life.

Robert Schuman, a devoutly Roman Catholic diplomat from Luxembourg with whom Monnet worked to produce the very first embryo post-war European Union,* seems to have shared Monnet's misgivings. He issued an even clearer warning: 'we have not sufficiently taken into account the needs and aspirations of human development and its cultural enrichment. Our concern with technical progress has led us to ignore the need for a balance between the two factors which make up real progress: material know-how and moral control.'[lxiv]

Like Schuman† and Monnet, my Icelandic novelist friend Arni Bergmann had also recognized the soul's imperatives. I vividly remembered him chuckling his own objection to the new united Europe. 'I'm against homogenization. It's better *dlya dushi* – for the soul, as the Russians would say – to be a little eccentric.'

On the television evening news that night I recognized Gniezno sweltering in its ersatz summer. There was that chief pastor of souls Archbishop Muszynski with the heads of government of various central European states and Germany – sweltering too in their uniform white shirts and ties – planting commemorative trees.

~

Waiting for a train to transport me on another westward tack, across to Reims, in a station so shiny, well ordered and light that a person from somewhere more colourful and chaotic might have mistaken it for heaven, I bought a newspaper in which I read the headline 'THE DREAM OF ONE BIG HAPPY EUROPEAN REGION'.[lxv]

* The European Steel and Coal Community.
† Robert Schuman is a candidate for canonization. The qualifying two miracles are being sought.

The article proceeded to describe the invention of a new region to be known as Saar-Lor-Lux. It sounded as evocative and appealing as a brand of biological washing powder, I thought, reading on with interest. The idea would gain substance, it said, by creating schoolchildren bilingual in French and German through the agency of teacher exchanges. Twenty million Euros would be spent on a park straddling the old national borders, and Robert Schuman's homeland, Luxembourg, would be the heart of the new region and home to its central office.

Minutes later I was gazing out of an oddly tinted train window at the usual unremarkable signs of prosperous organized living. There were flying clusters of neat pale houses with dark roofs, speeding dots of cows in fields and metallic flashes of passing cars. This same heartland of western Europe, the lands between the Somme in eastern France and the Rhine in western Germany, had marched in the vanguard of economic and social development in the eleventh century too. The region included Flanders, home to western Europe's medieval wool industry. Towns and populations grew throughout the century, too fast for the countryside to support. What one historian has described as the continent's first poor, insecure and resentful urban proletariat was born here. Thousands of them would flock to join the First Crusade in 1095. Had not the prophet Isaiah said, 'As one whom his mother comforts, so I will comfort you: and you shall be comforted in Jerusalem. You shall see and your heart shall rejoice'?[lxvi]

Sharing my train compartment was a large German woman who produced from her bag a children's puzzle book and a rainbow pack of felt pens. Spreading the book on his lap, her chubby son set to work. I watched him joining dot to dot, flipping over page after page as he efficiently filled in the blanks, sorted out the anagrams and spotted all the differences. In my own lap was a book describing how the seeds of a new – in fact recognizably modern – way of thinking about and making sense of the world were sown in the eleventh century. As I watched the boy, now busy sucking on the end of his orange pen as he turned his book upside down to gain a fresh perspective on a puzzle, it occurred to me that the genesis of the mind games he was engaged in might – by a highly improbable leap of imagination admittedly – be traced in a straight line all the way back to this new way of thinking, part of the rich intellectual legacy of the brilliant Gerbert of Aurillac, Otto's Pope Sylvester II.

While still a young man, long before Otto was even born and at about the time the pagan Thorvald was still raiding in Wales with Swein Forkbeard, Gerbert was scouring Europe in search of knowledge and enjoying himself exercising his mind in whole days of public argument about subjects as recondite as whether physiology was a branch of physics or something quite different. After mastering all there was to know at the time about mathematics, music, astronomy and theology, Gerbert had travelled the path I was now following, from Aachen to the famous cathedral school of Reims, on account of a deacon there who was equipped to teach him logic. This was a branch of knowledge which had been almost lost since the time of the ancients and Gerbert was powerfully drawn to it.

Before long Gerbert was a teacher. For Gerbert's students at Reims, logic in the basic form of Aristotle's categories must have been a new, intensely satisfying mind game, an excellent way to make sense of the world. It was simple. Each of Aristotle's categories was a different way of perceiving an object: according to quantity, quality, relation, position, place, time, state, action and affection. Thus, a single pen could be further described as long and thin, as mine, as resting on its nib, as lying on a piece of paper, at five in the morning, as filled with ink, as being in the act of making a blue mark, while in my hand. Sorting, classifying and solving according to simple principles was marvellous mental sport, although Gerbert himself neither recognized nor sought to develop this new weapon's potential because he deemed rhetoric – what we would call the gentle art of persuasion perhaps – the more important skill. He was always more interested in rediscovering and reincorporating the learning of the ancients than in fomenting any violent intellectual revolution.

But soon there were signs that the appetite for logic and the slow development of a scientific cast of mind that Gerbert had awakened at his cathedral school at Reims was growing. Logic had little to do with gently persuading anyone to do anything; it was a sharp, incisive, divisive tool and before long it was hacking away at the foundations of a society still painstakingly rebuilding itself on the scaffolding of the Christian faith. Midway through the eleventh century the heretic Berengarius had shocking recourse to logic in order to argue that the communion bread and wine did not literally change into the body and blood of Christ during the communion service. Later, St Anselm, a French monk and eminent theologian who had risen to become Archbishop of Canterbury in Norman England by the end of the century, set about trying to marry the new style of reasoning with the old faith. In 1079 he claimed, 'I do not seek to understand that I may believe, but I believe that I may understand: for this I also believe that, unless I believe, I shall not understand.'[lxvii] A very short time afterwards Peter Abelard was daring to turn that dictum on its head and arriving at a point any modern scientist would immediately recognize: 'By doubting we are led to enquire: by enquiring we perceive the truth.'[lxviii]

But Abelard had fared too fast and too far for most of his peers to follow and for the next couple of centuries theologians continued along St Anselm's earlier path, making superhuman efforts to force a fit between the new way of thinking and the Christian world view. Straining to produce logical proofs of God's existence, some calculated how many ranks and orders of angels there were in heaven and heatedly debated if angels could dance on a pinhead, and if so how many of them. Nevertheless and inevitably, the contradictions between the new way of thinking and the old faith became harder and harder to reconcile. The new thinking, nurtured in the universities of the twelfth and thirteenth centuries, was destined to win the contest.

Now, at this dawning of the third millennium, we can look back over the rise of the universities and science, over the Enlightenment and Darwinism and the twentieth century's technological progress, and marvel at how far that new thinking has brought us. If our pride in it is mixed that is perhaps because we fear that when men of the last century invented biological and nuclear weapons, when they engineered famines or ordered millions into gas ovens, it was not because they were out of their minds, but out of their souls. They had lost not their capacity to reason so much as their faith in all the old religions' teachings about the sacredness of individual human life and the judgement of an omniscient God.

'Finished!' shouted the boy, clapping his puzzle book shut. 'Do you want an apple juice?' his mother enquired dozily. 'I'm hungry,' said the boy. A salami roll, neatly wrapped in silver foil, was produced. While the boy crammed his mouth too full of bread and frowned over his Gameboy, the woman dozed off again.

With so little either inside or outside the train to interest or distract me from the eleventh century, I began to think ahead, beyond the year 1000 and the tragic demise of the young emperor who might have spared the continent some of its ills, beyond Gerbert's unwitting insertion of logic into the half-built edifice of a Christian society.

PART TWO

'the whole world overturned'
1048–1095

On that train humming through the well ordered heart of western Europe, I realized that the main action in my eleventh-century drama was filling me with more eager anticipation than the prospect of twenty-first century Reims.

Otto left no heirs, but a new German dynasty produced some Henrys and a Conrad to assume his mantle. The first of this fresh run of Henrys, Henry II, set about homogenizing religious practice and faith in his realm by forcing the pope to insert the *Filioque* clause which the Byzantines so detested into the Creed. When Charlemagne had tried to effect the same change two centuries earlier, the pope of the day had managed to resist the pressure. Heroically reinforcing Christian unity between Rome and Constantinople, he had ordered two plaques to be made and attached to the tombs of Saints Peter and Paul. One was inscribed with the *Filioque*-less Creed in Latin, the other with the same but in Greek. But by the early eleventh century the papacy was too weak to withstand any German emperor's pressure.

The next of the Henrys, Henry III, was an uncommonly pious monarch who, with his French wife Agnes, attended mass five times a day. Like St Adalbert, this imperial couple avoided laughter in memory of their saviour who had hung suffering to death on his cross while Roman soldiers jeered and mocked at him. There were no jesters at their wedding, one of the chronicles tells us. Henry III took his role as defender of the faith seriously enough to sponsor a radical overhaul of the Church. And not a moment too soon. The marks of decay were everywhere plain to see: in the grasping greed of priests, in the licentiousness of monasteries, in the very state of churches' altar furnishings. One outraged churchman asked himself how parish priests could 'indulgently allow chalices made of pewter or some baser metal to become horribly dirty and scurfy from long disuse'. Aghast, he continued, 'What should I say moreover of the torn and decaying altar linens?'[i]

The contrast between the high seriousness of some of the north European churchmen and the gross carnality and clannish infighting of the Roman popes had become too glaring to ignore by the turn of the second millennium. Three tenth-century Italian popes had died in the act of having sex: one of a heart attack and two at the hands of cuckolded husbands. By 991 a group of northern European prelates was bitterly complaining: 'it is notorious that there is no one at Rome with enough knowledge to qualify as a doorkeeper . . . It cannot be to monsters like these, utterly dishonourable, devoid of any knowledge either of things divine or things human, that countless priests of God throughout the world, conspicuous for their knowledge and virtuous life, should be legally subjected . . .'[ii]

The harmonious and effective partnership between Otto and Pope Sylvester had been too tragically brief to stop the centuries of rot. By the time Henry III assumed his throne in 1046 there were three scandalously competing popes in Rome.

Emperor Henry descended on the holy city to make a clean sweep of all of them. He then appointed his own candidate, an efficient and impartial German, the Bavarian Bishop of Bamberg, in their place. A period of fifteen years when a succession of northern Europeans, many of them from the dynamic half-French, half-German speaking area that is now Alsace-Lorraine, occupied St Peter's throne, began. Those first transalpine popes set the ball of eleventh-century Church revolution rolling. In the capable hands of teams of north European clergy wholly committed to the cause of Church reform, change was swift and radical. Beginning with a systematic rooting out of clerical abuses, the Church reformers proceeded to a repositioning and strengthening of the papacy. But what was conceived as a joint enterprise of the German emperors and north European popes soon exceeded anyone's expectations or plan.

By the close of the century, the happy old era of popes and Holy Roman emperors ruling in partnership would be gone for ever. The Roman Church would be strong enough to stand alone. Setting itself above and beyond the reach of any emperor it would be a fundamentalist Church and the most powerful single institution in western Europe. By 1095 the Roman pope could command kings and summon armies of Western Christians to do his divinely inspired will. When the First Crusaders battled their way into Jerusalem in 1099, a mere fifty-three years had elapsed since the first of the reforming north European popes had arrived in Rome.

How had it been done?

Looking for inspiration and ideas to two groups of impressively organized French and German monasteries clustered in the Alsace-Lorraine region and Burgundy, the reformers had concluded that the millennium-old project of building Christ's kingdom on earth was doomed unless the clergy were forthwith removed, like those monks, from the temptations of piling up fortunes and founding dynasties. Two rampant evils – simony and nicolaitism – had to be eradicated. The first was the widespread and long-established* practice of buying and selling positions in the Church hierarchy, which amounted to disgraceful trading in the grace of the Holy Spirit. The second was the equally widespread and even longer-established† norm of married or fornicating clergy.

The task of imposing celibacy on the clergy was a superhuman undertaking and one that naturally met with plenty of opposition. Had not St Paul himself written, 'To avoid fornication let every man have his own wife'? But the reformers couched their arguments in terms that strongly appealed to the common man and ensured

* Since the eighth century.
† There were fourth- and fifth-century rulings on celibacy for higher ranks of clergy.

popular support for their programme. Logic was a useful weapon, as was a deliberate emphasis on Christ's human attributes. The reformers were appealing to men not unlike the freshly converted Icelanders, who had no trouble picturing their supreme Lord Jesus holding court up in heaven like a feudal lord or king: 'if our Redeemer so loved the integrity of flowering chastity that not only was he born of the womb of a virgin, but also cared for by a guardian who was also a virgin, and that, when he was still a baby crying in his crib, by whom, I ask, does he now wish his body to be handled as he reigns supremely in Heaven?'[iii]

Appeals to conventional sexual mores were popular too. The Church, the reformers reasoned, was so broken and neglected because no one had been bothering to defend her honour, to fight for her chastity. They also argued that priests who dallied with flesh and blood women were repeatedly insulting the Church, which was Christ's bride, when it was their high duty to honour and serve her on behalf of her heavenly bridegroom. The reformers' chief propagandist, Humbert, a monk from Moyenmoutier in Lorraine, railed against the married priests of the Byzantine Church in graphic terms: 'Completely enervated and exhausted by the recent pleasures of the flesh and thinking in the midst of the holy sacrifice about how to pleasure their wives, they handle the immaculate body of Christ and distribute it to the people. Immediately afterward they turn their sanctified hands to touch the limbs of women.'[iv]

The reformers' onslaught on the practice of buying and selling Church offices was presented in a similarly vivid fashion. The central notion was that the Church, the bride of Christ, was turned into a common prostitute every time an evil simoniac instead of a true representative of the Lord succeeded in coming between her and Christ with a false offering of the sacraments.

The third and most effective of the northern European popes was a cousin of Emperor Henry III. A handsome Alsatian nobleman, Pope Leo IX was only forty-six when he arrived in Rome, but he had already proved himself a committed reformer by taking an uncommonly hard line on simony and nicolaitism in his diocese of

Toul. In the manner of all the versatile German higher clergy he had also covered himself with glory on the battlefield. The Romans accepted him easily; they probably appreciated the tactful way he refused to be installed until he had assured himself of their support. They might also have heard how when a ghastly malady had ravaged the five-hundred-strong company of pilgrims he was leading on one of his annual pilgrimages to Rome, Leo had healed the sick with wine in which his personal collection of saints' relics had been marinating a while.

Filled with reforming energy, Leo set about organizing the papacy's finances and rationalizing Church administration. Cardinals were no longer superannuated Roman churchmen enjoying empty honours, but reform-minded, younger men appointed to go forth and spread the message. Pope Leo and his cousin Emperor Henry were in perfect agreement that the best way to enhance the prestige and authority of the papacy was to take it on tour. If the reform was to take root there must be close monitoring and good communication. The shepherd must keep watch over his flock, rounding up the laggards and urging them on.

A far-farer to rival John Paul II, Pope Leo would spend no more than six months of his five-year-long pontificate in Rome. The first of his eight journeys north of the Alps was made in order to combine the consecration of a new cathedral with the convening of a first reform council in Reims.

~

Outside another pristine railway station I found the fine spring gone. A thick grey sky had replaced Aachen's blue one and a wet wind blew in irritated gusts. It was mid-afternoon but Reims looked lifeless, almost deserted and bleak. Only the cobbled expanse in front of the cathedral was alive, filled with tour buses and crowds of elderly tourists in pale primrose, pink, pistachio or baby-blue anoraks whose hurriedly opening umbrellas lent darker splashes of colour to the scene.

The taxi driver dropped me off near a crowd surrounding one of the British coaches. A couple of elderly women hurried past me, making for one of the gift shops. 'Come on, Molly! We've just got time to get a bottle of that brandy you wanted. Come on; you haven't bought anything yet, have you?' 'That reminds me, I need to spend a penny,' shouted Molly, tying her plastic rain bonnet under her chin and stumbling after her friend.

At first I did not notice the cathedral itself. Gazing up at the Gothic immensity of its flying buttresses, sculptures and towers and rose window and pillars and doors, recalling the stark but harmonious simplicity of Quedlinburg's Romanesque church, I was almost as blind to its beauties as I had been to those of the baroque confections Waldemar had shown me in Poland. Magnificently but madly overwrought, with a vault so high it shrank everyone to the size of insects, Reims Cathedral suggested not so much faith unlimited as ingenuity unleashed, power unbounded and riches untold. Here, it seemed to me, was northern Europe's new spirit of reason and science, harnessed in the cause of not so much an almighty God as an almighty Church which had learned to strut its stuff like any nation state of the time. The harmony of Romanesque proportions had been forgotten in favour of exaggerated Gothic height, depth and over-adornment. Built in the thirteenth century, Reims Cathedral seemed to proclaim the reformed, but by then also deformed, Church.

When I found a guidebook indicating that the cathedral Pope Leo had travelled all this way to consecrate in 1049 was about half a mile down a road to the left of the cobbled square, I abandoned any idea of visiting the treasury for a glimpse of the golden cross reliquary which Otto III had removed from around Charlemagne's neck in the year 1000. Towards the end of a wide, straight street lined with ugly, dark buildings, closed tourist restaurants and a parrot-coloured tour bus, was the Basilica of Saint-Remi of Reims. Driving rain had deterred other tourists from finding their way there. I was alone inside but for a courteous, elderly man wearing a faded blue worker's jacket and carrying a silver chalice and a duster.

I liked the building's three aisles divided by two lines of Roman arches, and the simple solidity of its stonework. There was no question of feeling ant-like or diminished. The magic darkness of such early Romanesque churches – that determined celebration of the ancient world's lost civilization – moved me again. I felt at home and soon settled down with my bags in a chair towards the back of the church to ponder the extraordinary crowd scenes this empty place had witnessed in 1049.

Pope Leo, who had offered to consecrate the new church while still a bishop, crossed the Alps and took a roundabout route via Aachen and Mainz to Reims in order to honour his pledge. He must have calculated that a church consecration, guaranteed to attract thousands of people from miles around, in a city with as excellent a reputation for learning as Reims had enjoyed since the days of Gerbert of Aurillac, was the ideal setting for the launch of his reforms. He needed to impress upon the high-ranking churchmen who would gather for his synod there that he expected them to take his new directives on simony and nicolaitism seriously. They must be in no doubt that he expected action, not just words.

Pope Leo reached the city's stone walls on the eve of Saint Remi's feast day to find so gigantic a crowd of the faithful gathered for the grand occasion that 'one would think that the whole world had sent its pilgrims'.[v] Such a show of popular love for Remi's relics and for the new *papa mirabilis* who had condescended to venture out of Rome to visit his flock must have been heartening. But there was disappointment too. Conspicuous by their absence were most of the French bishops Leo had summoned to his council. Clearly signalling that they wanted nothing whatsoever to do with his reform project, they had taken their cue from the equally absent French king and gone off campaigning with him. Leo had to content himself with a mere twenty bishops, including an Englishman and five Normans, but the stalwart support of Abbot Hugh of Cluny, whose monastery was the most impressively reformed, the richest and most powerful in Europe at the time, with a small army of his monks, must have been reassuring.

After saying mass and getting a night's sleep in the archbishop's castle Leo was up early the next morning, hiding himself away in the Monastery of Saint Remi in an attempt to avoid the clamouring crowd who were camped all about, singing around their camp fires, shouting his name. But three times he was forced to oblige the patient faithful by appearing on the balcony to bless them, and still they could not be persuaded to vacate the area to make room for the procession. The new church, which needed to be quite empty for the solemn ceremony, was also still full – of monks and peasants and priests who had spent the night praying. Only a dire threat to indefinitely postpone the great event could persuade them to evacuate the building.

At last the ceremony could begin. As the doors of the monastery swung open and Pope Leo emerged with the relics of Remi in a casket and Abbot Hugh of Cluny at his side, a 'tremor of joy'[vi] rippled through the crowd. The faithful went wild, singing praises to the Lord, clapping and clamouring for a chance to carry the casket. Soon tempers were flaring and vicious fights erupting. People were swept off their feet in the surging, pressing throng and trampled underfoot. 'The cries of the injured mingled with the chanting of psalms,'[vii] noted one eye-witness, while St Remi's precious relics travelled on around the town at the head of a giant procession which wound its way back at last to the new church. The high altar of the brand new building received the saint's ancient remains. Another night-long vigil was held, with ceaseless singing of praises.

The following morning, the opening day of Pope Leo's council, there was such a gigantic crowd still pressing at the doors of the monastery that no one could leave to do the pope's bidding. Leo had decided that the exceedingly delicate nature of the council's agenda called for some supernatural reinforcement and had requested that the casket of St Remi's relics be transferred from the high altar of the new church to a hall in the monastery where the meeting was about to begin. He calculated that it stood a better chance of success if St Remi rather than he were presiding. At last, the precious box was roughly handed out of one of the church windows and over the heads of the clamouring crowd. Not just the few summoned bishops and abbots but also hordes of monks and laypeople hastened to attend the council.

Leo opened proceedings with a pastoral sermon about such matters as the *sodomitico* vice and then resolved a difficult question of precedence between the archbishops of Reims and Trèves by arranging the seats in an egalitarian circle, before adjourning proceedings until the following day. The next morning there were no more delays. The pope plunged straight into the main matter with a direct demand that each bishop and abbot swear on St Remi's relics that he had paid nothing for his own position and sold no position to anyone else.

The archbishops of Trèves, Lyons and Besançon had no trouble doing just that, but others were thrown into confusion by this public confession session in which Remi's relics performed the work of a most efficient lie detector. Leo's host, the Archbishop of Reims, and four other bishops requested leave to consider the matter for a day. The Bishop of Langres, a well educated man who stood accused of not only buying his post and selling holy orders, but also of adultery, sodomy and even murder, arranged to have his case defended by two archbishops. But one of his advocates was miraculously struck dumb while the other made a partial admission of guilt on his client's behalf. The potency of the relics and the extraordinary significance of what was happening escaped no one. Pope Leo interrupted the proceedings to rise and lead the singing of a hymn of praise.

By the next morning the Bishop of Langres had fled Reims in fear and shame. On this second day of the council another bishop confessed that he had not been aware of it at the time, but he knew now that his parents had bought his post for him. He was so well respected by his fellow prelates that when he moved to surrender his pastoral staff it was immediately returned to him. There was also the highly thought of Norman Bishop of Coutances who, having told the assembly that his brother had bought him his job, tried to flee but was forcibly returned to the chamber and promoted to the rank of archbishop. The similarly well regarded Bishop of Nantes admitted that his father, a bishop and clearly a fornicator too, had paid out a large sum to the local count for his post. Stripped of his pastoral staff and ring, he was demoted to the rank of priest. Three prelates who had stayed away from the council to go campaigning with the French king were summarily excommunicated and a Norman bishop who had burnt down a church while warring with his neighbours was despatched on a penitential pilgrimage to Constantinople. When it was Abbot Hugh of Cluny's turn to make his confession, his denial of any wrongdoing was deemed exemplary in its humility and truthfulness: 'The flesh was willing, but mind and reason revolted,'[viii] he said simply.

At the close of the council Pope Leo hoisted the casket of five-hundred-year-old bones onto his own shoulder and carried it back to the new church to set it down on the high altar. He would always credit Saint Remi with the startling success of the Reims council. On his way home to Rome, Leo reached the famous Benedictine monastery of Reichenau on its island in the Bodensee* at the end of November. There he deposed the community's simoniac abbot and, after consecrating the monastery's new church of the Holy Cross, rested awhile before braving a winter crossing over the Alps.

Back in the twenty-first century, the kind man with the silver chalice and the duster was discreetly motioning to me that the cathedral was closing. I took his hint, hoisted my bags and made for the exit. But I had mistaken his meaning. He intercepted me, keen to show me what he judged to be the cathedral's true treasure – a large crude wooden crucifix on which a crowned Christ, decently attired in a red robe with a rich belt around his middle, was hanging in triumph.

'We think it was brought home from the Middle East by fourteenth-century Crusaders. They must have stolen it, probably from the Eastern Christians who always like to show the crucified Christ as a king like this, in triumph,' he told me, in a reverent whisper.

* Lake Constance.

'Of course, now we know that the Crusades were not a completely good thing . . .'

'No,' I agreed.

I was marvelling at how long and stubbornly our medieval forbears had persisted in their ultimately doomed efforts to conquer and keep the land in which their Lord Jesus Christ had lived and died. After capturing Jerusalem in the last year of the eleventh century, the Crusaders had held the city itself for less than a century, and the rest of their puny colonies – Outremer – for less than a hundred years longer. Jerusalem lost again, the Crusading energy of northern Europe turned in on itself. Crusades were proclaimed against not just pagans holding out in the forests of north-east Europe but heretic Cathars and Waldensians, and even entire enemy nations. There was talk of launching Crusades against England's King Henry VIII and Queen Elizabeth I.

A last Crusade to the east was preached as late as 1464 – by a pope too sick to lead the expedition and too hopelessly moribund to be told that his ships' crews were deserting before setting sail and that no Christian king had volunteered an army. And even after this pathetic finale, the great sunlit dream of northern Europeans would survive through centuries of their own wars, to re-emerge in the late nineteenth and twentieth centuries amidst the ruins of the Ottoman Empire, which ruled the Holy Land for the second half of the second millennium.

Outside again, rain was pouring down from a darkening sky onto workers hurrying frowning from the doors of office blocks, struggling to hoist their umbrellas while dodging the spray from passing cars. Sheltering for a moment in a second-hand bookshop, I flicked through a dog-eared school history textbook which explained, with the help of colourful pictures and diagrams, how the great powers of western Europe which had between them ruled the world at the start of the twentieth century forfeited it all in two world wars. When I emerged it was much later, dark, still raining, and I had not yet found anywhere to stay.

I was dreaming my own sunlit dream, of being instantly

transported out of this wet northern European city, south across the Alps to Rome. I could jump on a train to Paris and, from there, take a direct flight to Rome, I thought. Where Pope Leo IX had taken a couple of months to get home to Rome from Reims, I could do the journey in three or four hours and arrive in time for a late dinner. But as I paused on a dark street corner for a British tour bus to pass me in a shower of spraying tyres, I realized that the homesickness I had not felt aboard the *Bruarfoss* had finally found me here. Home, not Rome, was where I wanted to be. My spirits were dampened by this rainy phase of my voyage through a part of Europe that seemed to have little but old stones to show for its eleventh-century past.

Staring out of a rain-streaked hotel window overlooking Reims' empty main shopping street with its brightly lit shopfronts, I thought of Saint Adalbert's *peregrinatio* – his lifetime's wandering, as the word 'pilgrimage' meant before the twelfth century – his yearning 'to grow old in poverty under a foreign sun', and how 'all hard and bitter things seemed sweet to him because of Jesus'.[ix] Adalbert had fared far and wide through some of the least sunny parts of Europe as well as France and Italy but, like Otto III, he had never joined the new millennium's 'innumerable multitude of people from the whole world, greater than any man before could have hoped to see' who took advantage of the new stability in the Balkans since Byzantium's crushing of its enemies to travel overland to 'the Sepulchre of the Saviour at Jerusalem'.[x]

In that rainy city where the only other travellers were day trippers or businessmen I was for the first time struck by the lonely eccentricity of my plan to travel from Iceland to Jerusalem. Lying awake into the small hours, watching the reflection of a blinking pink shop light on the ceiling, I decided I was suffering from a mild case of what medieval monks, but especially hermits in the solitude of their hideaways with their poor diets and unvarying prayer routines, would have called *Accidie*. This startlingly modern-sounding malaise was one of the eight deadly sins listed by St Cassian. Later merged with the sin of *Tristitia*, sadness, to make sloth, *Accidie* is what we would now call depression – an all-enveloping negativity. Nothing is worth doing, nothing matters, hope is crushed and the spirit numbed. But, switching on the bedside light, I jumped out of bed, suddenly certain that somewhere in his imaginary tale of Thorvald the Far-farer's wanderings through Eastern and Western Christendom Arni Bergmann had described this grievous affliction. In the bottom of my suitcase was an English translation of a few pages of Arni's novel and there, just as I had remembered, was a perfect profile of *Accidie*, often called the Midday Demon:

> He it is who poisons the soul with nausea and loss of appetite for everything. The hermit considers nothing to be of importance any more, neither prayer nor sin, nothing cheers him or makes him sad, his mind wanders far and wide but stops nowhere . . . The hermit has no ease in his bones, cannot endure his solitude, is constantly looking whether somebody is taking his way past his hut, or he will run from his cell and rush off without even knowing where he is going . . .[xi]

All the fathers and doctors of the Church agreed that the way to banish the Midday Demon, the only sure cure for *Accidie*, was incessant and fervent prayer. But how could those poor starved monks, let alone an agnostic such as myself, have managed to pray while in such a condition?

I must have fallen asleep. On waking the following drizzly morning, I resolved on a cure. Hiring a car, I would head east for a while through the Alsatian homeland of Europe-builders Jean Monnet and Pope Leo IX. Once back in Germany, I would speed south on the autobahn in search of the Bodensee, Reichenau Island with its view of the Alps, and sunshine.

~

Sunshine at last.

I had passed a day trailing fuming lorries through Alsace and a sleepless night in a rainy Stuttgart watching a televized Byzantine Christian church service. Finally, a long, fast drive down the autobahn had brought me on a hot May bank holiday afternoon to the banks of the hazy blue Bodensee, a wide and glittering expanse festively dotted with white-sailed yachts. My relief at seeing the water, which many a foot- or saddle-sore eleventh-century pilgrim must have wishfully mistaken for an ocean, was overwhelming. I consumed the last square of a bar of Polish chocolate Sister Consolata had given me and noted that *Accidie* had fled.

With a right foot numb from long hours of pressure on the accelerator pedal, I inched my way west along the crowded north shore of the lake behind monster tour buses, roaring black motorbikes and cars laden with luggage, children and bicycles. Every German in Germany seemed to be converging on that inland southern sea that afternoon. Tempers and cars were overheating, but to my left was the lake, the Alps a hazy smudge on the horizon. To my right were hillsides lined with orchards of apricot trees and tidy rows of spring-leafed vines. Pretty little eighteenth-century resort towns with impossibly steep and narrow streets and expensive-looking *Gasthausen* whose fancily ironworked balconies overlooked the water further graced the scene. The light was golden and kind, the air balmy. Nothing could spoil my mood, not a wrong turning into a pedestrianized modern resort and a couple of wagging fingers from a pair of elderly men in white tennis shorts, nor a curse from a young mother with a pushchair for executing a three-point turn on a footpath.

The old lakeside town of Konstanz, at the mouth of the Rhine on the border with Switzerland and the closest point on the mainland to the monastery island of Reichenau, was where I was headed first, to deposit my hire car. Motoring slowly across a bridge over the Rhine, along a tree-lined ring road encircling a barely glimpsed cobbled town and gracious medieval cathedral, I could very well imagine that in this comfortably warm south German settlement the strictness of the new German pope's clerical celibacy directive would have been as welcome as a blast of winter wind. Three thousand six hundred clergy of the Konstanz diocese protested against Pope Leo's order, enough to earn the town a special mention in the chronicles of the time.

While Leo IX found room for cast-off priests' wives in the servants' quarters of his papal palace in Rome and warned the faithful that they were automatically excommunicating themselves by accepting Holy Communion from the hands of married priests, Bishop Otto of Konstanz blithely ignored the new ruling. He let his married priests be and allowed the unmarried ones to take wives. The bishop might have been among the clutch of German prelates who later resisted not so much reform in general but specifically the celibacy rule with forceful good sense. 'The Pope must be a heretic or madman. He would compel all men to live like angels,' they wrote. 'Then let the Pope who thought men too grovelling for him, see if he can find angels to govern his Church.'[xii]

I found a bikers' *Gasthaus* near the railway station and took the last room they had. The young woman serving me my breakfast the next morning could not direct me to the car-hire office but assured me that her boyfriend, who happened to work for a rival car-hire company, would know where it was, and she kindly offered to ask him before accompanying me there.

A plump girl of nineteen with flawless pale skin and long, straight, jet-black hair that she was allowing to revert to the original reddish gold which already showed in her parting, Anya was dressed entirely in black with clumsy platform shoes to match. As we drove around the light-industrial outskirts of Konstanz that bright early Sunday morning, she told me that her English-born father was an army officer currently serving with Germany's NATO forces in Kosovo who did not care about her. Her brother, also a soldier serving in the Balkans, was similarly uncommunicative. Anya had seen neither of them, nor her invalid Dutch mother in Amsterdam, for years. She claimed her parents' early divorce had meant nothing to her but she resented having had to leave home at sixteen.

'Not that it was ever much of a home; we lived in ten different places between Hamburg in the north and Berne in the south before

I was sixteen. You know, I don't like being from nowhere, but that's how I feel – from nowhere at all . . .'

Anya was trying to make a home here in Konstanz with her German boyfriend Patrick but the outlook for a 'happy ever after' was not good. Patrick was fighting a losing battle to evade ten months' military service.

'I've lost my father and my brother to the army already and now Patrick is going too. I'm scared and, you know, I shouldn't be alone. I may look very healthy but I should *never* be left alone . . .'

Was she hinting at an affliction as serious as epilepsy, a weak heart or schizophrenia? I could not be sure, but there was something about the way she was staring at me through her grown-up spectacles that discouraged me from delving into the matter. The demon taunting Anya was not *Accidie*, I decided, but another at least as dangerous. Nervous, over-communicative but oddly opaque, she was angry and afraid. In an effort to distract her from her multiple woes, I changed the subject to explain my presence in Konstanz. She did not seem in the least interested in medieval history so I was astonished and touched when, a few minutes later, she offered to spend her day off showing me around the town.

'I've no idea if there is anything from the eleventh century here but we must start with the cathedral,' she decided for us, walking me down a narrow cobbled street ending in the tree-shaded cathedral close.

The clear blue sky was clouding over and beginning to promise rain, but there was a crowd of excited little girls gathered like a bunch of white flowers in their frilly First Communion dresses outside the cathedral doors. All around them, like a bouquet's greenery, were their parents in their church-going best English tweeds. Smart, shiny cars blocked the side streets. Anya scowled at the scene. The crypt of the grand cathedral might have been eleventh century but it was also still closed. As we left the building I noticed how Anya dipped her hand in the holy-water stoup by the door. Was she, by any chance, a practising Christian?

'No, of course not,' she replied with a frown and a toss of her two-tone hair. But she was a believer of a sort because she went on to explain that 'I only do that because I believe that if you dip your fingers in and then shake your hand it keeps all religion well away. If you dip your fingers in and then cross yourself it means you'll get sucked into all that God stuff.'

We wandered on around the town, past a clothes shop styling itself in English 'More & More – a whole philosophy of life'. We were in search of first an eleventh-century monastery I had read about but, 'No, no – there's no monastery there; I'm sure it's a police station,' said Anya, and then an eleventh-century chapel. 'No chapel there. Far as I remember there's just a baker's which does *Wurst* and chips with mayonnaise and ketchup,' she assured me. She may have been right because we did not find what I was looking for, but her brusque negativity was beginning to wear me down. We parted company after agreeing to meet up again, with her boyfriend Patrick, in the evening.

Patrick was a soberly dressed young man who smoked a pipe and greeted me with stiff-necked formality. The son of a border guard and grandson of an airman shot down over London in World War Two, he laughed with a loud 'Ho,ho,ho!' When he spoke it was often about the Second World War and how, thanks to being so close to the border with neutral Switzerland, Konstanz had kept its lights burning all night and so tricked Allied airmen into thinking that it was a Swiss town. A fatherly sort, he indulged Anya like a child.

'Patrick, let's go to the funfair . . . Oh, please . . . You know how I love it!' she wheedled as we sat finishing our beers in the courtyard of a hotel where she had worked. She had only chosen the hotel because she wanted to take revenge on the manageress who had sacked her a few days before. No turning the other cheek for Anya. She wanted to humiliate her enemy by forcing her to serve her a drink, but the woman did not appear to recognize her and was busy elsewhere. Narrowing her eyes spitefully at her foe's retreating back, Anya loudly commanded Patrick to leave a wildly overgenerous tip.

On the other side of the old town were the garish lights of a small travelling fair, thronging with Turkish *Gastarbeiter* and their children. Anya begged Patrick for some money to buy her favourite, candyfloss, and then for some more for a go on her favourite attraction, the dodgems. Next it was the Magic Carpet, a stomach-churning, neck-wrenching ride that whisked our red plastic chariots high above the town and over the border into Switzerland, before shooting them back down to earth in Germany, over and over again. Pink in the face and bright-eyed with excitement, Anya made Patrick buy her an outsize *Wurst* before scrambling aboard a dodgem car again. When at last Patrick suggested finding a bar for another beer, she was desolate at leaving all the fun.

'*You* enjoyed it, didn't you?' she enquired of me anxiously, as we headed off towards a bar. I had, in a way, and said so, but Patrick wanted a grown-up talk about politics so I raised the subject of the failing Euro currency.

'You can forget the Euro,' he said, *Stein* of beer in one hand, pipe in the other. 'Of course, the Euro makes travelling and doing business with France, for example, much easier – you British are mad not to see that – but the US dollar is the only currency I'm interested in.'

Anya did not want to be left out of the conversation, and was interestingly keen to take a longer view than Patrick.

'Well, if you want to know what I think,' she began, with a pout and a shrug of her shoulders, 'I think it's a kind of sick irony that we're joining up all our economies before we've all learned to really love each other and feel united . . .' I thought Jean Monnet and Robert Schuman might have nodded sagely, and Otto III could have sympathized.

The next morning there was no Anya to serve me breakfast. The receptionist coolly informed me that she had just been 'let go' before handing me a badly spelt note from her. It said, 'We will go to your Reichenau together. Meet at the opposite café at 10 – A'. I had hardly mentioned my plan to visit the monastery island and had certainly not suggested she accompany me there. But once again I was surprised and touched, even charmed, by her brusque friendliness. So we met up as she had commanded, with Patrick and a car. The morning was bright and already warm. Anya was clutching her identity card.

'This will be fun,' she announced. 'I need my identity card because we have to cross the border into Switzerland to get there. You know, when I was much younger—'

'Perhaps you mean last year? Ho, ho!' interjected Patrick.

'When I was much younger,' she began again patiently, 'I was so excited to have my identity card that I used to cross the border just for fun. Sometimes I would dress up as a Turkish woman with a headscarf and long skirt, hoping that the guards would stop me. Sometimes I went to take photos of the guards. Once I had an idea to make a bucket filled with little bags of white sugar . . . You know, to look like drugs.'

Taking my cue from Patrick, I said nothing. We crossed the border without incident and were soon driving over the long, poplar-lined causeway known as Philosopher's Way onto the island. Neither of them had ever set foot on the island before.

'So what's so great and interesting about this place?' said Anya.

It was all the encouragement I needed and certainly the first I had had. I launched into a mini-lecture on the history and attractions of a place that was already two hundred years old and famed throughout Christendom 'as far as the mist-enshrouded land of the Britons,'[xiii] by the middle of the eleventh century when Leo IX had halted there on his way home to Rome after his Reims council.

'You have to imagine,' I told my companions in as lively and engaging a style as I could manage, 'that Reichenau, cleverly and delightfully situated just before the northern foothills of the Alps here, was where the pilgrim routes from northern Europe met before parting in different directions again towards the various mountain passes. The place was fabulously rich thanks to all the pilgrims as well as the patronage of the German kings and the generous donations from nobles who had their sons educated here. It must have been covered in vineyards and colourfully frescoed churches, bustling with holiness – monks and pilgrims everywhere. There are ten thousand pilgrims' names in Reichenau's visiting book for the period between the middle of the ninth century and the end of the eleventh. About forty of those names are followed by the words "*ex Islant terra*". Just think of that! Icelanders travelling to and from St Peter's tomb in Rome or the much longer *Jorsalaferd*, the pilgrimage all the way to Jerusalem—'

'You know what?' interrupted Anya.

'What?' I asked eagerly, prepared to answer any of her questions, to encourage any glimmer of interest in my subject.

'I could eat a horse. I didn't even have time to have breakfast before I was sacked. Patrick, why don't we just go to America?'

He laughed and patted her hand and I continued to think – rather than talk – about Reichenau. Otto's Granny Adelheid and his mother Theophano had visited the place and doubtless tasted its famously 'bulging grapes'. Pope Sylvester II, or plain Gerbert as he still was at the time, had penned his ecstatically exhortatory epistle to Otto III, 'Ours, ours is the Roman Empire . . .' from Reichenau in 997. Young Otto would certainly have called in with his retinue on his way south to quell his Romans or north to soothe his Saxons. He had one of his favourite saints, Bartholomew, honoured with a church here and another, dedicated to St Adalbert, was begun. The abbey produced the best art – gospel covers, illuminated manuscripts and frescoes – of his reign. In 1029, an abbot of Reichenau wrote to the pope of the day proudly confirming that the community remained the top breeding ground for the ecclesiastical civil and military service the German emperors used to run their empire. 'In the monastery there have always been and are now only monks of illustrious and noble birth.'[xiv] One such nobleman's son, whom Pope Leo would certainly have encountered on his stopover at Reichenau in late 1049, was one of my favourite eleventh-century characters, a certain Brother Hermann the Lame.

Hermann had been deposited at the monastery at the age of seven, so severely handicapped that he was unable to either sit comfortably or speak clearly. Apparently, the sounds he made were 'barely intelligible'[xv] and he can never, in all his life, have felt healthy. But he made up for all he lacked in physical strength with extraordinary intellectual gifts. Only the long-dead Gerbert could match Brother Hermann's genius. He composed passionately poetic hymns to the Virgin Mary, including the famous '*Salve Regina*', but also weighty treatises on multiplication and division, and he invented a complicated game based on Pythagorean number theory. More usefully, he explored Arabic science in sufficient depth to be able to introduce vital instruments for navigation and measurement – the astrolabe, the portable sundial and a quadrant – into western Europe. Stargazing and music were his passions, and on the latter he held pungently purist views.

> We have to realise that the whole point of music is that we should construct a science of composing a reasonable tune, of judging a tune correctly, and singing it properly . . . The blind run of singers pays attention to the third point only, I mean, to singing, or rather, to howling, giving heed to nobody's ideas, accepting no one's opinion . . . [They are those] to whom loud voice is everything! Herein you will be right in rating such as lower and clumsier than donkeys, who after all make a great deal more noise, but never mix up braying with bellowing! Miserable idiots![xvi]

In spite of such sneering and his incessant physical discomfort Brother Hermann seems to have been so *hilarissimus, amabilis* and *benevolus* that he was especially loved by his fellow monks and hailed by them as 'the miracle of our century'.[xvii]

I could hardly wait to see Reichenau. Surely I would find there a monk to talk to, or some pilgrims. Perhaps someone could tell me whether the Reichenau monks of almost a thousand years ago had supported Pope Leo's reform programme, or what kind of anti-celibacy protests the Konstanz clergy had mounted, or something new about Brother Hermann.

'About half of the island is now devoted to market gardening – a very profitable business,' Patrick informed me.

'So the monks are still growing their vegetables and cultivating their vines then,' I commented approvingly, wishing it was the season for their 'bulging grapes'.

'Monks?' he queried, as we drove past acres of plastic green-houses, sprinklers and neat, furrowed fields frilled with the first green shoots of vegetables. The island seemed deserted. The wooden shutters on a few houses were still closed. 'I don't know if there are any monks. I've lived in Konstanz all my life but I've never heard of any monks at Reichenau.'

'At the monastery, I mean. There *is* a monastery here, isn't there?'

'I don't know. There are some churches, I think . . .'

There must still be a monastery, I insisted. Catholic southern Germany had not suffered the sixteenth-century Protestant Reformation so there can have been no smashing of reliquaries or stripping of monasteries down here. I could not think of a single good reason why there should no longer be a Benedictine monastery on Reichenau. Patrick did not argue with me.

We stopped the car at the main abbey church. The carefully restored tourist attraction, which I could not imagine Pope Leo entering, was flanked by pristine pale yellow buildings with tidy red-tiled roofs. On one of those pretty yellow walls was a striking sundial such as Brother Hermann might have designed. The neat outline of a kneeling monk beside it and a painted banner inscribed with the Benedictine motto *'laborare est orare'** below it suggested to me the presence of at least a token community of monks on the island. Inside the bare church, all that recalled the zenith of Reichenau's fortunes were the rounded arches of its three Romanesque naves.

'Well, you can find out if there is still a monastery here – just ring that doorbell,' suggested Patrick, who was starting to take an interest in my hunt for monks. Anya sat on a low wall and yawned. Climbing a flight of stone stairs in one corner, I duly rang a bell:

* To work is to pray.

once, twice, three times. The sharp electronic noise was audible through the wooden door but there were no answering footsteps. At last a verger, an elderly man in a checked shirt, jeans and gumboots who might have been a market gardener, informed us that I had been ringing the parish priest's doorbell, and he was not at home.

'Please, are there any monks on Reichenau today?'

'Monks? No.'

'The big monastery. Are there any ruins to see?'

'No, no ruins. There are some churches . . .'

Accidie was back again, and Anya swearing that if she did not have breakfast soon she would surely faint. The eleventh century was not here, any more than it had been outside St Remi's basilica in Reims.

On the way back to Konstanz I was flicking through a guide to the island I had found at the back of the church when I discovered why there is no longer a monastery on Reichenau. It seems that the community's policy of exclusivity was its undoing. In the twelfth century the cream of the German nobility had insisted on barring all but the most aristocratic from entering the monastery. By the fourteenth century a pope was complaining, 'At one time sixty to seventy monks wore Benedictine garb at Reichenau. But then years ago a nasty practice crept in whereby no more monks were admitted unless both parents were of noble blood.'[xviii] A hundred years later there were only two monks at Reichenau.

Fortunately, I thought, as I idled away the rest of the day back in Konstanz, I had had plenty of advance warning that there was no longer a monastery at my next destination, Cluny in Burgundy. The miserable fact that the most influential, reform-minded and effective Benedictine house in Europe for the last hundred years of the first millennium and the first hundred years of the second had been closed by zealous French Republicans at the end of the eighteenth century and then ransacked for scrap stone would not come as a shock to me. Nor would I experience another bout of *Accidie*; I was planning to come as close as I could to living eleventh-century

Cluniac life by spending a week with *Frère* Roger at the Christian Communauté de Taizé, only four miles from Cluny.

The next morning I hired another car from Patrick's firm and drove the mostly mountainous route numerous monks of Cluny and Reichenau must have taken, back and forth about their Church business.

~

I was back in France, but only just and keeping an eye out for a *chambre d'hôte*. Swerving abruptly to my right off the main road with its twin lines of plane trees and square detached houses down a rough track indicated by an arrow on a green sign, I stopped the car outside a large modern house set in a tidy garden. The middle-aged woman at the door showed me straight upstairs to a bedroom hung with a large crucifix.

Monsieur and Madame Brard accommodated only pilgrims that night. There was me and a ruddy-faced dairy farmer and his wife from the Pas de Calais, on their way south to Rome to visit the tomb of St Peter and glimpse Pope John Paul II in this jubilee two-thousandth year since Christ's birth. As night fell the five of us gathered round a long wooden table with a pool of yellow lamplight in the middle of it. Sustained by a roast chicken and home-made cake, we lingered late, talking.

Monsieur Brard and the dairy farmer compared their families' Second World Wars and my mind wandered backwards. Eleventh-century peasants crouching around their night fires might have swapped old tales about Viking raids and Saracen bandits still lurking in the Alps, but in about 1050 they would have had more recent terrors to regale passing travellers with. The century's terrifyingly frequent outbreaks of *ignis sacer**, holy fire, made for fine horror stories.

Ignis sacer sent whole peasant communities screaming mad with

* *Ignis sacer* was known as St Anthony's Fire by the late fourteenth century.

visions both heavenly and hellish, burning genitalia, giddiness, sweating, diarrhoea and spells of suicidal depression interspersed with
bouts of macabre merriment, absurd elation and convulsions. We
know what this hell's torment was like and even that its victims
gave off a telltale stench of dead mouse because there were two
outbreaks of it as recently as 1951, in a southern French village.

The violent disorder of mind and body gripping the inhabitants
of Pont Saint-Esprit was eventually traced to a batch of bad
baguettes, but not before the village had witnessed a woman
screaming that her children had been hung, drawn and quartered
to make sausages hanging from the rafters in her attic, not before
an eleven-year-old boy had turned on his mother and clawed her
face to shreds while his father lay in bed quaking with his own
horrible hallucinations, and not before a former pilot had climbed
out on to a hospital window sill shouting 'Look at me! I'm an
aeroplane!'[xix] and then jumped and broken both of his legs. There
were those who claimed to be experiencing a euphoric sense of
blessing and enlightenment; while as yet unaffected members of the
community charged through the village wielding crucifixes and
rosaries to ward off the evil. Animals in sixteen neighbouring villages were hideously afflicted. Cats screeched and clawed and
dragged their paralysed hindquarters along the ground. Dogs
smashed their teeth on rocks, or pulled them all out by gnawing
the bark off tree trunks. The high tide of lunacy – appalling delusions
brought on by traces of the hallucinogen LSD in ergot mould
growing on wheat used in the baguettes – took three weeks to
subside.

Eleventh-century victims of *ignis sacer* would have prayed to
God and his saints to spare them, quaked at their clergy telling
them that the Almighty was punishing them for their wickedness,
and fearfully recalled a description in the Bible about how the end
of the world would come about: 'Their torment was the torment of
a scorpion . . . and in those days shall men seek death and shall not
find it; and shall desire to die and death shall flee from them.'[xx]

Miracles worked by holy relics bred more tales. This was an age in which it was generally believed that there could be no more direct means of tapping into the supernatural and improving one's chances of health and happiness than by being in the presence of a piece of clothing, a bone, a hair, a toenail, even a droplet of spittle of a saint. God was way on high but his saints were masters of bilocation – on high but also down here on earth, in the neighbouring town's cathedral, in the crypt of the monastery down the road, in a bag around one's neck. They were wholly present and powerful in every bone, excrescence or fluid of their mouldering corpses. Relics were an insurance policy against chaos and misfortune, a trusted means of exacting order and justice from a hostile universe which denied people both those luxuries. The impresario monks of the age perfectly understood all this and wittingly or unwittingly exploited simple people's love of the uncanny. The more miraculous a monastery's relics, the more widely they became known and the more pilgrims travelled there to experience their good effects. The more pilgrims came, the larger the monastery's revenues and the greater the monks' influence.

But there was a price to pay. The sort of rowdy rumpus seen in Reims on the occasion of Pope Leo IX's visit in 1049 was not uncommon. In Limoges in 1018 a crowd of pilgrims gathering to attend an early-morning mass stampeded suddenly, leaving fifty-two of their number trampled to death. A German abbot was driven to beg the patron saint of his monastery to curtail his miracle working because the crowds of pilgrims he attracted were uncontrollable and the monks could get no peace. The monks of the monastery and pilgrimage church of Sainte-Foy in Conques scored a notable failure with their attempts at crowd control. When lusty peasant pilgrims keeping vigil in the church one night set up an 'abominable shouting and unruly singing'xxi the monks decided that the church must be emptied after vespers, locked up for the night and the *rusticana multitudo* made to bed down outside. A miraculous unlocking of the doors and repossession of the church by the peasants forced the monks to conclude that God willed that his house be overrun by his unruly children.

The chronicles of Brother Raoul Glaber, a Cluniac monk born in the same year as Otto III, are full of such tales and plenty more about devastating famines. His native Burgundy was terribly cursed in the early 1030s. It was commonly believed – as in our own age of global warming and climate change – 'that the order of the seasons and the elements, which had ruled all past ages from the beginning, had fallen into perpetual chaos'. Apparently, starving men's voices 'piped like dying birds' while wolves 'gorged themselves on corpses' dug from mass graves at crossroads. The famines made cannibalism commonplace. 'Travellers were set upon by men stronger than themselves, and their dismembered flesh was cooked over fires and eaten,' wrote Brother Raoul, and a ravenous peasant might tempt a child with an apple or an egg before dragging the unfortunate away to a lonely spot to kill and eat. Brother Raoul also dolefully noted how 'the custom of eating human flesh had grown so common that one fellow sold it ready-cooked in the marketplace of Tournus'.[xxii]

I recalled seeing a black-and-white photograph capturing exactly such a scene during famines engineered by Stalin rather than God in 1930s Ukraine: two shawled peasants of indeterminate sex standing with staring, emptied eyes behind a market stall heaped with frozen lumps of human flesh. It struck me that a millennium ago, in the 1030s, Ukraine might have been a happier place, not wrecked by purges of the peasants but prospering and well integrated with the rest of Europe. The early medieval principality of Kiev with its Byzantine Christianity was ably and piously governed by Prince Yaroslav the Wise, a descendant of the Scandinavian Vikings who had settled the place and pioneered the Varangian trading route two centuries before. Prince Yaroslav 'applied himself to books . . . by night and by day'[xxiii] but also to building churches and monasteries, and to marrying his sisters and children into some of the most powerful ruling families of Western Christendom. Yaroslav's three sisters wed rulers of Hungary, Poland and Nordmark.* His

* Today's Denmark.

son and successor, Vladimir Monomakh, married King Harold of England's sister, Gytha, after she fled to Kiev from the catastrophe of the Norman conquest.

Fuelled by the fine local *vin de table*, I had fared as far as Ukraine and the late eleventh century in my thoughts but now dragged myself back into the present to hear Monsieur Brard explaining how his parents had run a farm before the Second World War. The French army, he was saying, had requisitioned every one of their horses.

'We weren't as mechanized as the Germans at the start of the war – you remember that, Monsieur, don't you?' he said, refilling his guest's brandy glass. 'Our lot still needed horses to pull the gun carriages around. It makes you think how much has changed, doesn't it?'

The dairy farmer shrugged and sighed, and Monsieur Brard continued: 'My father was taken prisoner by the Nazis and sent to work in a factory in Vienna because he was too proud to do any German's farm work for him.'

We all expressed our appreciation of his heroism.

'But he died there . . . My mother got back home in forty-five. Nothing left of the farm of course, just one crippled rabbit! She lassooed some horses she found roaming free.'

I thought I heard the same bleak note of *fin du monde* despair that someone like Brother Raoul must have felt in the early 1030s. Could a man-made twentieth-century catastrophe have seemed as dismaying as a natural eleventh-century one? Perhaps more so. There was a certain simple logic to God's divine justice, meted out to wicked mankind in the shape of periodic famines, droughts, storms, outbreaks of *ignis sacer* and earthquakes. Then, there had been no doubt whatever that mankind was wicked, or that God was omnipotent and just. The reasons for the twentieth century's two total wars were more complex and much more mysterious. Jean Monnet and Robert Schuman had simply noted the sad salient fact that both victors and vanquished had lost by the conflicts and had bravely embarked on their rebuilding project in a spirit of not so much Christian forgiveness and reconciliation as sober self-interest.

Monsieur Brard swilled his cognac in its glass. 'The family had to start from scratch again. We managed to build this house about twenty years ago. We breed bulls now, do a bit of market gardening.'

'Got a son to take over the reins of the place from you, have you?' asked the dairy farmer.

'No, a daughter,' said Madame Brard with a sigh as she helped us each to a second slice of cake. 'But she has no motivation to do anything, let alone farming. Sits around smoking all day. She's got all the qualifications you can think of, even speaks perfect English, but you try getting her to do anything! She just says "What's the point!" It's *affreux!*'

A chronic case of *Accidie*, I decided.

'*Bon Dieu!*' breathed the dairy farmer's wife in sympathy as Madame Brard continued with a glance at me:

'Now that I come to think of it, she once went to Taizé for a weekend. That impressed her, livened her up for a time, you know, made her think about things . . .'

While the two Mesdames cosily compared notes about all the pilgrimage centres they had ever visited – Lourdes, Loreto, Fátima, Santiago de Compostella – the two Messieurs quizzed me on my travels. Iceland and eastern Germany were beyond their ken, the west of Germany they knew, but they were interested in my impressions of Poland.

'Poles are everywhere these days,' the dairy farmer mumbled into his cake. 'Our local baker's a Pole. That's fine, I say. Someone's got to bake bread and if we haven't got enough of our own to do it . . . But do we really need them in the EU? They're at least fifty years behind us with their agriculture.'

Monsieur Brard nodded and shrugged as if to say 'And what can we, the little people, the peasants, do about this latest man-made catastrophe in the making?' It was too late to embark on a discussion about the European Union. Madame Brard glanced at her watch. We all retired for the night.

Over breakfast the following morning the dairy farmer and his wife regaled me with the tale of a young woman who had visited a monastery and succeeded in seducing a monk from his celibacy. 'There must be lovely clean and serious young monks at Taizé . . . What a waste!' observed the dairy farmer's wife, munching ruminatively on her brioche.

When I left, Madame Brard saw me to the door, wished me God speed and added, 'Have a – how shall I say – reflective time at Taizé. Whatever else you do there you will have to reflect.'

That early on a rainy Sunday morning the only signs of life in the villages I drove through were a few elderly men stepping out with their small dogs to purchase baguettes from strip-lit bakeries. Through the streaked windscreen the sunny golden brown of those bread crusts made cheerful spots of colour in streets lined with grey apartment blocks and shuttered supermarkets. My stubborn determination to avoid the autoroutes was soon costing me dearly in time and fuel. The dog-eared printout of my e-mail from Taizé informed me that the community expected visitors to check in by six in the evening, but I was already lost for the second time in two hours with incessant heavy rain further impeding my progress.

By mid-morning there were more people in the villages I passed through, families of church-goers and fragile, bowed old women answering the call to Sunday worship. Rain muffled the ringing bells. Shortly before noon the churches opened their doors to emit colourful bunches of the faithful and their umbrellas. People headed back to cars parked in shiny lines down main roads to left and right of the churches, and grabbed the hands or coats of small children to prevent them running into the road. Young fathers carried fancy white boxes of pâtisserie tied up with ribbons. Restaurants were opening for Sunday lunch.

The rich medieval towns of wine-producing Burgundy – Beaune and Nuits-St-Georges – were choked with anoraked tourists consulting signs directing them to *caves* for tastings. In the wide spaces between the towns, tidy rows of vines stretched as far as the eye could see into the hills rising in the distance on either side of the road. Taizé, I found to my dismay, was not marked on either of my maps, but the sun was making a shy appearance at last and the signposts told me that I was nearing Cluny, only four miles from my destination. I had time to spare.

~

Snug in a valley of the River Saône and bathed in watery afternoon sunlight I found a small town grown fat on its tourist trade since the end of World War Two. But all Cluny's well-organized coach and car parks, helpful signposts, a museum of the Romanesque, handy tourist information offices and expensively attractive eateries could not conceal the dismal truth: the French revolutionaries had done a commendably thorough job. There is precious little left of Cluny's *raison d'être*, the great monastery which replaced Rome as the heart of Western Christendom during the first half of the eleventh century.

There are some once giant now brutally truncated pillars and a single tower belonging to what had once been the biggest church in the West. They did not help me conjure up a candlelit vision of glittering gold altars and hundreds of tonsured monks performing the *Opus Dei* – the unceasing liturgical round of sung services that was Cluny's speciality and hallmark. Climbing to the top of the tower for an overview, I could see how the main street – two crooked lines of pretty tiled roofs – had grown up around one of the outside walls of the monastery. But so what, when there was no monastery?

I had devoured bookfuls about life at Cluny. I wanted to hear bells calling the monks to matins, prime, terce, sext, none, or – glancing at my watch – 4.15 p.m. vespers, before supper and compline. But buildings and bells were not everything. Monks – hankering after heaven and marking out their ordered days in a ceaseless round of holy time – were what was missing.

I would like to have seen the brothers kissing their abbot's hands every time they entered his presence and bowing at the mention of his name, or to have attended a chapter house meeting to witness a monk being chastised for drunkenness or talking to a woman, or to have eaten in the one-hundred-foot-long refectory, half-listening to some spiritual reading while silently signing for a brother to pass the bread. Where were the *circatores*, trusted monks whose task was to patrol every nook and cranny of the church, the cloisters and the dormitory, keeping a sharp watch for monks dozing through their night prayers, or sleeping with bare arms and legs indecently escaping from linen sheets in summer or rough wool blankets in winter? Where were the oblates – the often slightly handicapped young lads donated to the monastery in infancy like Reichenau's Brother Hermann – being shepherded about the place by a monk with a lantern in one hand, a rod in the other? I missed the bustle of monks lining up along the cloister wall for their weekly shave, their excitement at collecting a new pair of shoes on Maundy Thursday. Where was the brother in charge of making Holy Communion bread, with his assistants washed and combed and ready to set to work while singing psalms? What about the keeper of the fish ponds, the only monk permitted to ride in through the abbey gates straight to the fish kitchen, and to leave his cell after vespers if he had fishing to do?

Brother Raoul's enthusiastic observations about Cluny seemed more evocative than a few broken stones.

> Let every man know that this convent has not its equal anywhere in the Roman world, particularly when it comes to delivering souls that have fallen under the demon's sway. Communion is taken there so frequently that virtually not one day passes but that this never-ending link [between man and God] makes it possible to wrest some soul from the power of the evil spirits. I myself am witness that in this monastery it is a custom, made possible by the very great number of monks, that masses be celebrated constantly from the earliest hour of the day until the hour assigned for rest; and they go about it with so much dignity and piety and veneration that one would think they were angels rather than men.[xxiv]

A hermit living on an island in the Mediterranean, plagued by visions of demons chucking sinners' souls into the smouldering entrails of a nearby mountain, once heard those devils complaining that too many were escaping their clutches thanks to all the prayers from Cluny. He sent urgent instructions back to Burgundy to keep up the good work.

I pictured Otto III's Granny Adelheid here, kindly received by the two successive abbots of Cluny whom she revered as her spiritual fathers. Not long before she died, in 999, she had approached the second with a characteristically pious request: 'Know that this is the last time I shall see you with bodily eyes. I hope that your brothers will do me the favour of praying for me before God.'[xxv] If, on account of weather or war, Otto III had been obliged to take a more westerly route across the Alps to Italy than that leading to the Bodensee and Reichenau, he would surely have spent a night or two at Cluny, as would his friend Gerbert. The German Holy Roman Emperor Henry II, father of the dour Henry III, must have breathed the superior air of Cluny on a visit in the 1030s because he bequeathed to Cluny 'his gold sceptre, his gold orb, his imperial robe of gold, his gold crown and his gold crucifix – all of these together weighing a hundred pounds'.[xxvi] Pope Leo IX, passing on his way back and forth across the Alps, certainly used the magnificent monastery as a stopping place, and Cluny backed all his reforming initiatives. Pope Leo's aim, to divide all churchmen from the wicked world by means of monastic celibacy and ecclesiastical independence, reinforced everything Cluny stood for.

Back at ground level it began to rain again. Walking down the high street, I discovered two old men sitting on folding stools in plastic rain capes guarding the entrance to an alternative pilgrimage site: a small exhibition about the Second World War. Beside them, lit by a dangling naked light bulb, was an untidy display of second-hand books about the region's wartime resistance movement. Behind was a roughly drawn map indicating that Cluny – and nearby Taizé too, I noticed – had fallen inside the *zone libre* of unoccupied Vichy France. Just how un-*libre* that zone had been, how tainted by collaboration with the Nazis, was graphically illustrated by a rough grey and blue striped prison uniform hanging on the opposite wall, as silently reproachful as a crucifix. A label saying '*Tenue appartenant à Madame Georgette Colin (clunisoise) déportée au camp de Ravensbruck*'* was pinned to it.

Like the tenth-century invaders of Europe, the twentieth-century Nazis had, for a time at least, spared this mountainous area of Burgundy their closest attention. A thousand years ago this remote region was rich in monasteries and hermitages. As early as 910 Duke William the Pious of Aquitaine had sought to secure his entry to heaven by donating his favourite hunting ground at Cluny to Saint Peter. The duke must have been not only more pious but also more canny than most of his contemporaries because in the monastery's lengthy foundation charter he clearly stipulated two important departures from the norm. First, he set up a barrier to simony by stipulating that the monks of Cluny be free in perpetuity to elect their own abbots without interference from local lords or bishops. It was a foretaste of the measures Pope Leo IX and his reformers would take almost a century and a half later to separate the Church of Christ from the evil world. Secondly, and just as significantly, the generous duke commanded that the abbots of Cluny be answerable and accountable to no one but the pope in Rome, who was St Peter's direct representative.

Cluny was thereby invested with a huge measure of *libertas* – freedom. But it was freedom as medieval Western Christendom understood it. The logic of the feudal order dictated that everyone had some form of lord or protector, so what counted was how highly placed and how far away that lord or protector was. The popes were not only highly placed but also across the Alps in Rome. In effect, Duke William was granting Cluny total independence, and prescribing horrible tortures for anyone who dared to infringe it. 'Let God remove him [the meddler] from the land of the

---

* 'Suit belonging to Mme Georgette Colin (of Cluny), deported to Ravensbruck [Nazi concentration] camp.'

1 An eleventh-century map on vellum showing Jerusalem at the centre of the world and Britain in the lower left-hand corner.

2 The ridge of Thingvellir, the site of Iceland's open-air parliament.

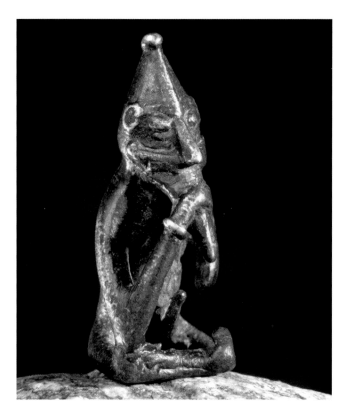

3 Seven-centimetre-high bronze statue of the
Viking fertility god, Freyr, from Sweden.

4 The teenage Holy Roman Emperor Otto III (980–1002)
on his throne. From the illuminated *Gospels of Otto* c.998.

5 The story of St Adalbert's life and violent death in 997, told on the twelfth-century bronze doors of Gniezno Cathedral.

6 Holy Roman Emperor Henry III (1017–1056), Pope Leo IX's partner in church reform and father of Henry IV; with Apostles Simon and Jude. From the *Codex Caesareus Upsaliensis*, c.1045.

7 Emperor Constantine IX of Byzantium with his wife, Empress Zoe (Otto III's former fiancée) on his left and Zoe's sister, Theodora, on his right. From a Greek codex of 1042–50.

8 On the right, Pope Leo IX (1049–1054) excommunicating
Patriarch Michael Kerollarios of Constantinople in 1054.
From a fifteenth-century Greek manuscript.

9 Holy Roman Emperor Henry IV who fought
Pope Gregory VII for supreme command of western Christendom.
From a twelfth-century German chronicle.

REX ROGAT ABBATEM: MATHILDIM SUPPLICAT ATQ;

10 Holy Roman Emperor Henry IV on his knees at Canossa,
pleading with Countess Matilda of Tuscany and Abbot Hugh
of Cluny to intercede for him with Pope Gregory VII.
From a twelfth-century Italian Life of Matilda.

living ... his members putrefying and swarming with vermin,'[xxvii] was how his charter of donation concluded. William must have had in mind Burgundy's plethora of petty lordlings with their bands of armed followers jockeying for land and livelihood by ceaseless skirmishing and plundering.

By the eleventh century St Peter's Cluny was renowned throughout Christendom, East and West, as an exemplary house of God staffed by monks truly living the *vita angelica*. The brothers and their *Opus Dei* were inviting comparisons with heavenly choirs of angels, and Cluny's abbots with archangels. Popes and kings came seeking spiritual counsel and mediation in their quarrels. Pillaged peasants sought and sometimes gained the abbots' protection from rapacious lordlings, the very men who were proving – ironically enough – to be the source of much of the monastery's wealth.

Those bellicose benefactors were like Thorvald the Far-farer or Otto III in that they retained a sharp awareness that they were doing a grievous wrong to their Lord Jesus by devoting their days to warfare and the plundering of castles, land, livestock and peasants. But, also like Thorvald and Otto, they were still locked into ancient Germanic tribal mores which exalted combat and personal honour above all else. They knew all about loving thy neighbour and turning the other cheek but could not marry those fine ideals with life as they felt they had to live it to survive. They were simple *milites* – armed and mounted fighters – not yet knights endowed with a certain respectability by a code of Christian chivalry, but most of them were desperately anxious to spare themselves an eternity of roasting in hell and desired to make amends for their multiple misdeeds before they died. Amends might take the form of a pilgrimage, or two or three, to Jerusalem,* Rome or Santiago de Compostella. Generous donations to ensure burial in Cluny's graveyard so as to be ready and waiting first in line at St Peter's gates

* The ferociously bellicose Frenchman, Fulk Nerra, made three pilgrimages to Jerusalem – in 1003, 1010 and 1038–9.

on Judgement Day, were also highly rated, as were large donations of land.

Between 1027 and 1030 alone thirty-one separate parcels of land were made over to Cluny, plus some lucrative salmon fishing rights on the Loire. Cluny also acquired churches and whole monasteries, complete with all their contents, inmates included. Each new monastery underwent a thorough purge and was reformed to observe Cluny's punishing daily round of church services and reinforced Benedictine discipline. By the mid-eleventh century the rigidly centralized Cluniac order was proving so popular that the same prayers, music, timetable, rituals, sign language for use during periods of enforced silence, architecture, diet and monastic garb were to be found at religious establishments from Spain in the west to Asia Minor in the south, to England and Sweden in the north. A year after the First Crusaders' conquest of Jerusalem in 1099, the Italian Norman Prince Tancred of Galilee endowed a Cluniac monastery on Mount Tabor, where Christ had undergone his Transfiguration.

Cluny's order and uniformity were reassuring in a western Europe studded with castles erected by rampaging *milites* who had filled the power vacuum created by the ravages of Magyars, Saracens and Vikings during the tenth century. Her inexorable expansion was not viewed with anything like the sort of suspicious distaste many of us feel today for the garishly homogenizing march of a fast-food chain or soft-drinks maker. Saint Augustine of Hippo's famous work, *City of God*, was widely read by churchmen of the time who found in it a useful message for their flocks. Order in heaven, St Augustine seemed to be saying, must be matched by order on earth. And there could be no order without peace.

Alongside their work as spiritual advisers to kings, pedlars of salvation to the *milites*, protectors and keepers of magic relics to the peasantry and stalwart supporters of the reforming popes in all their projects, a series of long-lived and piously energetic abbots of Cluny worked hard to bring peace first to their region and then, as their order spread, to Western Christendom. Neither Cluny's develop-

ment nor its contribution to public peace could have happened
without them.

In the mid tenth century Abbot Odo of Cluny was the first to
acknowledge the existence of the *milites* and penned a popular saint's
life aimed at showing members of this unruly new class a way to
reconcile their violent worldly calling with non-violent Christianity.
'It is legitimate,' he declared in approximate agreement with St
Augustine's views on fighting just wars,* 'for a layman in the order
of warriors to carry the sword to defend people without arms.'[xxviii]
The Western Church's campaign at the start of the new millennium
– to re-establish peace and order by co-opting *milites* away from
their land grabbing to the project of expanding and defending
Christendom – was launched.

Odo's successor, Abbot Maiolus, a spiritual father to Otto III's
Granny Adelheid and famous for his piety, turned down the job of
pope but took a leading role in promoting an initiative known as
the Peace of God, the brainchild of some Aquitainian bishops
who judged that church-plundering urgently needed curbing. The
movement organized councils attended by churchmen of every rank,
by monks accompanied by the choicest of their holy relics, by local
milites and by peasants. In front of a vast crowd gathered in an open
field, with holy relics serving as lie detectors and seals of divine
approval, *milites* were publicly shamed into swearing to keep the
peace. Not just the fearful threat of excommunication† but the presence of a posse of peacemakers prepared to fight on the side of right
ensured the efficacy of the procedure. Wildly popular with the put-
upon, relic-relishing peasantry, the number of Peace of God councils
grew, boosted by serial outbreaks of *ignis sacer*. At one council, in
989, it was declared that stealing peasants' cattle, robbing churches

---

* St Augustine seems to have thought that a just war was one waged to avenge an
injury. Injuries done to God – heresy – could also be punished with war.
† Excommunication meant no receiving of Holy Communion, no burial on sacred
ground and certain residence in hell. It was said that the ground could not take the
body of an excommunicant but would five times hurl it out of its grave.

and mugging churchmen were crimes punishable with excommunication.

Abbot Maiolus' successor, the aristocratic Odilo, was even more closely identified with the Peace of God, and with the later Truce of God which aimed at restricting the warring and outrages of the *milites* to certain days of the week. In 1042 Abbot Odilo of Cluny and the southern French bishops wrote to their Italian counterparts to encourage them to follow their lead:

> From the hour of vespers on Wednesday until sunrise on Monday, let there reign a settled peace and an enduring truce between all Christians, friends and enemies, neighbours and strangers . . . Whosoever shall kill a man on a day of truce shall be banished and driven out of his country, and shall make his way into exile at Jerusalem . . .[xxix]

Brother Raoul's lively chronicles are all dedicated to Abbot Odilo. After describing the appalling famine of the early 1030s during which Odilo ordered the opening of Cluny's granaries to the poor and sold many of its treasures to local Jews so as to be able to feed his starving monks, he lovingly recounts how relics turned a peace council held during Abbot Odilo's period of tenure into a gruesome-sounding spectacle of mass healing: 'Lest any doubt this, let it be recorded that as bent arms and legs were straightened and returned to their normal state, skin was broken, flesh was torn and blood ran freely . . . such enthusiasm was generated that the bishops raised their croziers to the heavens, and all cried out with one voice to God, their hands extended "Peace! Peace! Peace!" '[xxx]

Both the peace movements were marvellous, confidence-inspiring successes, a sign – like the new Romanesque churches – of the hopeful times, but in 1038 a place called Bourges witnessed the birth of a dilemma familiar to this day to all peace-keepers and - makers. In that year the local bishops commanded defenders of the Peace of God to take up arms against violators. An all-out battle ensued. Overzealous upholders of the Peace of God burnt down a castle with fourteen hundred *milites* and their followers inside. A revenge attack ended with the slaughter of seven hundred churchmen. It was a grisly foretaste of how difficult it would be to wean *milites* away from their fighting. Cluny's attempts to find them a role more in keeping with the tenets of Christianity was showing ominous signs of leading to the militarization of the Church rather than to the demilitarization of the *milites*.

Abbot Odilo's energies were also devoted to supporting the eviction of the Moors from the Iberian peninsula. He masterminded the monastery's strategic expansion with a string of new houses along the busy pilgrim trail through southern France and across northern Spain to the popular pilgrimage destination of Santiago de Compostella. Spanish riches adorned the new church he built at Cluny. One Spanish king loved Cluny and Odilo so well he made over a first Spanish monastery to the order and donated a thousand pieces of gold a year in return for prayers. There were Spanish monks at Odilo's Cluny and even a Pole, whom the pope of the day ordered back to Poland in 1043 to claim the Polish throne, as Casimir I.

Odilo fared far on church business but did not share the age's taste for pilgrimage. What need had his monks to go seeking Christ in Jerusalem when they could find him at home at Cluny? Aged eighty-five, in 1046 Odilo managed to journey south across the Alps to Rome to see the dourly pious initiator of Church reform, Emperor Henry III, crowned on Christmas Day. Two years later the great abbot was on his deathbed and asking one of his monks to fetch an abacus – part of Gerbert's legacy to Europe – to calculate the number of masses he had said every day of his life since ordination. The miracles he worked from beyond the grave soon qualified him for canonization.

While the popes in Rome had wallowed in their mire of corruption, discrediting the papacy and disgusting German churchmen, Abbot Odilo's Cluny had come to represent all that was best and most useful in the Church. When choosing between visiting St

Peter at Rome or St Peter at Cluny, many pilgrims opted for the latter.

Within a year of reforming Pope Leo arriving in Rome, Cluny was celebrating the instalment of a new young abbot, the nobly born Hugh of Semur, who would prove a staunch supporter and mainstay of at least the first phase of Church reform for the next half-century. Shrewd Hugh could discern the monk in a man and 'through him the great of many ranks and walks of life were converted from their turbulent and restless ways into the calm of monastic peace'.[xxxi] Under his direction the number of Cluniac monks would treble and the number of monasteries living by Cluny's order rise to over a thousand, scattered from Sussex to Hungary, from Castile to Sweden.

Repelled by the warrior future his father had mapped out for him, Hugh had entered Cluny at the age of seventeen. By the time his father and one of his brothers were killed by rival *milites* he was sufficiently advanced along his spiritual path to be able to forgive the murderers and even welcome one of them as a brother monk at Cluny. He was a compassionate man. When a novice of noble birth confessed that he could only bear the monk's hard life if he could wear silks and furs under his cassock, Abbot Hugh permitted this gross infringement of the Benedictine rule for as long as it took for the aristocrat to come to his Christian senses. Hugh was loved for his charity too. Beside his bed in the dormitory he shared with his monks there were always piles of old clothes which he cut up and re-stitched into garments for distribution to the poor.

Abbot Hugh undertook the building of Cluny's third church, a gigantic Romanesque extravagance with an ambulatory designed to accommodate thousands of pilgrims. Begun in 1088, it was the biggest and most splendid church in Western Christendom until Rome's sixteenth-century St Peter's was built.* Lavishly adorned with jewelled crosses, gorgeous cloths, priceless relics and seven towers, it boasted richly detailed frescoes much like the interiors of

---

* Cluny's third church was 525 feet high, St Peter's is 675 feet high.

Eastern Christian churches today. Sumptuous textiles imported from Byzantium inspired sculptors to carve exotic beasts around the capitals of its marble columns.

Most impressive of all perhaps was an eight-foot-tall candelabra donated by William the Conqueror's wife, Queen Matilda. William himself sent Abbot Hugh a magnificent golden cope embellished with amber and pearls and trimmed with gold bells 'delightful in melodiousness to the ear'[xxxii] while his queen followed that gift up with yet another, a vestment 'so stiff with gold that it could not be folded'.[xxxiii] Although the royal couple's names were added to the long list of those for whom the Cluny brothers said prayers every day, Hugh refused King William's request for six Cluny monks to oversee the reorganization of the English church after 1066. Generally, William was not as obedient to the reforming popes as Hugh would have liked,* and he had ignored the provisions of the Truce of God by invading England on a Saturday.

More even than Abbot Odilo, Hugh busied himself with brokering peace between popes and emperors, and making his mark at papal synods like Pope Leo IX's at Reims. Like Odilo he was also concerned with Spain, finding time to court and support King Alfonso VI of Leon and Castile in his outpost of Latin Christendom. Alfonso responded by turning more Spanish monasteries over to Cluniac rule and doubling his father's annual tribute to two thousand pieces of gold. He then married Abbot Hugh's niece and chose a Cluniac monk as archbishop of Toledo, which he had just recaptured from the Moors.

In the 1070s Abbot Hugh would see the Roman Church use the shining example of Cluny's *libertas* as a model for its own liberation from the control of Holy Roman emperors. He would be a sad witness to the dramatic destruction of the old ideal of partnership between pope and emperor. But that important part of my saga

---

* Norman England did not become a fief of the papacy – accept the pope as lord and protector and pay tribute in the form of Peter's Pence – until the early thirteenth century, in the reign of King John.

belonged to Italy, I reminded myself, splashing back to my parked car through a sudden downpour.

Driving the four miles north from Cluny towards Taizé, on a gently winding road swept by curtains of rain, I marvelled at how a monastery remote from any port or big town had become such a bastion of the reforming Church in the eleventh century, such a magnet for travellers from all over Western Christendom. In one year alone Cluny had welcomed seventeen thousand visitors. Then I noticed that the cars behind and in front of me had foreign number plates – one German, one Dutch. Like me, they were indicating an imminent turn to the left, to where a white, hand-written road sign pointed up a steep hill to the Communauté de Taizé.

~

Rain bucketed down out of an iron-grey sky. Bells clanged from a tall wooden structure that reminded me of a prison watchtower.

A neat sign in German, French and English on the door of the reception centre informed anyone arriving after five o'clock in the afternoon that they were at liberty to leave their luggage inside before heading straight to the church for evening prayers.

Feeling in greater need of physical than spiritual comfort, I reluctantly deposited my bag and followed a straggle of people striding, heads down and umbrellas up, across a muddy central compound surrounded by lines of wooden cabins and a huge open tent furnished with wooden benches and outsize cauldrons. Making for the large brick building that looked more like an aeroplane hangar than any church I had ever seen, I was wrestling with a devil more ferocious than *Accidie*. This devil was rudely arguing that the Communauté de Taizé was no place for me, that I did not need to damply suffer for days in the bosom of a crowd of Christians. Not so much will power as peer pressure defeated him. A smiling young German wearing rain-spattered spectacles was politely holding open the church door for me.

Inside, I found myself in a softly lit carpeted space at the far end of which, exactly where one would expect an altar to be, was a pleasing arrangement of candles set in a decorative wooden frame. Down the middle of the church were two straight rows of shoulder-high shrubs in white boxes and between them two long lines of monks in full-length creamy robes. The carpeted spaces to right and left were dotted with a couple of hundred pilgrims like myself – crouching, kneeling, lying prostrate or sitting cross-legged or, more comfortably, on steps and benches around the edges.

During the fifteen minutes allotted for silent meditation I glanced around at all kinds of people: a sturdy girl with a loud, German-accented singing voice, a young and unmistakably French couple, both elegant in neatly pressed jeans and polished shoes, a tall big-boned elderly woman with thick grey hair who must have been a north European, some stocky young Americans in T-shirts and trainers, and a middle-aged man, conspicuously English in his green corduroy trousers and Viyella shirt. There was nothing to mark me out as very different and I relaxed. *Ubi caritas et amor, ubi caritas Deus ibi est* – where there is charity and love, where there is charity, God is there – sung by hundreds of voices over and over again and embellished with the descant of a single male voice acted like a sedative on my attack of new-girl's nerves. Soon I was singing along from a booklet of sung prayers in French, Spanish, English, Russian, German, Polish, Hungarian, Greek and Latin. Outside, gusts of wind were lashing the brick sides of the church, vividly recalling my first stormy night aboard the *Bruarfoss*.

The end of the service was signalled when from the very back of the church a tall old monk began walking forward, hand in hand with a child on either side of him, towards the distant arrangement of candles. Behind this trinity the two lines of monks rose from their knees in a ripple of fluid movement, and followed. The old monk, looking as much an archangel among angels as Abbot Odilo must have done, was *Frère* Roger, the founder of Taizé, the white-robed man with the sweet smile and neat haircut who had won Aachen's Charlemagne Prize in 1989.

If not as influential in this comparatively irreligious age, *Frère* Roger is probably as famous in Europe today as either Odilo or Hugh were in their time. Every year, more and more pilgrims – currently up to six thousand a week – find their way here to Taizé. Just as Cluny's beautifully chanted *Opus Dei* was copied in Cluniac houses throughout Europe, so Taizé's style of sung prayer has spread to churches as far away as Scandinavia in the sixty years since the community's beginnings in 1940.

Like those tenth- and eleventh-century abbots of Cluny, Roger grew up in a Europe convulsed by conflict. That was the First World War, but there was conflict again in 1940, when he was finishing his studies in Geneva. Of almost the same generation as Jean Monnet and Robert Schuman, he was as anxious as they were to ensure that a world war never happened again. But his contribution to the rebuilding of Europe would be different to theirs. He would devote his life to healing the wounds inflicted by the Reformation's division of Western Christendom into its Catholic and Protestant camps.

Most of France had just fallen to the Germans and communications between neutral Switzerland and France's *zone libre* were down when Roger set off in search of somewhere to begin his work, cycling over the frontier into Vichy France. He arrived at Cluny expecting to find only ruins. The existence of the small town surprised him, as did the news that there was a house for sale for the price of two cars in the nearby village of Taizé. He found the phylloxera-stricken former wine-making village on top of its hill, noted the good condition of the vacant property and bought it. Taizé, only two miles from the border with Nazi-occupied France, was ideally placed for the secret and dangerous other work he wanted to do: sheltering and assisting refugees, mostly Jews, as they fled from occupied France to neutral Switzerland.

Frère Roger's triple life as farmer, resistance fighter and hermit began to take shape. But in 1942, after escorting a refugee over the border to Switzerland, he found himself stranded there. The Germans had invaded Vichy France and a friend sent him word that the Gestapo had twice visited Taizé. 'I discovered that the so-called *zone libre* was not free at all,' Roger recalled many years later. 'Someone had been interrogated and had denounced me and what I had been doing.'[xxxiv]

Temporarily exiled in Geneva, Roger gathered three old university friends together to form the nucleus of his dreamed-of community. When France was liberated in 1944 they moved back to Taizé to devote themselves to the work of befriending the German prisoners of war who had been farmed out to work in the area. One terrible day the young men were forced to witness the old *milites* spirit resurgent when some local women, wives of men whose husbands had died in Nazi prison camps, vented their fury in a revenge attack on a German prisoner who happened to be a Catholic priest. Thrashing him with leather straps used for cattle, they beat him to a pulp. He was praying for peace and forgiveness when he died.

The community grew. Soon the little Romanesque church of Taizé was too small to accommodate the numbers of pilgrims drawn from all corners of Europe. However, when a German charity offered to build the community a new church, *Frère* Roger was wary, determined not to stray from his narrow path of simplicity and poverty. Cluny's architectural grandeur was not for Taizé. Roger informed the well-meaning Germans, 'We are not going to construct buildings. We are not builders.'[xxxv]

Nonetheless, this gigantic Church of Reconciliation in which I was sitting listening to the last strains of the music while watching Taizé's eighty monks of all nationalities rise and follow their leader, was eventually built. *Frère* Roger was reconciled to its existence one evening by the appearance of a rainbow arching over it. 'I said to myself: "There is God's answer. This church will not immobilise us. It's an ark. It will be filled." '[xxxvi] Many times over. On summer evenings, when the flood of young pilgrims is at its fullest, a later extension is used and the doors are opened.

Back at the reception centre I was handed a photocopied map of the settlement. The plan showed me that the Communauté de Taizé is as impressive as Cluny in its heyday. Almost the size of a village, its amenities include asphalted roads, numbered dwellings, public telephones, a bar, a children's playground, a gift shop and a bus stop. On one side of the main hedge-lined road running along the crest of the hill are car parks and fields filled with neat rows of tents for younger visitors. On the right-hand side of the road are the reception centre, the bell tower, the church and barrack-like accommodation blocks for adults, in one of which – No. 159 – I was billeted.

No. 159 contained three pairs of bunk beds and five middle-aged women from Karlsruhe. As we all unpacked, apologizing for getting in each other's way in the extremely confined space, I learned that they were close friends who had travelled here together for this, their ninth visit to Taizé. Not until they tentatively drew attention to my lack of bedding did I learn that I should have brought a sleeping bag with me.

By the time I had borrowed one, the rain had stopped and iron-grey clouds were parting sufficiently to reveal a sky coloured the yellow and violet tones of an old bruise. From the communal wash-room behind No. 159 came the sound of someone taking a shower and whistling a Taizé tune. Outside in the dripping trees birds were singing. As I stood sniffing the freshened evening air, it seemed to me there were more birds at Taizé than anywhere I had ever been.

In the queue outside the supper tent a fresh-faced young Swede called for volunteers to perform a variety of kitchen duties. Offering to help distribute the evening meal would be my first contribution to the community, I decided. Soon there were six of us – myself, two Norwegian social workers, a bearded Methodist minister from Lancashire and his wife, and an elderly woman from Cornwall on crutches – hygienically attired in plastic gloves and aprons standing behind trestle tables doling out a modest repast of soup, bread, pasta, fruit and yoghurt from giant tureens and trays. The last to fill our trays and take our places on the long wooden benches, the Methodist minister, his wife and I fell into conversation.

'I'm on a six-month sabbatical,' George confided, 'sort of

checking out other faiths and spiritualities. This place is a very long way from anything we're familiar with, I must say . . .'

He and his wife Elizabeth were luxuriating in the superior amenities of the house I had borrowed my sleeping bag from. Zipping up her fleece to ward off the early evening chill, Elizabeth remarked with satisfaction on the electric kettle in their room and then mentioned the packet soups they had thought to bring with them.

'I think they were having something different for supper up there,' she observed, unenthusiastically picking at her plastic plateful of overcooked pasta bake. 'I'm not saying this is not nice; I'm just saying that whatever they were having smelled really tasty.'

Allergic to fruit, she offered me her apple and kindly promised to slip me her daily ration.

'It'll be nice for you to have something to keep you going in the morning before breakfast,' she said, and she was right. The food we ladled out was never tempting or plentiful.

Every morning Taizé's single Korean monk, the smiling *Frère* Hanyol, cycled up to our meal tent to conduct Bible readings. While we pored over passages from the Gospels and the day warmed up, birds flew in to twitter and nest-build among the electric light fittings in the tent roof.

Once I was cast straight back to Gniezno again, to Father Waldemar's stirring Easter Saturday sermon about how desperate and abandoned the Apostles must have felt between Christ's Crucifixion on Friday and his Resurrection on Sunday. Picking up the story a little later on, Hanyol wanted us to imagine how let down the Apostles must have felt again, once the excitement of the Resurrection was passed. Fixing a glossy magazine photo of the Sea of Galilee onto the canvas tent wall behind him, he joked that we were not with Club Med, but Club Matt – St Matthew – and then bid us open our Bibles at his Gospel. Into a crackling microphone he spoke, first in English and then in German.

'So there were the Apostles. They'd been fishing for a whole night and caught nothing. They were feeling exhausted and thinking that Jesus had risen, but so what? What had really changed? They didn't see that he was just there on the shore waiting for them until he shouted, "Children, have you any fish? No? Well throw your nets over the right side of the boat." Of course they did as he told them, and they caught so, so, so many fish!'

Delighted by the idea of such abundance, *Frère* Hanyol mimed grappling with a huge net full of fish. His knees in their grey corduroy trousers buckled as if under a huge weight.

'Yes?' he said, recovering himself and pointing to one of the British pilgrims, a middle-aged man with a beard and white hat, who had raised his hand.

'I think they would have hesitated to do as Christ told them, actually, because it's far harder to cast a net on the right side of a boat. Most people are right-handed, aren't they? Most of us haven't got enough strength in our left arms to give a net a really good throw.'

There followed a protracted and pedantic exchange about net-casting technique between the speaker and a German pilgrim. I was reminded of Gerbert's intellectual legacy. Hanyol smiled, waiting patiently for these logicians to finish their wrangle.

As the days passed he would stray from Bible reading, sometimes allowing us to glimpse the dynamics of life with his brother monks.

'It's not always easy for us. Although you see us all in our white robes, looking like angels, we're not angels. I notice that the older brothers especially are very patient and very accepting of us younger ones. There is no pressure on us to become exactly like each other. Look how St John's Gospel tells us that when the Apostles counted all those fish they had caught, they found a hundred and fifty-three different kinds, all of them big, and still the net was not torn! Our *communauté* is a bit like that.'

Frère Hanyol's mind was still running on fish the next day, when he improvised a parable about the kind of love that bound the community.

'You know, fish is absolutely *Frère* Roger's favourite food, so when he invites each of us sometimes for a private supper with him, it's always fish. Of course, some of the brothers can't stand it! But none of us will ever complain out of love for him and we know the menu will never change.'

The smaller afternoon discussion groups, conducted in the field outside the meal tent in the sunshine, furnished me with more food for thought. Lancastrian George and Elisabeth were not members of my group, but there was a charity worker from Oslo who had abandoned a career in journalism because he wanted to belong to some kind of community – to be able to use the pronoun 'we' instead of 'I'. Intending to make a real pilgrimage, he and a large group of his fellow countrymen and women had fared far: from Norway to Cluny by train, and then up to Taizé on foot. There was Frieder, a German social worker I dubbed the Guru of Stuttgart on account of Indian mannerisms he had acquired during years spent soul-searching in Indian ashrams. His brother, he told me, had filmed the Eastern Orthodox service I had spent a wakeful night watching in a hotel on my way to Reichenau. Frieder had come with his wife Susanna, a kind quiet woman who worked with disabled children, and with two of his cases, both of them impress-ively reformed alcoholic down-and-outs. These burly, gruff men's sweetness to the small children camping with their parents in the end field was extraordinarily touching.

Heidi, a peroxide blonde who wore high heels and black leather at Taizé but spent her working days caring for sick and crotchety pensioners, made startlingly honest contributions to our dicussions. The golden youth of the German contingent was a handsome doctor struggling to mend his broken heart. 'For me, love is the key to everything,' this son of a Protestant pastor announced quietly at our first meeting. Laetitia, who worked with recovering alcoholics in Devon, was a recent and fervent convert to Christianity and more practised than I was at group discussions. A German Protestant minister, another German woman, en route to a canoeing holiday on the Loire with her husband, a young Portuguese woman doctor and an American housewife completed our excellent company. Unaccustomed to contemplating questions such as 'How can we bring understanding and peace where there is tension?' or 'What acts as life-giving bread for me and my community?' I was more interested to hear what they all had to say than in dreaming up answers of my own.

Uncomfortable on my top bunk in barrack No. 159, I woke early every morning and, for an hour before the eight o'clock morning service, sat on a bench near the church gratefully munching the apples Elizabeth gave me while perusing a book entitled *Taizé: A Meaning to Life*. It was written by an Orthodox Christian theologian who deemed Taizé's work of making Christianity relevant by striving to reconcile the various branches of the faith so vital that he described the community as having 'a prophetic character'. 'It is truly the twenty-first century that is getting underway!'[xxxvii] was his happy conclusion.

Glancing up from my reading one morning to feel the warm sunshine on my face and enjoy the view across green-clothed hills, I noticed for the first time that there were five or six little Russian Orthodox-style onion domes gracing the roof of the gigantic Church of Reconciliation. Their presence backed up what the Orthodox Christian theologian had asserted, that Taizé was no longer restricting itself to healing the breach between the Christians of western Europe; *Frère* Roger and his brothers were reaching out to Eastern Christians too, going for the grandest reconciliation of all.

~

Western historians have usually apportioned equal responsibility for the ancient scar which still runs through the heart of the Christian Church, dividing Western from Eastern Christendom, to Pope Leo IX and his fanatically reform-minded propagandist Humbert of Moyenmoutier on the one hand, and Patriarch Michael Kerollarios of Constantinople on the other. And certainly these three characters all played their parts in killing off Otto III's millennial dream of one united Christian Church in harmonious partnership with a loosely federated Holy Roman Empire. What happened in 1054 was

– like Otto III's early demise, like Pope Leo's energetically undertaken reforms, like the peacemaking initiatives that entailed the
gradual militarization of the Church – another milestone on the way
to the bloodbath in Jerusalem in 1099. But the crisis of that year
was only one dramatic episode in the long, slow slide into the
division of the Church of Christ that persists to this day.

With hindsight, one might describe omissions such as failing to
include Otto III's cousin Bruno, Pope Gregory V, in the list of
Church hierarchs prayed for by the patriarch of Constantinople, as
not careless but deliberate. And there can be no doubt that Constantinople deeply resented Emperor Henry II's forced insertion of
the *Filioque* into the Roman Creed in 1014. But where the early
decades of the eleventh century – after the deaths of Otto III and
Pope Sylvester – were difficult for Western Christendom, Byzantium
was thriving. Emperor Basil the Bulgar-slayer was strong. He had
defeated the Bulgars and won traditionally Byzantine possessions in
south Italy back from the Saracens. Orthodox spirituality of the
kind practised by the ancient hermit St Nilus, of whom Otto was
so fond, was blossoming in the caves and rocky reaches of southern
Italy and spreading north to Tuscany. For Constantinople, the time
was well suited to taking advantage of Western Christendom's comparative weakness.

In 1028, the patriarch of Constantinople sent ambassadors to
Rome to suggest a live-and-let-live sort of arrangement between the
Churches of East and West. The pragmatic message they took with
them was, more or less, you, the pope, can be spiritual boss of
the western part of the old Roman Empire if I, the patriarch of
Constantinople, can be spiritual boss of the eastern part; and you
are welcome to your *filioque* and unleavened communion bread just
as long as you do not try and impose them on us. It was to be more
than twenty years before Henry III set the ball of Church reform
rolling by installing his reforming German popes, so lax old Pope
John XIX enjoyed the gorgeous gifts the Easterners had brought him
and let them know he had no objection to their suggestion.

However, the terrible row which erupted when news of this deal penetrated north of the Alps to Burgundy was reported by Brother Raoul at Cluny. He gives us a clear impression of how legalistically literal the northern European churchmen were already inclined to be by quoting a letter to the pope from the abbot of the Cluniac house in Dijon. The abbot reminds the pope, just in case he had forgotten, that he, *in loco* Saint Peter, had the supreme power of 'binding and loosing' on earth and could never share it with any patriarch of Constantinople. The transalpine objectors to the pope's submission were angry enough to secure the deal's reversal. Brother Raoul tells us that the ambassadors from Constantinople were sent packing, 'their pride checked and their presumption deflated'.[xxxviii]

By 1050 more bad feeling was being stirred up. The reformers were trying to order and homogenize Christian worship by foisting Latin Church usages onto the Greek Christians in the Byzantine areas of southern Italy. The Byzantine Patriarch Michael retaliated by closing down Constantinople's three Latin rite churches – one frequented by Scandinavian mercenaries in the Byzantine emperors' Varangian Guard, another built by a Hungarian king as a token of his personal sympathy with Eastern Christianity and a third, an Italian church used by merchants from Amalfi. A shocking story filtered back to Rome, about how one of the patriarch's right-hand men was seen trampling on the unleavened bread of the Roman Catholic communion host.

The Byzantines had a further reason for righteous anger when they learned that Pope Leo had promoted his propagandist Humbert of Moyenmoutier to the post of archbishop of Sicily, although that island – still under Saracen rule at the time – rightfully belonged to the Eastern Christendom. Relations suffered yet another grievous setback when the Byzantines did not keep their promise to help Pope Leo defeat a troublesome and growing band of Norman *milites* who had been settling in south Italy for the past thirty years or so and unsettling everyone else there – Eastern and Western Christians – with their violent land-grabbing and plundering.

Pope Leo in Rome had been shocked by a stream of victims,

people 'with their eyes popped out, their noses cut off, their feet and hands mutilated, miserably bewailing the cruelty of the Normans'[xxxix] and had been stirred into action on their behalf. A German churchman, he was used to fighting and had satisfied himself that a campaign against the Normans was just, even if they were Christians. But in 1053, at the head of a small ragtag army, he was left to face the Normans alone, lost the battle and was ignominiously taken prisoner. The Byzantines had failed to play their part because they suspected that the pope would continue trying to impose the Latin rite on their territories in southern Italy once the fighting was over. Anyway, they heartily disapproved of such an eminent Christian as the patriarch of Rome, as they called the pope, leading an army into battle. So for that matter did the then abbot of Reichenau, who also strongly objected to the way Pope Leo had recruited his fighters – with promises that they would be martyrs on the fast track to heaven, with all their sins forgiven them, if they should happen to die while fighting the Normans.

In letters to the Byzantine emperor of the day, Pope Leo regularly advanced the supremacy claims of the Roman Church. These were based on Christ having told the first bishop of Rome, Saint Peter – rather than any bishop of Constantinople – that he was the rock on which the Church would be built. A famous forgery, a two-hundred-year-old document stating that the first Christian Roman emperor Constantine had granted the patriarch of Rome supremacy over all the other patriarchs of the Church and various kingdoms in western Europe, was unearthed and repeatedly cited. Half a century earlier Otto III had spotted that the 'Donation of Constantine' was a fake, but it was too useful to the reformers to jettison. All claims to the large area of central Italy known as the Papal States until their dissolution in the late nineteenth century rested on this forgery.

Wild rumour and shameless exaggeration, rife in a world plagued by slow communications, seem to have hastened the breakdown of relations between the twin hearts of Christendom. On the strength of a snippet of gossip, Pope Leo penned the following furious letter to Patriarch Michael Kerollarios of Constantinople:

> God forbid that we wish to believe what public opinion does not hesitate to claim has happened to the Church of Constantinople; namely, that in promoting eunuchs indiscriminately against the first law of the Council of Nicaea, it once raised a woman onto the seat of its patriarch. We regard this crime as so abominable and horrible that, although outrage and horror of it and brotherly goodwill do not allow us to believe it, nevertheless . . . we consider that it could have happened because even now you indifferently and repeatedly promote eunuchs and those who are weak in some part of their body, not only into clerical office but also to the position of patriarch.[xl]

Patriarch Michael, at heart a nit-picking and intemperate Byzantine bureaucrat rather than any kind of spiritual leader, wrote a huffy letter to his friend, fellow Orthodox patriarch, Peter of Antioch,* complaining about a powerful Constantinople monastery which seemed to be espousing Catholic Latin ways: 'Ought those who lead the same life as the Latins, who are brought up in their customs and who abandon themselves to illegal, prohibited and detestable practices to remain in the ranks of the just and orthodox? I think not.'[xli]

There were some – Patriarch Peter of Antioch, a holy man and a wise theologian – who feared schism above all. What could be more blasphemously sinful than the division of Christ's one, holy and apostolic Church into two hostile halves? His counsel of moderation to Patriarch Michael Kerollarios was couched in apocalyptic terms:

> I beg and implore you Divine Beatitude . . . Consider the obvious result of all this, I mean the yawning gulf that must ultimately separate from our holy Church that magnanimous and apostolic

---

* Rome, Jerusalem, Antioch and Alexandria are more ancient and senior centres of Orthodox church government than Constantinople.

see [Rome]. Life henceforward will be filled with wickedness and the whole world overturned. If the two queens of the earth are at loggerheads, then alas! – abundant sorrow will reign everywhere . . . [xlii]

Held under house arrest by the Normans in south Italy and trying to teach himself Greek in his ample free time, Leo penned two letters: one to Constantinople's patriarch whom – thanks to Humbert of Moyenmoutier's free translation – he mistakenly addressed as a mere bishop, and a second to the Byzantine emperor. These epistles were almost posted when two more arrived from Constantinople, one from the emperor, the other from Patriarch Michael. Both were disarmingly conciliatory except in two tiny details. The patriarch had addressed Pope Leo as 'brother' rather than as 'father' and signed himself with a title implying that the authority of a Byzantine patriarch was as universal as that of the Roman pope. Humbert of Moyenmoutier, recently honoured with the title of Cardinal of Silva Candida, had Pope Leo sign the replies, both calculated to fan the flames of the feud. Next he chose a pair of fellow countrymen from the Alsace-Lorraine region – veterans of Pope Leo's doomed anti-Norman campaign and anti-Byzantine – as his travelling companions. Together they set off down to the south Italian port of Bari and took ship for Constantinople.

Arriving in April 1054 in a city that was richer in precious relics and churches even than Rome, they called on the patriarch and were greatly offended by the manner of their reception. Patriarch Michael was in his turn offended by the letter they had brought him, but also deeply suspicious as to how Pope Leo – still under Norman arrest, as far as anyone knew – had been able to go about his usual papal tasks, writing letters and sending embassies. He decided that Cardinal Humbert and his friends were impostors. The legates' meeting with the emperor was more successful, but he was not as popular with his subjects as the patriarch.

A few weeks later Pope Leo IX died. On hearing this sad news Cardinal Humbert and his friends should immediately have abandoned their foolish enterprise and headed home to Rome. Instead, fired up with reforming zeal and still intent on getting the Byzantines to acknowledge the supremacy of Rome, they stayed on, sniping at Byzantine Church customs and making enemies.

The Byzantines were appalled by this first glimpse of the revolutionary changes wrought by less than a decade of Church reform in Western Christendom. Cardinal Humbert and his companions were treating them to a shocking display of Roman tyranny, dangerous deviation from ancient custom, boorish arrogance and almost overt aggression. Admittedly, this was the ugliest part of a wider picture. The Byzantines had not been to Reims to attend the inspiring launch of Pope Leo's reforms nor participated in any of the ecstatic peace councils. Nor had they witnessed Cluny's impressive reordering of monastic life, so they could not have known how desperately Western Christendom longed for stability, law and order after its centuries of turmoil and dark disorder, how papal control and the policy of homogenization had grown up naturally, in the long vacuum of miserable insecurity which the Holy Roman emperors had only partially been able to fill. The sophisticated Byzantines only saw what they saw, and knew that they hated it.

Cardinal Humbert and his friends had been three long months in the richest city on earth, working themselves into a furious lather against the patriarch, when they decided to disgrace Western Christendom with a last breathtakingly arrogant gesture. At three o'clock in the afternoon of 16 July 1054, just when Constantinople's top churchmen were about to celebrate a solemn liturgy, the three visitors marched into the great candlelit cathedral of Ayia Sophia, laid a document excommunicating the Patriarch Michael from the Church of Christ on the high altar, and marched out again. Riddled with demonstrably false accusations against the head of the Byzantine Church, this piece of parchment so angered the Constantinople mob that they gave it a public burning and then threatened to depose their emperor if he did not pronounce revenge anathemas on the three legates.

The mutual anathemas did not add up to a schism, but the

weight of all that had gone before and all that would follow by the close of the eleventh century and afterwards did. The anathemas were lifted when Pope Paul VI met Patriarch Atenagoras of Constantinople at an ecumenical council in 1965, but the schism remains to this day. With the end of Communism in eastern Europe, the location of the majority of Eastern Christian countries, the ancient scar is showing up again. Running from north to south and a little to the east of the old Iron Curtain, it divides the comparatively prosperous traditionally Catholic or Protestant countries of western and central Europe from most of the poorer traditionally Eastern Orthodox ones.* Behind it, Orthodox churchmen from Siberia to Cyprus are responding to a deluge of the crudest elements of Western culture with about as much enthusiasm as those Byzantines showed towards Pope Leo's ambassadors and their culture. A thousand years after Cardinal Humbert brandished the 'Donation of Constantine' and reminded Constantinople that St Peter, the first bishop of Rome, was the rock on which Christ had built his Church, papal claims to supremacy are still the main stumbling block to reuniting the two halves of the Christian Church.

~

Frère Émile, a young French monk as carefully dressed as Father Waldemar in a neat green crew-neck sweater and matching trousers, led me around the back of the community's reception centre and out into an overgrown little garden shaded by fruit trees where he found us a pair of folding chairs to sit on.

He could, he said, confirm for me that the community was making every effort to reach out to Europe's Eastern Christians. But he admitted that, although a group of Russian monks had recently visited and a Bulgarian monk had stayed for months, none had yet joined the community. He went quickly on to detail the impressive numbers of Eastern Orthodox visiting Taizé every summer, especially

---

* The exception is Greece, which is Orthodox but inside the European Union.

from Romania and Russia, but also from Ukraine, Bulgaria and even Kosovo.

'We have so much to learn from the Orthodox. You see, Christianity has given us all a sense of the uniqueness of the human being. It's a sense we still have in the West, enshrined in our human rights legislation, for example. But what we've lost and what the Orthodox have somehow kept is a sense of the resurrection – that mystery, that miracle, that hope that we will all triumph over death. *Frère* Roger speaks of it as "a sense of eternity". We were so pleased when a Romanian Orthodox bishop visited us here and told us that he breathed an "air of resurrection"!'

When I described my project to Émile he very gently suggested that I should not waste my time lamenting the lost Christian unity of the early eleventh century and telling tales of the Western Church's transformation from a spiritual community to a papal monarchy. Instead, I might think about the resurrection and go in search of signs that modern Europeans are triumphing over their hateful divisions and experiencing a spiritual rebirth.

'Wouldn't it be wonderful, and also very helpful, to be the first to detect early signs of a new spiritual unity of Europe?' he asked, leaning forward in his chair, his dark eyes glowing with enthusiasm.

Would I find green shoots of Taizé-like hope in Rome or Constantinople or Jerusalem? Would they necessarily be Christian, I wondered as, to the usual loud accompaniment of birdsong, I headed back along the hedge-lined road just in time to perform my evening kitchen duty. Elizabeth, distributing her watery soup next to me and my mountain of sliced ham, was interested to hear about my talk with *Frère* Émile but even more interested in sharing a discovery she had made during the meditation period in church.

'Victoria, have you noticed that all the monks have the same haircut?'

'I hadn't actually . . .'

'There must be a barber who comes and does them all at once, don't you think?'

'Maybe . . .' I said, reminded of the pedant *Frère* Hanyol in the

Bible studies class and of Gerbert's introduction of Aristotelian logic and all that had flowed from it in the way of deduction, reason, the scholastic method, science.

'I know I should have been praying but I couldn't somehow. I did some mental arithmetic instead. If there are eighty monks and it takes about twenty minutes to give them each a haircut, that would be about twenty-five hours, wouldn't it? Quite a lot of hair-cutting! Although I suppose they'd spread it out over two or three days . . .'

There were times when, a prey to mild *Accidie*, I felt imprisoned in that hill-top encampment. One morning I set off on a long aimless walk by myself. Descending the mountain, I had crossed the main road in the valley, trudged through a forest, skirted the edges of two fields, reached a crossroads and was beginning to think of my excursion as a metaphor for my life, when I found that I was lost. In the distance, across some fields filled with Charollais cows as creamily clad as Taizé's monks, I spied a small village with a Romanesque church. Not far from the church, on a gentle slope with a small furrowed vineyard in front of it, was a two-storey faded yellow building with white shutters and a steeply sloping red roof. As close to a child's picture of a home as one could hope to see, it seemed to me perfect in every detail. I began to covet it in a way I had never in my life before coveted real estate. How much could such a place cost? I asked myself, rapidly computing the sum of my assets and wondering if the house's closed shutters meant that it was uninhabited, for sale.

Approaching it and the village along the quiet country road I soon succumbed to another appetite. Hungry after all my walking, I was dreaming of a modest but decent French meal and telling myself that no harm would be done and no one would miss me if I skipped Taizé's midday church service and lunch. Anyway, what could I do? I was lost. In the village I found exactly what I sought, a simple restaurant with a shady terrace, a view of the house and a three-course *carte du jour*. It was some time later, after I had enjoyed a simple beetroot salad and a salmon steak followed by a large slice of lemon tart, washed down with some local white wine, when I realized that another devil was stealing my soul. His name was probably the Latin for greed or gluttony and I imagined him looking much like the demon of one of Brother Raoul Glaber's night visions: 'His nostrils were pinched and he had a wide mouth and blubbery lips. His goat-like beard covered a receding and pointed chin, while his ears were shaggy and pointed. His hair was a disordered mop and he had dog-like fangs. He had a pointed head, a swollen chest, a hunch-back and mobile haunches . . .'[xliii]

I felt as feeble-spirited as the Cluny monk whom Abbot Hugh had permitted to wear silks and furs under his cassock. The Communauté de Taizé was in the business of reminding people of the value of and need for things that money cannot buy. In Cluny and Taizé terms, comforting oneself with quick emissions of cash – on silks or furs, sixty francs on a meal, six hundred thousand francs on a house – was a miserable cheat. Just as the young German doctor in my discussion group had discovered and *Frère* Hanyol had illustrated, community, other people and love were the treasures to be seeking.

In church that evening I was happily singing along, asking Jesus not to let my shadows talk to me, when I felt tears running down my cheeks. Locked into my Western Christian heritage with its scholastic colouring, I reminded myself of the known physiological link between singing and emotional release. Drying my eyes, I quickly calculated that I had been singing three times a day for almost a week. Three times fifteen minutes made forty-five minutes a day. A total of almost six hours, I marvelled, just as obtusely as Elizabeth doing her haircut sums or as the men arguing about net-casting techniques.

After my kitchen duties and supper that warm spring evening, the sky turned a pretty golden pink and the birds sang even more loudly than usual. I wandered down to the bar, where some of the younger pilgrims were playing their guitars and drinking their Taizé ration of one beer or glass of wine. The Guru of Stuttgart was there and asked me how I was feeling.

'As if my heart's been cracked open,' was all I could tell him.

~

On a Sunday morning as wet as the evening on which I had arrived, I downed a tepid instant coffee in the sodden meal tent, said my farewells and departed.

Driving away down the steep hill from Taizé I imagined the countryside of Burgundy, of France, of western and central Europe, of Europe and beyond, dotted with spiritual powerhouses like Taizé. The startling, unstoppable spread of the Cluny order through Europe in the eleventh century must have been something like that, I decided, only more so. The solid splendour of Cluniac buildings, the magnetic appeal of precious relics, the splendour of their sung services and processions, the legions of monks and the prestige of its abbots, would all have enhanced its impact. And everything had to be viewed against the black background of famines, plagues and warring *milites*. After western Europe's terrifying tenth-century invasions Cluny had cracked its heart open again.

After Chambéry the Alps loomed massively ahead, their summits still covered in snow, silhouetted against a ribbon of pink-gold Italian sky far beyond the blanket of French rain clouds. Tired of losing my way in a series of run-down small towns with featureless outskirts recently regenerated with the flimsy prefabricated premises of light industries, I stopped for the night in a large village only to find the little hotel on its deserted main street closed. Another, tucked away on the edge of town on top of a hill and surrounded by pines, was undergoing wholesale refurbishment. Its owners – two sisters and their husbands – were hard at work washing and cleaning after the crowd of Sunday lunch guests. One of the sisters dried her hands on a tea towel, shrugged and told me that, if I wanted to, I could stay in a room piled high with boxes of cupboard kits waiting to be assembled and rolls of fabric for curtains and bedspreads. The price she named was discouragingly high, but I had no choice.

Waking to utter silence the next morning, I missed Taizé's birdsong and lay there a while wondering why *Frère* Roger had not followed Cluny's lead by establishing Taizé communities all over western Europe. The old monk's stalwart resistance to empire-building or constructing a bigger church, keeping any archives or mapping out any long-term future for his community seemed to spring from an impulse to beware the temptation to organize and aggrandize, to control and legislate for the spiritual.

The eleventh-century Church reform revolution, which Pope Leo IX had launched with Abbot Hugh of Cluny's support and such high drama at Reims in 1049, was turning out to be all about aggrandizement, control and legislating for the spiritual. The campaigns to root out simony and nicolaitism were under way and Pope Leo IX had restored the prestige of the papacy by far-faring and good management. Now the third and most revolutionary phase of the Roman Church's project to reform itself for the new millennium was about to begin.

Pope Leo's demise in 1054, while Cardinal Humbert and his two friends were busy in Constantinople disgracing all Western Christendom, was followed two years later by the death of his loyal partner in reform, the sternly pious Henry III. During the decade-long new emperor's minority, the Holy Roman Empire was ineptly ruled, first by the child's thirty-year-old mother. Like Theophano and Otto's sister Sophie in their day, the dowager Empress Agnes was accused of *obscoeni negotii* with a churchman; she then suffered her little Henry IV to be kidnapped by an archbishop before giving up the struggle and retiring to Rome to spend the rest of her days as a *paupera et peregrina*. Into the power vacuum stepped a succession of squabbling German churchmen, none powerful enough to govern the empire.

The Church reformers were quick to exploit this opportunity to assert the supremacy of the papacy over the empire. In 1058 Cardinal Humbert was thundering that the German emperors' habit of appointing popes as well as their own bishops was not the proud prerogative of a divinely appointed Holy Roman emperor and defender of the Church, but a crime akin to rape. Only a year later the bond of harmony and cooperation linking the two institutions was severed. Useful relationships of the sort that Otto had enjoyed with his friend and mentor Pope Sylvester II, and Henry III with his cousin Leo IX, became a thing of the past. The reformers wanted the sort of *libertas* Cluny enjoyed in electing its own abbots. In 1059, at Cardinal Humbert's instigation, the pope of the day* decreed that popes would be elected by cardinals.

The two difficult men who succeeded in bringing the rivalry between Church and empire to a dangerous climax during the following twenty years were Pope Gregory VII and the young German monarch Henry IV, who took up his birthright in 1066 at the age of sixteen. Abbot Hugh of Cluny, who was both the emperor's godfather and the pope's supporter, and the formidable young Countess Matilda of Tuscany, who was the emperor's cousin as well as the pope's most devoted ally, were also caught up in the drama. In the bitterly cold January of 1077 all four were gathered at Matilda's castle at Canossa, on the south side of the Alps in the northern foothills of the Apennines. Lying there in that cluttered hotel room with morning sunshine pouring in through the window and a view of freshly snow-dusted pine trees, I made plans to be at Canossa in time for the annual re-enactment of what was surely one of the most dramatic episodes in western European medieval history.

Ignoring the fresh snowfall, I set off boldly in the direction of the Mont Cenis Pass, a favourite with the German Holy Roman emperors because – despite the forbidding height of the mountain – it was the most convenient route from their possessions in Burgundy to their lands in Italy. Cruising along a good road filled with lorries whose number plates proclaimed the continent's new unity, I marvelled at how completely late twentieth-century engineers had conquered Europe's largest natural barrier. For a time I raced a train watching it weaving to left and right of me on its track, sometimes higher, sometimes lower than the road. Another half-completed motorway soared past me, high up between the mountain sides, its green plastic barriers shining. Such aids to communication, comfort,

* Pope Nicholas II.

convenience and prosperity might be seen as the fruit of the seeds of logic and rationalism that Gerbert of Aurillac had planted in late tenth-century Reims. Another perhaps not as useful fruit was the overly literal and legalistic mindset of a reforming Church that had set its sights on controlling Christendom, body as well as soul, by three quarters of the way through the eleventh century.

Picturing the growing traffic of pilgrims, traders, fortune-seeking Normans, freshly appointed bishops and itinerant monks over the Alps in the eleventh century was not easy in that fine spring weather. An account of one group of pilgrims' disastrous winter crossing came to mind:

> as though fixed in the jaws of death, they remained in peril by night and by day. The small village was overcrowded with the throng of pilgrims. From the lofty and rugged heights above it fell often huge masses of snow, carrying away everything they encountered, so that when some parties of guests had found their places and others were still waiting near the houses, these masses [of snow] swept the latter away and suffocated some, whilst crushing and crippling others of those in the buildings.[xliv]

Local guides, known as *marones*, had come to the remaining pilgrims' rescue, offering to open up a road for them. Swathing their heads in felt, the *marones* had donned high boots 'the soles of which were armed with iron spikes' and started out ahead while the pilgrims were still in church praying for a safe journey. But another avalanche had buried many of the intrepid guides and 'a most sorrowful lament sounded through the village'.[xlv]

I needed to be above all this hubbub and speed, high among the snow-covered mountain tops where nothing lived, in as pitiless a wind as I had experienced in Iceland, to recapture even a hint of the atmosphere of those times. Thoughts of Iceland and how far I had fared set me calculating that three quarters of the way through the eleventh century I was only about halfway through my journey. Crossing the Alps in a warm Renault 5 with Taizé tunes on the cassette player I calculated I had time to consider the background to the century's central Church-versus-empire mini-saga.

~

Pope Gregory VII was not a German, nor was he any sort of legal genius like Cardinal Humbert or even a born leader like the aristocratic Leo IX but, equipped with the extraordinary energy of a principled fanatic, he towered above any other churchman of the eleventh century. He would hurl himself headlong at the task of imposing order and justice on Christendom.

The son of a Tuscan carpenter, Hildebrand, as he was known prior to his election as pope, had joined the Roman monastery where the abbots of Cluny were wont to stay on their trips to Rome. A devoted supporter of one of the three competing popes whom Henry III had sacked on becoming emperor back in 1046, Hildebrand struggled off into exile north of the Alps with that pontiff.* At a monastery near Cologne he seems to have been inspired by energetic notions about overhauling the Church generated in a German monastic revival as impressive, though not as independence-minded, as Cluny's. Hildebrand visited Aachen and met Emperor Henry III and the future Pope Leo IX.

Once elected in 1048, Leo took Hildebrand back to Italy with him. Familiar with both German and Roman customs, he would make a skilful church bureaucrat and the Romans, wary of the sudden influx of northerners into the higher echelons of the Church, were mollified to see the barbarian influence diluted by one of their own. Although not much of a theologian, Hildebrand was every bit as convinced a reformer as Pope Leo IX or Cardinal Humbert, and he put at the service of the eleventh-century German popes his fiery Latin fervour, his temper 'like a blast of the north wind',[xlvi], his burning belief in the wisdom of radical Church reform and a taste for bold adventure. It was Hildebrand who saw to it that

* Pope Gregory VI.

William the Conqueror was provided with the pope's blessing and a papal banner of St Peter to wave during the invasion of England in 1066.

Short, burly and famously unattractive to look at, Hildebrand was liked by women. Two of his most devoted friends were a mother and daughter, Countess Matilda of Tuscany and her mother Beatrice, whose family had long been supporters of the reforming papacy. One of Matilda's uncles had accompanied Cardinal Humbert on his ill-starred mission to Constantinople in 1053 and been pope for a brief period. Hildebrand had known Countess Matilda a long time; with Pope Leo IX he had been a frequent visitor to the pious and glitteringly learned court her mother presided over. There he would have pitied the little girl who had lost her father in a mysteriously violent hunting accident and then her brother and sister too. He would have become acquainted with this polyglot *puer senex* – a Latin oxymoron for a child wise beyond its years – and been impressed by the courage and determination with which, at the tender age of fifteen, she led her *milites* into battle yelling, 'St Peter and Matilda!' According to one story, it was Matilda who at Hildebrand's suggestion, stitched the papal banner for the Norman conquest of England.

Becoming Pope Gregory VII in 1073, Hildebrand soon found himself at odds with both the German and French rulers. He did manage to maintain good relations with William the Conqueror, but only by calling him *potentissimus rex* and turning a blind eye when the Norman ignored his directives. From all sides danger seemed to threaten, not least from the south where Pope Leo's old foes, the Italian Normans, were still stealing papal lands and eyeing Rome itself in their insatiable hunt for new territories to seize and despoil. From further afield came the still more desperate tidings of the shrinking of Eastern Christendom with the loss of Asia Minor (most of today's Turkey) after the Byzantine army's shameful defeat by the Seljuk Turks at the battle of Manzikert in 1071. The holy places of Palestine were already in infidel hands, and returning pilgrims' tales of harassment during their pious progress were commonplace. The hastily broken relations between Rome and Constantinople cried out for mending. Amidst all this unquiet, it seemed to Gregory that when it came to practical support and disinterested advice he could rely only on his Tuscan women friends.

In 1074 Gregory dreamed up a bold plan designed to rid him of his domestic foes as well as reunite and reinforce Christendom, East and West. Knowing that what amounted to a crusade would have an irresistible appeal for the feisty Countess Matilda, he wrote to her:

> There are some whom I blush to tell, lest I should seem to be led by mere fancy, how firmly my mind and heart are set upon crossing the sea, in order that, by Christ's favour, I may bring help to the Christians who are being slaughtered by the heathen like cattle. But to you, my most beloved and loving daughter, I do not hesitate to disclose any of these thoughts, for even you yourself can hardly imagine how greatly I may count upon your zeal and discretion . . .[xlvii]

He was counting on her happily volunteering thousands of her *milites* for his expedition, and informed her that he was sending the same request for armed forces 'to those beyond the Alps'. Daring to hope that Henry IV would care to donate some of his men to the project, he was confident at least that Henry's mother, the dowager Empress Agnes, would happily sacrifice 'her corruptible flesh for Christ'. Gregory fondly imagined that Matilda's mother Beatrice and Henry might be left in charge of Western Christendom while he, Matilda and Agnes led a mighty army east for an all-out war with the Muslims.

> If moreover, the empress [Agnes] came and devoted herself to prayer, she in concert with you might encourage many to take part in this work. As for me, furnished with such sisterly aid, I would most gladly cross the sea, if need be to lay down my life for Christ, with both of you whom I always desire should cleave to me in the heavenly country.[xlviii]

Gregory was the first pope to articulate the notion that dying in a war waged in Christ's name was a privilege and could take the place of doing penance. Countess Matilda would not have been startled by the innovation because it had originated among her Tuscan circle of intellectual churchmen who had developed a useful style of Bible commentary – political allegory – to promote Gregory's aims and interests. They had read their Gospels and noted the fact that when an angry St Peter cut off the ear of a servant of the high priest, Christ had only told him to sheathe his sword, not to throw it away. This had persuaded them that there was nothing inherently unchristian about violence.

Pope Gregory confidently imagined that his army, recruited from all points north of Rome, could easily deal with his chief domestic care on its way south to take ship for the east. 'As for those vile little Normans,' he wrote to Matilda, 'with 20,000 men, if it pleases God, we can attack and vanquish them.'[xlix] Matilda's reply injected a first note of realism into the ambitious enterprise. She begged leave to suggest that a 20,000-strong army might not suffice to do the Norman part of the job, that the whole venture could backfire and fail before they even boarded ship for the east. She wrote:

> All the world would say, those women occupy themselves with what is not at all their affair, and it is just that they should bear the blame, since they preferred to assume the role always reserved for princes. We must act like men therefore . . . May your holiness permit us to bring as many men as may be required, we shall thus have the honour of victory, and oblige the enemy to restore what he has stolen from the Prince of the apostles [St Peter].[l]

Just as Matilda feared, the leader of the south Italian Normans, Robert Guiscard, mocked Gregory's lack of male support and his shameful reliance on his women friends. In fact, the male ruler of Aquitaine *had* offered to contribute a few of his *milites*, but Henry IV did not relish the tedious task of holding the fort in the West while Pope Gregory sallied out on a glamorous expedition to repel the Muslims who had invaded Eastern Christendom. He ignored Gregory's call.

The crusade had to be aborted. Squabbles broke out between those who had been willing to take part. Countess Matilda soon had a rebellion to contend with at home, and the army's paymaster was complaining that the would-be crusaders were kitted out with 'Indian girdles and bands and cheap cloths, fit only for girding women and equipping servants, or for adorning walls'.[li] Sick and discouraged, Pope Gregory wrote to Abbot Hugh at Cluny in early 1075, complaining, 'I convict those amongst whom I live, I mean the Romans, Lombards and Normans, of being, as I often say to them, worse even than Jews and pagans.'[lii]

But he had not abandoned his dream of mustering a *militia sancti Petri* to stand up to the armies of wicked earthly rulers and enforce his papal will for him. In the same letter he sought Abbot Hugh's support for the Church's continuing campaign to tame the *milites*, apparently blind to the fact that he was hastening the militarization of the Church.

> With brotherly charity we enjoin you to the best of your ability to extend your hand with watchful zeal by warning, beseeching and urging those who love St Peter that, if they would truly be his sons and *milites*, they should not hold secular princes more dear than him. For secular princes reluctantly grant wretched and transient things; but he, by loosing from all sins, promises things blessed and eternal, and by the power committed to him he brings them to a heavenly home.[liii]

Abbot Hugh was a Burgundian nobleman and Pope Gregory only a carpenter's son but the two men got on well enough. Gregory always revered Cluny, once describing it as having 'come to such a state of excellence and religion under its religious and holy abbots that it surpasses all other monasteries, even much older ones, as well I know, in the service of God and in spiritual fervour'.[liv]

Abbot Hugh, for his part, had good reason to admire and even fear Gregory. Once, when Gregory was still only Hildebrand the high Church official, Hugh had witnessed his reaction to a reception laid on in his honour and thought, 'this little man of despicable parentage and small stature, surrounded by such riches and the homage of the great must doubtless be puffed up and, in giving sentence, must be influenced by the obsequiousness of those around him'. Hildebrand had wheeled around on his horse and shouted back at Hugh, ' "You think wrongly, and falsely suspect an innocent man. I do not consider this glory – if what passes so quickly can be called glory – as mine, but impute it to the apostles and wish others to do so." ' Red-faced and baffled, Hugh could only reply, ' "I ask, lord, how you knew my thoughts which I told to no one?" ' Hildebrand had said,' "They came from your mouth to my ears, as if by a string." '[lv]

Abbot Hugh was one of the first people Gregory wrote to on being elected pope. The tone he used to address him was warmer than he employed to anyone but Matilda. If Cluny was no longer quite as firmly identified with the papal reform project as it had been in the good old days of Pope Leo IX that was probably because Pope Gregory's fanatical energy was sowing dissent wherever it was felt. For a man as actively engaged with this world as Gregory, the great monastery was doubtless too focused on the next.

Pope Gregory had sufficiently recovered his spirits and confidence to intensify the flagging campaigns against simony and nicolaitism and draw up a highly illuminating list of twenty-seven ideal papal attributes, a blueprint for a reformed papacy that was beginning to look like a powerful and worldly monarchy. Never intended for public scrutiny, the Dictatus Papae was written in the form of a memo and slipped inside the pages of another book, but a few highlights indicate precisely where Gregory's ambitions lay and where he perceived threats to his power to originate from. Attribute number two baldly states that 'Only the Roman pontiff can lawfully be called universal', a clear dig at the patriarchs of

Constantinople who styled themselves universal and still do today.*
Number nine – 'The pope is the only man whose feet all rulers kiss'
– confirmed the repositioning of the Church above all merely earthly
rulers, Holy Roman emperors included. Number nineteen placed
the pope out of reach of the law; the Church had its own body of
canon law by which to judge its personnel, but not the pope.
Number twenty-two claimed that 'the Roman Church has never
erred nor will she ever err'.[lvi] Even Cardinal Humbert had never
dared claim that, in effect, pope and God wielded the same
authority; that to disobey the pope was to disobey God. If the term
'fundamentalist' describes a person so literal-minded as to believe
that the absolute sovereignty of God must be expressed in a practical
dictatorship of priests, rabbis or mullahs, then Pope Gregory VII
was a Christian fundamentalist.

How different from his saintly father who, inspired by the Peace
of God movement, had addressed a synod in Konstanz in 1046 with
a plea that any injuries he had done anyone be forgiven him, as he
forgave any done to him! Early led astray by an archbishop of
Hamburg and Bremen who was 'talented and witty but gay and
immoral',[lviii] Henry IV had had no saintly spiritual father figures like

Henry IV never saw the twenty-seven items on Pope Gregory's
extraordinary list. Doubtless the investiture crisis would have
exploded earlier and even more dramatically if he had because,
after an appalling childhood and famously dissolute early manhood,
Henry was a sovereign very jealous of his dignity and not one to
shrink from confrontation. Handsome, almost six feet tall, with a
bad temper and a poor eye for choosing his counsellors, he was
about as entrenched in his Germanic tribal mores and incapable of
turning the other cheek as Thorvald the Far-farer: 'As he saw it, to
submit to an insult without seeking satisfaction was an ineradicable
blot of shame. Indeed, he considered it highly laudable and something worth striving for, even at the cost of one's life, to let nothing
untoward that befell him go unavenged.'[lvii]

How different from his saintly father who, inspired by the Peace
of God movement, had addressed a synod in Konstanz in 1046 with
a plea that any injuries he had done anyone be forgiven him, as he
forgave any done to him! Early led astray by an archbishop of
Hamburg and Bremen who was 'talented and witty but gay and
immoral',[lviii] Henry IV had had no saintly spiritual father figures like

* The first word of the title 'Ecumenical Patriarch of Constantinople' means universal.

Otto III's Nilus or Adalbert to instil in him a pious reverence for men of God and the Church.

Pope Gregory deeply regretted that Empress Agnes had not raised her son as well as Beatrice had Matilda. By retiring from the world to become a *paupera et peregrina*, she had failed to direct young Henry into the paths of righteousness. Gregory was inclined to frown on pious laymen and women abdicating their temporal responsibilities to go and save their souls in the cloister. When Countess Matilda abandoned her two-year-old marriage to a gloomy Lorrainer called Godfrey the Hunchback and asked Gregory's permission to become a nun, he firmly refused it. He needed her where she was, with her *milites sancti Petri* at the ready. Similarly, he was furious with Abbot Hugh for enticing a powerful and pope-friendly Burgundian duke into impotent retirement at Cluny. Gregory VII would have had no time for Otto III's agonized soul-searching about whether to go on a pilgrimage to Jerusalem or crack down hard on his Romans, whether to remain an emperor or become a monk.

In the mid 1070s Henry's flouting of the Church's new ban on lay rulers appointing their own churchmen became too serious to ignore when he dismissed a reformer and installed his own candidate in the important archbishopric of Milan. This was one insult too many after a series of offences, humble repentings and speedy re-offendings. Pope Gregory's stern letter of protest began: 'Bishop Gregory, servant of the servants of God, sends King Henry greetings and apostolic blessings, provided that he obey the Pope as behooves a Christian king . . .'[lix]

Pope Gregory threatened the young man with the ultimate sanction of excommunication. Of course Henry's disrespectful behaviour was exasperating but Gregory seems not to have understood that to deny the German monarch the right to appoint his own churchmen was tantamount to deposing him and dismantling the Holy Roman Empire. Since the time of Charlemagne, on into Otto III's reign and under Henry III, the German lands of the empire had been ruled by civil servant bishops, appointed by the emperor. For all their worldly wrangling, these aristocratic prel-

ates – at once churchmen, administrators, judges and generals –
were what united the Holy Roman Empire and made it strong.
Henry must have asked himself how he could hope to run his realm
if his bishops were to be appointed by an ambitious plebeian of a
pope who seemed determined to usurp his position.

Ignoring the gains in prestige and power which the reformed
papacy had made in the thirty years since Henry III had swept down
to Rome and got rid of three competing popes, the young monarch
decided to follow his father's example and rid himself of this Gregory,
who had behaved as if the Holy Roman Empire were his to
command 'and not in the disposal of God'.[lx] In January 1076, in a
blizzard of propaganda about Gregory's ungodly presumption, scandal
about his relationship with Countess Matilda and rants about how
the Church was being run by 'this new senate of women', twenty-
four German bishops, two archbishops and Henry met at Worms to
depose the 'false monk'. The proclamation they signed worked up
to a terrific climax: 'Let another sit upon St Peter's throne, one who
will not cloak violence with a pretence of religion, but will teach
the pure doctrine of St Peter. I, Henry, by God's grace king, with
all our bishops say to you: come down, come down!'[lxi]

Gregory was in Rome presiding over a synod of a hundred
bishops when the news of his sacking reached him. Rattled by the
challenge, he lost no time in turning to St Peter for support. The
public letter he penned finally deposing and excommunicating
Henry was in the style of a confessional address to that Apostle and
designed to be read in all the parishes of Western Christendom. It
was prefaced with a long, self-justifying complaint about how he
had never wanted to be pope in the first place and was only doing
his papal duty now by excommunicating and deposing Henry.

Who had heard of such a thing? A pope and an emperor at
loggerheads, each determined to unseat the other. There was a
growing sense that the perilously achieved order of things might
collapse back into the dark chaos of the previous century. 'Our
whole Roman world was shaken,'[lxii] wrote one monk. 'Who does
not grieve at so great an upheaval in the Church? What else . . . is

talked about even in the women's spinning rooms and artisans' workshops?'[lxiii] How could a pope and a king – each divinely appointed to advance God's project on earth – be pummelling each other like a pair of common *milites*? The resounding clash of personalities generated the first Europe-wide controversy the continent had ever seen. The crisis was so serious that both sides felt constrained to call a ceasefire. Pope Gregory was persuaded that Henry should be given exactly a year to examine his Christian conscience and mend his ways before his deposition took effect. February 2, 1077 was the deadline. At a meeting in Augsburg on that date, Henry, the pope and an army of bishops would judge whether Henry was fit to rule.

No fool, Henry suspected he might fail the test. He worked out that his best chance of retaining the throne was by making a direct appeal to the pope in his capacity as chief dispenser of Christian forgiveness. Surely a pope could not refuse to pardon a poor sinner? Gregory would have no choice but to cancel his excommunication and the looming danger of Augsburg would disappear. But this ingenious loophole occurred to Henry rather late. Gregory had already left Rome and begun heading north for the scheduled Augsburg meeting when Henry, having gathered up his wife Bertha, his baby son Conrad and a retinue of loyal *milites*, began journeying south in the hope of intercepting him.

There was not a moment to lose. Henry's was a desperate remedy for desperate times. Appalling weather conditions not to mention the usual hazards of travel meant he was risking life and limb to save his throne. The eleventh century was cold and damp in Europe, hence the high incidence of ergot mould on grain and the resulting plagues of *ignis sacer*. But cold was one thing, this winter quite another.

From early November 1076 until April 1077 Europe's great rivers – the Rhine, the Rhône, the Elbe, the Danube, the Po and even the Tiber – were frozen so hard they were 'impassable to ships, but passable for men, horses, donkeys and carts as if it had been solid ground'.[lxiv] To add to his worries Henry discovered that the shortest and lowest pass over the Alps, the Brenner, which was within easy striking distance of southern Germany and much used by Otto III and Pope Leo IX in their times, was unusable. Some disloyal south German dukes would not give him safe passage through their lands. He and his party had no choice but to tackle the long way round, west through Burgundy, the way I was driving over the Mont Cenis pass. Henry was fortunate to have even this option. A decade earlier he had tried to divorce Bertha because he found her hideous, but one of his counsellors had pointed out that this would be unwise since members of Bertha's family controlled the Mont Cenis pass over the Alps. 'Then I shall control myself and continue to bear as well as I am able the burden I cannot lay down,'[lxv] he had conceded grudgingly.

In order to have recorded their crossing of the Alps in such hair-raisingly vivid detail, the monk-chronicler Lampert of Hersfeld, must have been a member of that miserable cavalcade.

> When, with the greatest difficulty, they reached the mountain's crowning height, led by guides, they found they could go no further since the mountain's ice-covered slopes were frozen so hard and slippery that descent seemed impossible. The men then attempted to overcome the dangers by sheer physical force, sometimes crawling on all fours, sometimes clinging to the shoulders of the guides. Often one would lose his foothold on the ice, and slither and tumble a considerable distance in mortal danger before reaching a flat surface. The Queen [Bertha] and other ladies of the retinue were seated on cow-hide mats and hauled by the guides leading the way. The horses were brought down, some with the help of various contrivances. Others, with legs securely bound together, were slid down the icy slopes – in the course of which many were killed and many gravely injured. Only very few arrived safe and sound. [lxvi]

Reaching the 'mountain's crowning height' almost a thousand years later, I stopped the car on the excellent, empty road. Only the charms of a restaurant with a next-door gift shop selling postcards would slightly delay my own comfortable descent into Italy.

Settled at a table by a picture window with a dish of pork stew in front of me, I surveyed snow-capped mountains under a royal-blue sky. But the foreground was more intriguing. Across a stretch of new grass speckled with pink Alpine flowers and beside a small reservoir filled with turquoise water stood a pyramidal grey stone structure with a few small windows in it. Neither an artfully designed pump house nor a hikers' hut, it was, the Italian waiter informed me, a *chiesa*. He pointed out the tiny cross on top of it. As soon as I had eaten and handed some scribbled postcards to the postman drinking coffee at the bar I set off to investigate, but the church door was locked and the basement *salle d'histoire* closed for the day. A plaque on the building did not inform me that Henry IV had slithered about in the snow and ice here before descending to rendezvous with the pope, Countess Matilda and Abbot Hugh of Cluny at Canossa in January 1077; instead, it commemorated the studious and virtuous life of a local clergyman.

AU CHANOINE JEAN BELLET,
1899–1978
HOMME DE SCIENCE ET HISTORIEN DU MONT CENIS
IL FUT AUSSI UN HOMME DE COEUR

Suspecting that a Frenchman 'of heart' who was also a historian and a scientist might have had wise things to say about Pope Gregory, Henry IV, and the birth of western European science in the eleventh century, I felt extremely sorry to have missed him. Measured against the whole of the past millennium, the twenty-two years since his demise seemed the merest *ictus oculi* – a twinkling of an eye – the smallest particle of time known to medieval Europeans.

The southern side of the Alps looked less tamed and more densely wooded than the north. A happy golden light shone through new leaves on the trees overhanging the road. I passed a sturdy woman hiker with short silver hair, a white smile in a tanned face and a stout staff in her hand. Through the open car window came a tinkle of cowbells and a whiff of wild garlic. The descent was swift and pleasant into the narrow shadowy streets of Susa, an ancient pilgrimage stop where Henry and his companions must have paused after their arduous descent. The town's bustle of colourful activity was exciting after the quiet of south-eastern France. There were mothers walking schoolchildren home to lunch, old women dressed in black with shopping baskets over their arms filled with greenery and golden bread. A pair of white-veiled nuns sat waiting for a bus. Boys in luminous blue, pink or yellow shirts and sunglasses were roaring around on motorcycles. A young priest trotted down the steps of a dark Romanesque church, and *carabinieri* lounged in the front seats of their little jeeps with the doors open, watching girls with long hair and tight trousers prance past them on high heels. Everywhere, Fiats bounced over the cobbles. When I strayed down a one-way street the driver of one wound down his window to hurl a furious '*Cazzo!*' at me. But nothing could dampen my delight at having reached Italy at last.

I did not need to share Otto III's half-Byzantine background, much less his golden dream of recreating the Roman Empire, to be able to empathize with his helpless love for the most troublesome extremity of his empire. After the low grey skies and heavy rains of Reims, the pleasant but prosaic orderliness of Aachen and Konstanz, and the reasonable piety of Taizé, the reckless glamour of even this remote little town was exhilarating. If *Accidie* attacked me here I would have only myself to blame, I decided, speeding onward past Milan in the direction of Reggio nell' Emilia, the nearest big town to Canossa.

The cool blue-green Apennines in the distance on my right were beckoning, but it was only Friday. Since the pageant re-enactment of the great drama did not happen until Sunday and I was consumed with a sudden desire to enjoy some superior ham and cheese, I left the motorway at Parma. Taizé's good effects were wearing off.

In the throes of its annual food fair, Parma was loudly

proclaiming the excellency of its delicacies from every billboard and that evening's *passeggiata* was carnival-like. There were parties of suited German businessmen hitting the bars for an evening of unwinding after a hard day's work, elegant women with mobile phones weaving their way slowly on bicycles through the colourful throng and elderly men in their shirtsleeves walking dogs and greeting friends. Children were playing tag around lamp posts whose soft yellow glow only enhanced the natural beauty of the failing light. At the end of the main street, in a wide cobbled square dominated by the cathedral, I found the city's treasure, an eleventh-century baptistery built of rosy marble, which the evening light was painting a deepening pink. Momentarily inspired, I paused by a shop selling gleaming icons and statues of the Virgin Mary to scribble in my notebook 'this light suits spirit and body, not mind'.

Wandering back the way I had come, my eye was suddenly caught by the sign, 'Bar Cluny'. Seating myself at one of its outside tables, I asked the proprietor how the place had come by its name. A fine figure of a man with forearms as solid as Parma hams and a bushy black moustache, he politely concealed his surprise at my question. A long time ago, he told me, he had read about the great monastery of Cluny and been astonished to learn that during most of the tenth and eleventh centuries its abbots had wielded more power and influence in Europe than the pope himself. Cluny had stuck in his mind as an auspicious name, and, 'Now, whenever I see the priest from the cathedral up there,' he said, gesturing in the direction of the baptistery square, 'I tease him, I say, "Watch out! I'm much more important than you!"' He then directed me to the restaurant serving the best ham and cheese in Parma.

Cluny was still on my mind the following bright morning so I decided to visit the Cluniac monastery of Polirone on the banks of the River Po not far from Mantua. Matilda had presented Polirone to Pope Gregory, who had passed it straight on to Abbot Hugh, who had transformed it into a stronghold of his order. Matilda had funded the building of its new church, a copy of the one Abbot Odilo had built at Cluny, with a generous *ambulatorio* for pilgrims to wander around revering the relics of a certain Saint Simeon. In 1510 Martin Luther happened to visit the place and, disgusted by its worldly splendour, had announced that 'the worship of God is not manifested by wealth' – or power, he might have added. Luther hated everything Gregory VII had stood for. He always referred to him as Höllenbrand, a corruption of Hildebrand meaning hell's fire. The Austrian historian Friedrich Heer has emphasized the vital link between the Church's eleventh-century reformation and Luther's sixteenth-century one: 'Monk Luther's revolt is inconceivable without monk Hildebrand's. The German answer to the desacralisation of the Empire and the Emperor was to desacralise the Papal Church and the Pope.'[lxvii] The eleventh-century's investiture crisis was still a live issue at the start of the nineteenth century. Following his defeat of the Austrian Holy Roman Empire at the Battle of Austerlitz in 1805, Napoleon is said to have crowed, 'Si je n'étais Napoléon, je voudrais être Gregoire VII.'[lxviii]

Crossing the sluggish Po I drove for miles and miles under a wide pale blue sky, across flat arable land dotted with ornate picturesquely ruined stone gateposts, entrances to long-abandoned estates. The remains of the monastery are in the middle of the little town of San Benedetto Po, behind a giant, mostly baroque basilica which was about to host a wedding. I watched the last guests disappear inside and then the arrival of the white-suited groom astride a silver motorbike with his best man riding pillion behind him. Roaring up to the front of the church, they hopped off their steed, ran combs through their windswept hair and dashed up the church steps. Unable to imagine how any bride could match their glamour, I did not wait for one and instead wandered around the back of the church in search of the eleventh century.

There it was, in a quiet Romanesque cloister named after the monastery's obscure Saint Simeon, an Armenian whose canonization Matilda's father Bonifazio had sponsored and whose relics had turned Polirone into a great and lucrative centre of pilgrimage. A short handwritten biography tacked to one of the cloister's columns informed me that Simeon had died in 1016 after a lifetime's far-

faring. In Jerusalem, possibly in the fateful year that a lunatic Muslim caliph had ordered the destruction of all the city's dogs and churches,* Simeon had cast the devils out of seven possessed persons. In Rome he had been accused but then exonerated of heresy, before travelling on to Compostella and Tours. When he finally settled in a specially constructed hermit's cell at Polirone he was already an old man.

There are no monks at Polirone any more, but once the wedding had finished and the happy couple had roared off on the motorbike together I ventured into the cathedral to discover a grand monument to Countess Matilda. The great lady had rested here awhile after her death in 1115. Twice disturbed in her tomb, in the fifteenth and early seventeenth centuries, she had been judged as miraculously uncorrupted as Charlemagne, with every one of her white teeth in place. Disinterred a third time, at the height of the Counter-Reformation in 1633, she was upgraded to reburial in St Peter's in Rome, as befitted such a devoted daughter of the Church. As if to compensate for the sad absence of her mortal remains, a recent portrait of her had been affixed to the monument. But the artist had equipped her with improbably yellow tresses, baby-blue eyes and full, pouting lips. She looked like a Disneyland fairy-tale queen. Her original long-winded epitaph read touchingly, and concluded with a hint of the sort of ancestor worship I had encountered in twenty-first-century Iceland.

By this marble sepulchre am I entombed,
Countess, once called Matilda.
When the years passed were one thousand, one hundred and ten years
    plus six,
    I was released from the flesh.
I lay before the Lord, eight days before the end of July, the fifth month
    of the year.
Mantua, for whom I was your lady, praise the divinity.

* In 1009, al-Hakim destroyed all Jerusalem's churches including the Church of the Holy Sepulchre, built by Emperor Constantine in the fourth century.

I was generous to the pious people, the monks here, for whom the
   memory lives on that this monastery and this chapel
Were founded by Tedaldo, my sweet forefather. [lxix]

The tourist information office in Reggio nell' Emilia's pretty
main square had a poster-portrait of quite another sort of Countess
Matilda on prominent display. Primly buttoned up to the throat in
a red robe with a high mandarin collar, this Renaissance-era Matilda
was wearing what looked like a yellow turban. Her face was darkly
handsome, its expression tight-lipped and grim.

After receiving directions to Canossa and checking the time of
the pageant, the *corteo*, I fell into friendly conversation with the
men who ran the office. Massimo, a shy academic sort, was pleased
I was so interested in their local heroine.

'Some people say Matilda had a love affair with the pope,
but—' he began.

'Ah! *Certamente!*' interrupted his colleague, the long-haired,
chain-smoking Fabrizio, before mentioning a nonagenarian local
history professor who knew Matilda 'better than he knows his own
wife. He's the man who organized the first *corteo* at Canossa in the
early 1950s. The only thing Professor Sparggiari doesn't know about
Matilda is—'

'What's that?'

'Not for translation. Actually, she was no beauty. We think
that poster there is probably a good likeness.'

I begged Massimo to put me in touch with Matilda's elderly
devotee.

'Usually *il professore* drops in here for a few minutes every
morning, after drinking a coffee next door. He could be here any
moment . . . Ah! What did I tell you?'

Professor Sparggiari looked wonderfully fit for his advanced
years. He was bursting with funny, proud stories about his four great-
grandchildren with which he insisted on regaling Massimo and
Fabrizio before attending to me and swiftly deciding the prickly
question of whether Gregory and Matilda had ever had *obscoeni*

negotii. 'Pah! The Germans always say that but it's not true,' he said, with a dismissive wave of his hand. As an Italian he was on the whole a staunch supporter of Pope Gregory in the investiture crisis, but he loved Matilda especially 'for her strength and her courage. It seems she had no failings at all!' he said. As children growing up before World War One, he told me, his older sisters had joined the Matildini, a sort of devout Roman Catholic girl-guide association which Mussolini had later abolished. Mussolini reminded Professor Sparggiari of World War Two, World War Two of Germany again, and Germany of Count Otto von Bismarck, who in 1872 famously assured the Reichstag of a united and ecstatically proud new Germany, 'We will not go to Canossa.'

Germany's Iron Chancellor set out to break the power of Pope Pius IX – who had vigorously opposed the 'springtime of nations' – over German Catholics. Bismarck's *Kulturkampf* against Catholicism entailed the persecution and imprisonment of priests, the closure of Catholic printing presses, the banishment of the Jesuits and a ban on teaching by religious orders. The religion of a new Germany must be German nationalism. The new nation state would never humble herself before Pius IX as Henry IV had before Gregory VII at Canossa.

'But Germans especially have been coming to Canossa ever since Bismarck said that.' Professor Sparggiari laughed, rising to his feet and shaking my hand. 'Enjoy the *corteo* tomorrow!'

As the door closed behind the old man, Fabrizio lit another cigarette and shook his head in affectionate wonder, 'You won't find a fellow like Sparggiari on the Internet!'

The *corteo* would take place at Ciano d'Enza, a few miles from the mountain-top castle of Canossa, at four o'clock the following afternoon. So, having driven south from Reggio nell' Emilia towards the foothills of the Apennines, I spent the night in a small town between the two places and rose early the following morning. By eight, I was motoring up into the rolling hills, through dense woods and sunlit glades, enjoying the crisp clear air and bright sunshine. Across a high meadow Canossa appeared at last, looking as if it had sprouted organically from a high white spur of rock in a setting of lush dark woodland.

Passing a posse of fancily kitted out Italian cyclists, I climbed as far as I was allowed to by car and set off to walk the rest of the way up a shaded cobbled path punctuated by shallow steps. Inserted at intervals in a new grey stone wall on my left were delightful small bas-reliefs of scenes from the castle's history, reminding me of Stations of the Cross. First there was Azzo Adalberto, Matilda's ancestor, who built the castle back in the tenth century. Next, I was delighted to see, was one depicting none other than Otto III's dour Granny Adelheid as a young maid, in the castle here at Canossa besieged by her fiancé, Otto I. Apparently opposed to the marriage, Granny Adelheid had fled here. Otto I had pursued her, 'in hot haste'[lxx] but, unable to break in, had eventually won her over by shooting arrows tagged with love letters up at the windows of her tower. Last came the scene which unfolded at Canossa in January 1077. There were Matilda, Gregory, Henry and Abbot Hugh, each of them naively fashioned to look as tall as the castle itself.

Ignoring a sign barring entrance to the castle ruins themselves on account of construction works, I reached the top at last and perched on a broken wall to admire a sunlit view of undulating wooded hills patched with meadows and delightfully empty of any suggestion that it belonged in the twenty-first century. No distant roar of traffic on a motorway or hum of an aeroplane overhead disturbed the silence of that morning. One high half-ruined wall looked a good thousand years old to me, but a long-haired workman who appeared in a T-shirt and jeans at the entrance to his hut to stretch his limbs and greet the new morning could not tell me a thing about the place. It did not matter because, aided by that excellent chronicler monk, Lampert of Hersfeld, I was having no trouble imagining the details of Canossa's finest hour.

After telling us that Gregory and Matilda were together in Mantua when news of Henry's daring expedition reached them, Lampert proceeds to a lengthy digression on that same old moot point: did Matilda and Gregory have carnal relations with each other or not? He blames disgruntled German churchmen for spreading foul rumours that Gregory 'shamelessly wallowed, day and night, in her [Matilda's] embraces, and so closely bound was she to the Pope by her illicit passion that she had declined to marry again after the death of her husband'. Having given the rumours a brand new lease of life with this colourful retelling, the hypocritical Lampert then tries to conceal his prurient malice by adding, 'It was as clear as daylight however, to all reasonable persons that these accusations were false. The Pope, in fact, led so pure and apostolic a life that no rumour could cast the least slur on his sublime behaviour.'[lxxi]

For all Pope Gregory knew, Henry was on his way with an army to do battle with him so, not for the first time, he heeded Matilda's sensible advice and retraced his steps a short way to take up a safe position in her castle to wait for him there. About six miles north of Canossa as the crow flies over rolling green hills, Henry and his retinue took up their own position in Bianello Castle, today a private property on the edge of the little town of Quattro Castella, where I had spent the night. There he prepared for his assault on the pope's mercy by collecting mediators to plead his cause.

Chief among them was Matilda, whom Henry had known since they were children and whose influence over the pope, *obscoeni negotii* or no *obscoeni negotii*, was considerable. But Henry's godfather, Abbot Hugh of Cluny, was also conveniently to hand. Abbot Hugh must have cursed his luck at finding himself there because he had never wanted to be Henry's godfather and had twice refused the honour, pleading that he would be too far away from Saxony to do the job properly. Henry III had had to beg him to accept and had showered him with rich gifts when he finally gave in. Abbot Hugh's conception of his duty as godfather included continuing to pray for Henry's soul after his recent excommunication, which resulted in his own excommunication and the need to travel across the Alps to Rome and Pope Gregory to have the ban lifted. Hence his presence at Canossa and availability to help Matilda plead Henry's cause.

Gregory loved and trusted both Matilda and Abbot Hugh but was wise to Henry's tricks and therefore wary. He reasoned that 'if the king felt himself to be blameless, he should confidently present himself without fear or worry in Augsburg'.[lxxii] When Abbot Hugh and Matilda protested that Henry was only asking for Christian mercy, Gregory fired back, ' "Let him send me up his crown and sceptre then. If he be truly contrite, he must acknowledge himself unfit to wear them." ' Hugh and Matilda were dismayed by Gregory's righteous intransigence. For some days the peace brokers shuttled back and forth through the heavy snow, between castles and conveniently situated chapels until, at last, Gregory relented sufficiently to suggest that Henry come to Canossa. He would see for himself if the king 'was really prepared to do penance for his misdeeds'.[lxxiii]

On the morning of 25 January, Henry left Bianello. Barefoot and dressed only in a penitent's robe, he struggled up the hill to Canossa and was allowed to penetrate the first of the castle's three walls, the one at the bottom of the hill which enclosed the peasants. For three days he remained in the thick snow before the castle gate, fasting and praying and begging for admittance. The letter Pope Gregory sent to his German supporters once the drama was past conveys the effect of Henry's penitential posturing and his own agony of spirit:

> He [Henry] did not cease with many tears to beg the help and consolation of our apostolic mercy, until he provoked all who were either there or in receipt of tidings of what was happening to such great mercy and pitying compassion that they interceded for him with many pleadings and tears. For all marvelled at the unwonted harshness of our attitude; indeed, some complained that we were showing, not the strictness of apostolic authority, but a cruelty that was a reminiscent of a tyrant's inhumanity.[lxxiv]

On the morning of the fourth day, Gregory gave in and revoked Henry's excommunication. A rather confused oath was sworn on some relics by all present except Abbot Hugh, who deemed oath-swearing incompatible with his monk's calling. There was great rejoicing and a happy feast at which Henry, after his long fast, ate much and said little. The question of his fitness to rule was left unresolved, but he had got what he had come for.

Both men had lost and gained by this drama. Henry lost face because he had not achieved his aim of sacking the pope, but he had won back the loyalty of the German prelates without which he could not rule. Gregory won the submission of empire to Church by asserting his spiritual overlordship, but lost his battle for the right to depose a ruler. Henry was soon back to his old tricks and Gregory felt constrained to excommunicate him all over again. The story would end happily for neither of them.

Under Gregory VII the reformers overreached their spiritual remit and worldly rulers began losing respect for the Church. Its new fundamentalism, its meddling in the affairs of the world, its acquisition of lands, laying down of laws and attempts to raise armies were beginning to contradict the early reformers' humbler aim of raising the Church above the secular sphere in order to set an example of purity and virtue. By the 1080s the Roman Church was well on its way to becoming the powerful papal monarchy of the later Middle Ages. Without Pope Gregory and the monarchy he had inspired there might have been no fifteenth-century Martin Luther to lambast the Church for having mistaken its mission. And without Luther the seeds of our modern secular West would not have begun to sprout – for better or for worse – in the space between Western Christendom's disgracefully warring Catholics and Protestants.

The cyclists had arrived at the bottom of the hill where Henry had spent his three days and nights of penance. They were resting at a café, the sun warm on their backs after their ride, or hobbling about in their cycling shoes refilling their water bottles. After pondering all that dark and difficult history, I enjoyed their lewd wisecracks about Countess Matilda and cheerful chat about their kit. Restored, I set off to nearby Ciano d'Enza for the *corteo*.

The small town was already humming with excitement. Its main square was filled with stalls selling coloured sweets, cheap underwear, pickled wild mushrooms, plastic toys, brooms and baskets, jeans and *parmigiano* cheese, while local artists and craftspeople were hopeful of making a financial killing from their embroidered doilies, fancy wickerwork and crude landscape paintings. Attracted by the bursts of mirth from the people surrounding one stall, I wandered over to investigate. In the middle of the crowd, on a rickety trestle table with a scrap of white paper tacked to it, was what looked at first sight like a large boulder.

It turned out to be a powerful evocation in stone of the grand drama at Canossa. There, below the castle tower, on expertly chiselled battlements, was mitred Gregory with his crozier. There was Matilda shielding baby Conrad's eyes. I could not see an Abbot Hugh, but Henry IV – roughly engraved onto rather than properly chiselled out of the raw stone base of the sculpture – was an outsize figure in full chain mail instead of penitential robe, lurking by a marvellously convincing castle gate. The sculptor, a small bright-eyed man with a wide smile beneath his Zapata moustache, was delighted with his handiwork and the admiration it was provoking, but also with the snatch of dialogue he had scrawled on the scrap of white paper tacked to the edge of the table.

Gregory VII:	Apologise, Henry! Repent!
Henry IV:	Holy Father, I repent!
(*He curses the pope with a rude sign and whispers.*)	
The Baby:	Daddy Henry! Come, Daddy!
Matilda:	Hush! Keep quiet so Pope Gregory VII won't end up excommunicating the lot of us!

Signor Germano Musi was a builder by trade but a Renaissance *uomo universale* by soul; sculpture was only one of his rich store of talents. Invited back to his home for lunch, I admired the house's outside walls which he had decorated with vivid murals and examples of his speciality, sundials. Next he drew my attention to the universe he had cunningly worked into his crazy-paved driveway. A round red tile represented Mars, a black spot of a tile was Pluto and Saturn had a ring around it. The blue-green Earth, a whitish Moon and a sandy-coloured Sun were easily recognizable. Signor Musi had included Hale Bopp and Halley's Comet and had not forgotten to add the name of Jehovah in Hebrew lettering and the descending dove shape of the Holy Ghost in pebble-dash. My host, I concluded, was a man intent on locating himself in a post-Christian universe, covering all bases for good measure. But by the standards of any religion his hospitality to a stranger was simply good. While eating our takeaway pizza lunch in his gloomy main room he insisted we watch a video of himself starring in some humorous musical skits which he had written and performed with a couple of friends in the 1980s. From time to time, overcome with shyness at my enthusiastic appreciation of his dancing, singing and acting, he left the room to shout 'Marta! Maaar-ta!' up the stairs. He needed me to admire yet another product of his inexhaustible creative urge, his daughter.

At last she appeared, a slight, pale girl of about twenty with lashings of black kohl around her sad dark eyes. The fact that she was dressed from head to toe in black and the aura of unhappy intensity surrounding her immediately reminded me of Anya back in Konstanz. But she offered to accompany me to the *corteo* and I was relieved to see that, on hearing the sound of horses clip-clopping along the road outside, she ran to the window in genuine excitement at the forthcoming fun.

With only an hour to go before the entertainment began, the main street was jammed with traffic. As well as cars and buses there were large sleek horses ridden by handsome youths who spurred their mounts forward, calf muscles rippling manfully in the tight leggings of their medieval costumes. They and crowds of small children in sacking shifts, women in wide-sleeved jewel-coloured robes, teenage boys in jerkins and tights and monks in cassocks were all heading towards the middle of town and then up the hill to an open-air theatre. Marta and I found ourselves trudging up the hill beside a stern, grey-bearded Pope Gregory in a green velvet chasuble with yellow trimmings. 'It's our butcher!' she giggled. A few paces ahead was a monk who might have been Abbot Hugh. By running up the verge we overtook the bulk of the crowd and reached the front, where we found the heroine of the piece, the *donna nobilissima* Matilda, on a large white horse. Wearing a gorgeous green robe, a richly jewelled headdress and golden slippers, she had thin, dyed yellow hair and a brightly lipsticked pout. Marta explained that she made a particularly popular Matilda because she was currently starring in one of Italy's favourite television soap operas.

The scene – once all the costumed locals, mounted and unmounted, had arranged themselves in front of the backdrop of Canossa's façade – was splendid. On the battlements stood a line of helmeted *milites*; the various villages around Canossa had sent their costumed representatives, each with their own rich banner to display. There were more banners twirling, long golden horns blowing and drums rolling. Matilda processed around the stage in her golden slippers waving to the audience, saying how honoured she felt to have been invited to Canossa to star in the *corteo* and shouting '*Grazie bambini, grazie!*'

It soon became clear that the purpose of the Canossa *corteo* was not to faithfully re-enact that miserably perilous winter of 1077. The aim was to have fun, so the humbling of Henry was a perfunctory affair compared to the entertainments that followed. Henry entered centre-stage, stripped down to a penitential robe with Abbot Hugh's assistance, approached Matilda and the pope, did the historic deal and then took a seat near them. The real entertainment started when a troupe of girl dancers in floaty pink dresses was followed by another of banner-twirling boys in yellow tights under red tunics. Next came the strongmen of the local villages, their heavy haunches straining in red or black leggings, who competed in a daft tug of war. Finally, and most entertainingly of all, the handsome young fellows on horseback raced each other in heats in a contest which involved galloping full pelt in one direction, picking up a hammer, galloping back and throwing the hammer into a central slot as they passed. The crowd roared and gasped and cheered on the various village teams. Between charges the horses wheeled and snorted while the riders mopped their brows. Marta clapped loudly for the winner, a burly young man from the village of Trinità.

Soap star Matilda, seated on a throne with the butcher-Pope Gregory at her side, merely enjoyed the spectacle. She presented prizes to the winners and received bouquets from all.

~

Lying on my hotel bed, half-watching a noisy Italian soap opera starring Matilda of Canossa, I was enjoying the letters of the eleventh-century Italian saint Peter Damiani:

> At times lustful desire is enkindled and flares up within me, agitates my whole being, causing my genitalia to grow hard . . .[lxxv]

In a colder clime and slightly earlier time this engaging Italian hermit might have been a passionate devotee of the Icelandic Vikings' fertility god Freyr. It was his bad luck that he hailed from the ancient heartland of Western Christendom and lived in the era of Church reform when clergy had to be celibate or the entire Christian project would fail. Nevertheless, Freyr seems never to have renounced his claim on him.

Peter Damiani had started life as a humble north Italian swine-herd, but gained a good classical education in Ravenna in the 1010s at a school founded by the genius Gerbert. It was while he was engaged in further studies in Parma that Freyr's first rude promptings coincided with his shock at the moral laxity of the clergy. He was aghast at how a priest neighbour of his, who wore elegant shoes which 'did not puff up to a curved point like an eagle's beak', used to sing and wink and tell 'scurrilous jokes' to his lady love every day. Describing this scene in a letter when an old man, Peter Damiani asked, 'What could I do when I saw all this happening? I was so tempted by sexual excitement . . .'[lxxvi] Fleeing Freyr's urgings and the evil city, he became a hermit and eventually prior of Fonte Avellana, a hermitage high in the mountains near the modern Adriatic port of Ancona. Only a life lived according to the strict rule of St Romuald, who was one of Otto III's three favourite spiritual fathers, could save his soul.

An early and ardent supporter of Church reform, in the early 1050s Peter Damiani presented Pope Leo IX with a detailed report on the regrettable sexual practices current among churchmen of the day. 'Alas! It is a disgrace to speak, it is a disgrace to intimate such a foul crime to holy ears,' he began, and went on to explain, 'There are some who pollute themselves; there are others who befoul each other by mutually handling their genitals; others still who fornicate between the thighs, and others who do so from the rear . . .'[lxxvii] The Church reformers, but especially Hildebrand, were so impressed by this learned Italian hermit's passion for chastity among churchmen that they coaxed him down from his mountain-top to offer him the office of cardinal. Only the threat of excommunication could induce him to accept the honour. While far-faring to Milan to preach against simony and nicolaitism and crossing 'over the lofty peaks of the horrible Alps'[lxxviii] to Burgundy to champion Cluny's precious *libertas* or to save Henry IV's miserable marriage to Queen Bertha in Saxony, he dreadfully missed the 'beloved solitude' of his hermitage. Once he protested that if St Adalbert had been allowed to abandon his post as bishop of Prague to become a simple missionary monk, why wasn't he allowed to retreat to the peace of his cell? Peter Damiani may have been a martyr to his lusts but he never doubted that the first and worthiest work of a churchman was the most austere form of monasticism as pioneered by the desert fathers of the East in the fifth century.

In his beloved solitude he fought off the devils of sex and *Accidie* by writing hundreds of fancily phrased letters of spiritual counsel. One hundred and eighty of them have survived, thanks to the careful way he first dictated them to a scribe equipped with a quill and wax tablets, and then had another scribe make two copies on parchment; one for the addressee, the other for storage in Fonte

Avellana's library. Letter writing was the safest form of intercourse with young women, he admitted to a young countess: 'It is safer for me to converse in writing with young women in whose presence I am apprehensive . . . I guard my eyes at the sight of more beautiful and attractive faces.'[lxxvix] He must have been a man of heart; his writings are full of the poignant humanity of Christ and his mother.

Most of his correspondents were bishops, monks and nobles who play no part in this eleventh-century saga, but there are plenty of familiar names. In 1042 he was warning Matilda's father, Count Bonifazio of Tuscany, that hellfire awaited him unless he took active steps to stop his *milites* ransacking local monasteries. Thirteen years later he was congratulating Matilda's mother Beatrice on her pious decision to forgo sex with her husband, claiming that he had 'shouted with joy'[lxxx] at the news. Later still he was telling Beatrice's second husband and Matilda's stepfather, Duke Godfrey the Bearded of Lorraine, that he should crack down as hard on the criminals in his duchy as Otto III had on John Philagathos and two Roman rebels back in 998. Before visiting Abbot Hugh at Cluny in the 1060s, he had written to say that the Cluniacs' diet and daily regime did not strike him as quite ascetic enough. 'If for two days more you could abstain from fat in your food, you who are so perfect in most other matters . . .' he ventured to suggest. Hugh had politely refused, saying, 'Beloved father, before we try to increase our merits by increasing our abstinence, try yourself to endure our labours for a week and then you will judge whether it is possible to add anything to our austerities . . .'[lxxxi] When Peter Damiani did visit Cluny he was so impressed he immediately withdrew his criticisms and enrolled his young nephew there. Abbot Hugh took a special interest in the lad, personally hearing his confession twice a week.

Peter Damiani's relations with the future Pope Gregory VII seem to have been more strained. He once called Hildebrand 'my Holy Satan' for torturing him with ecclesiastical responsibilities. In 1060 he protested his affection for him but complained of being ignored: 'why do I go on with this letter since I have no hope that you will ever read it? Certainly there is no one alive to whom I would rather write, if only you would condescend to read it . . .'[lxxxii] It seems likely that Hildebrand, busy with politics and church organization, had little time for the sort of reclusive religious practice Peter Damiani valued above all others. Although the two men were agreed that the world was evil and urgently needed subordinating to Christ, they inhabited different spheres. By *milites Christi Petri* Peter Damiani would have understood a monk engaged in fighting Satan with a lifetime of constant prayer and self-denial. But when Gregory VII coined the similar term, *milites Sancti Petri*, he was bravely but brutally fitting words to actions in the name of order and justice, and talking about warriors physically fighting his wars for him.

Peter Damiani may have seemed an eccentric outsider to most Church bureaucrats busy implementing their reforms, but there were plenty of ordinary Christians – men and women – who felt as sickened and alarmed as he did by the character of Western Christendom's revival. Its new litigious spirit, the hectic new love of money, the growth of urban living, worldly learning, trading and travel did not seem to be bringing the kingdom of God any nearer. Many were out of sympathy with the changes and sought comfort in simpler, stricter, older certainties.

Like Peter Damiani, thousands followed the lead of St Romuald, the hermit who had almost succeeded in turning Emperor Otto III into a monk. These back-to-basics Christian fundamentalists headed off into the dense forests and the mountains to save their souls. Beginning their lives again, creating their own pared down order, far from where the law operated or money changed hands or 'where the shouts of young men and the singing of young girls could be heard',[lxxxiii] they cleared the land, built churches, fasted, tended the sick and repented. In his biography of St Romuald, Peter Damiani captured the fundamentalist zeitgeist, with 'it seemed as if the whole world would be turned into a hermitage.'[lxxxiv]

By 1030, as the Peace of God movement took hold, this radical rejection of the world and all its works was spreading northward to the French lands, to Aquitaine, to the dense forests of Brittany and into the lands of the Germans. Sixty years later a churchman of Konstanz was marvelling at how 'whole villages' were handing 'themselves over as communities to religion so that they may compete ceaselessly to attain holiness in their lives'.[lxxxv] The craze would peak by the end of the century and give rise to new, more ascetic monastic orders than Cluny – the Cistercians and Carthusians. It also fuelled the wave of popular enthusiasm for large pilgrimages to Jerusalem which culminated in the biggest mass pilgrimage of all, the First Crusade.

Inspired by the idea of forested mountains dotted with hermitages full of people so dismayed by the complexity and materialism of modern eleventh-century living that they had given it all up for the good life, I cast aside my copy of St Peter Damiani's letters and unfolded my road map. It seemed to me that if I were to drive on through the Apennines in a south-easterly direction towards Ancona, where I had arranged to deposit the hire-car before taking a train to Rome, I could visit St Romuald's most famous foundation at Camaldoli as well as Peter Damiani's hermitage home of Fonte Avellana.

~

Passing through thickly forested mountains along a road darkened by pine trees planted so close together their bare trunks looked like lines of crucifixes, I reached Camaldoli. First came the monastery with its eleventh-century cloister, founded as a pilgrim's hostel on the busy mountain crossing between Ravenna and Rome, and then – eight kilometres away and much higher up a side road strewn with leaves and branches blown down by the previous night's gale – the holy hermitage.

Its lofty remoteness was pleasant and the cold air, laced with the delicious scent of wood smoke, a tonic. On that damp grey morning a thick mist blurred the view across a courtyard through a high wrought iron fence to the tiny village of hermits' cottages. Crossing the courtyard I stood at the gate, staring up the stone-paved path that divided the hermits' village in two, waiting for a glimpse of a white-robed and hooded monk, perhaps on his way to the little church whose bell tower was just visible at the end of the path. None came. I tried to picture the phenomenon Peter Damiani described so vividly: 'men preciously dressed in silken and golden robes, escorted by cohorts of servants, and accustomed to all the pleasures of affluence, now content with a single cloak, enclosed, barefooted, unkempt and so parched and wasted by abstinence . . .'[lxxxvi]

Behind the little church rose a dark wall of dense trees, once the property of the monks. When one of Countess Matilda's illustrious forebears gave this land to Peter Damiani's mentor St Romuald to build his hermitage on, he also entrusted to him a gigantic area of the forest. Generations of Camaldoli monks took excellent care of their little earthly paradise and even incorporated into the rule of the order a directive concerning the planting of four or five thousand tree seedlings every year. The monks also produced a first Italian compendium of ecological knowledge. In the mid-nineteenth century not a single tree in the forest was felled without the say-so of the entire community of monks. Today the forest is a treasured national park.

St Romuald's greatest contribution to Western Christendom was his introduction of this especially ascetic style of monasticism, until then only found in the East. A halfway house between the utter solitude of the lone hermit and the enforced sociability of an ordinary monastery, the arrangement proved popular. Romuald's saintly inventiveness and his ability to make 'the great of this world quake in their bowels before him as if before the majesty of God'[lxxxvii] drew thousands to him. Perfectionist, driven and urgent about the business of building God's kingdom on earth, Romuald founded dozens of the new communities.

> The holy man burned to do good so that he was never content with what he had done and while at work on some project would soon be rushing off to something different, so that it looked as if he wanted to turn the whole world into a hermitage and for everyone to be joined together in the monastic order.[lxxxviii]

St Romuald died when Peter Damiani was twenty but remained his preferred role model. In his biography of his hero Peter Damiani tells us that Romuald first became a monk at a monastery in Ravenna to do penance for a murder his father had committed. However, violently set upon by his brother monks when he complained of their laxness, he fled into the woods near Venice to learn how to be a hermit. There he apprenticed himself to an old monk who made him sing twenty psalms under one tree, forty under another, and clouted him over his left ear every time he made a mistake. For five long years he battled demons at one of his new hermitages, during which time if any brother monk knocked at the door of his cell he would assume it was the devil come hunting for his soul, and yell ' "What now wretch!? What is there for thee in the hermitage – outcast of Heaven! Back, unclean dog! Vanish old snake!" '[lxxxix] Peter Damiani described him as a doughty *miles Christi* and noted his tremendous capacity for penitential weeping and miracle working. Romuald was considered so holy by the inhabitants of one town he visited that when they heard he was planning to move on, they plotted to murder him for his valuable relics. He foiled their wicked scheme by shaving his head and pretending to be raving mad. At a later stage of his life he 'dwelt for a while in a swamp' until, driven out by the stench, he emerged bald and swollen, 'as green as a newt'.[xc] Back in Ravenna he fought off a bishop intent on strangling him. Romuald spent four years in silence in an Umbrian hermitage before dying in June 1027 at the age of eighty-five. Such was the larger than life character who very nearly persuaded young Otto III to abandon his crown for a monk's cell. Such was the man whose life and works inspired thousands to flee the bustling world for the wilderness of mountains and forests.

By the time St Romuald died, his hermitage here at Camaldoli consisted of five stone huts clustered around a small chapel. Today there are twenty cells, each modelled on the one in which St Romuald spent two years of his life and one of them named after Peter Damiani. Abandoning my patient wait for a glimpse of a monk, I followed a sign directing me to St Romuald's old cell, which has somehow been preserved, incorporated into the hermitage's library and opened to the public. It was a squat whitewashed one-storey cottage set like all the others in a small walled garden. Through a low wooden door on which a rusty iron cross was nailed, I passed into a wood-lined chamber furnished with a high-sided bed like a coffin, a writing table, a little altar and a hatch through which the hermit's daily ration of bread and vegetables was posted. It was cramped but cosy and I was fascinated to note that Pope John Paul II had paid the place a visit in 1993. He has voiced a forlorn wish to honour St Romuald and end his days as a Camaldoli hermit.

The hermitage's main church had a dark baroque interior. Almost every painting and statue was framed with gilt bars radiating outwards, a little like blazes of heavenly glory but more like freak stalactites. Two red marble columns reminded me uncomfortably of mortadella sausage. I did not linger there and, once outside again, found something far more interesting. Fixed to the wall of the church porch was a typewritten notice concerning the acquisition of plenary indulgences from this church in this jubilee two-thousandth year since the birth of Jesus Christ. Wiping one's soul clean of all its sins, bypassing a period of suffering in purgatory and securing oneself direct access to heaven was dependent, it seemed, on the fulfilment of five simple conditions.

1. A full confession.
2. Holy Communion.
3. The recitation of an Our Father and the Creed.
4. A sincere spirit of repentance for all one's sins – mortal or venal.
5. A prayer for the intentions of the pope.

Underneath this mystifyingly simple recipe for eternal salvation was a bishop of Lourdes's almost equally baffling definition of the term 'indulgence': 'An indulgence is like a superabundance of grace received in a particular way, in solidarity with all other Christians – dead and alive – in order that the grace of pardon and reconciliation should extend for the rest of our lives . . .'

Plenary indulgences were invented by the reforming popes of the eleventh century and have been described by one eminent medieval church historian as 'a peculiarly personal expression of the papal plenitude of power'.[xci] Effectively another brick in the fortress of worldly power the reforming popes were steadily erecting for themselves, they had their critics even then. In 1053 an abbot of Reichenau protested against Pope Leo's offering of what was a plenary indulgence in all but name to those who fought in his doomed battle against the Normans of southern Italy. But the mostly French *milites* who rode off to help conquer parts of northern Spain from the Moors in the 1060s were offered the same incentive. When, in 1095, Pope Urban despatched those First Crusaders to Jerusalem, they were all promised plenary indulgences, whether or not they died battling the Infidel.

At the end of the eleventh century a plenary indulgence was still relatively hard to come by. By the beginning of the thirteenth century the process of devaluation was well under way and a generous contribution to the expenses of the Fourth Crusade was all it took to acquire one. When in 1300 the pope of the day decided to institute a jubilee to be repeated every hundred years, he ruled that anyone completing a pilgrimage to Rome in a jubilee year automatically merited one. By the mid-fourteenth century it was possible to quickly and quite cheaply purchase a plenary indulgence from a parish priest on one's deathbed. In the hands of unscrupulous travelling salesmen like Geoffrey Chaucer's pardoner, the currency of plenary indulgences sank to rock bottom. Martin Luther's sixteenth-century revolt against the papacy was fuelled at least as much by his loathing for the sordid industry of indulgences as by his dislike for the ostentatious wealth of Cluniac monasteries like Polirone.

I was astonished, even shocked, to discover that such a quintessentially medieval phenomenon had survived into the new millennium. Why had they not been quietly phased out, as relic-gathering, the mortification of the flesh by flagellation or the Latin mass had been? Were there really Roman Catholics who, in this jubilee year, would follow points one to five, earn themselves a plenary indulgence and know they would be counted among the angels? Surely only God could decide who deserved salvation and eternal life? Something about the prescriptive simplicity of plenary indulgences was reminding me of the way Iceland's first priests, most of them former pagan *gothar*, had decided that there must be room in the Lord Jesus Christ's feasting hall in the sky for as many of their followers as could fit into the churches they had built. Nothing like plenary indulgences developed in Eastern Christendom and I guessed that neither St Romuald nor Peter Damiani would have approved of so formulaic a route to salvation.

On my way east, out of Tuscany into Umbria, towards Peter Damiani's hermitage of Fonte Avellana, the light seemed to change, along with the scenery, which became less greenly lush and gently rolling, less formed for human convenience. There were still forests but the mountains were barer, and under that high, bright sky it was not hard to see why this more austere region once abounded in disciples of St Romuald waging their life-long, lonely battles for salvation.

Gubbio, the nearest town to Fonte Avellana, was a revelation. Built entirely of limestone, like Jerusalem, it sat up high on a mountain side, the forested summit behind it. I spent an hour or so of deepening pink twilight wandering its back streets, delighted by nothing in particular but by the perfect arrangement of all its parts: steep, grey cobbled alleys, tall, white-grey stone houses with narrow windows, shadow shapes, damp smells, strangely amplified voices and footsteps, whiffs of cooking suppers, tinkles of cutlery. While stopping to admire a giant statue of St Peter keeping watch at the end of a long cobbled street over the quarter of the town that bore his name, I was hailed by a couple of cheery Albanian builders, hard at work up on their scaffolding, grouting one of the stone façades. They asked me in Italian what I was doing in Gubbio. When I told them and mentioned I would be passing through their country soon, they were touchingly pleased, and I walked on. By the time I had climbed up the steep mountain side to the northern edge of the town the setting sun was casting a blood-red glow over Gubbio's bleached-bone stones.

Higher and higher into the mountains I went the next morning, up into the clouds almost, past a glossy mare with her foal, expecting to see Peter Damiani's Fonte Avellana – 'the poor little place' he had entered at the age of twenty-eight – around every corner. Today it is a tidy little place fashioned in the same old bone-coloured limestone as Gubbio, with terracotta roofs, a large coach-park, a snack bar, a picnic area and signs requesting visitors to respect the environment. The oldest part of the complex, the monastery's north-facing scriptorium, whose rows of arched windows along three sides let in plenty of light, had been designed though never used by Peter Damiani. Of the hermitage – little cottages grouped around a church, such as I had seen at Camaldoli – there was nothing left but the church crypt. Nor was there a single monk in sight.

A party of pilgrims who had arrived by coach from a nearby town poured out of the church after a final hymn and stood around chatting in the bright sunshine. A large family, hauling baskets and plastic cooler bags, was making for the picnic area behind the monastery. I was beginning to doubt that Fonte Avellana was still a monastery until, wandering through a dark cloister richly scented with the aroma of simmering tomato sauce, I spotted an ancient, bowed figure in the distinctive white cassock of a Camaldoli monk. As he approached me out of the shadows I thought I recognized the telltale marks of an ardent ascetic: hollow cheeks, papery white skin and exhausted red-rimmed eyes. He was proceeding painfully slowly and passed me without a glance. But for the navy-blue canvas lace-ups he was wearing on his swollen feet, he could have been the ghost of one of Peter Damiani's hermit brothers.

We know a good deal about those humble hermit brothers who lived in fearful austerity in their separate cells and only met once a week for mass because Peter Damiani loved to mention them in his letters to some of his more worldly correspondents. Praising to the skies their feats of holy endurance, he offered them as role models. There was Brother Peter, who refused a bed and slept naked on the floor of his cell in summer and winter, a Brother Lupus who never touched soup, and a Brother Leo who wore tight iron chains next to his skin to stop himself overeating. But Peter Damiani's favourite seems to have been a master of the logic so commonly applied to matters relating to salvation and the hereafter in that age before the crack between faith and reason appeared, before logic separated itself from belief and gained a life of its own. Brother Dominic had calculated that by flagellating himself a certain number of times while saying a certain number of psalms he could pay off a century's worth of suffering in purgatory. Peter Damiani wrote approvingly of this holy hero, who frequently appeared 'as if he had been bruised like barley in a mortar':

> a hundred years of penance, as I learned from Dominic himself, is performed in this way. While three thousand blows regularly count as one year of penance here, chanting ten psalms accounts for a thousand blows, as we have often proven. Since we know that the psalter contains one hundred and fifty psalms, five years of penance, if we count correctly, are contained in disciplining [whipping] oneself throughout one psalter. Now, if you multiply five by twenty or twenty by five, you arrive at a hundred. And so, when one has chanted twenty psalters while taking the discipline, one is sure that he has performed a hundred years of penance.[xcii]

I could see how a new and valuable commodity called plenary indulgences had cornered a part of the salvation market.

Although the Cluniacs had busied themselves with altering and reordering the world and these Italian hermits had preferred to reject it, both monastic reform movements had worked hard at spiritually renewing Western Christendom for the new millennium. Which had weathered the past thousand years better? I asked myself as I drove down the mountain and on towards the coast and Ancona. Cluny had been demolished two hundred years ago but had inspired the creation of other monastic orders, all of them as usefully employed in the selfless work of education, healthcare, land cultivation and the relief of poverty. Camaldoli and Fonte Avellana had survived. Contemplative orders like the Camaldoli are now attracting more vocations than the active ones.

Peter Damiani had always hated to leave his hermitage for Rome and his onerous duties as a cardinal, but I was looking forward to reaching the noise and vitality of the capital. Hermit-like myself, I had barely spoken to anyone since leaving Canossa and was wearied by long hours spent driving up and down mountains.

Noise and vitality had lost much of their appeal by the time I reached Rome the next day. Soon after pulling out of Ancona, my train compartment had erupted into loud and lively political debate. One of its five male occupants was a gangly young man wearing a rose-pink open-necked shirt, grey flannels and scuffed trainers. He had blundered in, turfed a dozing Albanian agricultural worker out of his reserved seat, and glanced out of the window to rail about the poor state of the houses he was seeing. Five minutes of angling for an argument sufficed to provoke an older man sporting sky-blue socks and yellow moccasins into exclaiming, 'Now don't let's get on to politics. We'll never reach Rome if we start on politics!' Too late. Politics was exactly what the young man wanted to talk about. To and fro, back and forth went their salvos about trade unions, a new labour law, the abominable corruption of the government, the merits and demerits of the Christian Democrat party, taxation. The young man's hands made fists and flicks and signs; the other man nervously folded and unfolded his newspaper. 'When you've quite finished . . .' he huffed. Outside in the corridor the Albanian, precariously perched on a fold-down seat, was trying to sleep. Trapped in the crossfire, an elderly man frowned over his *Corriere della Sera* until the noise and heat of the debate became intolerable. Rising to his feet he opened the compartment door and gestured to the Albanian to have his seat.

When I joined him outside in the corridor his rueful smile of complicity made me laugh. He must have read the title of the book on my lap because he addressed me in perfect English: 'I'm afraid you won't get much reading done in there.'

A mathematician, he had spent two years at an institute near

Oxford. Retired now, he occupied himself with mastering the gamba-viol, 'a very popular instrument in Shakespeare's England,' he said, sketching a widened, six-stringed viola in my notebook. Reminded of Gerbert of Aurillac and Brother Hermann at Reichenau, I remarked that the combination of mathematics and music sounded marvellously medieval.

'Yes,' he said. 'They connected all these things. They were trying to hear the music of the spheres, weren't they? Unfortunately I know nothing about astronomy.'

His polite interest in my project and particularly in Emperor Otto's efforts to unite Europe a thousand years ago led us on to consider the latest attempt to unite the continent. In his regret at the 'flattening' of everything, I heard Arni Bergmann's distrust of 'homogenization' again.

'Look, for example, there is a place just outside Ancona where I like to buy my white wine. Just recently they've started making the wine much sweeter, for export to Scandinavia. I don't like it any more; I won't buy it. And there are things I used to buy in Amsterdam – my wife is Dutch – that I just can't find these days, not in Amsterdam, not anywhere!'

It occurred to me that one of the prices of the Poles' admission into the European Union might easily be the disappearance of their butter *Agni Dei*.

'But I hope northern Europe will come and give us some good laws,' he was saying. 'Actually, I'm very happy to see that it's happening already, slowly, slowly. There are certain conventions now, certain expectations – of responsibility, reliability, honesty . . .'

Had there been Italian churchmen in the eleventh century, Peter Damiani perhaps, heaving similar sighs of relief at Emperor Henry III's decisive intervention south of the Alps, applauding his sacking of three popes and his determined efforts to reform and reorganize the chaotically corrupt Roman Church? An older, milder man than Pope Gregory, Peter Damiani always approved of emperors and popes working together for the good of Christendom. The two institutions of papacy and empire, he once wrote, should 'be so closely united by the grace of mutual charity, that it will be possible to find the king in the Roman pontiff and the Roman pontiff in the king'.[xciii] By dying in 1072, at the age of sixty-three, he had spared himself the shocking spectacle of Pope Gregory VII falling out with Henry IV and the events culminating in that desperate snowbound meeting at Canossa, let alone what followed.

Canossa proved no more than a flimsy sticking-plaster on the suppurating sore of Church versus empire. Henry IV went on outraging the pope by nominating his own bishops and Pope Gregory went on protesting until, in the spring of 1080, he felt obliged to re-excommunicate Henry. Back came the old retort: Henry and his bishops demanded that Gregory 'Come down!' off his throne. Gregory ignored the call, but this time the Germans followed through with the old and disgraceful ploy of appointing their own antipope. Support for Pope Gregory waned fast. If Countess Matilda was still loyal enough to make all her lands and riches over to the papacy, most cardinals were beginning to miss the good old days of Henry III and Pope Leo. Pope Gregory's head-to-head confrontation with Henry IV was jeopardizing the entire reform project.

In 1081 the rivalry burst into open war. Henry marched down Italy through Countess Matilda's Tuscany with an army, forcing her to strip churches and monasteries of their treasures to pay for her defence. Henry laid siege to Rome. Holed up in the papal fortress of Castel Sant' Angelo and fearing for his life, by 1084 Gregory was a spent force.

～

A colossal circular fortress, Rome's Castel Sant' Angelo still dominates the eastern approaches to the tomb of St Peter and today's Vatican City.

Leaving behind the old city's bustling narrow streets, its rackety traffic and alternating play of black shadow and sudden blinding light, I had crossed the river by an old stone bridge whose Roman arches were perfectly mirrored in the Tiber's still green water, and reached the great fortress at last. In the cool of a balmy early evening I sat in the shade of its walls a while, watching boys kicking their football hard against its ancient stones, or expertly bouncing it on their knees while waiting for mothers with pushchairs or pairs of old men to saunter by.

A two-minute stroll further on, down the wide avenue of the Via della Conciliazione with its long view of St Peter's vast dome glowing pink in the failing light, brought me to the vast open space of the square. Equally dwarfing but not as decorative as Reims's Gothic cathedral, baroque St Peter's – built with the proceeds from sales of indulgences – looked much more like a palace than any church. Gregory VII was not a builder-pope but, it occurred to me, if he were reincarnated here on the cobbles of St Peter's Square, he would blink and gape before clapping his hands and shouting for joy. A headquarters as magnificent as this was surely proof positive that his successors had taken his vision, run with it, and been righteously ruling the world – temporal and spiritual – for some time. A flight over the rest of Rome might have puzzled him though; he could not fail to notice that St Peter's is now far too monumentally formal and quiet for such a colourfully, casually lived-in city.

Thinking that an edifice like St Peter's really belonged in the capital of an empire as grand but defunct as the Hapsburgs', I was not at first startled when a gigantically amplified German voice suddenly blared an urgent 'Achtung! Achtung!' and went on to say, 'You are invited to holy evening prayers, to live a moment of spiritual communion with the pope and with the whole Church at six forty-five p.m.!' The announcement was repeated over and over in Italian, English, German, French and Polish. With only five minutes to go before the 'moment' began, I settled on one of the sun-warmed steps under the colonnade to the left of the basilica to witness what I later discovered was a nightly event in this jubilee year 2000.

On the step above me I heard two women greeting each other happily. Below me a group of American tourists were laying down their cameras and unlacing their shoes. The square in front of us started filling up with pilgrims and uniformed Church personnel. There was a small army of young ushers wearing baseball caps and royal-blue tabards advertising the jubilee. Groups of nuns in the brown, eau-de-nil, black, sky-blue, white with blue borders, navy-blue and grey habits of their different orders took their places in the rows of seats immediately facing the basilica. Friars – Franciscans in brown, Dominicans in black – mingled with a few policemen and the odd Swiss Guard in his plumed helmet, high white ruff, and striped doublet and hose. The colourful mêlée and the appearance at the top of the steps of four Franciscans with flaming torches in their hands transported me straight back to Canossa's *corteo*.

A familiar Taizé tune set to Latin words was followed by an amplified announcement concerning the availability of plenary indulgences. After a welcome had been extended to two Spanish pilgrims who had cycled the 1,500 kilometres from their home town of Tarragona, the choir began to sing the Latin Creed I had not heard since the sleety Sunday morning I had taken refuge in Rejkyavik's bare Catholic cathedral. I was enjoying that memory when a young man came down a couple of steps towards me and handed me a scrap of paper. The scribble was hard to make out, but it seemed to be a poem.

> Dark is coming on St Peter's Square, pilgrims and colonnades.
> Vespers' hymns are gently fondling a blonde woman's
> Profile on ancient marbles, she's watching
> Silent, in a holy kiss of bells.

'Wait a minute, I'll sign it so that when I get famous you can sell this piece of paper,' he said, scribbling a barely legible signature. 'I'm a poet you see ... And here is a book of my poems. It's the last copy,' he added with a flashing smile, drawing a slim work entitled *Fragments about Women* out of a sports bag. 'Of course, it's strictly forbidden to sell anything here in St Peter's Square, but if I get inspired I sometimes write a poem for a girl – to use as an icebreaker. That's the right word? And if they like it I show them this book. Often, they are happy to buy it . . .'

He must have read my expression because he quickly changed the subject.

'But I'm also a salesman for Herbalife. Have you heard of it? It's a food supplement. I take it myself three times a day. Perhaps, if you are not interested in my poetry, I can show you . . .'

'*Et unam sanctam catholicam ecclesiam apostolicam*' went my favourite part of the Creed as I thanked him for his poem, got up and walked away.

The desperate salesman's eleventh-century counterpart would have been plying a trade equally geared to ensuring his customers a long life, but one which relied on the supernatural rather than the natural for its good effects. Lurking about the holiest sites of the city on the watch for likely customers, with their leather pouches or perhaps sacks stuffed full of yellowing teeth, knuckles, withered foreskins, femurs, scrapings of fingernails, phials of blood and breast-milk, relic-sellers would not have been so easy to shrug off.

In an age when everyone coveted those instant instruments of heavenly assistance and having acquired one or more never moved without them, when saints' relics were employed in fund-raising for new churches, to validate oaths and to enhance the economic viability of a monastery or even a town, the business of these tradesmen must have been at least as good as that of mobile phone or personal computer companies today. Gregorovius once described the city as a giant mouldering cemetery in which rival relic-gatherers squabbled over the parts of decayed corpses. But this nightmare vision needed modifying; Rome must have been an extraordinarily lively place to visit.

Ownership of its crumbling ancient ruins was much prized, especially by monasteries, which charged pilgrims a fee to see them, but often they were used by Rome's most powerful clans – the Tusculi, Crescenti, Cenci and Aldobrandeschi – as strongholds in bloody skirmishes against their rivals. When the Cenci clan built themselves a high tower overlooking the main pilgrim route across the bridge to Castel Sant' Angelo and St Peter's, Pope Gregory VII – a member of the rival Aldobrandeschi clan – ordered it demolished.

Once the malaria-breeding heat of summer was past the city teemed with pilgrims from all over Europe, trailing around its three hundred or so churches intent on tapping the spiritual power of the largest concentration of relics in Western Christendom. The armies of religious tourists were easy prey for the native population of innkeepers, moneylenders, relic-sellers, guides and clergy whose livelihoods depended on them: 'over the very bodies of the holy apostles and martyrs, even on the sacred altars, were swords unsheathed and the offerings of pilgrims, 'ere well laid out of their hands, were snatched away and consumed in drunkenness and forni-cation'.[xciv]

There were periods in the eleventh century when Rome was so infested with criminals that it was boycotted by 'every nation, as each had much rather contribute his money to the churches in his own country, than feed a set of plunderers . . .'[xcv] In 1002 Pope Sylvester had to threaten to excommunicate those who had stolen the bronze peacocks on the gates of the chapel of St Michael the Archangel on the Castel Sant' Angelo. The eleventh century's reforming popes, Gregory VII included, issued decrees threatening anyone who robbed or harmed pilgrims with excommunication.

Inspired by the example of a tenth-century archbishop of Can-terbury who had managed to take in St Peter's and fifteen lesser churches on his first day in Rome and eleven more churches as well as an audience with the pope on the second, I set off to explore the city the next morning. My progress was abysmally slow by comparison. For an hour or so I was imprisoned in St Peter's' vast marbled interior by uniformed ushers who had cordoned off most of the basilica and all the exits to allow free passage to hundreds of processing churchmen in pristine lace surplices. On Tiber Island in the middle of the river I sat and waited patiently in a shady café for someone to come and open a basilica church on the site of the one Otto III had built to house the arm of St Adalbert which he

had acquired on his pilgrimage to Gniezno. Not knowing or caring
very much about an obscure saint from distant central Europe, the
Romans had been more impressed by a relic of the higher-ranking
Apostle Bartholomew and had soon renamed the church after him.
By the early seventeenth century, when the church was rebuilt, a
home-grown Italian saint was taking precedence over even Bartholomew. I was sorry to see that Adalbert was not even mentioned in
the matter-of-fact Latin inscription over St Bartholomew's marble
doorway: 'IF YOU WISH TO KNOW WHICH PRECIOUS BODIES ARE
KEPT IN THE CHURCH, YOU MAY KNOW THAT THEY ARE THOSE
OF PAULINUS AND BARTHOLOMEW .'

At last a van drew up in front of the church and disgorged a
number of busy women who opened the doors and began ferrying
flower arrangements and long bolts of fabric and carpet inside. They
set to work preparing for a wedding by draping the pews in blue
velvet and covering the aisle in blue carpet while I wandered around
and discovered what could only have been a product of the eleventh
century: a well head fashioned from a hollowed out column of
Roman marble. The grooves cut by the ropes were clearly visible
around its rim and four sculpted figures – sombre, big-eyed and as
touchingly solid as those I had admired on the articles in Quedlinburg's treasury – adorned its exterior. There was St Adalbert, long
bishop's crozier in one hand, Bible in the other; and there was
young Otto with a medallion showing a miniature model of the
original church he had built here. The well itself had been a source
of healing water from the time when the ancient Romans wor-
shipped their god of healing, Aesculapius, on the island.

I was especially pleased to find this object. Rome's ancient,
Renaissance baroque and nineteenth-century pasts were everywhere
plain to see but I had almost abandoned hope of finding any trace
of the eleventh century. Archaeologists have not been able to locate
Otto's palace on the Aventine Hill overlooking Tiber Island. The
half-Byzantine, half-Roman monastery where St Adalbert loved to
stay up there has been transformed into a neglected and unremarkable church surrounded by diplomatic residences. The only sign of

Pope Leo IX I could find was a tiny side alley bearing his name. But St Bartholomew's wondrous well head had amply compensated me for all these disappointments.

The great pilgrimage church of Santa Maria Maggiore was crowded with foreign pilgrims, many of them slumped in the rows of orange plastic chairs exhaustedly fanning themselves with leaflets while they waited to make their confessions. A Spanish pilgrim reminded me that confession was one of the conditions for a plenary indulgence, and added that although she herself was not in the process of acquiring one most of her group were. For a time I rested in the cool gloom, studying a larger than life-size white marble sculpture of the newly beatified Pius IX, who ruled the Church for much of the mid nineteenth century and once declared himself frankly opposed to 'progress, liberalism and modern civilisation'.[xcvi] Pio Nono, as he was called, had fretted and fumed while the new Italian state smashed his temporal power by confiscating all but a hundred acres or so of the Papal States, a large swathe of the peninsula since the Middle Ages. The statue betrayed nothing of the man who had had to flee a republican mob besieging his summer palace disguised in an ordinary priest's soutane and a pair of extra-large spectacles. Kneeling, his hands piously joined in prayer over a luxurious-looking stone cushion, Pio Nono was smiling smugly, his blind stone gaze tilted heavenward.

Long before I reached St John Lateran, after catching the wrong bus and toiling through the honking midday traffic, I had had my fill of baroque sculpture and mortadella marble work. The promise of cool was all that could attract me inside. But when I noticed that a priest, looking like a lottery ticket seller in his wooden confessional, was experiencing a temporary fall-off in demand and whiling away his time leafing through a book, I approached him. The sign on his booth said 'English' and he turned out to be an Australian Franciscan. As an icebreaker I explained that I had come to Rome in search of the eleventh century and was finding the superabundance of baroque 'rather confusing'.

'To be honest I can't stand it either. Lovely in a ballroom or a lounge,' he went on, 'but not in a church. In fact this book here is all about the latest directives on how to serve the liturgy. It mentions baroque churches, to say that their altars are useless!'

'Oh?'

'They're not designed to draw the attention to the main business of the Holy Sacrament, you see. You'll find the focus tends to be on a great dark painting of the Virgin Mary with little left to the imagination, if you know what I mean. Excuse me now, will you?' A teenage girl needed to make her confession. A queue formed. I had to wait forty-five minutes before the Franciscan became free again, and then he was shutting up shop.

'Father, I'd like to continue our conversation . . .'

'Actually, I'm a bit washed out,' he said with his back to me, gathering his books together and locking the doors to his booth. He moved slowly and his shoulders were bowed.

The next day, my impression of a Church similarly bowed under the weight of its powerful, worldly past but still doggedly engaged – as it had been since the mid eleventh century – in organizing and legislating for the spiritual, was reinforced.

Months before even embarking on my pilgrimage I had discovered that the nearest I could come to securing an audience with Pope John Paul II was to attend one of the weekly mass gatherings in St Peter's Square. But procuring a ticket to such an occasion was no simple matter. I had had to telephone the British ambassador to the Vatican to request my name be added to a list of United Kingdom citizens desiring tickets for a certain date and receive instructions on how to collect my ticket the evening day before the audience, from an office accessible through a pair of high bronze doors located just to the right of St Peter's.

On the appointed day I stood for twenty minutes in a queue moving slowly up the steps towards the bronze doors where a Swiss Guard in his bizarre uniform waited, halberd at the ready. But once inside the dark and crowded office I discovered that my name was only on the computer list. There was no ticket made out for me. The official suggested it must be with the British embassy. I had half an hour to get to the embassy before it closed, he informed me. Where was the embassy? In the Via Condotti, Rome's busiest shopping street, back on the other side of the river. I caught a taxi, which inched its way slowly through the rush-hour traffic, down the Via della Conciliazione, past the Castel Sant' Angelo, across the bridge and through the old city's narrow cobbled streets towards the Spanish Steps at the far end of the Via Condotti. But in my hurry to find the British ambassador to the Holy See before he left his office, I had forgotten to ask for the exact address. The taxi driver had no idea where the embassy might be. Fortunately, I had the telephone number. Fortunately, the ambassador answered his telephone and sounded suitably concerned about the mix-up. But he did not have my ticket so there was no point in my visiting the embassy. I waited while he contacted a Monsignor Malloy in charge of the ticket office, but he could not discover the cause of the mix-up. Finally he suggested I ring Monsignor Malloy myself, but the monsignor sounded as if he had better things to do than attend to me.

'You should be able to pick up a ticket in the morning before the audience starts,' he drawled.

'I'm afraid that's leaving it a little late. How can I be sure there will be one tomorrow morning?' I countered mistrustfully, imagining another long queue, another official shaking his head. It struck me that a direct ticket to heaven and eternal bliss in the form of a plenary indulgence was easier to come by in Rome than one to a papal mass audience here on earth.

'OK, OK,' the monsignor drawled back at me, with a hint more irritation in his voice. 'If you get back to the bronze doors by eight tonight you should find your ticket waiting for you.'

I did not care for the way he had again qualified his promise with the word 'should' but thanked him anyway.

Back I went on foot, through the crowds taking the evening air and shopping in the glamorous boutiques of the Via Condotti, over the bridge where I watched how traffic fumes blended with the heat haze over the Tiber, past the boys playing football in the shade of the Castel Sant' Angelo, down the wide Via della Conciliazione with its shops full of religious books and paraphernalia – noting that it was strewn with empty plastic water bottles this late in the day – across St Peter's Square where exhausted pilgrims sat around the fountain with their shoes half off, fanning themselves with pieces of paper, past the long line of stinking blue or beige Portaloos under the right-hand colonnade, and back up the steps to the bronze doors. At the top I discovered that the office had already closed. Consumed by anxiety and struggling to catch my breath, I told a Swiss Guard with a sheaf of green cards in his hand, 'Problem . . . My ticket's waiting for me in there . . . All the way to the Via Condotti . . . Talked to the ambassador . . . Monsignor—'

'Someone's been pulling your leg. Never mind,' he said with a smile, handing me one of the cards, a ticket.

I was one of around ten thousand taking my seat in St Peter's Square the next morning for a glimpse of Europe's last absolute ruler, the two hundred and sixty-first pope of Rome. Alone in a crowd of groups, each differentiated by coloured sun hats and base-ball caps, I felt as if I had strayed into a noisy political rally. As the blaring tannoy voice named one group after another – members of a Neapolitan aeronautics association, boy scouts from Reggio nell' Emilia, pilgrims from holy Poznan, the choir of the Music University of Hiroshima, crew members of HMS *York*, miners from Katowice, members of the Association of Widows from Sevilla, employees of Telecom Italia – each group announced its presence by rising to its feet, cheering, wolf-whistling and hooting. The imminent arrival of John Paul II was signalled by excited shouts of '*Il papamobile!*' All but the elderly and infirm clambered onto their chairs for a better view of one of the gigantic video screens positioned around the colonnades. There was the pope in his open-top car, a tiny bowed figure in white clutching a safety rail in front of him, skimming through the crowds on his way to St Peter's. Soon he was up above the crowd, at the top of the steps, safely seated but almost invisible in the shade cast by a dark red canopy.

'In the name of the Father, Son and Holy Ghost,' he began in Latin, his voice faint though amplified, his words slurred.

There followed prayers, readings and songs in a medley of different languages. 'Mama mia!' muttered a bored Italian in the row in front of me as the pope slowly welcomed Croats, Slovenians, Czechs and Slovaks in all their different Slav languages. The group of young Polish pilgrims beside me waved their red and white national flags and cheered when he switched to his native Polish, his voice trembling. A priest announced that the Holy Father extended his blessing to all rosaries brought along to the audience. The sun rose higher and higher in the sky. All around me pilgrims were taking photographs of each other or, with their zoom lenses at full stretch, of the group of robed churchmen under the canopy. Women were solicitously draping the backs of their husbands' necks or bald patches with scarves. Foreheads glistened and reddened, plastic water bottles appeared, fans flapped.

By the time the pope dispensed his final blessing, his voice was cracking and so faint it was barely audible. I was flooded with pity – shedding tears, I found to my surprise – for the old man who longed to be allowed to retire to the Camaldoli hermitage. Was it the self-flagellating example of hermits like Peter Damiani's Brother Dominic, or of tirelessly far-faring predecessors like Leo IX, or of pilgrim missionary monks like St Adalbert that kept him on his gruelling treadmill of foreign trips and mass audiences?

But my tears dried when I noticed that Pope John Paul was not, after all, as exhausted as I had imagined. He spent the next half-hour blessing, first visiting bishops with paternal pats on their shoulders, and then young married couples arrayed in their wedding finery with kisses on the brides' young cheeks. All around me the faithful gazed at the giant video screens, ooh-ing and aah-ing over the beautiful wedding dresses.

The novelty of the first non-Italian pope for over four hundred years has evaporated by this twenty-first year of his pontificate. The extraordinary respect he won for helping to bring down the Iron Curtain and for far-faring about the world tending to his flock remains, but it is increasingly tempered by misgivings among both churchmen and laity. One of the criticisms levelled against him these days is that he has proved an authoritarian defender of the old-style papal monarchy founded by Gregory VII and is a throwback to more recent predecessors like Pio Nono. Some complain that his pontificate has been long on showmanship but short on real content and progress, that when he talks about re-evangelizing Europe he is only talking about Catholicism, that his spirit is far from ecumenical.

His inflexible opposition to contraception, women priests and married priests has won him many critics. There are plenty who believe he has betrayed the hopes raised by the Second Vatican Council of the early 1960s, that joyful promise that the Church would simplify and return to its roots for fresh inspiration and energy. He has brooked no dissent in the Church, however loyally expressed. Dr Hans Küng, an eminent Swiss German Catholic theologian whose loyal criticisms cost him his job as a Church-accredited professor of theology at the Catholic University of Tübingen in 1979, speaks for many, especially north European and American Catholic churchmen and laity, when he sums up John Paul II's contribution to the Church in the following withering words: 'Despite countless speeches and expensive "pilgrimages" (with debts running into millions for some local churches), hardly any progress worth taking seriously has been made in the Catholic Church or the ecumenical world.'[xcvii]

What Dr Küng goes on to say tallies with what Father Waldemar in Gniezno had told me about ignoring the pope's teachings on contraception and homosexuality. Küng notes that what is happening at ground level in the Church bears less and less relation to what is being decreed and preached from the top. It is as if the pope and his *Curia* were high on the battlements of the old fortress Church busily extending and reinforcing its towers while far below foundations were being quietly dismantled and rebuilt to a simpler, low-rise open-plan design by a devoted lower clergy and laity who know that Christ did not envisage a fortress garrisoned by a 3,000-strong bureaucracy and an absolute ruler. Those first German popes of the eleventh century had diligently and sincerely set about purging and reorganizing the Church, but their successors – starting with Gregory VII – had proceeded to lay the foundations of a structure that was not so much Christ's Church as the West's first superpower.

Sitting there in that broiling heat, at that oddly dated-seeming event, I began to imagine John Paul II as possibly the last in a long line of popes reaching all the way back through the second millennium, popes who had extended and defended the fortress Church on the foundations the eleventh-century reformers had laid. I guessed that his twenty-first-century successors might want to make changes as least as radical as those set in motion a thousand years ago.

Although Pope John Paul may not be fully aware of what is going on at the foundations of his fortress, his distant predecessor Gregory VII – caught up in a crisis that was very largely of his own making – cannot have failed to notice that even the cardinals were abandoning his cause by the early 1080s. In 1083 Henry's besieging troops destroyed a section of the walls of the old Leonine city* and were brought at last to St Peter's. Nervous about breaking down the doors of so sacrosanct a shrine, they smashed a window instead. Young Godfrey of Bouillon, the Lorrainer who would lead the assault on Jerusalem and be crowned Defender of the Holy Sepulchre in 1099, was the first to enter. Abbot Hugh hurried across the Alps from Cluny to try and mediate a peace between pope and emperor. Making straight for the Castel Sant' Angelo where the pope was hiding he delayed calling on his godson Henry and venerating the tombs of the holy Apostles Peter and Paul. When criticized for these omissions, Hugh replied that the Apostles and his godson would forgive him quicker than Pope Gregory for not visiting them first. Henry did forgive him, but the peace mission failed and the siege continued. In the spring of 1084 Pope Gregory, holed up in

* Wall erected by the ninth-century Pope Leo I around St Peter's, defended by Castel Sant' Angelo.

his castle, received the bitter tidings that Henry had had himself crowned by his antipope, Clement III.

I was surprised to see that the ugly but important dual car-riageway snaking around the southern edge of the Vatican City had been named after Gregory VII. The Romans have little reason to celebrate the pope whose clumsy politics invited not only Henry IV's invasion but the first wholesale sacking the city had experienced since the visitations of the Goths, Visigoths and Vandals in the fifth and sixth centuries. Gregory's only allies by the 1080s, the Normans of southern Italy who had once tried the patience of Pope Leo IX, were responsible for this final catastrophe.

In the spring of 1084 their leader Robert Guiscard belatedly answered Gregory's cry for help and marched north with an army to rescue him. News of the impending arrival of Christendom's most fearsome warlord sowed panic in the German camp. The freshly crowned Emperor Henry and his antipope fled Rome, leaving behind a garrison of soldiers to mark their intention to return. The Normans arrived and set fire to the heart of the old city before liberating Pope Gregory from his fortress. The Romans rose in protest at this pointless vandalism, but one of Robert Guiscard's sons appeared with reinforcements and the Norman reprisals were terrible. Nuns were raped, monks murdered and Roman aristocrats taken as slaves south to the Norman heartland of Calabria. Churches, palaces and towers were all destroyed. In a matter of days the city was reduced to a heap of smoking ruins. An Italian historian of Rome has cautiously noted, 'In all honesty we cannot directly blame Gregory for the Normans' destruction of the city. Nevertheless the tragic event was to some extent the product of eight years of radical and extremist papal policy.'[xcviii]

~

Those Normans had fared very far indeed since around the year 1000 when a small group of them, sailing home to northern France after a pilgrimage to Jerusalem, had called in at the shrine of

St Michael on the south-east coast of the Italian peninsula, been offered work as mercenary *milites* by a local noble, and decided to stay where 'the soil was fertile and the people were by nature listless . . .'[xcix]

Half a century before the Normans gained a rich new English *Lebensraum* for their growing population, southern Italy began taking the overflow. Freelancing Norman fighters, especially ones trained in Normandy which was the military superpower of the time, were assured a good living in this beautiful but unquiet land where East and West Christendom as well as Islam had been overlapping and colliding for centuries. Perpetually warring populations of Byzantine Greeks, originally Germanic Lombards who were loyal to the Roman popes and Muslim Saracens guaranteed that the Norman adventurers were never short of work. At first they were temporary economic migrants but because land was their preferred form of payment they soon constituted a fourth political force in the region.

By the late 1030s the three eldest sons of an impoverished Norman landowner named Tancred of Hauteville had established the Norman presence in Italy. But it was Robert Guiscard, Tancred's eldest son by his second wife, who transformed that presence into a power more feared and effective even than its counterpart in northern France and England. William the Conqueror himself, asserts one chronicler, 'was accustomed to stimulate and incite his own valour, by the remembrance of Robert Guiscard, saying it was disgraceful to yield in courage to him whom he surpassed in rank'.[c]

At the peak of his powers in the early 1080s when he was over sixty, Guiscard bested the Byzantines in a mightily hard-fought battle on what is now Albania's Adriatic coast. His army was pushing on across today's northern Greece towards its final glittering goal, the conquest of Constantinople itself, when Pope Gregory's cry to be rescued from Castel Sant' Angelo reached him. Small wonder that the news of Guiscard's approach with a gigantic army,* caused Emperor Henry and his Germans to flee Rome ahead of his advance.

---

* 6,000 horse and 30,000 foot soldiers.

Guiscard's subsequent reduction of the city to ruins was only to be expected. He was the *Terror Mundi*. Such wanton wastage was entirely consistent with the scorched-earth tactics he had favoured from the outset of his extraordinary career. Down in southern Italy his *milites* had been leaving ruins and smoking wastelands in their wake for almost half a century.

Back in the 1040s Guiscard's older half-brothers had not welcomed his first appearance on the Italian peninsula. He had had to carve out his own little realm in a spot that was 'airless and rank with malaria',[ci] gather his own following of *milites* and prosper by ruthless brigandage and the sort of rare daredevilry that breeds marvellous myths. One such tale recounts that, intent on seizing a mountain-top village, he had one of his men climb into a coffin which was then borne into the village in doleful procession by some of his fellows. Once safely inside, brought to the monastery and laid in the church, the coffin opened. Out leapt the play-acting warrior, fully armed and combat-ready. The fraudulent funeral became an orgy of looting and slaughter.

It is hard to imagine Thorvald or Otto III abusing the Church like this. Thorvald's Christian conscience was so sensitive that when he recognized the incompatibility of Iceland's code of honour with Christ's teaching he resolved never to return to his homeland. Otto III did not conceive of any wily plan to marry his need to be an emperor with his wish to become a monk by getting himself tonsured while still on the throne. It seems that by the late eleventh century the Roman Church had waxed rigid, bureaucratic and powerful enough to be treated as a temporal power like any other, an obstacle to be got round, tricked or used. Guiscard staged faked funerals in much the same spirit as Henry IV play-acted the penitent at the gates of Canossa, but with far less excuse.

Guiscard belonged to a modern species of hero ideally adapted to benefit from western Europe's new vigour and confidence. His particular strengths would have won him renown and fortune in any century in the second millennium. Clever, boundlessly energetic, exuberantly aggressive and vaultingly ambitious, he was admired as much by his enemies as by his followers. The historian daughter of a Byzantine emperor who spent the best part of his reign fighting to curb Guiscard's ambitions noted the Norman warlord's 'overbearing character', 'thoroughly villainous mind' and matchless skill at justifying his nefarious activities by recourse to 'incontrovertible argument'.[cii] In today's terms, Guiscard combined the cruelty and ambition characteristic of Balkan warlords with the equally ruthless sort of intellectual dexterity found in top American lawyers. Anna Comnena has also left us the best physical description of this captivating colossus.

> He was a man of immense stature, surpassing even the biggest men; he had a ruddy complexion, fair hair, broad shoulders, eyes that all but shot out sparks of fire. In a well-built man one looks for breadth here and slimness there; in him all was admirably well-proportioned and elegant. Thus from head to foot the man was graceful . . .[ciii]

Guiscard's willingness to misuse the Church, tales of his arrant knavery and the stream of pitiful refugees pouring into Rome with their terrible tales of Norman cruelty were what had finally prompted Pope Leo IX to turn soldier again and lead his ragtag army down south. Guiscard, by 1053 the acknowledged leader of the Italian Normans, fought Leo at the ensuing battle of [Civitate]. Three times he was thrown from his horse, three times he remounted. Thanks to the way he sent heads 'spinning with a blow of his sword'[civ] and the manner in which his Calabrian *milites* routed the papal forces, the Normans scored a stunning victory. At the last minute they had been spared the impossible challenge of facing the combined forces of Christendom because the Byzantine emperor had not sent an army to support the pope. Emperor Constantine hated the Normans, but his powerful patriarch Michael Kerollarios mistrusted the intentions of the reforming papacy more. Guiscard therefore had much to be grateful for and was lenient with Pope Leo. Treating him as an honoured guest, 'furnishing him continually with bread and wine and all that he might need',[cv] he took him back to Benevento. There Leo languished for the last nine months of his life, a pope in nothing but name. While Cardinal Humbert and his friends busied themselves in Constantinople wrecking the unity of the Christian Church, Leo tried to learn Greek so as to be able to win the Byzantines' help with ridding the world of the Norman menace. In a letter to the Byzantine emperor he wrote that he was still looking forward to the day when 'this enemy people will be expelled from the Church of Christ and Christianity will be avenged'.[cvi]

The mortal danger posed by the predatory energy of the south Italian Normans was perhaps the only matter East and West Christendom could agree upon by the middle of the eleventh century. But even this small degree of unanimity would not endure. To the dismayed disgust of the Byzantines, the Roman Church suddenly executed an about-turn and concluded an alliance with those same Normans. In 1059, by the solemn Treaty of Melfi Robert Guiscard gained the grand and solid-sounding title of Duke of Apulia and Calabria – two large regions which he had seized from the Byzantines – and the promise of dominion over the former Byzantine territory of Sicily if he could wrest it away from the Saracens. In return he promised to help the Roman Church 'preserve and acquire the revenues and domains of St Peter'.[cvii] He also guaranteed – again, by force of arms if necessary – the successful implementation of the reforming papacy's most recent innovation: papal election by cardinals instead of German Holy Roman emperors. The Roman Church had won itself an army, but there was no question of emulating the old harmonious bond between pope and emperor that had existed in the times of Otto II and Gerbert, and Henry III and Leo IX. Guiscard's first care was never the creation of the city of God on earth; his alliance with the papacy came low down on a list of priorities that began with his breathtakingly bold ambition to conquer Constantinople. Like his distant Scandinavian forebears, he was dazzled by the idea of Mikligarthr's fabulous riches.

The person responsible for brokering the volte-face Treaty of

Melfi was Desiderius. A former hermit, he was the illustrious abbot of the famous southern Italian monastery of Monte Cassino, founded by St Benedict in the sixth century. In that wild region where so many peoples and religions fought for survival Monte Cassino had long ago mastered the art of realpolitik, but befriending a Norman robber baron – in our terms perhaps, a terrorist leader – was a breathtakingly bold step and it certainly exacerbated the widening rift between Rome and Byzantium.

Abbot Desiderius was risking Monte Cassino's privileged position as a vital point of contact between East and West Christendom. Way back before the turn of the second millennium two of Otto III's favourite spiritual fathers, the great practitioners of Byzantine spirituality Nilus and Adalbert, had met and delighted in each other at Monte Cassino. The appearance of Nilus at the monastery had been celebrated like a holy feast day; the Monte Cassino monks had marvelled at his 'spiritual bliss' and he at their 'discipline and well-ordered pattern of existence'.[cviii] A handful of Monte Cassino Benedictines had been so inspired by Nilus' example they departed to Jerusalem and Mount Athos to immerse themselves in Byzantine spirituality. Otto III made a pilgrimage to Monte Cassino after his coronation as Holy Roman emperor in 999, and that other connoisseur of Eastern spirituality, Peter Damiani, often visited the place. True to his Cluny form, Peter Damiani voiced his concern that Monte Cassino's rule – especially with regard to fasting and self-flagellation – was too lax.

Abbot Desiderius' strategy was to cultivate anyone and anything conducive to the enrichment and prestige of Monte Cassino. His fortuitous discovery of the relics of St Benedict and his sister St Scholastica at Monte Cassino in about 1068 inspired him to build a glittering new church embellished with the handiwork of Byzantine craftsmen. Its consecration in 1071 merited eight days of festivities. All the great, good and not so good of the day attended, except for Robert Guiscard and Peter Damiani. The first was away conquering Sicily, the second was ill.

Henry IV's *paupera et peregrina* mother Agnes spent six months at Monte Cassino in 1072. Her sumptuous gifts included 'a chasuble of white silk completely interwoven on all sides with gold',[cix] a vestment embroidered with elephants and two silver candelabra weighing twelve pounds. When Henry IV himself once mooted a visit, Desiderius hastened down to Amalfi on the coast to purchase twenty Constantinople silks of the richest, triple-dyed variety to offer him as presents. From the pious Countess Matilda Desiderius won a useful guarantee that his monks would not have to pay tolls when travelling through her dominions. While Pope Gregory was suffering Henry IV's siege of Rome in 1083, Abbot Desiderius and Abbot Hugh of Cluny were cementing a fond union between the two greatest and wealthiest Western Christian monasteries of the day. The sight of Abbot Desiderius' new church inspired Abbot Hugh with ideas for the even larger one he would start building at Cluny five years later.

But Abbot Desiderius' championing of the Norman cause was surprising because he had as much reason to loathe those northern interlopers as Pope Leo. His own father, a Lombard noble, had been killed by a Norman and they had even attacked Monte Cassino. But the abbot had recognized what the pope in Rome was much slower to understand: that the Normans were the dominant power in south Italy, that the Byzantines were fast losing their territories on the peninsula and that the reforming Church needed an ally and protector because the Holy Roman Empire could no longer be relied on to fulfil that role. After the nimbly negotiated 1059 Treaty of Melfi, all communications between the papacy and its new allies were mediated by Monte Cassino. Guiscard, the terrorist turned shield of the Roman Church, might never have gained his grand title and recognition of his conquests without Abbot Desiderius' support. Among many other rich gifts the monastery received from its new Norman friends was an oven so large and handsome that many mistook it for a chapel.

Pope Gregory's relations with his Norman allies, whom he reviled as 'worse than Jews or pagans',[cx] were predictably stormy during the 1070s. He and Guiscard got off to an ominous start when

Gregory overreacted to a wild rumour that Guiscard had died by sending a condolence letter to his wife. Guiscard did not take offence but nothing Desiderius said could dissuade Gregory from punishing the wily Norman's repeated and shameless encroachments on 'St Peter's domains'. Three times Gregory excommunicated Guiscard and it was not until the year before Henry IV marched on Rome that he realized with alarm how badly he needed his pesky Norman ally. As usual, it was Abbot Desiderius who facilitated the rapprochement. The Byzantines' deepening disgust at the warrior 'Norman pope' of the Western Church was well-expressed by Anna Comnena: 'the abominable pope (when I think of his inhuman act [the alliance with Guiscard] there is no other word I could possibly apply to him), the abominable pope with his spiritual grace and evangelic peace, this despot, marched to make war on his own kindred [fellow Roman Catholic Henry IV] with might and main – the man of peace, too, and disciple of the Man of Peace!'[cxi]

Monte Cassino's reward for the eleventh-hour reconciliation between Pope Gregory and Guiscard was no fewer than nine monasteries and churches plus some valuable warehouse facilities on the Amalfi coast.

My slow and almost empty train south from Rome seemed to be following the old Via Latina. After chugging slowly through the pretty green Alban hills to the south of Rome it had meandered on along a river, weaving to left and right of a noisy new motorway linking the capital to Naples and Salerno. Almost three hours later we were in a wide valley and within sight of a large town. There at last, on the left-hand side but so high up I had to crane my neck to see it, was the vertically steep mountain crowned with its vast white monastery.

Far below, an empty tarmac platform was sliding into view. 'Cassino,' said a faint voice over the crackling tannoy.

~

On a patch of well tended grass in the middle of its main square was Cassino's monument: a rusted World War Two tank treading a pile of artfully arranged stones under its tracks. In a nearby bookshop window was a slim work entitled *Cassino 1944 (Before, during and after)*. While waiting to catch the bus up the winding mountain road to the monastery and the eleventh century, I would read this book and quickly inform myself about the history of the town and its great monastery in the middle of the twentieth century.

The bookseller, a tiny elderly man with an enthusiastic manner but little business sense, had stocked his shelves with Italian translations of D. H. Lawrence, Keats and Longfellow. He turned out to be the publisher of the work I wanted and was easily drawn into conversation about its contents. During the hour I spent in his shop, customers requiring fashion magazines, computer manuals and school textbooks were curtly dealt with and sent away empty-handed. Signor Lamberti wanted to talk to me about the war.

He told me that when the Allies invaded southern Italy in the autumn of 1943, they had advanced up the west side of the peninsula, over the only terrain suited to tanks. The Germans meanwhile had orders to make a stand here at Cassino. Although the German general, a devout Oxford-educated Catholic who ended his days as headmaster of a school near Reichenau on the Bodensee, saw very clearly that the war was already lost, preparations for a great battle were set in motion. Like a couple of his junior officers, General Frido von Senger und Etterlin also realized that the monastery might become part of the battlefield. Its priceless treasures – the relics of St Benedict and his sister, some 70,000 handwritten parchments which included letters to Abbot Desiderius from Robert Guiscard and papal bulls regarding Monte Cassino dating back to the eleventh century, as well as Renaissance masterpieces by Breughel, Titian and Raphael – were in peril. The Germans therefore decided that this priceless Western Christian heritage should be packed up and evacuated. Desiderius' mid-twentieth-century successor wept as 387 wooden crates, including the two sets of precious relics in their narrow wooden boxes covered with silken cloths, were loaded onto a long convoy of German army trucks for the journey to Rome and safe storage in the Castel Sant' Angelo.

'You see,' said Signor Lamberti, 'there were cultured people among those Nazis.'

'Hermann Goering, of course,' I remarked.

'Actually he stole fifteen of the crates but they were found after the war and returned. Anyway, after this removal of all the treasure, the Germans promised the Vatican that their troops would not occupy the monastery.'

'Oh, so the monastery wasn't damaged in the war?' I said, happy to be able to visit so substantial a relic of the eleventh century as Abbot Desiderius' famed basilica church.

'Wait! Be patient; the story is not finished. The fighting had not started yet. There were four battles here in 1944.'

The Allies reached Cassino in January 1944. The first battle lasted twenty-two days and cost some 14,000 Allied lives but did not dent the Germans' Gustav Line. Allied morale was low and suspicion grew that the Germans had occupied not just the slopes of Monte Cassino but the monastery itself. It stood to reason. How could they resist making use of what was in effect a mighty fortress with commanding views over the valley and all the surrounding countryside? Suspicion hardened into certainty as in the minds of the disheartened and exhausted Allied soldiers the monastery came to symbolize the German enemy. Soon, bombing it from the air was a vital 'military necessity'.

'Oh, no!' I gasped. Steeped in the eleventh century, I had temporarily forgotten that holding high ground is no absolute advantage in the age of the aeroplane.

'Look – look here. In this book it tells you exactly what the Allied planes dropped on Monte Cassino in the second battle. Here it is. Read!' Signor Lamberti was commanding, jabbing at the page with his index finger. I did as I was told.

From a cold, blue sky, between 0925 and 1005 hours, 135 Flying Fortresses dropped 257 tons of 500lb bombs and 59 tons of 100lb incendiaries on and around the abbey... 87 medium bombers (47 Mitchells and 40 Marauders) dropped 126 tons... US II Corps artillery fired 266 rounds from 240mm and 8' howitzers and 4.5' and 155mm guns...[cxii]

At first my mind boggled at the numbers and unfamiliar names and reeled back irrelevantly to Taizé and monks' haircuts. It was hard to imagine a better illustration of where the creeping militarization of the Roman Church at the beginning of the second millennium had led Western Christendom to by the end of it.

The author described the ruins as being as total and irreparable as those left behind by Guiscard in Rome in 1084. Worse still, the entire operation had been just as futile and senselessly destructive. Not a single German soldier but some four hundred Italian refugees sheltering inside the monastery's ten-foot-thick walls had died in the hellish onslaught. During the third battle the Allies razed the town of Cassino. In the fourth the Gustav Line gave way at last.

A year to the day after the raid on 15 March 1945, the foundation stone for a new monastery was laid. Old Cassino, at the foot of the mountain, had to be abandoned and this town which now sprawls across the wide valley built from scratch.

'So there's not much love for the Allies here in Cassino...' I ventured.

'Of course it's long ago now. But people still remember how hungry they were – starving – and how the Americans and the British set up their military kitchens all around, and the smells of their cooking...' said Signor Lamberti, before mentioning that he had met the American who had led the bombing raid on the monastery. 'He came here into my shop not so long ago. He had come back to apologize. He embraced a monk from up there. I have no words for the emotion I felt on that day.'

Signor Lamberti has done his own brave bit to promote turn-the-other-cheek forgiveness. In 1989 he helped to arrange for five hundred British veterans of the battles of Cassino to visit the town. The trip had taken two years to organize and he remembered how the mayor of Cassino, whose father had been killed by a British bomb, had slammed the door in his face when he first mooted the idea.

It was time to go. The bus to take me up Via Serpentina was due in five minutes.

'If it's the eleventh century you're really interested in you should talk to Don Faustino; he's the monk in charge of the archives up there. Even ten years ago I would never have recommended him to speak to but now it's a little easier.'

Thanking Signor Lamberti profusely for his time and advice, I bought the book and made for the door.

'Wait! Take this souvenir,' he said, pressing a metal ashtray decorated with a painted scene of the new monastery into my hands. 'The metal is taken from shells used in the bombing.'

The day had turned swelteringly, muggily hot. As the bus slowly negotiated the five miles of hairpin bends up to the monastery, I gazed down into the broiling plain with its ugly new town and pondered the miserable job of clearing half a million cubic metres of destroyed monastery after the war. The German prisoners of war, Allied soldiers and local Italians engaged in that work cannot have felt anything like as spurred by faith as the people who had helped Abbot Desiderius build his magnificent new basilica church. Then, there had been staggering quantities of precious building materials and decorations to haul up rather than down the mountainside.

Abbot Desiderius had sent some of his monks on a shopping expedition to Constantinople with thirty-six pounds of gold and instructions to purchase fifty candlesticks, innumerable icons and a silver candelabra 'made in the form of a huge crown, twenty cubits in circumference and weighing about 100 pounds, with twelve projecting turrets and thirty-six lamps hanging from it'.[cxiii] He himself went shopping in Rome. There, by activating all his connections and 'generously and prudently' disbursing 'large sums of money', he was able to invest in 'huge quantities of [ancient] columns, bases, epistyles and marbles of different colours'[cxiv] which he arranged to be shipped down the coast and transported inland to the foot of

Monte Cassino by wagon. From there, a chronicler tells us, 'a large number of citizens by themselves assumed the burden of the first column on their neck and arms'[cxv] and toiled up the mountain.

I was thinking to myself that Peter Damiani had had a point when he once suggested that Abbot Desiderius was a mite too concerned with material wealth, when I felt a tap on my shoulder.

'Monte Cassino? *Polski kladbishe?*'

The only other passenger on the bus was a Russian who had journeyed here all the way from Murmansk inside the Arctic Circle to pay his respects at his father's grave and now wanted to be quite sure that this bus would bring him to his final destination, the Polish war cemetery near the top of the mountain. Clutching a black briefcase in one hand and a wilting bunch of flowers in the other, this far-farer was sweating profusely in his formal pinstriped suit. He exuded anxiety, perhaps because his career in the Soviet navy's Baltic fleet had barred him from ever travelling abroad before. It had taken him five years to discover how his father had died and where he was buried. Now, the prospect of fulfilling his filial duty at last was bringing tears to his eyes.

'But why is he in a Polish cemetery?' I asked.

'He was a Polish Catholic from Lithuania, which was annexed of course by Stalin in 1940,' he began, and then launched into a bizarrely tragic tale about how his father had been one of some 50,000 Poles who, in the misplaced belief that the Allies – if and when they emerged victorious – would make sure that there was a free Poland, left Russia to go and fight the Germans in western Europe. They had embarked on a long and arduous trek down through Soviet Central Asia to Iran, and then on west to Iraq and British-controlled Palestine. The British had loaded this army onto ships bound for Italy. Reaching Cassino in time for the fourth and finally successful attempt to break the Germans' Gustav Line, some of them had had the honour of raising their red and white Polish flags among the ruins of the monastery.

'My father died of gangrene, but look at this,' said Anton Alexandrovich, snapping open his briefcase to produce a dark photocopy of a press cutting. It showed a defence attaché from the British embassy in Moscow handing him the medals owing to his father.

He was touchingly proud. I congratulated him before asking how he was enjoying his first trip abroad, and what he thought of Italy.

'Oh, this is obviously a very good country. As soon as I arrived in Rome this morning I saw that everything was clean and that everyone had cars and that the roads were beautiful. I was so shocked. I asked myself "What have they done to *my* country?" '

His answer made me as sad as his story of those poor Polish soldiers whose hopes Winston Churchill had betrayed with an agreement placing post-war Poland in the new Soviet sphere of influence.

'My country had diamonds, uranium, gold! Everything, everything! Every mayor of every town in Russia should be forced to come here and see this town. The mayor here must be a good, honest man who cares for the people and wants his town to be beautiful.'

Cassino's chipped concrete buildings and no more than adequate amenities were eliciting the same sort of praise from Anton Alexandrovich as the unparalleled splendours of Constantinople had from eleventh-century European visitors.

I had a sudden inkling of the great burden of grief borne by so many of eastern Europe's elderly. The morose stoicism of *Herr Doktor* Leike back in Quedlinburg and the despair of Waldemar's mother in Gniezno seemed all of a piece with Anton Alexandrovich's heartbroken bewilderment. 'It's so hot here!' he said, opening his briefcase and producing a crumpled handkerchief. He set to, mopping away his sweat, and tears.

We parted company at the top of the mountain but not before he had snapped open his briefcase once more to produce a handful of Russian sweets in shiny coloured wrappers. These he pressed on me, along with a pen inscribed with the word 'Fatherland', some Soviet-era tin badges and a bar of Russian chocolate with a polar bear on its wrapper. Two coach-park attendants, cheerful Italian lads in baseball caps who prided themselves on having picked up a smattering of every European language but spoke no Russian, were also recipients of his kingly largesse. When they tried to refuse the sweets, Alexander Alexandrovich laughed and scattered them, like glittering jewels, all over the tarmac. Then he strode off in the direction indicated by a signpost to the Polish war cemetery on its *Monte Calvario*.

Passing a coach from Hamburg disgorging elderly German passengers dressed in light summer casuals and armed with cameras, I reached the gates of the reconstructed monastery. At the lodge just inside I asked to talk to Don Faustino, as Signor Lamberti had recommended. The archivist monk was not immediately available but might be if I returned in an hour. Wandering about the pristine white complex, I passed through a doorway and across a cloister cum courtyard in which a neo-classical marble statue of a mighty ROBERTO GVISCARDO occupied one of the niches reserved for the monastery's greatest patrons.

A long, wide flight of steps brought me to the 1066 bronze doors of the main church. Its interior was as far removed from the early Romanesque I loved as any of the palace churches I had seen in Rome. It was as oppressively baroque as any Father Waldemar had shown me. Unmoved by the painstakingly recreated splendour, I stood in the gloom and imagined instead the marvellous handiwork of the Byzantine craftsmen Abbot Desiderius had employed to work on his new church. In Desiderius' church the steps leading up to one altar had been 'inlaid with precious marbles of harmonious diversity'. Mosaics were so cunningly crafted that the figures looked alive. On the floor, marble 'of every colour bloomed in wonderful variety'.[cxvi]

Abbot Desiderius was quite as interested in recapturing the glory days of the old Roman Empire as Otto III and Gerbert had been. Keenly aware of all that western Europe had lost during what historians used to call the Dark Ages, he knew that Byzantium had preserved it all and 'in his wisdom decided that a great number of young monks should be thoroughly trained in these arts lest this knowledge should again be lost in Italy'.[cxvii]

An ominous low rumble followed by a deafening crash of thunder directly over the monastery jolted me back into the present and then immediately back again half a century to the Allies' savage bombing raid. More rolls of thunder and forked lightning split the iron-grey sky. When the rain poured down, cold and hard, the elderly German tourists cowered under the new Romanesque arches. From the courtyard balcony no town or valley was visible, only low grey cloud drifting like battle smoke.

I went in search of the monastery's museum. Its exhibits were poorly lit and lamentably labelled but there was one happy surprise. The Allies' bombing had destroyed the eighteenth-century church floor but revealed patches of Abbot Desiderius' gorgeously marbled one, which everyone had supposed long lost.

Back at the lodge I was able to speak to Don Faustino on the telephone and explain my business with him. Crossing the puddled courtyard again, I mounted the long flight of steps, found the right entrance and rang a bell. The door opened to reveal a youngish monk with shockingly sad green eyes and a pile of books under one arm. I had expected an elderly Don Faustino, one whose bitter memories of 1944 could account for the chilliness Signor Lamberti had warned me about. This young man had not been born in time to harbour grudges but his welcome was markedly cool. Ushering me into a high-ceilinged gloomy room, he sat down opposite me across a wide table and began talking about the books. One of them, a thick volume, was a collection of talks about eleventh-century Monte Cassino delivered at a conference here in 1987. On its cover was a charming eleventh-century illustration showing Abbot Desiderius, handsomely robed in blue and green with his tonsured head meekly bowed, receiving a rolled parchment from a Lombard prince seated on a throne and just as handsomely attired in a blue cloak and leggings with knee-high red boots.

'You may have this book and also these ones,' said Don Faustino. 'You will find them all very useful for your project.'

I thanked him, uncomfortably aware that he was already preparing to usher me straight back towards the door and out into the
rain again.

'Don Faustino, could you please explain the meaning of a plenary
indulgence?' I asked him quickly.

He shifted in his chair, frowned and began to fumble his way
through a confused account of purgatory and earthly penitence.

'But the most important thing about a plenary indulgence is
that one must be in the right mood to receive it. One is not always
in the right mood, is one?' he said with a wan smile that did not
reach his sad eyes, and rose from his chair.

He had a point. I was obviously not 'in the right mood' to
acquire a plenary indulgence, but I could not help regretting that
he was not 'in the right mood' to show me the correspondence
between Desiderius and Guiscard, or to hazard an opinion as to
whether Abbot Desiderius' pro-Norman policy had been cynical
and self- rather than Church-serving. Clearly, he did not want to
consider the extent to which Desiderius' diplomacy had contributed
to the deterioration of relations between Rome and Constantinople.
There would be no relaxed chat about Guiscard's son, the ferocious
First Crusader, Bohemond. I was back out in the rain, down the
mountain and another hundred kilometres or so south in Salerno –
the Lombards' then the Normans' capital* – before I remembered
that I had also meant to ask Don Faustino if the grave of Guiscard's
doughty Lombard wife Sichelgaita had survived the Allies' bombing.

~

'SICHELGAITA REGNA!' shouted some large red graffiti on the wall
of a shoe shop in Salerno's town centre where the locals were performing their *passegiata* in the cooling evening.

As I strolled down the ancient port-city's crowded main shopping street and on into the narrow dark streets of its old quarter in

---

* Robert Guiscard besieged and captured Salerno in 1076.

search of the *duomo* Robert Guiscard had built at Pope Gregory's command to house some relics of St Matthew, it struck me that the last time I had been favoured with such a startlingly direct line back to the eleventh century had been in Gniezno. I had had the politically engaged Archbishop Muszynski to thank for that one. There was no knowing who in Salerno today loved Guiscard's famously warlike wife enough to immortalize her in this fashion. Perhaps a fledgeling Lombard independence movement on the lines of the Northern League had claimed her as its figurehead. Just possibly but more ominously, the graffiti was a protest against the flood of Albanian migrants who, despairing of their broken homeland, have flooded into southern Italy in search of a living during the past decade. Sichelgaita's finest hour had come in 1081 when, on a battlefield on the other side of the Adriatic Sea in what is now Albania, she had rallied her husband's *milites* for a final victorious attack against the Byzantine emperor's forces who included the ancestors of modern Albanians.

The *duomo* Guiscard had built to much the same simple basilica plan as Abbot Desiderius' using many of the same craftsmen had a large enclosed courtyard. At last there was no longer any need to imagine the eleventh century because there it was. The rounded forms of the Romanesque arches providing a shady cloister were decoratively picked out in different-coloured marbles. Each arch was supported by marble pillars, some of them fluted, some grey, some white, some red, suggesting that Guiscard or his minions must have been on a shopping expedition to Rome like Abbot Desiderius. Above the arched cloister was a loggia with more arched openings and more intricately worked marble. The proportions of the place were elegant, not absurdly dwarfing in the manner of a Gothic cathedral or St Peter's in Rome. Dim gold lighting and a splashing fountain only accentuated its charms, as did a crowd of the faithful clustered chatting around the church door.

After Robert Guiscard had rescued Pope Gregory and allowed his army to run amok in Rome, he and the pope had travelled to Monte Cassino where Gregory rested a while and hoped to stay until the time was right to re-enter Rome. But Guiscard must have realized that the pope's return to Rome was out of the question. Gregory's enemies were legion. Not only Henry IV but some of his cardinals, most of the northern Italian bishops and huge numbers of clergy still opposed to celibacy were ranged against him. Guiscard wanted Gregory safe in his capital and succeeded in gaining the broken pontiff's helpless agreement to the onward journey to Salerno by inviting him to consecrate this delightful *duomo*. That happy occasion coincided with the arrival of some good news for Gregory: far away to the north, the armies of the ever faithful Countess Matilda had scored a marvellous victory over Henry IV.

According to a slim hagiography of Pope Gregory which I picked up at a book stall just inside the entrance of the *duomo*, Salerno in 1085 was 'surrounded by impregnable walls, crowned with green hills, rich in sumptuous buildings'.[cxviii] In this attractive place where the archbishop was a close friend of Abbot Desiderius and a keen reformer, Pope Gregory convened a poorly attended council and issued a final blistering encyclical against all his enemies, inside and outside the Church. He noted – never for a moment blaming himself – that the Church had 'sunk so low, as to become an object of mockery, not just for the Devil, but for Jews, Saracens and pagans'.[cxix]

In May 1085, less than a year after consecrating Guiscard's new *duomo*, Pope Gregory was on his deathbed, stubbornly explaining to his friends that the only reason why he had to die an exile from his beloved Rome was because he had 'loved righteousness and hated iniquity'.[cxx] An attendant bishop's reply must have been marvellously soothing: 'No, you cannot die in exile. You are the Vicar of Christ who gave you all the peoples, and the borders of your realm are the confines of the world!'[cxxi] Just before he died Pope Gregory absolved all those he had excommunicated with two exceptions, Henry IV and his antipope.

He was buried with honour in the south-east apse of the new church. According to a Burgundian bishop who happened to have stopped off in Salerno on his way home from a pilgrimage to

Jerusalem, some robbers were prevented from stealing the corpse's precious vestments when the lamps in the crypt were miraculously extinguished. Pope Gregory VII was not canonized until the height of the Counter-Reformation five hundred years later. By 1606 his brand of unbending fanaticism appealed to a Roman Church busy retrenching after its battering by the Protestants; the most warlike pope the Roman Church has ever known proved the perfect model for those later times. But the Germans' abiding hatred for the pope who had humiliated their emperor at Canossa and fatally weakened the Holy Roman Empire meant that his feast was only celebrated in Italy. When, just over a hundred years later, another authoritarian pope tried to extend its observance to the entire Catholic Church, the move caused an international outcry.

Walking out of the church into the humid night, I wandered the back streets of Salerno's old town a while, enjoying the whiff of salt air from the sea, the sounds of television soap operas and the sight of a large sign announcing that the EU was subsidizing the conversion of an old monastery into a 'centre of touristic welcome'. The open doors and bright lights of a small art exhibition drew me inside. The works, as far as I could tell, were Dali-esque commentaries on the death of the Catholic religion – meticulously painted heaps of chalices, crucifixes and monstrances, and empty vestments soaring across a night sky being barked at by mangy dogs.

'Is this an anti-clerical exhibition?' I enquired.

'No.' replied the startled curator.

'But where's the person inside this vestment, for example?' I persisted, surprising myself with my strong reaction to this facile mockery of the Roman Church.

'The person inside the vestment dies, the objects live on,' said the curator.

'The spirit is more important than the objects though,' I rejoined huffily, before setting off into the night again in search of my hotel.

Guiscard had been back at work, campaigning against the Byzantines in the Ionian islands just off the coast of modern Albania, when the news of Pope Gregory's death reached him. The chronicler insists that 'the death of his own father could not have made him weep more, nor the view of his son and his wife in their last moments'.[cxxii] Before the year was out, the wily old *Terror Mundi* himself would be dead.

Aged sixty-eight in the summer of 1085, he was trying to retake Corfu when he fell mortally ill of a fever at Cape Ather on the neighbouring island of Cephallonia, at a place later named Fiskardo in his honour. Guiscard knew his end was near when an elderly monk of the island of whom he begged a glass of cold water told him about a cool spring in the long-ruined town of Jerusalem on the neighbouring island of Ithaca. The monk's words struck terror into the old warrior's failing heart. Soothsayers had once predicted: 'As far as Ather you will bring all countries under your sway, but from there you shall depart for Jerusalem and pay your debt to nature.'[cxxiii]

He would never conquer Constantinople and the Byzantines had no more to fear from the Italian Normans, for a while at least. A distraught Sichelgaita hastened to his deathbed and threw herself on him 'tearing at his clothes and weeping . . . scratching her cheeks with her nails and tugging out handfuls of her hair'.[cxxiv] When he died she set about arranging for his body to be transported back to Italy for burial alongside those of his half-brothers and first wife in the monastery church of Venosa. Guiscard was duly packed in salt, laid in a coffin and loaded aboard a ship, which foundered in a savage storm. The coffin was washed overboard but subsequently retrieved, only a little damaged.

Once a favourite stopping place on the busy pilgrims' route from Rome to the Adriatic ports of Bari and Brindisi for ships to Palestine, Venosa, where those first Italian Normans were buried, is on the way to nowhere now, far from any large town or motorway.

The midday local bus there from Melfi, the Italian Normans' almost equally forgotten first capital, was crowded with teenagers on their way home for lunch. Chattering into their mobile phones, they laughed and yelped and fell off each other's laps as the bus careered along narrow country roads, through hilly but bosky countryside which looked ideally suited to the sort of guerrilla warfare Guiscard, his half-brothers and his sons had waged.

Gaining admittance to the low monastery church of Santissima Trinità on the very edge of the eerily quiet little town proved unexpectedly difficult. I asked a woman in the ticket office attached to Venosa's main archaeological attraction, some ancient Roman ruins, if she could let me in. No, she could not, but she directed me some way back down the dusty road to a hospital run by some monks. They would know who had the key, she said. At the hospital a kindly doctor informed me that I would have to wait three hours to see the church, but then asked a friend of his to give me a lift to the *municipio*. This turned out to be a grand nineteenth-century town hall flying the EU and Italian flags. A young security guard asked me my business before leading me through an arch into a surprisingly squalid rear courtyard littered with a rusting pram, some disembowelled car seats, old cans, plastic bags and broken toys. In one corner was a derelict stone dwelling that might once have been a stable. Picking our way towards it through the rubbish, past a skinny cat lunching off scraps of macaroni and peas, we arrived at its filthily curtained entrance. A man in a soiled vest appeared and shouted for his wife. She had the key to the church but would not hear of escorting me there until she had had her lunch. Fortunately for me, their daughter, a lively young woman wearing high heels, grabbed the key from her mother's hand and bade me follow her.

'Are you a student?' she began, and continued without waiting for an answer, 'There was a student here for about a month who spent every day studying every stone of Santissima Trinità. People come from all over the world, you know. Only the other day millions and millions of Chinese tourists arrived in a terrible rainstorm. Some of us locals don't appreciate what we've got in this church or even realize that the place is open again after twenty years.'

The British travel writer Norman Douglas, who visited Venosa and its monastery a century ago, had also noted the locals' 'Mephis-tophelian spirit of modern indifference' and lamented the church's falling into ruins when a paltry ten pounds would have gone far 'towards arresting its fall'.[cxxv] It was interesting to learn that a good deal more than ten pounds had been spent on its preservation in the past five years. The locals might not appreciate their Norman treasure any more than they had a century ago but they – or at least someone at the *municipio* – had learned to appreciate its potential as a tourist attraction.

The interior of the church, all that remains of the monastery Guiscard had re-staffed with eighty monks from the monastery of St Evroul in Normandy in 1063, was spacious and the plain grey marble tomb of the de Hauteville brothers stood on the right-hand side, adorned with fragments of frescoes that had no bearing on the eleventh century. There was no trace of the original inscription which had begun, 'HIC TERROR MUNDI GUISCARDUS . . .' Beside the tomb stood a black plastic stand designed to hold a page of explanatory notes, but it was empty. The same sort of stand had been placed beside the tomb of Robert Guiscard's first wife and mother of his almost equally famous eldest son, Bohemond. A Latin inscription on the tomb simply informed all visitors, 'SI GEMISTUM QUAERES HUNC CANUSINIS HABET' – 'If you are looking for my son here, Canosa has him.'*

My guide apologized for the lack of notes. 'Everything was supposed to be ready in time for this jubilee year 2000,' she said, 'but I imagine we'll be waiting another thousand years for those notes to arrive!'

I laughed but recalled how those first Normans to arrive in Italy had judged the land fertile but the people 'by nature listless'. My guide was more interested in the recent theft of a baroque altar painting than in any Italian Norman and I was feeling almost as disappointed as I had been by Reichenau. Italian Normans were as utterly absent from this place as blue-blooded German monks had been from that one. Embarrassed to have dragged the young woman away from her lunch for such a small return, I made a great

* Canosa is a small town between Venosa and Bari.

show of interest and joy in everything she showed me, which included the relics of a Santa Dominata, 'the mother of four martyrs'. Kept in a small box under the altar, they were visible through a square grating like the entrance to a rabbit hutch.

At last I told her that I had a bus back to Melfi, a train to Bari on the Adriatic coast, and another *corteo* to catch.

~

In 1071 Robert Guiscard's three year-long siege of Bari had ended almost a hundred years of uninterrupted Byzantine rule in southern Italy. Two years after his death, in 1087, the busy port would win itself marvellous renown in Western Christendom and shameful notoriety in the East.

Some sixty Barese merchants, nobles, sailors and churchmen decided that their city's fortunes – sadly flagging since the Norman siege and now badly threatened by the waxing maritime might of Venice – needed swift restoration. This club of concerned citizens reached the conclusion that a simple *furta sacra*, the holy theft of an important saint's relics, would work the economic miracle Bari needed. A big saint's name attraction was just the thing to bring pilgrims, merchants, churchmen and rulers flocking to the city to fill its empty coffers. After all, had not the Apostle St Mark done wonders for Venice since some ninth-century Venetians had stolen his relics from Alexandria? They decided that St Nicholas, a third-century bishop of Myra, patron saint of all kinds of far-farers from pilgrims and sailors to bargees and revered in both halves of the Christian world, could be guaranteed to do the same for Bari. And so, with the backing of Guiscard's son Bohemond, an expedition to Myra on the south-western coast of what is now Turkey, near Antalya, was planned and launched in 1087.

The Barese were in a hurry. Grim tidings had reached them that their Venetian rivals were planning to steal St Nicholas by breaking into his tomb with iron crowbars and the Barese were determined to beat them to it. When they disembarked at Myra, a group of local Eastern Christian monks kindly showed them the church, the tomb of St Nicholas, and the miraculous flow of sacred liquid the relics produced. But something about the merchants' nervily furtive manner – they would have been keeping an eye out for Venetians, of course – must have aroused the monks' suspicions because soon they started protesting that, actually, they were not certain this *was* the real tomb of the saint. At this, the Barese abandoned all pretence of being pious pilgrims and began spinning a tall but impressive tale.

> Look you . . . we have been sent by the Pope of Rome and by the archbishops and authorities at Rome associated with him and the whole Council. For all of these arrived in our city of Bari with a large host and the diverse armies of the west, enjoining us to accomplish this work, and bring back to the Pope the remains of the saint without fail. Why, even the saint himself, appearing in a vision to the Pope, bade him do this with all haste.[cxxvi]

When this softly-softly approach did not work, nor an offer of payment for the precious booty, the Barese began threatening to murder the monks and destroy the church. The terrified monks gave in and admitted that, as it happened, the year before one of them had experienced a vision of St Nicholas in which he had mentioned that he was ready for a change of scene.

The tomb proved hard to smash open but the heavenly fragrance of the saint's relics was so powerful that the Barese 'seemed to be standing in Paradise'.[cxxvii] Wafting out of the church and over Myra, the glorious scent alerted the town's Greek inhabitants to the imminent loss of their protector. ' "Who are you and from what land have you dared to bring such calamity upon our See?" ' they wailed. The bold Barese kept a tight grip on their booty and shouted back, ' "Realise brothers that we are Christians, and that the saint appeared to us in a vision and bade us disembark here and carry away his venerable remains . . . now his will is to give light to the western world." '[cxviii]

By an extraordinary accretion of myth and nonsense St Nicholas would become Western Christendom's rotund and rosy Father Christmas. By the end of the twelfth century he was the patron saint of little children on account of a tale about his miraculous resuscitation of some children who had been chopped up into little pieces and salted down for use as food by a wicked innkeeper. Another tale, about him secretly providing rich dowries for three poor girls, is the root of his reputation as an invisible gift-giver. In the East his loss was mourned and deeply resented. The Byzantines' hatred for the Italian Normans, who had deprived them of Bari, their last foothold in Italy, sixteen years earlier and then gone on to menace Constantinople in the early 1080s, was reinforced. For them St Nicholas remained the bishop of Myra who later became Russia's patron saint. In the icons of the Greek and Russian Orthodox Churches he is always a tall, gaunt figure with a swarthy complexion, dressed in the dazzling black and white robes of a Byzantine bishop.

The Barese placed St Nicholas' relics in a small wooden chest in the prow of one of their boats but bad weather hampered their progress westward among the Greek islands until the leaders of the expedition concluded that the sailors must be to blame. Any sailor who had dared help himself to a little relic of the saint during the journey was ordered to return it at once and do penance for his sin. The weather improved. Back in Bari the precious booty was received with loud rejoicing; 'the sacred and holy ministers of the archdiocese and the clergy of the other churches, garbed in their holy vestments and singing a heavenly hymn, departed straightway for the harbour to receive the holy remains of the Blessed'.[cxxix] Only one of the thieves – who had undressed St Nicholas' corpse and been violently sick immediately afterwards – suffered enough pangs of conscience to become a monk, at Venosa's Santissima Trinità.

St Nicholas' relics were reverently laid in one of the city's many monastery churches and a guard provided. The latter was a wise precaution because a posse of *milites* commanded by a greedy arch-bishop who wanted the treasure for himself soon attacked the place.

The resulting skirmish left three dead but St Nicholas safely in the hands of the townspeople. A staunch Church reformer, Abbot Elias, was then entrusted with the relics and the job of building them one of the handsomest churches I have ever seen.

Only a sight as enchanting as a flock of starlings swirling around the towers of the Apulian Romanesque basilica of San Nicolo di Bari in the pinky-gold glow of early evening could have distracted me from my enjoyment of a large slab of delicious herb-scented *focàccia* bread I had picked up from a bakery in one of the dark side alleys leading towards the church. As gracefully proportioned as Salerno's *duomo* but built entirely of dazzlingly clean white lime-stone, with its small arched windows and asymmetrical flanking towers the basilica looked more like a fortress than a church. The sturdy stone oxen standing on either side of the main door, each supporting a column on its broad back, were one of many quaint reminders that, before the good Abbot Elias began building his basilica for St Nicholas, a grand palace had occupied this prime site between the sea and Bari's old town. The headquarters of the Byzantine *catapans* who ruled southern Italy from Bari for exactly a century – from 970 until their final eviction by Robert Guiscard in 1071 – the palace must have been a gorgeous sight with its four churches, barracks, offices, throne room and port, all embellished with marble shipped ready-dressed from Constantinople. It had taken Abbot Elias two months to demolish the splendid complex, but he must have been as aware as Abbot Desiderius at Monte Cassino of the superior craftsmanship and artistry of the Byzantines, for he was careful to salvage not just the oxen, but other fragments of sculpture, some Greek-inscribed tablets and perhaps even a tower from the *catapans'* palace.

On my first evening in Bari the courtyard in front of the church was thronged with people and there were clear signs that prep-arations for something out of the ordinary – namely, the annual celebration of St Nicholas' dubious *translatio* from Myra to Bari – were in progress. In front of the main door with its oxen was a lovingly laid semicircular carpet of flower petals coloured like

Neapolitan ice-cream, and on either side of the church strapping young men in T-shirts were rigging up the giant black boxes of sound systems. A crowd of elderly pilgrims, some leaning on sturdy walking sticks and all wearing yellow kerchiefs around the necks, trainers and knapsacks on their backs, sang a hymn to St Nicholas. They clustered about the door of a small shop doing a brisk trade in little bottles of the same deliciously fragrant *manna** St Nicholas' relics had been producing on the occasion of their theft from Myra.

Down in the crowded crypt of the church, just next to where the ornate reliquary containing St Nicholas' relics lay behind bars in a snowdrift of banknotes donated by the faithful, I found a little Eastern Orthodox chapel hung about with lamps and icons. It had been consecrated in 1966, a year after Pope Paul VI and Patriarch Atenagoras of Constantinople had signalled a cautious thawing in relations between East and West Christendom by lifting the mutual anathemas pronounced by Cardinal Humbert and Patriarch Michael Kerollarios in 1054. On one of the pews I found a handy leaflet informing visitors of the serious differences still dividing the Churches: Orthodox priests are not required to be celibate; the Orthodox do not recognize the supremacy of the pope; they do not believe in purgatory where sinful Catholic souls must (unless, of course, they have acquired a plenary indulgence) serve a term before being admitted to heaven; the Orthodox have never allowed the addition of the *Filioque* to their Creed; neither have they created a dogma out of the Virgin Mary's Immaculate Conception.†

All those negatives were giving me pause for thought. Until as recently as the mid nineteenth century, when Pio Nono promulgated the prim dogma of the Virgin Mary's Immaculate Conception and another defining papal infallibility, the Catholic Church has expanded on the basic tenets of Christianity. Such alterations have been bricks in the walls of the fortress Church whose foundations were laid by the eleventh-century reforming popes. The all-powerful

---

* Pure water formed, the faithful believe, by the relics or by the marble of the tomb.
† A dogma promulgated by Pope Pius IX in 1845, it stated that the Virgin Mary had been conceived without stain of original sin.

papacy is the real reason why the oldest scar in Christendom is still not healed in spite of the good start made by Pope Paul and Patriarch Atenagoras in 1965 and Pope John Paul II's recent brave forays into parts of Eastern Christendom.*

A saunter through Bari's old town furnished me with a few more reminders that Byzantium had ruled southern Italy before the eleventh-century Norman conquest. I spotted a brown signpost tactfully indicating the way to the basilica in Russian. Souvenir shops were selling statues of a distinctly Byzantine St Nicholas and there were pictures of him on posters advertising the *corteo* in every shop window. But there was so much else to see that I soon forgot about the schism between East and West.

Bari's old town is undergoing a happy renaissance after years of being so infested with pickpockets and muggers that tourists were warned not to go there. Amidst the noisy renovation work and the hordes of people in town to enjoy the *corteo* I passed old men sitting quietly smoking outside their front doors and wives knitting by trestle trays of drying home-made pasta. Children shrieked from balcony to balcony; televisions blared through open windows. Mothers laden with shopping bags who had paused to gossip glanced at their watches as church bells chimed out the quarter hours. I lingered a while to watch a line of old women in black sitting on a bench in an alley saying their rosaries while boys on Vespas roared past, obstructing their view of the opposite wall where a shrine dedicated to 'Maria Santissima di Constantinopoli' was decked in fresh flowers, candle-lit and daintily adorned with a white lacy cloth. There were dozens of these little shrines, often prettily illuminated by a halo of electric light bulbs, beneath balconies festooned with underwear, dripping jeans and trailing pot plants.

The next morning I learned that Bari's *corteo storico* – for the first time sponsored and organized by the Banco Populare di Bari instead of by the Catholic Church – would be a great deal more lavish and splendid than Canossa's. A whole series of events,

* Romania 1999, Greece and Ukraine 2001

happening in different parts of the old town and spread out over two days, would make this millennial year's *corteo di San Nicola* one to remember. Determined not to miss the highlight – the placing of St Nicholas' relics on a boat to be taken out to sea for the day – I made my way down through the old town to the harbour where fishermen were slapping octupuses on the stone steps leading up from their bright-blue fishing boats and stalls selling nuts and sweets and toys were setting up in expectation of big holiday business. Strolling on along the wide harbour esplanade I headed for the far end where a crowd had gathered around a red-carpeted motor launch. Decked with fluttering coloured pennants and flags – Barese, Italian and EU – and carrying a large glass case in which a life-size statue of the saint stood on a gorgeous casket presumably containing his precious relics, the vessel was just leaving the crowded quay. St Nicholas' travelling companions included a white-robed monk and representatives of the armed forces. From the cheery owner of one of the little blue fishing boats I discovered that when the sun went down thousands would take to boats of all kinds to go and pay a visit to St Nicholas on the one day a year he spent 'enjoying the sea – just like all sailors.' If I liked, the man said with a winning smile, he would be happy to ferry me out there later in his boat; I would see St Nicholas but also some *spettacolari* fireworks. The price he named seemed reasonable, so we shook hands and I promised to meet him exactly where I stood at seven.

'*Arrivedérci*, Victory!' he called, politely doing his best to translate my name into English.

With thousands of excited Italians of all ages frantically scrambling onto boats, there was chaos at the quay that evening. But Vincenzo was as good as his word and waiting for me. Soon we were slowly phut-phutting out into the harbour with fibreglass speedboats whizzing about, more little fishing boats, and rubber dinghies filled with teenage boys drifting dangerously across the paths of great gin-palaces packed with overdressed Italian matrons. I also spotted a smart grey Guardia di Finanza speedboat and a single orange canoe being expertly paddled by a person wearing goggles and a wetsuit.

Hailing his friends and cursing the gin-palaces, Vincenzo kept me supplied with snacks of sunflower seeds and raw runner beans. The mood on the water was hilariously festive and the sky darkening fast. Behind me the brilliant illuminations of Bari's harbourside St Peter's Square, like the interior of an Orthodox church, grew steadily brighter and smaller. Up ahead, surrounded by smaller craft, was St Nicholas on his colourfully lit launch. As we drew closer I began to make out a grey-suited official standing in front of the saint's glass case. Using a white bag fixed to a long pole he was fishing for donations from the boatloads of the faithful drawing alongside. In return for my small contribution I received a souvenir poster of St Nicholas.

Suddenly, the warm air was riven by loud heavenly music. Vivaldi's exhilarating 'Gloria! Gloria!' came blasting from the gold-lit splendour of St Peter's Square, out across the harbour and over the boats on the dark water.

'Look, Victory, look!' yelled Vincenzo, pointing behind me at a gigantic projected image of St Nicholas on the wall of the quayside fish market. No sooner had I swivelled around to appreciate this miracle than he was shouting again.

'Look, Victory, look!'

The night sky was exploding in shower after shower of fireworks, whose accompanying explosions ricocheted around the harbour like an exchange of cannon fire. Shouts and hoots of glee greeted every fresh eruption of silver, red and green stars. A light wind rose, whipping up waves and rocking the little boat.

'Victory, San Nicola is dancing!' Vincenzo laughed as I shivered.

High on his launch, St Nicholas passed us on his way back to the shore, and Vincenzo turned our boat to follow in his wake. As we drew closer the dazzling lights of St Peter's Square illuminated a crowd of churchmen gathered on the quayside – just as their predecessors had been in 1087 – waiting for 'the Blessed' to reach them. A final mass would be said before the relics were carried in solemn procession back home to the basilica.

If late eleventh-century Bari had been even half as enchanting as its early twenty-first-century counterpart, I could understand why Robert Guiscard had suffered the teasing taunts of its Byzantine inhabitants who paraded along the city walls flashing their gold and jewels during his long siege of the city. I was liking Bari so much I decided to delay my departure on a ferry across the Adriatic Sea to Albania by a couple of days. With the *corteo* over I could turn my attention to developments here in Bari which, when taken together, seemed to constitute another step on the road to the First Crusade and Jerusalem.

Two years after the *translatio* of St Nicholas' relics, in 1089, Abbot Elias and Guiscard's eldest son Bohemond invited the newly elected Pope Urban II to Bari to lay St Nicholas' relics under the altar in the just completed crypt of the new basilica. Educated at Reims, Urban had been a monk at Cluny and risen to the position of Abbot Hugh's second in command by the time he was made a cardinal in the late 1060s and sent on a delicate mission to Quedlinburg to bring the German Church to heel. In 1089 he had been pope for less than a year and had not yet managed to enter Rome on account of Henry IV's antipope. A careful, diplomatic sort of person, Urban had not tried to raise an army of *milites sancti Petri* to force a passage back to the Eternal City, as Pope Gregory might have done if Guiscard and his health had permitted. Instead, he had been biding his time, slowly coaxing support back for the reformed papacy by modifying Pope Gregory's inflexible reforming style. His power base comprised the French, who had never supported any German antipope, and the Italian Normans. Despite his close association with the latter, he was also managing to mend some fences with the Byzantines.

Byzantium's Emperor Alexius Comnenus had climbed onto a throne at least as shaky as Pope Urban's and now shrewdly calculated that if he improved his relations with the pope, Urban might use his influence to curb the Italian Normans' greed for Byzantine land. Pope Urban was able to accept the invitation to Bari because he was in the region, holding synods at Monte Cassino, Melfi and

Sicily,* assuring himself that his Norman allies were not about to spoil all his careful diplomacy by embarking on another expedition against Byzantium.

Guiscard's widow Sichelgaita, who died the following year and was buried at Monte Cassino, must have attended the consecration because the inside of St Nicholas' tomb bears an inscription in her name. But it seems that a certain bedraggled and long-faced French monk, lately arrived in Bari after a pilgrimage to Jerusalem, was also there. Peter the Hermit as he would later become known, seems to have been one of those disaffected seekers after the good life who had taken their cue from saints like Romuald and Nilus. Utterly unprepossessing he was nevertheless uncannily charismatic, for there was something 'half-divine' in everything he said. He had arrived in Bari claiming that while in Jerusalem's Church of the Holy Sepulchre he had been granted a marvellous vision. Christ himself had favoured him with a moment of his majestic presence and commanded to him to get a letter of authorization as his envoy from the patriarch of the city. Armed with the letter, Christ had told him, he was to go home and 'rouse the hearts of the faithful to come out and purge the holy places'.[cxxx] The patriarch of Jerusalem had obligingly provided Peter with the required authorization. The story goes that by brandishing this document Peter the Hermit managed to win the ear of Pope Urban in Bari in 1089 and implant the idea of the First Crusade, which the pontiff would go on to proclaim six years later.

During my happy wanderings around an old town that seemed comatose and deserted after three days of pious revelry, I found a street named after Peter the Hermit and another called Via della Crociata – Street of the Crusade. A third – with drying sheets billowing from its balconies like spinnakers – was named after Guiscard's first-born, Bohemond. He would be accompanying me all the way now, over the Adriatic to Albania, across northern Greece

---

* Sicily was mostly conquered by Guiscard's brother Roger between 1060 and 1091. Guiscard helped.

to Istanbul, once Byzantium's Constantinople and east across Turkey to the Syrian border. Bohemond led the last mighty leg of what one historian has lyrically described as the Norsemen's centuries-long 'glissement vers le soleil' [cxxxi] or, less lyrically, their migration south and east to warmer climes.

~

The night ferry to Albania was late leaving Bari. I stood on the upper deck as a last lorry raced up to its slowly rising back door and watched the door lower again and the lorry drive on with a speedy rumble. Its glancing headlights, like the harbour lights and the fluorescent strips of the Montenegrin boat moored alongside, outshone the pale crescent moon.

Boarding had been arduous. After an hour's wait on the quay, the crowd of leather-jacketed Albanian men laden with amorphous loads of baggage, a handful of Italians and I had begun a painfully slow progress onto the boat and up the stairs to its decks. The cause of all the delay was a scruffy Albanian immigration official sitting behind a plastic picnic table at the top of the stairs, laboriously inscribing visas and demanding payment in dollars only, no change. Smartly turned out Italian ship's officers stood by, rolling their eyes heavenward, glancing at their watches, muttering *mamma mias*. A broadcast announcement about the opening of the self-service restaurant, in Italian, English, French, German and finally Albanian, sounded to me like a deliberate assurance that, until we reached Albania the next morning, we were still safely inside the EU.

In the comfortable privacy of my Formica-walled cabin I slept well, better than the young Albanians who crowded on deck to watch a dull sulphur-yellow dawn break over the pale sea and the uneven black line of their country's mountains. Most of them looked as if they made the journey often and all were as exhausted as the Albanian agricultural worker I remembered trying to sleep on the train from Ancona to Rome. Hollow-eyed and hunch-shouldered, unshaven, they leant against the rails smoking, not talking. We had not yet reached Albania but I had already arrived in the poorest country in twenty-first-century Europe. Back in the late eleventh century Albania was Byzantium's province of Illyria, her cherished westernmost outpost after the loss of southern Italy.

In 1081 a flotilla of sixty ships had ferried the army Guiscard had mustered for his bold campaign to conquer Constantinople across this stretch of water now used by smugglers of Albanians into Europe. I guessed it had been a happier sight than either those smugglers' boats or this grumbling grey ferry laden with unwashed and sleep-starved *Gastarbeiter*. Back then, before the sacking of Rome and Pope Gregory's disgrace, the *Terror Mundi* had been at the height of his powers. His lifelong ambition to rule over the richest empire on earth whose manners, dress and rituals he had been copying for decades was about to be realized. Pope Gregory had given him his blessing and a papal banner to brandish, and he had succeeded in allaying his dear Sichelgaita's doubts about waging an unjust war against fellow Christians by engineering a characteristically colourful *casus belli*.

Eight years earlier the Byzantine Emperor Michael VII had been desperate to neutralize the Italian Norman threat to his empire by marrying one of his sons to Guiscard's eldest daughter. Flattered, Guiscard had done the deal, but shortly afterwards Emperor Michael had lost his throne and Guiscard's daughter all her bright prospects. Here was a mini-*casus belli* which Guiscard then worked hard at inflating into a grievance large enough to warrant a full-scale invasion of Byzantium. First, he had play-acted the indignant father bitterly grieving for his beloved daughter. Next, discovering a deranged monk masquerading as the deposed Michael VII, he had pretended to believe the impostor's story, dressed him up in the finery of a Byzantine emperor and begun championing his cause. Following this up with indignant declarations about feeling it incumbent upon him to defend his daughter's dignity by returning this wickedly wronged 'Emperor Michael' to his throne, Guiscard had gleefully set about mustering an army and readying his campaign. He would be accompanied by Sichelgaita, 'Michael' and an arm of St Matthew. Bohemond, his first-born, would be his second in command.

Guiscard had christened his strapping eldest son Marc but nicknamed him Bohemond after a fairy-tale giant of the same name. Raised alongside the children of his father's second marriage, Bohemond did not take to his stepmother Sichelgaita, who wanted her own progeny to inherit all the territories their father had conquered. There is a remarkable tale about how when Bohemond once fell dangerously ill Guiscard immediately suspected Sichelgaita of poisoning him and threatened to plunge his sword into her bosom if his son died. Bohemond survived his sickness and was a handsome blond giant in his late twenties, whom one chronicler admiringly described as 'the exact replica and living image of his father',[cxxxii] by the time the Italian Norman army set out east across the Adriatic Sea to conquer Byzantium. The same chronicler, the Byzantine Emperor Alexius' historian daughter, Anna, has left us a richly ambivalent description of him: 'His skin was marvellously white, and in his face the white was tempered with red. His hair was yellowish, but did not hang down to his waist like that of other barbarians ... A certain charm hung about this man but was partly marred by a general air of the terrible.'[cxxxiii]

But Bohemond was about to exhibit early signs of being not precisely the colossus his father was. Bohemond lacked his father's luck. He would bluster and boast, but then bungle. What any twenty-first-century psychoanalyst would term 'childhood insecurities' dogged his long career.

The Byzantine Emperor Alexius had only just gained his throne from the deposed Michael VII when fearful intelligence concerning Pope Gregory's support for Guiscard's expedition against his empire reached him. An alliance with seafaring Venice was hastily bought with the promise of generous trading concessions and a mighty Venetian fleet sailed across the Adriatic to do battle with the Italian Normans who were already besieging Dyrrachium – today's Durres, where my night ferry would dock. Guiscard sent Bohemond to parley with the Venetians and demand that they immediately acclaim the

Normans' false Michael VII as emperor, but they mocked Bohemond's youth. 'Unable to bear the insult',[cxxxiv] Bohemond launched a disastrous attack on them. He and his cohorts were soon put to flight by a hail of wooden blocks hurled from the small boats which the Venetians had hauled up their ships' masts. On hearing about this too hastily joined and speedily lost battle Guiscard may have cursed his son and boxed his ears but he did not give up the war. Instead he suffered a harsh winter outside Dyrrachium, block-aded by the Venetians, watching his troops starve and sicken for lack of adequate supplies. By the following spring Emperor Alexius himself, at the head of a large, fresh army he had mustered in Thessaloniki, was on his way.

The ferry slowed. The early morning was brightening and Durres taking shape. Below the line of dark mountains were the city's drab high-rise concrete blocks and in the foreground the harbour's yellow cranes. The quay was crowded with freelancing taxi drivers furtively muttering their business. By means of pidgin Italian I discovered from one of them that ten dollars would buy me a ride to the Albanian capital Tirana, about an hour's drive away. Only a couple more dollars would secure help with locating the nearby battle-ground where the Italian Norman and Byzantine armies had clashed, and the ruins of a church I was especially keen to see. We set off south along the potholed coast road. Between it and the shining blue sea was not a beach but a long, untidy string of half-finished hotels. Some of them had black gaps where the windows should have been, some sprouted clumps of rusting iron rods from their open tops, some were still only concrete shells, but they were all deserted.

'There used to be flowers all along here,' explained the driver, 'then Communism ended and everyone came and started building what they wanted. Now they have no money to finish anything and there is no electricity, no running water.'

We turned off to the left, inland, up into some gently rolling hills roughly divided into small green fields sprinkled with white bungalows, the odd tree and some cows. I asked the driver to stop while I got out to survey what, by my reckoning, must have been the late-eleventh-century battlefield I was looking for. Although Guiscard and Bohemond had been up all night praying for victory and had urged their forces to fight 'as if this battlefield were the birthplace of their tombs',^{cxxxv} the Italian Normans were having a bad time of it. Everything looked lost until Sichelgaita, an awe-inspiring sight in a full suit of armour, rallied the troops for a final great push. Anna Comnena describes how Sichelgaita saw the runaways and glaring fiercely at them shouted in a very loud voice something like, 'How far will ye run? Halt! Be men!' When they paid no attention she 'grasped a long spear and charged at full gallop against them', which immediately 'brought them to their senses'.^{cxxxvi} The Italian Normans' forces, a motley but mettlesome mix of Normans, Saracens and Lombards, fought on against the equally variegated Byzantine army, whose elite fighters were a corps of several hundred Englishmen.

Northern Europeans of various sorts had provided the backbone of the Byzantine army since 988, when Prince Vladimir of Kiev had signalled his thanks to Byzantium for baptizing him a Christian with a gift of dozens of Scandinavian mercenaries. Known as Varings, these descendants of the Vikings who had pioneered the route down the Russian rivers from the Baltic to the Black Sea, made up the emperor's elite Varangian Guard. Their love of combat and ancient Germanic custom of pledging unquestioning loyalty to their lord made them invaluable servants in a society which glorified neither war nor loyalty. By the 1020s the ranks of those first Scandinavian Varangians were being swelled by freelancing Norman mercenaries but the latter's reputation was besmirched when a couple of them betrayed their oaths of loyalty and began carving out territories of their own. Combined with the Byzantines' mounting hatred for the Italian Normans who were busy grabbing the empire's westernmost provinces at the time, this made the Varangian Normans' situation untenable. New recruits were needed.

In 1070 a Byzantine agent, a certain Ioannia Rafailis, travelled to England to find some. He must have known that, only four years after the Norman conquest, the misty little island between Normandy and Scandinavia was far from peaceful, filled with young Anglo-Saxons seething with resentment against their new overlords. His tales about the other Normans' dastardly activities in Byzantine southern Italy must have struck just the right note. By 1075 over two hundred and fifty shiploads of disaffected English were departing for a new life in distant Micklegarth,* where many of them joined the Varangian Guard. By 1082, they would have needed no encouragement to enlist in an army mustered against the Normans, whom Emperor Alexius was viewing as a greater threat to the integrity of his empire than the Turks.

Face to face with such uncommonly well-motivated Englishmen on this battlefield just south of Durres, Robert Guiscard and his son must have thought that they had met their match. The English, fighting on foot with the sort of lethal double-bladed axes the Vikings favoured, terrified the Italian Normans' horses. But Sichelgaita's rallying cry restored the Normans' morale and the Byzantine forces were soon disabled by the efforts of Bohemond's crossbowmen. Some poorly motivated Serbian and Turkish mercenaries also proved easy to bribe away from their loyalty to Emperor Alexius. Before long the Italian Normans had stolen the advantage.

Now I needed to see the church in which Guiscard's forces had roasted hundreds of those Englishmen alive.

'We need the village of Arapaj, which must be very near here,' I told the taxi driver, studying my guidebook. 'It says, where the road from Durres to Kavaja crosses the road from Peza to Tirana . . .'

'Here,' he said, stopping the car by a corrugated iron shack advertising spare tyres in loud red graffiti on its side.

'*Impossibile!*' I told him. 'There must be a village and some ruins . . .'

With a smile and a shrug he entered into the spirit of my treasure hunt. First he asked the tyre seller and then a head-scarved old woman leading a cow up the road if they had heard of any

* Anglo-Saxon for Constantinople.

ruined church at Arapaj. They had not. Then, after driving back part of the way we had come, he asked a couple of young men running a roadside car-washing business but they too shook their heads and shrugged. I was about to do the same and instruct the kind man to drive me on towards Tirana, when he swerved the car into a petrol station. A very old man sitting smoking on a stool in the forecourt surrounded by a small herd of goats knew exactly what we were talking about. He sent us off the main potholed road up a steep mud track to a village of crumbling little stone shacks, each of them crowned with a tin or plastic water cistern and a television aerial.

In the middle of this village, where two muddy tracks intersected, stood an outsized concrete mushroom. While my companion went in search of yet more precise directions to the ruined church, I had plenty of time to study the odd object. Albania's Communist dictator Enver Hoxha,* as fearful of invasion from across the Adriatic as any Byzantine emperor, had planted these concrete bunkers with room enough inside for one soldier the entire length of the Albanian coast. When the driver returned we drove on, down a narrowing and muddier track towards a rustily padlocked metal gate.

'Here!' he announced.

'Where?' I asked, getting out of the car. Through the wire fence I could only see a lumpy plot of grassy land and a cow.

'Come,' said the driver, helping me through a gap in the fence, delighted at having found the treasure I was after.

Outside the fence, with a fine view of the empty site, were new three- and four-storey houses in the by now familiar state of incompleteness, but once inside the low ruins of some walls were visible and it was possible to discern the outline of a church large enough to hold hundreds.

By sunset on 18 October 1082, all that remained of Emperor Alexius' mighty army were some exhausted Englishmen who had fled for sanctuary to this church of the Archangel Michael. 'All

* Hoxha led Albania from 1944 to 1985.

who could,' wrote Anna Comnena, 'went inside the building; the rest climbed to the roof and stood there, thinking that would save their lives. The Latins [Italian Normans] merely set fire to them and burned the lot, together with the sanctuary.'[cxxxvii] I struggled to picture the flaming carnage and to recreate the hellish cacophony of Anglo-Saxon curses and screams as the fugitives realized that the Normans were not going to respect their place of sanctuary. But my ears were assailed instead by the unmistakable strains of a pop song I had not heard since Poland. 'Sex bomb! Sex bomb! You're my sex bomb . . .' was drifting towards me from a nearby bungalow sporting a satellite dish on its side. The sound transported me back north a thousand miles, to a warm night's drive with Waldemar's army chaplain friend Father Christopher, past fields filled with flowering cherry trees and out-of-town supermarkets lit up like airports.

Emperor Alexius, 'dusty and bloodstained, bareheaded, with his bright red hair straggling in front of his eyes',[cxxxviii] fled the battlefield, pursued by a posse of Normans. His daughter describes the miraculous manner in which he escaped them, by taking flight on an aerodynamic warhorse draped with a purple silk saddlecloth. 'Indeed it was a most amazing thing,'[cxxxix] she admits. Victorious, Guiscard slept in the imperial tent that night. He and Bohemond then proceeded to conquer the rest of Illyria and make good speed towards their final destination, Constantinople. By Christmas they were some two hundred kilometres east of Durres by the lake of Kastoria in northern Greece, putting another garrison of Varangian English to flight. By early spring 1083 they were still further east and almost within striking distance of Byzantium's second city, Thessaloniki, which was only a few days' march from Constantinople. But Guiscard received two items of bad news: a rebellion had erupted back in southern Italy, and Pope Gregory in Rome urgently needed his help against Henry IV. Telling Bohemond that all the lands they had conquered were his, Guiscard left him in charge of consolidating their conquests while he made a quick trip back to Italy.

Bohemond, proud lord now of most of the southern Balkans, was so keen to prove himself his father's equal that he disobeyed him. Instead of working to consolidate his colossal gains by winning over the locals' minds and hearts, he continued to force his way east towards Constantinople, plundering as he went. But his communication lines were dangerously extended and the Byzantines developed a devastating new tactic. Instead of aiming their arrows at the warriors, they targeted the horses only. A Norman *miles* without his horse was about as effective as a tank driver minus his tank. 'All Kelts [Normans] when on horseback are unbeatable in a charge and make a magnificent show, but whenever they dismount, partly because of their huge shields, partly too because of the spurs on their boots and their ungainly walk, they become very easy prey . . .'[cxl]

Bohemond was at his headquarters on a little island in the middle of a river when the news of the defeat his *milites* had suffered in one such encounter reached him. According to Anna Comnena he was eating grapes, 'bragging loudly, full of his own vainglory' and endlessly repeating, ' "I've thrown Alexius into the wolf's mouth" '.[cxli] But he was riding for a fall. His captains began revolting over unpaid wages and demanding that he go back to the Adriatic coast to wait for his father to bring some money from Italy. Desperate and humiliated, Bohemond had to do as he was told. Naturally, Emperor Alexius wasted no time and offered Bohemond's captains their four years' unpaid wages if only they would desert and join his army.

Guiscard must have been busy in Rome rescuing Pope Gregory because Bohemond waited in vain for funds to arrive. At last he sailed back to Salerno to tell his mighty father that his great golden dream of capturing Constantinople was very far from being realized. Anna Comnena's talents as a popular historian more gifted even than Cluny's Brother Raoul or the German monk who chronicled Canossa are especially dazzling in her description of the reception Guiscard gave Bohemond. 'Robert, who saw the terrible news in his son's face and knew that the glorious hopes he had placed in him had gone astray (like a coin falling the wrong way up), stood for a long time speechless, as if struck by a thunder-bolt.'[cxlii]

When he died of his fever on Cephallonia in 1085, the old

Terror Mundi had been trying to correct his son's bungling by making another attempt on the southern Balkans and Constantinople. Eight centuries later a French historian was still bitterly mourning the ruin of Guiscard's great ambition to conquer Byzantium.

> In his [Guiscard's] powerful hands, in those of his son Bohemond, so worthy to succeed him, the decrepit [Byzantine] empire which no longer knew how to manage the admirable resources which nature and the inheritance of the Romans had given them, would have woken from its lethargy . . . Islam would have rolled back to the Asian steppes, into the depths of Africa. Asia Minor, Syria, would be Christian perhaps. Constantinople would not be Istanbul and the question of the East would not periodically cause alarm in the governments of Europe.[cxliii]

Musing about one of history's many might have beens, Héon omits to mention that the Byzantine Empire survived another three and a half centuries and that, with the Ottomans at the walls of Constantinople in 1453, many Byzantine Greeks calculated that life would be bearable under Turkish rule. The price of accepting help from Western Christendom would have been the intolerable sacrifice of their Church.

~

Tirana did not exist in eleventh-century Illyria, but I was headed there anyway for a meeting. Albania's deputy foreign minister Pellumb Xhufi had been recommended to me as the country's leading expert on the historical period I was interested in, and had e-mailed me a hearty welcome.

Tirana was less welcoming. Its monstrously wide and unmarked streets teeming with cyclists and cars whose drivers obeyed no known traffic rules belonged in Beijing, the din of its blaring car horns in Bangkok. Pedestrians, often long-skirted gypsies carrying filthily bundled babies, ventured across these thoroughfares at their peril. In the shade of a dusty tree, on a square of dirty cardboard, a baby slept while its mother begged. As we idled at a rare traffic light I watched a young able-bodied man hunched over a small brazier on the pavement roasting a couple of corncobs for sale. Others hawked paper twists of sunflower seeds. A monumental Communist-era building hung with red and black Albanian flags dwarfed them all as efficiently as any Gothic or baroque cathedral. We passed a large Western-owned hotel, as shockingly glamorous as a Roman *palazzo*.

'Down there is where the Communist party top dogs used to live,' said the driver, gesturing off left towards a quieter, leafy-looking suburb. 'Now all the foreign banks and companies and charities are there.'

On the north side of a gigantic traffic-filled expanse called Skanderbeg Square, conveniently next door to the little hotel I was staying in, loomed the sky-scraping hotel on whose chipped concrete steps I had arranged to meet Mr Xhufi.

The shiny black Mercedes carrying the deputy foreign minister swooped up to the front of the hotel a few minutes late. Out stepped a handsome young man in a smart dark suit with a mobile phone pressed to one ear. He raised his eyebrows, smiled a greeting and snapped his phone shut.

'I trust we shall have a few minutes of quiet now!' he said in excellent English, trotting briskly up the hotel steps and ushering me through the revolving door. In the sanctuary of an air-conditioned coffee shop, we ordered drinks.

Pellumb Xhufi had been pursuing a humble academic career when he had received the call to serve his country. 'But politics is not really my cup of tea,' he told me. 'Already I dream of being allowed to go back to my institute to finish my book about Albanian relations with Byzantium and Italy during the Middle Ages. You should know, by the way, that the word "Albanian" to describe the indigenous non-Greek population here was first used in the eleventh century – if I am not mistaken, by the wonderful Anna Comnena.'

While he took a stack of papers and pamphlets from his briefcase, we agreed that Emperor Alexius' daughter easily outstripped any saga writer or church chronicler of the era with the depth of her psychological insights and the vividness of her physical descriptions.

'Oh yes, what does she say about Guiscard? Something about his being a clever conversationalist with a loud voice and hair always the right length . . .?'

Overjoyed to meet someone so attuned to the eleventh century that he could recall passages from the *Alexiad* I made Mr Xhufi laugh by reminding him of boastful Bohemond eating grapes, and then described my hunt for the 1082 battlefield and the ruined church outside Durres.

'Of course, Durres – Dyrrachium – was a vital strategic fortress. It marked the start of the old Roman Via Egnatia, the main route to Constantinople across the southern Balkans, the first great road the ancient Romans built outside Italy. Whoever hoped to control that road first had to control Durres.'

He took an unexpectedly sanguine view of the Italian Normans' invasion of his country in the early 1080s. Despite his respect for Anna Comnena, he reserved the bulk of his distrust for her fellow Byzantines.

'I suppose we Albanians have usually distrusted the Byzantine Greeks more than the Latins,' he explained. 'We had to deal with Greek nationalism in the nineteenth century. Even today, many of us are uneasy about our Albanian Orthodox Church having a Greek archbishop.'

'But isn't that because Albania's Communist regime did such a good job of eradicating religion that there was no Albanian fit to be archbishop when Communism ended?'

'Yes, yes, you're right, but the Greeks have a different, more nationalistic, feeling than us about religion. When the Communists banned religion it was no great tragedy for most Albanians because we've never taken religion too seriously.* We are a country of

---

* Albanians are reckoned to be 65% Moslem, roughly 20% Orthodox and 10% Roman Catholic.

heretics, a people without many moral scruples, you could say,' he added with a carefree laugh. I was reminded of the morning I had spent in Reykjavik's Café de Paris, listening to Jörmündur Ingi Hansen and his friends telling me that, after all, Iceland had never really been converted to Christianity. It seemed to me that most of Thorvald's contemporaries would also have felt comfortable with Albania's famously violent code of honour, the *Kanun*. Although the Communist regime did its best to stamp out the custom, blood feuding is now back in fashion. Experts reckon there are some two thousand feuds still in progress today.[cxliv]

'Well, never mind about all that! Let's get back to our mutual passion before my telephone rings again.' Plucking one of the papers from the pile in front of him, he said, 'I think this will interest you.'

On a poorly photocopied page from an Austrian work on archae-ology, was the outline of a tombstone discovered in Albania, engraved with a Greek inscription at the top, Latin at the bottom.

'Now, this is quite common; a tombstone could be reused. The Latin inscription is the one to concentrate on. You read Latin, of course?'

'Not too well,' I admitted, peering at the ancient text which looked as baffling as a website address. Mr Xhufi set to work with enthusiasm.

' "*Hic est suppositus de Forti Monte Robertus . . .*" So, "Here lies Robert et cetera, et cetera, beautiful of body, a good soldier, a generous man . . . Under a leader he commanded all the Normans as well as the English . . . While rich in youth his years bloomed . . . He served the world seeking the Sepulchre of Our Lord." ' We pored over the next line together. ' "*Hic obit Phoeb[o] [I]a(m) sub Libra quater orto. Det roberte tib[I] [s]ua gaudia rex para[disi].*" '[cxlv]

'Hmmm, now what's this about?'

'Something to do with the sun being in the sign of Libra when he died? And then "Robert, may the King of Paradise give you his joy"?' I hazarded. I was heartily enjoying myself but had always found Latin as challenging a discipline as mathematics.

'Probably something like that,' said the deputy foreign minister kindly.

'Wonderful! But he wasn't one of Guiscard's Italian Normans. You would never have had Italian Normans and English fighting on the same side back then, would you? Then there were no English to speak of on the First Crusade, were there? He must have been later . . .' I enthused.

Mr Xhufi's phone rang. His Mercedes awaited him.

'Here you can keep this paper – and these other pamphlets. Good luck!' he said, speeding towards the hotel's revolving door, briefcase in one hand, mobile in the other.

Early the next hot, bright morning I made my way to Tirana's litter-strewn bus station and boarded a bus south towards the Greek border and the formerly predominantly Greek town of Gjirokastra. There I hoped to find a friend of a friend, the same controversially Greek archbishop of the Albanian Orthodox Church whom Mr Xhufi had mentioned.

The bus rattled its way slowly along roads used by carts and tractors, through pleasantly undulating countryside marred by more half-constructed dwellings and bungalows topped with metal cisterns. Every time we lumbered into the muddy narrow streets of an ugly little town whose centre was a jumble of rotting concrete in which bored men sat on plastic chairs outside darkened coffee shops, I found myself praying that my destination would not look like this. The bus began climbing into some hills and then paused at a roadside canteen where a few turkeys gobbled about in the dust and weeds. I watched one of my fellow passengers, a young woman carefully and fashionably dressed in black, emerge from the squalid outdoor lavatory, frown at the bright midday sunshine and then down at her high-heeled sandals, before disdainfully making her way back up the steep muddy incline to the sanctuary of the bus.

Eleventh-century Illyria must have been a happier, more prosperous place than twenty-first-century Albania, I guessed. Back then the importance of the Via Egnatia as a major route for pilgrims travelling from Rome to Constantinople would have ensured its people a living. During most of the latter half of the twentieth century, isolated from the rest of Europe under a Stalinist regime, Albania had been plunged into so benighted a state of poverty that its progress towards democracy and the free market since 1989 has been more difficult than that of any other country in the old Communist bloc. In 1990 crowds of Albanians invaded western European embassies in Tirana, demanding visas abroad. A year later, 20,000 more hijacked Durres harbour and commandeered boats to ferry them across to Bari. In 1997 the country erupted into civil war. Thousands of guns were looted from arsenals and anything associated with the old Communist regime – factories, for example – destroyed in an orgy of bitter, vengeful fury.

As I sat on that bus peering out of a dirty window at scenery that was sometimes as wildly, mountainously beautiful as any in the Balkans and sometimes as bleakly unearthly as Iceland, it struck me that twenty-first-century Albania was hardly habitable.

To my relief, the historically strategic mountain stronghold of Gjirokastra near the Albanian-Greek border was a good deal more attractive than any of the other towns the bus had passed through. A low setting sun gently illuminated its fortress and the splendidly half-timbered Ottoman-era mansions which had once doubled as more fortresses in a place where Greeks, Turks and Albanians had often battled for a living. As a taxi sped me uphill from the bus station towards the town's Orthodox church, I concentrated on these old buildings, trying to ignore the smashed windows of abandoned factories, looted in the 1997 free-for-all.

The wall and metal fence surrounding the courtyard and new white stone buildings around the church suggested that something of the old siege mentality remained. Within the enclosure all was ordered and calm. The courtyard was illuminated by yellow light from a gallery room at the top of a flight of wooden stairs. After the jolting bus ride to this stern stone town on its mountain and the taxi ride through deserted streets lined with vandalized factories and shops, this Orthodox stronghold was a sanctuary.

To my enormous relief I learned that I would not have to wait until the morning or another day entirely to meet the living link with Albania's eleventh-century Byzantine Orthodox past. Archbishop Anastasios Yannoulatos was upstairs and could receive me. A few minutes later he descended to welcome me in the English he had perfected while a missionary in Kenya.

A slight figure dressed in a wide-sleeved black robe, he had a thin white beard, thick spectacles and a blissfully happy smile. Upstairs, in a long white room simply furnished with a table, some chairs and a single icon, he asked a young monk to serve us coffee and little dishes of marmalade. After I had given him news of our mutual friend, I asked him how being the Greek archbishop of the Albanian Orthodox Church compared with being a missionary in Kenya.

'You have to remember,' he began carefully, 'that Albania was the only country where Communists succeeded in destroying an Orthodox Church. If the ambassador of the patriarch in Constantinople had asked me to transfer to a big European city, for example, I would have refused and said, "No thanks, I must stay in Africa," but Albania? Well, how could I say no?'

'It must have been such a dramatic change . . .'

'Of course. In Africa I never met with the suspicion and hostility I have found here. I have to keep reminding myself that no African was ever forced to stop praying or dancing for his God. Albania is my hermit's cell, my desert.'

I guessed that Peter Damiani and St Romuald would have understood him perfectly.

Archbishop Anastasios had been warding off *Accidie* by striving to render his 'desert' more habitable for himself and others. In order to allay fears that he was secretly spearheading a Greek separatist movement to claim some of this south-eastern corner of the country, he had learned fluent Albanian. Flipping over the pages of a calendar he wanted me to have, he pointed out photographs of the seventy-five Orthodox churches he had built or restored in the past ten years and all the social projects he had undertaken: a children's holiday camp in a disused monastery, a mobile dentists' clinic, a refugee camp for Kosovar Albanians, a boarding school here in Gjirokastra. The picture for May 2000 showed him standing in his black robes in brilliant sunshine beside a long new sewer ditch which went snaking back across a bright green field towards the distant speck of a yellow bulldozer still at work against a backdrop of smoke-blue mountains.

'All this is our service of love! What makes a Christian? Freedom and love!' he said, his tiny, bright eyes twinkling behind the thick lenses of his spectacles.

I described my project to him. We discussed the fortress Catholic Church which the eleventh-century reformers had started building, and my impressions of St Peter's.

'For the first time when I saw St Peter's,' he agreed, 'I could sympathize with Protestantism. I think that in Rome the power of love has become very confused with the love of power and, of course, it's very easy to lose the love of freedom within a big institution. And these big audiences and travels of the pope are typical manifestations of Catholic fundamentalism. Certainly John Paul II has a genius for working with the mass media but none of it is real. Reality is so different! But wait!' he exclaimed, as I nodded in agreement. 'Don't misunderstand me! I am not claiming that we Orthodox are perfect in every way. Oh no, certainly not! The hateful nationalism infecting many of our churches at the moment shows that the confidence in God which gives hope is very lacking.'

Shaking his head sadly, he paused for a mouthful of coffee and a stroke of his beard before continuing in a quieter tone, 'The main problem – you could say the devil – we all face is egoism. Let me tell you something— No, first you must have more of this,' he said, piling my saucer high with marmalade. 'All of us need to remember that the opposite of love is not hate. Oh no! Hate is too easy! Love's true opposite is egoism, and egoism has many, many faces!'

I admired the way he had gently steered our conversation away from an invidious comparison between the Christian Churches of East and West to the lighter upland of pure ethics. I also understood that his talk of egoism was intended for my personal edification. I resolved to redouble my efforts to imagine my way out of the twenty-first century and into the eleventh, to listen with all my heart to the people I had still to meet between here and Jerusalem, to refrain from swift judgement. This saga of mine must not be about myself, I decided. There must be no artful pretending that my travels and research were gently tipping me back into the arms of the Roman Catholic Church I had been born into. Nor would I pretend that meeting this remarkable archbishop and learning his truth about love's true opposite was about to turn me into an Orthodox Christian. But Archbishop Anastasios might be the nearest thing I had encountered to a true hero for my saga.

'Anyway,' he was saying, 'it is vitally important we all remain open to people of any and every faith, even to those who call themselves atheists, as so many Albanians do. That's the Christian way of freedom and love!'

If Nilus, Adalbert and Romuald – each of them steeped in Byzantine spirituality – had been anything like Archbishop Anastasios, I could quite understand how Otto III had loved and revered them enough to travel thousands of miles to visit them. Captivated by this prelate, by his fearless good cheer and hopefulness, I could imagine returning to this tiny ruined country for the sole purpose of speaking to him. Archbishop Anastasios was a perfect example of what I had been keeping an eye open for ever since Frère Émile back at Taizé had sat me down on a folding chair in an overgrown garden and suggested I forget about Europe's old divisions and go looking instead for signs of its spiritual rebirth.

'Have you, by any chance, heard of a Christian community at Taizé in Burgundy?' I asked the archbishop.

'Of course!' he replied with enthusiasm. 'I've never visited Taizé, but when it started – in the fifties – I knew Frère Roger. A very good man! But I think that Taizé has remained a beautiful island in the middle of the sea of Christian denominations – somehow not integrated.'

'But do you think that the reconciliation of all the Christian Churches they are aiming at is possible?'

'I believe in miracles! With freedom and love anything is possible!'

The following morning there was precious little freedom or love about the way the Greek border guards kept hundreds of transiting Albanians waiting in the hot sun while they took a long coffee break. But there was even less love as I strode past those same poor people, straight up to a window marked 'EU' and presented my passport for inspection before walking on into Greece.

A bus to one of the towns Bohemond had managed to capture before his captains started revolting about their wages was just about to leave.

PART THREE

The First Crusade
1095–1099

Bohemond had suffered a horrible setback as well as the death of his father, for which – if we credit him with a very modern sensibility – he might have felt partly to blame. If he had not wasted his time bragging about beating Alexius and his energies on overextending his communications he might not have lost the Balkans and given his father the chore of trying to win it back for him. But Bohemond would not forget his father's unfulfilled dream of Byzantium. He was back in the Balkans just over a decade later, this time his demeanour that of a pious pilgrim – a First Crusader – fired with the more popular dream of liberating the Holy Land frm the Muslim Infidel.

The bus purred along a wide new road, past small settlements of attractively built new houses and shiny EU-regulation roadsigns. While most of the other passengers – young Albanian *Gastarbeiter* and young Greeks on military service, to judge by their uniforms – tugged the flimsy curtains shut and snoozed, I immersed myself in Anna Comnena's description of the first the Byzantines heard of that First Crusade. Fourteen at the time, Anna remembers that her father had no sooner dealt with an enemy threatening the integrity of his empire from the north, than 'a rumour that countless Frankish armies were approaching'[i] reached him. She details precisely how Alexius felt about the prospect of another visit from the Normans who made up the bulk of the First Crusaders: 'He dreaded their arrival, knowing as he did their uncontrollable passion, their erratic character and their irresolution, not to mention other peculiar traits of the Kelt,* with their inevitable consequences: their greed for money for example, which always led them, it seemed, to break their own agreements without scruple . . .'[ii]

She then launches into a vivid account of the first plague-like wave of Crusaders, led by Peter the Hermit. But she omits to mention that this ghastly onslaught, like those that followed it, was partly triggered by a simple request her father had made to his new friend, Pope Urban II.

Pope Urban's patient efforts to rebuild the papacy after Pope Gregory's dreadful demolition job were bearing fruit by the early 1090s. He could rely on the goodwill of the Byzantine emperor, the loyalty of his fellow Frenchmen, the military protection of the Italian Normans and the stalwart faithfulness of Countess Matilda. By then in her forties, Matilda had assisted the pope by contracting a strategic second marriage to a seventeen-year-old German prince with lands adjoining her own.

Six years after his appointment, in 1094, Pope Urban bribed some of the antipope's minions to give him the keys to Castel Sant' Angelo and at last succeeded in entering Rome. By spring the following year he was confidently convening a council at Piacenza, near Parma in northern Italy. There he proclaimed his adherence to the Church reform agenda by issuing fresh decrees outlawing simony and nicolaitism. He also listened to Henry IV's Kievan Russian second wife complain about her husband's bad treatment of her and lent a sympathetic ear to some Byzantine delegates.

These Eastern Christians were on an urgent mission from Alexius: to win the Western Church's backing for a new army recruitment campaign. Beset on all sides by enemies, Emperor Alexius desperately needed fresh supplies of trained, loyal Western Christian *milites* to swell the ranks of his Varangian Guard and help him save his empire. The Turks had first begun migrating westward into Asia Minor in around 1000 and in the same year the Byzantines

* Anna Comnena refers to Normans – whether French or Italian – as Kelts, Latins or Franks.

had lost Bari to the Italian Normans, the Seljuk Turks had forced their way onto the Anatolian plain with a famous victory at Manzikert.* A Seljuk Turkish chieftain had then made his headquarters only a couple of days' march to the south of Constantinople itself, at Nicaea.

Emperor Alexius doubtless calculated that if Pope Urban II was sincere in his repeated expressions of goodwill towards Eastern Christendom he could prove it by backing a great mustering of *milites* to defend it, but the Anatolian plain meant precisely nothing to western European churchmen. So, clothing their imperial master's true agenda in what they considered to be the terms most likely to appeal to the pope and his prelates, the Byzantine delegates to the Council of Piacenza shifted the emphasis of their speeches away from the desperate plight of Asia Minor to that of Jerusalem, which had not been a Byzantine possession since the seventh century.† The gist of what they told Pope Urban and his council was roughly this: We miserably suffering Christians of the eastern empire are desperately looking to our Christian brothers in western Europe to help us roll back the advances made by the mighty Infidel who is occupying Jerusalem.

The word 'Jerusalem' was guaranteed to stir any Christian's mind and heart. The centre of the earth, an ancient town filled with relics and stones that would have known Christ, the goal of thousands of pilgrims, Jerusalem also symbolized the Church of Christ, the upright Christian soul, and heaven. If the idea had not struck him six years before, at his meeting with Peter the Hermit in Bari, Pope Urban would certainly now have noted the electrifying effect of the word on his prelates and begun hatching his revolutionary scheme to send thousands of pilgrims to the East to fight what St Augustine might have sanctioned as a just war for the reclamation of Christ's patrimony from the Muslims.

What Urban envisaged was an armed pilgrimage, the like of

* Today Malazgirt near Lake Van in eastern Turkey.
† Jerusalem was captured by the Arabs in 638.

which had never been conceived of before, not even by Pope Gregory. Gregory had never referred to his aborted 1074 expedition as a pilgrimage. Otto III, who was astute enough to spot the forgery of the Donation of Constantine, would surely have recognized the oxymoronic blasphemy contained in the concept; but Pope Urban recognized nothing of the sort. A combination of ancient German tribal mores, the new age's taste for law and righteousness and the crude literalism of Pope Gregory, who had transformed the *miles Christi* from a hermit battling devils into a *miles sancti Petri*, a soldier fighting in the pope's army, had all prepared the ground for Pope Urban's lethal initiative.

Urban was troubled by geopolitical concerns, including the spread of Islam and the dangerous enfeeblement of a divided Christendom, and must have reckoned that helping the Byzantines to repel the Infidel would earn Rome the undying gratitude of Constantinople. While battling together against a common enemy, Christians of East and West could learn to love each other again. The Byzantines might even feel constrained to return the favour by acknowledging Rome's supremacy.

The pope was also worried by the damaging activities of western European *milites*, who were still proving the chief obstacle to peace and good order. Although the Cluny-backed Peace and Truce of God movements had scored some dramatic successes, the old disorder, battling and pillaging was far from eradicated. Laws of primogeniture in western Europe, especially the French lands, meant that there were far too many younger sons with too much energy and not enough land to go around. Although some *milites* seem to have been sincerely troubled by finer feelings, of the sort ascribed to one of Bohemond's nephews who 'burned with anxiety because the warfare he engaged in as a *miles* seemed to be contrary to the Lord's commands',[iii] fighting remained the most prestigious career open to a free-born young man. Furthermore, if Pope Urban could rally warriors from all over Western Christendom and gather them into an army of his own, Pope Gregory's claim to rule over all worldly kingdoms would become no empty boast. The *militia sancti*

Petri – more powerful and righteous than any earthly ruler's army – would be a reality at last.

One might imagine that all but the most pious *milites* would have baulked at the idea of faring so far and so long on a pope's business, but it so happened that many of them had been falling badly behind with the strict penances the Church prescribed for their serious and frequently repeated misdeeds. The penance for murdering one's wife was entry into a monastery and abstention from all riding and battling. A murder committed out of hatred or greed was punished with a seven-year ban on bearing weapons. In an era when consulting a sorcerer, having sex during Lent, breaking open a tomb to steal a corpse's clothes, not purifying with holy water some wine in which a mouse had been found, talking to someone who had been excommunicated or even bursting out laughing all merited some form of penance, the soul of the average *miles* must have been black with sins awaiting expiation. Whether this was the case or not, the prospect of wiping one's slate clean with a plenary indulgence by joining the pope's armed pilgrimage to Jerusalem would have had an irresistible appeal. Instead of suffering in the knowledge that the only means of gaining a soul pure enough to enter heaven was by becoming a monk, a warrior could now look forward to fighting and slaughtering to his heart's content. A contemporary historian described the mind of one *miles* as 'divided, uncertain whether to follow in the footsteps of the Gospel or the world' until 'the call to arms in the service of Christ' arrived and 'the two-fold reason for fighting inflamed him beyond belief'.[iv]

But the First Crusade was not just Pope Urban's clever plot to reunite Christendom and neutralize the *milites*. A pilgrimage to Christ's Holy Sepulchre matched the fervently expansive spirit of the age. Hermits in the mould of St Romuald, charismatic freelancing preachers like Peter the Hermit, the mixed communities of devout poor who had fled the nascent urban centres between the Somme and the Rhine and taken to the forests to build simple Christian lives away from the world, the mass pilgrimages which had become a feature of eleventh-century western Europe all signalled a potent challenge to the centralizing legalism of the reformed Church. With an eloquent call to journey east to the holy places, Pope Urban could prove he was just as devout and inspiring, at least as charismatic, as any preacher or hermit.

Late summer 1095 found Pope Urban crossing 'the frozen Alps' into France. The launch of his holy *peregrinatio* cum military *expeditio* to the east – the word 'crusade' was not coined until the thirteenth century – was only two months away. He could not have imagined that what he was about to set in motion would remain a feature of Western Christian life for the next four hundred years, or that Crusader states in the Middle East would be the model for European colonies overseas which would reach their apogee in the nineteenth century. Nor, of course, had he any way of knowing that the expeditions would poison the West's relations with the East – Orthodox Christian and Muslim – for the rest of the second millennium.

He had countless important details to consider as he travelled. The project urgently needed the involvement of some respected and influential *milites* if it was to succeed. Much credibility would be gained if Count Raymond of Toulouse, for example, could be persuaded to volunteer the moment the appeal was made. Then there was the question of leadership. Pope Urban himself could not think of faring so far and so long from Rome, but hoped that Bishop Adhemar of Puy might consent to act as his representative.

In late October the pope arrived at his alma mater, Cluny, to consecrate the high altar of the magnificent church Abbot Hugh had begun building after seeing Abbot Desiderius' basilica at Monte Cassino. Abbot Hugh lent his support to his old friend's bold project and agreed to sponsor any deserving local *milites* needing help with acquiring equipment. Bishop Adhemar accepted the heavy responsibility offered him and the influential Count Raymond also agreed to play his part. The heavens themselves approved Urban's plan, sending a shower of meteors down over France. Pilgrimage and penance seemed a natural and urgent corrective to the flamingly hot summer which had been marked by a virulent outbreak of *ignis sacer*.

In November, Pope Urban and Abbot Hugh set out from Cluny on the three-day journey west to Clermont for another Church council. In the presence of a fragment of the true cross which he had brought with him from Rome and three hundred senior churchmen, Pope Urban issued some more decrees against simony and nicolaitism and proclaimed the Truce of God. He was saving his great announcement for a public session to be held on 27 November, in a field outside the city's eastern gate. On that day Pope Urban sat on a throne raised on a platform high above the excited throng which must have included the children and grand-children of those who had attended Pope Leo's first famous reform council at Reims almost half a century before. There is no single, definitive record of the precise words he used to preach the First Crusade but whatever they were they had precisely the required effect. A thunderous tide of cheers rose to heaven: '*Deus lo volt! Deus lo volt!*' – 'God wills it! God wills it!'

Bishop Adhemar of Puy dramatically cast himself down on his knees in front of the pope, begging for permission to volunteer; so did Count Raymond of Toulouse, and thousands followed their lead. Just as Christ had demanded of his true disciple, to 'deny himself and take up his cross, and follow me', so Pope Urban required that the *milites* sew a sign of the cross on the shoulders of their garments. To limit any wriggling out of an undertaking made in the heat and excitement of the moment, the volunteers were also asked to swear a solemn oath. By the following August they must be ready to leave their homes. Their families must be provided for, but the rest of their wealth exchanged for warhorses, suits of armour and the wherewithal to support a retinue of foot soldiers and attendants.

For a whole year Pope Urban continued to travel around the French lands, rallying support for the Crusade. So great was the popular enthusiasm that he soon found himself trying to curb its accompanying warrior spirit. Any lands conquered from the Infidel on the expedition must be returned gratis to their rightful owners, the Byzantines, he insisted, and footloose *milites*, tramps, adventurers of any sort would be surplus to requirements, he preached. But his efforts to exercise quality control over the thousands heeding his call and preparing themselves for the great *expeditio* east were bound to fail.

More marvellous heavenly portents seemed to approve the grand undertaking. Two knights were seen galloping towards each other across the night sky, one beating the other with a large cross. Favourable omens and curious happenings were so plentiful that one chronicler grew weary of enumerating them all: 'Why should I mention that in those days a certain woman continued pregnant for two years and at last brought forth a boy who could speak from birth?'[v]

Very soon the entire venture was slipping out of Pope Urban's hands and acquiring a momentum of its own. Like his friend Emperor Alexius, Urban had probably envisaged a force of a few thousand *milites* with a few more thousand retainers responding to his call. But his appeal had touched the hearts of tens of thousands of ordinary folk. A German chronicler set aside religious considerations to point out that, 'The western Franks [people of modern France] could easily be made to leave their lands, since for several years Gaul had suffered, now from civil war, now from famine and again from excessive mortality.'[vi] People without any experience of battle proved desperately keen to embark on the great trek south. There is a letter from St Anselm, archbishop of Canterbury and a close friend of Abbot Hugh's, to a Bishop Osmund of Salisbury, rebuking him for letting a local abbot buy a boat and send his monks off on the Crusade. Pope Urban had to write to various powerful counts ordering them to remain at home where there was work to be done. Everywhere, preachers and visionaries took up the theme of the Crusade, promising that Christ's second coming was imminent if only Jerusalem – a land flowing with milk and honey, the psalms said – could be captured by Christians. In northern France and the well populated cities between the Rhine and the Somme, Peter the Hermit was gathering a great multitude of the hungry and destitute, the feckless and the pious. Entire families were shoeing their oxen and loading worldly goods and children onto wagons in expectation of building a better life in the promised land. Because so many people needed to dispose of their assets as quickly as possible, famine disappeared: 'the cry of the Crusade, sounding everywhere at once, broke the locks and bars and closed the granaries. Provisions that had been beyond price when everyone stayed where they were, sold for nothing when everyone was stirring and anxious to depart.'[vii]

Months before any great lord had managed to muster himself a properly equipped army, a raggle-taggle 15,000-strong horde of the faithful led by Peter the Hermit descended on Cologne, near Aachen, prior to setting out. Swelled by a further 5,000 German pilgrims, it moved off south towards Hungary and the Danube, the frontier between western Europe and the Byzantine Empire. Unable to conceive of the distance still separating them from their goal, the pilgrims pathetically mistook every town they approached for Jerusalem. At Semlin, today a northern suburb of Belgrade, they brought down on themselves the first of their many troubles. An argument over the price of a pair of shoes flared into a riot and then a pitched battle in which four thousand Hungarians were killed. Fleeing across the River Sava into Byzantine territory on makeshift rafts, the pilgrims entered Belgrade, looted it and set it on fire. En route south-east again, battle was chaotically joined with the forces of the hitherto remarkably patient commander of the local Byzantine garrison. By the time the People's Crusade reached Sofia in July 1096 it had lost a quarter of its strength. But its fortunes were about to improve. The Byzantines, moved by piteous tales of their sufferings, began to give the pilgrims horses, mules and food, and on the grounds that God had punished them enough already for their barbarous blunderings, they were kindly received in Constantinople.

Emperor Alexius was quick to see that the helpless horde would be set upon by his Turkish enemies just as soon as it crossed into Asia. It was tempting to rid himself of the nuisance that way, especially as the pilgrims were already disgracing themselves by stealing lead from Constantinople's church roofs and robbing sub-urban villas. Instead, Alexius decided to transport his uninvited guests across the Sea of Marmara to the camp he had had built for his Anglo-Saxon Varangian Guards. He kindly advised Peter the Hermit to wait there a while in safety until he could unite his untrained and ill-disciplined forces with those of the more experi-enced Crusaders who would soon be arriving from the west. He also promised to supply them by boat from Constantinople so they would have no excuse to pillage the surrounding countryside. But Peter the Hermit was no longer an effective leader. A couple of hotheaded *milites* had each gained control over one half of the now fragmenting expedition. In competition with each other, they could brook no delay, nor could they see any reason to refrain from robbing and murdering the Eastern Christians living around the camp. Embold-ened by success and greedy for booty, they mounted forays as far as the Turks' capital at nearby Nicaea.

At last it happened just as Alexius had known it would: one half of the People's Crusade was destroyed in an attempt to take Nicaea. Soon afterwards, only three miles out of their camp at Civetot, in a thick wood on the road towards Nicaea, the other half was ambushed by Turks and wiped out. Anna Comnena writes: 'So great a multitude of Kelts and Normans died by the Ishmaelite [Turkish] sword that when they gathered the remains of the fallen, lying on every side they heaped up, I will not say a mighty ridge or hill or peak, but a mountain of considerable height and depth and width, so huge was the mass of bones.'[viii]

The Peoples' Crusade was over. Emperor Alexius generously sent a boat across the Sea of Marmara to rescue Peter the Hermit and a handful of other survivors but the Byzantines had had all their fears and worst prejudices about Western Christians confirmed. However, there were more to come. In the same month as the People's Crusade crumbled, Bohemond, accompanied by assorted members of his clan and a well-equipped and trained army, set sail from Bari.

Small, disorganized bands of north Italian Crusaders had set off for the east and joined Peter the Hermit in Constantinople, but the Crusading craze had taken time to reach southern Italy. It appears that Pope Urban deliberately failed to inform his closest ally – the doughtiest *miles* in all western Europe and the only one with long experience of the Byzantines and their terrain – about his great scheme to reclaim the Christian holy places. Urban knew Bohemond too well to imagine he would obey an instruction to return any conquests to the Byzantines, and he cared too much about his improved relations with Byzantium to want to risk jeopardizing them by inflicting on Emperor Alexius the Byzantines' deadliest foe.

It was only when bands of French Crusaders started marching through Norman Italy en route for the east that Bohemond learned that something very significant was afoot and decided that he needed to be part of it. What did he have to lose? His younger half-brother, Sichelgaita's eldest son, was inheriting Sicily; his other half-brothers, uncles, cousins and nephews all had their slices of southern Italy, but he had lost himself his allotted portion of the Balkans back in 1084. He was over forty years old already. His best chance of winning himself a fiefdom now lay in joining this armed pilgrimage and seeing what opportunities came his way.

Outside the walled city of Amalfi where he had just helped to put down a rebellion Bohemond told his men about the crusade. 'Moved by the Holy Spirit',[ix] he commanded that his richest cloak be produced and chopped up into crosses to be worn by any of his men who dared to accompany him east again. Volunteers flocked to him, among them four more grandsons of old Tancred de Hauteville and two great-grandsons. Arriving back in Illyria, Bohemond and his army were as tactfully and hospitably received by the Byzantines as the People's Crusaders had been. Returning the compliment Bohemond piously commanded his men to behave themselves: 'Take heed all of you, for we are pilgrims of God. We ought therefore to be better and more humble than before. Do not plunder this land, since it belongs to Christians,'[x] he told them. In that late autumn of 1096 he seems to have led his army off the Via Egnatia high up into the mountains, perhaps to escape the watchful eyes of Byzantine spies. By Christmas they had reached the rich and restful lakeside town of Kastoria.

~

For six hours the devil-may-care driver had been spinning his outsize steering wheel, sending his bus hurtling around the thickly wooded mountains. Higher and higher we had climbed, round and round, so that it was a relief to begin the abrupt descent to Kastoria.

A jumble of buildings set on a promontory overlooking a lake, old Kastoria had once been a place of exile for disgraced Byzantine courtiers who built themselves dozens of decorative little stone churches. These, the lake and centuries of prosperity derived from its lucrative fur trade are what give the place its charm today. The air smelt good that early evening, mild and sweet, but in the stiff breeze blowing off the lake and the scatter of fallen leaves along the esplanade, I detected the first signs of autumn. The next morning the old town's narrow winding streets were full of children excited at the start of a new school year. In the tourist shops the last of the summer's guidebooks were yellowing, and postcards curling. The fur merchants' emporia advertising their wares in Russian and Serbo-Croat were doing a brisk trade but the esplanade's open-air cafés were all empty. Kastoria would have been not just chilly but cold in December 1096, the lake perhaps frozen, and all the spiritual sustenance to be found in the myriad churches would not have compensated Bohemond and his Crusaders for the locals' frosty reception. The Kastorians refused to sell any of their livestock or food to the heavily armed pilgrims whom many remembered as the barbarian enemy of the previous decade. Impatient at their hostility, Bohemond instructed his men to help themselves to everything they needed.

I seemed to be the only tourist admiring all those little Byzantine churches tucked away in back streets, behind modern blocks of flats. There were at least two that Bohemond himself could have seen.

It was mid-afternoon when, outside the fifth or sixth church, I encountered a stocky man dressed in safari casuals with a couple of large cameras hanging around his neck. Running to the back of the church, squinting up at its roof, turning his camera this way and that and frowning into the sun, he was snapping away with more concentration but less enjoyment than an ordinary tourist.

Babis was sweating, tired, and even lonelier than I was after months of far-faring the length of the Via Egnatia. He had been commissioned by the Greek ministry of tourism to photograph the ancient road's architectural highlights for a brochure whose publication would coincide with Greece's hosting of the Olympic Games in 2004.

'Did you start your journey at Durres in Albania?' I asked him, remembering Mr Xhufi telling me how the road went from that port on the Adriatic all the way across northern Greece to Constantinople.

'Albania? No. The Via Egnatia starts at Igoumenitsa – in Greece,' he replied.

It transpired that each of us had a different Via Egnatia in mind. He was referring to a brand new twenty-first-century Via Egnatia, a four-lane motorway which – circumventing poor and unstable Albania – would do the job of the old road by linking Greece's Adriatic port of Igoumenitsa to Thessaloniki and Istanbul. Where the five hundred miles of the old road had taken twenty days to travel, this new motorway could be comfortably driven in a couple of days.

'Haven't you noticed it? Look out for big signboards. It's an EU-funded project so it's very well advertised,' said Babis. 'It has to be completed in time for the Olympics.'

For the rest of the golden afternoon I happily accompanied him on his hectic tour of Kastoria's sights, carrying his cameras for him and suggesting shots. He confessed he did not know much about the Crusades but expressed the startling opinion that the seeds of the Byzantine Empire's eventual demise in the middle of the fifteenth century lay in the fact that 'sixty per cent of Byzantine men were monks, only forty per cent soldiers.'

The Byzantines certainly never glorified war in the manner of western Europeans. Skilful diplomacy, judicious bribery and the sort of friendly alliances that Otto III had established with the Poles and the Hungarians in the year 1000 were the Byzantines' preferred weapons, not swords and axes. One reason why Emperor Alexius was forever recruiting foreigners into his army was that for Byzantines no merit whatsoever was attached to dying in war. Three years' excommunication was all the thanks a Byzantine Orthodox soldier could expect for killing in war. Priests and monks who took up arms risked defrocking or ejection from their monasteries. Anna Comnena was sincerely shocked by the comportment of Western Christian churchmen on the First Crusade. In one long footnote she explains: 'your Latin barbarian will at the same time handle sacred objects, fasten a shield to his left arm and grasp a spear in his right. He will communicate the Body and Blood of the Deity and meanwhile gaze on bloodshed and become himself "a man of blood" (as David says in the psalm). Thus the race is no less devoted to religion than to war.'[xi]

Unlike its Roman counterpart, the Byzantine Church never equipped itself with an army.

Early the next morning I caught another bus east to Babis's home town and Greece's northern capital, Thessaloniki. For a time the old dual carriageway ran parallel to a section of the new four-lane Via Egnatia. I tried to read the astronomical sums of drachmas inscribed on gigantic blue signboards marked with the European circle of golden stars, but they whizzed by too fast for me to count all the zeros. I wondered if Britain might feel more inclined to commit itself to the European project if it was similarly planted with loud reminders of how much it was benefiting from the EU. Thinking about Britain reminded me that it had been at least a fortnight since I had called home.

In Thessaloniki's noisy bus station, surrounded by eastern European traders and old women in black, I phoned London to discover that, after two emergency operations, my father had been in Charing Cross Hospital's intensive care unit for the past week. My elder brother wanted to reassure me but could not. When could I be home? Furious with myself for not calling sooner, I panicked. How was I going to get back? Just as at Monte Cassino, I had forgotten about aeroplanes but soon discovered that Thessaloniki is blessed with an international airport. There was a flight to London that afternoon. Less than eight hours later I was at my father's bedside.

For the three long months that he see-sawed between life and death in intensive care, we had to place all our hopes in the technological advances made in the field of medicine during the second millennium. In his lucid moments my father sometimes wondered at the purpose of being kept alive, and we wondered too. He turned the corner so suddenly and completely we more than half-suspected a miracle. One morning his face was a deathly grey and not his own. The next, he was back.

It would be a full six months, early spring 2001, before an ambulance ferried him home, and another fortnight before I felt able to return to the eleventh century and tales of the suffering those First Crusaders inflicted on themselves and others, not least the Jews.

~

'Today is a Christian holiday,' said a woman's voice. 'You must come on Tuesday.'

'But this is a Jewish not a Christian museum,' I remonstrated into the intercom. And if only I could come back on Tuesday I would, but I was leaving Thessaloniki the next day. Surely it was possible to admit me for a few minutes? I had come all the way from London . . .

The door buzzed open.

Out of the blinding spring sunlight, the crowds of people shopping for Easter and a stiff breeze blowing off the sea uptown from the port, I stepped into a cool stillness naturally lit from on high through a glass roof. Footsteps descended a flight of stairs at the far end of the marble-floored hall, and a small neatly dressed woman approached me.

'I am so sorry. You are very welcome,' she said. 'The museum has only been open for ten days so we are very happy to have a foreign visitor. But you must understand that the city authorities are very strict about closing on Church holidays. The Orthodox Church here is powerful.'

I was not surprised to hear it. The previous evening I had been happily loitering outside the famous St Dmitri Basilica, watching some boys playing football, when a pair of officious black-clad churchmen had approached and shooed us all away. They, and a group of monks by the church doors, had been awaiting the arrival of Thessaloniki's Metropolitan Panteleimon II who would preside over the long Maundy Thursday service. At last, his grand old black Mercedes sporting a silver number plate embossed with a gilt double-headed Byzantine eagle rolled slowly up to the church. The sight of the frail white-bearded prelate proffering his hand to the monks for kissing brought me marvellously close to eleventh-century Byzantium. The approach from all directions of hundreds of faithful bearing splendid red and white flower arrangements, the church filled with chanting and ablaze with candlelight reflected in the glinting gold backgrounds of its mosaics, and a red carpet richly woven with more Byzantine double-headed eagles brought me closer still.

For hours the metropolitan's amplified voice, almost sobbing with the pathos of the tale he had to tell about Christ's last supper with his beloved apostles, held the congregation spellbound. Crackling out from loudspeakers over the city, the Greek words for death, resurrection, man and glory followed me back downtown – *thanatos . . . anastasis . . . anthropos . . . doxa . . .*

In 1082 other metropolitans at least as venerably powerful as Panteleimon II who could dictate Thessaloniki's museum opening hours, had forcefully protested against Emperor Alexius' requisitioning of Church treasures to pay for his Dyrrachium campaign against Guiscard and Bohemond. 'Observe the holy monasteries and see how many have been sacked!' Metropolitan Leo of Chalcedon had railed. 'How many altars have been stripped of their beauties and are like stripped corpses!'[xii] Alexius had had to issue a decree promising that nothing of the sort would ever happen again and pay compensation to his Church. The emperor had also felt obliged to reimburse the Jews of Thessaloniki for the losses they, in particular, had suffered at the hands of the Italian Normans in the early 1080s.

The Jewish presence in Thessaloniki, the Byzantine Empire's second city after Constantinople, dates back to the second century BC. In the late eleventh century the community was thriving and the city became a noted centre of Jewish learning in 1096 when the eminent Rabbi Tovia ben Eliezer – son of a German rabbi from Mainz in the Rhineland but born in Kastoria – moved to Thessaloniki and founded a famous Talmudic school. In the same year rumours of a great stirring in northern Europe, of the lamentable side effects of the mighty First Crusade, began to reach the Jews of Thessaloniki by way of other Jews settled in French and German cities. Their blood already boiling, the soldier pilgrims of Western Christendom were practising for the great war against the Muslims by tormenting the race whose forebears had crucified their Lord.

The network of contacts between the Jews who had settled all over Europe, east and west, during the first millennium facilitated commerce and the passing of alerts. Jews had grown rich by efficiently managing the trade between the Christian and Muslim worlds. Unlike Christianity, Judaism enforced no ban or restriction on lending money at interest.* Loans and the other banking services the Jews offered Christian rulers and churchmen had guaranteed the German Jews in particular those lords' protection, the same sort of *libertas* Cluny enjoyed under the wing of the papacy.

But the spread of the cash economy and trade in the eleventh century meant that more and more people of all sorts were requiring financial services by the 1090s. Grumbling resentment at the interest rates the Jews were charging flared up into violence among some of

---

* Lending money at interest – usury – was a Christian sin because time was reckoned to be God's creation, a gift to everyone, and so not available to bargain over and profit by.

the German *milites* preparing to head off on the Crusade in the wake of Peter the Hermit. Many hated being forced to pay interest on the large sums of money they had borrowed from the Jewish enemies of Christ in order to buy the equipment they needed to go and fight the Muslim enemies of Christ. A knight might spend four times his annual income procuring himself a decent horse, a full suit of armour and a small retinue of followers. It was rumoured that Godfrey of Bouillon – Duke of Lower Lorraine and the same who had hastened Pope Gregory's ruin by climbing in through the window of St Peter's in Rome over a decade earlier – was so fired with fervour for Pope Urban's Crusade that he had sworn not to set out for the east until he had avenged Christ by killing a few Jews. This rumour reached Henry IV in Italy in a panicky letter from a German chief rabbi. Henry, who valued his Jews, issued decrees commanding that their safety be guaranteed but – to be on the safe side – the Jewish communities of the Rhineland began buying protection with vast sums of silver. To no avail.

In May 1096, a certain Count Emicho gathered himself a large army of Crusaders and launched his enterprise with a little pogrom in Speyer, where Jews had recently and happily begun settling at the invitation of the local archbishop. Twelve Jews who refused to convert to Christianity at spear-point were killed. From Speyer the count and his army swept on south to Worms, with them a woman and a goose which the woman claimed was filled with the Holy Spirit and just as eager as she was to be off on the Crusade. The Jews of Worms had had advance warning from their brothers in Speyer. Some fled for sanctuary to the local archbishop's palace; others shut themselves up in their homes. But virulently anti-Semitic local Christians seized the opportunity presented by the arrival of the count and his mob to unleash their sentiments. Some crafty citizens dug up a month-old corpse which they carted through the town shouting ' "Behold, look what the Jews have done to our comrade!" 'xiii They claimed that their Jewish neighbours had boiled the man alive and then poisoned the town's wells with the water. Count Emicho and his horde gleefully joined with the outraged locals in declaring, ' "Behold the time has come to avenge him who was crucified, whom their ancestors slew. Now let not a residue or a remnant escape, even an infant or a suckling in the cradle." '[xiv]

The archbishop's palace, where half the Jews had sought sanctuary, was broken into and five hundred of them slaughtered. One, a prominent and highly respected Jewess named Minna, managed to escape the horror by fleeing into the countryside. When a group of citizens discovered her, they urged her to take a look around at the corpses of her fellow Jews and draw the obvious conclusion: God no longer favoured Jews. But they were loath to kill her because 'her reputation was widely known, for all the notables of the city and the princes of the land were found in her circle'.[xv] On their knees, they begged her to accept baptism. She escaped, but in those terrible days there were plenty of Jewish suicides and cases of fathers killing their sons, of mothers decapitating their infants and of husbands plunging swords into their wives rather than accepting the religion of the Gentiles or even letting them 'be killed by the weapons of the uncircumcised'.[xvi] Hysteria reigned. Demonized by Gentiles, Jews responded by demonizing their tormentors. Casting aspersions on the Virgin Birth* of Jesus Christ, some alleged that the son of the Christian God had been conceived while his mother was menstruating. Sex during menstruation was, and is, taboo among orthodox Jews.

The German Crusaders' avenging bloodlust, amply fuelled by local anti-Semitism which no archbishop or ruler seemed capable of curbing, climaxed in the massacre of the Jews of Mainz. Events there in May 1096 furnished several eloquent Jewish chroniclers with the goriest tales of this first of the second millennium's countless pogroms. There was the 'perfectly pious' Rabbi Isaac, the famous dialectician, who humbly 'stretched forth his neck'[xvii] to have his head chopped off. There was the famously pious Rachel, mother of four, who slaughtered her own children rather than see them baptized. Her son Isaac, 'small and exceedingly comely', was despatched

---

* The belief that Jesus Christ had no human father but was conceived in Mary by the power of the Holy Spirit.

first, while his brother Aaron cried 'Mother do not slaughter me!' and ran off to hide under a bureau. Rachel sharpened her knife again to cut off the heads of her daughters, Bella and Matrona, and then called for her youngest son, ' "Aaron, Aaron, where are you? I shall not have mercy or pity on you as well." ' Rachel 'pulled him by the leg from under the bureau where he was hidden and she sacrificed him before the sublime and exalted God.'[xviii] A heroic Rabbi David pretended to agree to abandon the faith of his fore-fathers, but when a crowd of happy Christians gathered to witness his conversion, he told them, 'Lo, you are the children of lust. You believe in one who was born of lust.'[xix] He, his family and his servants were all killed.

The German Crusaders continued south, persecuting Jews all the way, until they reached Hungarian lands where they 'transfixed a certain Hungarian youth in the market place with a stake through his body'.[xx]. The Hungarian authorities cracked down hard and succeeded in dispersing the army, thereby ensuring that it never reached Constantinople, let alone Jerusalem. It is estimated that some three thousand European Jews were killed by Christians in 1096. Thanks to the second millennium's extraordinary advances in the technology of mass extermination the death toll of Jews in the pogrom to end all pogroms almost nine hundred years later would be two thousand times higher.

As grim tidings of the horrors befalling the German Jews began to filter down to Thessaloniki, the Jews there trembled in terror of attracting the same fate and a 'strange messianic movement grew up in the town'.[xxi] A rumour that the Old Testament prophet Elijah had assumed human shape and appeared in Thessaloniki spread around the city. Even Orthodox Christian townspeople saw him and a spate of miraculous cures followed. Studying their Book of Revelations, the city's Orthodox Christians concluded that God had sent his prophet to Thessaloniki to announce that Christ's promised second coming was at hand. Jews were convinced that Elijah's appearance meant only one thing: their true Messiah was on his way at last. Wise rabbis calculated that he must appear soon. They had done their sums by taking the second line of the seventh verse of the thirty-first chapter of the Book of Jeremiah, 'Sing aloud with gladness for Jacob', extracting the first letters of each main word in Hebrew, and adding together their mystical numerical values to arrive at a total of 256. This they understood to refer to the 256th lunar cycle since the creation of the world. Each cycle spanned nineteen years and they identified a nineteen-year period between 1086 and 1104. The year 1096 was the eleventh year of this cycle so the Messiah had eight more years to appear.

Fervently expecting the Messiah and everlasting joy, the Thessaloniki Jews mourned the fate of their brothers in the north but managed to extract a grain of comfort from the news that the Western Christians had embarked on a Crusade to liberate Jerusalem. They trusted that as soon as Christians and Muslims had exhausted themselves fighting a mightily impious battle in the holy city, it would revert to them, its rightful owners.* In much the same way as the Christians had made ready to set off on the First Crusade, Thessaloniki Jews began winding up their businesses, selling off their assets and setting off on a search for the ten tribes of Israel who had to be found before their Messiah could appear. Thessaloniki's Byzantine Greeks, as eager for Christ's second coming as the Jews were for their Messiah's first appearance and their return to Jerusalem, flocked to join their Jewish neighbours in the search.

The excitement stirred up by Thessaloniki's messianic movement spread through the Jewish communities of the Byzantine Empire. Kastorian-born Rabbi Tovia journeyed to Constantinople to tell one of his disciples about the miraculous goings-on in Thessaloniki. It was not until a highly respected Palestinian rabbi expressed his doubts about the veracity of the visions and the Crusaders conquered Jerusalem in 1099 that the movement expired and Jews everywhere sadly resigned themselves to an indefinite wait for their Messiah.

~

* The Jews were expelled from Jerusalem by the Romans in AD 70.

The exhibits on display in Thessaloniki's elegant new EU-subsidized Jewish museum could throw no light on such early history. They told the later story of the city's Jewish community, which had been enormously enlarged by immigration following the expulsion of Jews from Spain, Portugal and Italy from the end of the fifteenth century. By the nineteenth century the Jews were developing Thessaloniki's port and the city's reputation as a vibrant centre of commerce and industry. Up on the second floor I found the final instalment of their story. Among the selection of pathetic relics relating to the Holocaust was a blue and grey striped concentration camp uniform exactly like the one I had seen in the little exhibition I had visited on that rainy afternoon in Cluny.

'My father wore that at Auschwitz,' said the kind woman who had admitted me. 'He kept his uniform. It was his passport out of there; it entitled him to rations and so forth. Actually, he was not starving when he left. The Nazis had fed him well because he sang for them in the evenings. My mother suffered more. If you like we can talk in my office,' she said. 'By the way, I'm Erika Perahia.'

Seated at her desk, nervously fiddling with rubber bands and pens, she explained the genesis of the museum and then continued on a more personal note. 'Both my parents survived Auschwitz but I feel as if all my life I've been hearing about their wartime experiences. Every one of those survivors had to make up a story they could live with afterwards, you see.' I thought of the fairy-tale history of the Crusaders with which Western Christendom has been comforting itself for centuries. Erika went on: 'Of course, there were some who couldn't find a comforting story, and they committed suicide.'

She paused, on the verge of tears, before saying, 'In my twenties I went to France and Israel, really to escape my parents' suffering. Now I've grown up and come home again, but it wasn't until I read my father's book about his camp experiences that I became interested in the past. He had written about how proud and united the Greek Jews in the camps were, how they always spoke Greek and sang Greek songs, how patriotic they felt towards Greece.'

I wondered why the Thessaloniki Jews should have been as staunchly loyal to Greece as their eleventh-century forebears had been to the Byzantine Empire.

'It's simple really.' She explained: 'The Greek Jews belonged to the only nation that had fought and beaten a fascist power, Italy, and they could take pride in that victory. The other Jews only felt betrayed by their countries. And then, of course, the Greek Jews didn't speak Yiddish like most of the other Jews. But I think the most important reason was that most of the Greek Jews came from Thessaloniki, their home for hundreds of years. Jews had made this city what it was. Simply, they had never felt like a minority here.'

Erika told me that less than five per cent of Thessaloniki's pre-war Jewish community had survived, that almost fifty thousand of them had perished in the Nazi camps. In 1945, she said, her father had planned to escape from Europe to make a new start in Palestine, but her mother had wanted to stay put. They had managed to pick up the threads of a life although her father's family home had been occupied and his father's business stolen.

'There are between eight and ten thousand Jews in Thessaloniki today but only one famous Jewish business has revived since the war under the same family and in the same premises, the bookshop Molho. It's not far from here and very good. You should visit it.'

In brilliant afternoon sunshine the busy main shopping street was a warmer, kinder world, noisy with ringing church bells and motorbikes. I passed a More & More boutique like the one I had seen in Konstanz and fancy cake shops selling the Greek Orthodox Easter speciality, round loaves with red-painted eggs baked into their middles. Molho's two-storey emporium was everything a bookshop should be, every inch of its wall-space taken up by crammed book-shelves. Up a creaky wooden staircase, past piles of English dictionaries, past a table of second-hand books, in a far corner by the window, was its comprehensive Jewish history section. A hand-some man with a straggling foxy red beard, a descendant of the Molho who had opened the place in 1888 and son of another who had been forced to sell the business for a pittance and suffer all his books to be stolen in 1943, told me I was welcome to sit at a nearby table and read whatever took my fancy for as long as I liked. Soon I was settled amidst used coffee cups and full ashtrays with a work whose contents cast me straight back into the dark world Erika Perahia had grown up with. I found a song sung by Jewish women in the Nazi death camps.

> I was a little Jewess
> I wore the little star
> We were crushed by the soldiers
> Who took us away to Poland.
> We went to Poland
> Po, po, po, how we suffered
> They shaved off our hair
> And they dressed us like men . . .
> They took us to the baths
> They examined us for lice
> And our hearts beat tiki tiki tak
> For fear of being sent to the gas.
> I never stole my God
> Still less have I ever killed
> But I was a little Jewess
> And that's why I was imprisoned at Auschwitz.
> Blessings, my God
> Let blessings fall on the little English
> They are going to save us and free us
> Or, who knows, make things even worse for us . . .'[xxii]

Another book provided me with eye-witness accounts of how the Nazis terrorized Thessaloniki's Jews before despatching them north to the camps. After banning them from coffee houses, forcing them to wear yellow stars and expelling the sick from their hospital to make room for their own headquarters, the Germans had embarked on the wholesale destruction of the Jewish cemetery. They had used the gravestones from the vast necropolis dating back to the fifteenth century to build themselves a swimming pool and some roads.

11 Emperor Henry IV and his anti-pope forcing Gregory VII
to flee from Rome to Salerno; Gregory VII in Salerno, perhaps
presiding over his last council of bishops; on his death bed in 1085.
From a twelfth-century German chronicle.

12 View of Countess Matilda of Tuscany's
castle at Canossa, where Henry waited three days, barefoot
in the snow, to be pardoned by Gregory VII.

13 Basilica of St Nicholas of Bari, founded in 1087 on the site of a Byzantine
palace, to receive the stolen relics of the saint. Bohemond, the First Crusader,
sent the captured tent of a Moslem emir back to the church.

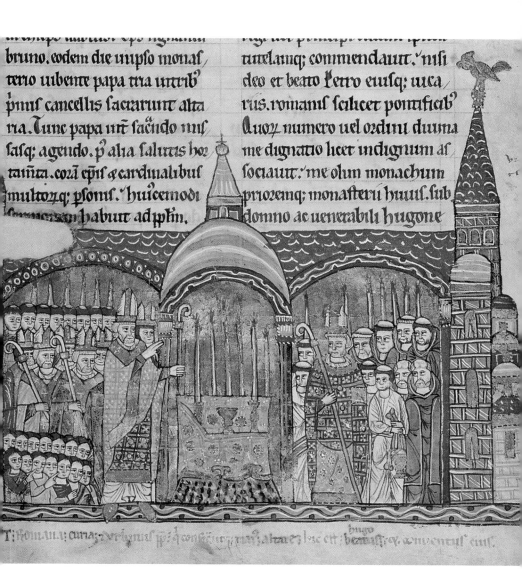

bruno. eodem die in ipso monasterio iubente papa tria inter bonus cancellis sacrarunt altaria. Tunc papa inter sacndo missasq; agendo. p alia salutis hortamta. cord epis & cardinalibus multoq; psonis. huiusmodi commeren habuit ad iptin.

tutelamq; commendauit. nisi deo et beato Petro eiusq; uicarius. romanis scilicet pontificib Quog numero uel ordini diuina me dignatio licet indignum af sociauit. me olim monachum priorenq; monasterii huius. sub domno ac uenerabili hugone

14 Consecration of Abbot Hugh of Cluny's church in 1095 by Pope Urban II before he preached the First Crusade at Clermont. It was Cluny's third church, designed to rival Abbot Desiderius' at Monte Cassino. From a twelfth-century chronicle of the Abbey of Cluny.

15 The arrival of Pope Urban II in France in 1095 and his preaching of the First Crusade at the Council of Clermont. From a fourteenth-century painting.

16 The four horsemen of the Apocalypse wearing the full armour of First Crusaders. From a twelfth-century Spanish manuscript.

17 (OPPOSITE) Emperor Alexius I Comnenus of Byzantium (1081–1118). From a twelfth-century mosaic in Hagia Sophia, Istanbul.

18 Peter the Hermit exhorting the multitudes to join
the First Crusade to recapture Jerusalem for Christendom.
From the *Histoire Universelle* c.1286.

19 The First Crusaders' Siege of Antioch, 1097–8,
as imagined by a thirteenth-century artist.

20 View of Krak des Chevaliers, the Crusader castle in Syria.

21 A fifteenth-century evocation of the First Crusaders'
sacking of Jerusalem in 1099.

22 The twelfth-century Crusader Church of the Holy Sepulchre, Jerusalem

The sight was terrible. People were scurrying among the workers begging permission to salvage the remains of their dead. At our family's burial site was the grave of my twenty-five year-old brother who had died during a trip to Rome ... When we opened the coffin, my brother was visible in smoking jacket and light coloured shoes, as though he had only been buried the day before. My mother fainted. A few months later my mother, my father and other relatives were all put to death in Auschwitz.[xxiii]

Five days after this brutal eradication of almost half a millennium of Jewish history, on 11 July 1942, nine thousand Jews were ordered to gather in the city's Elefteria Square, today a car park with a sea view. Erika had told me that her eighteen-year-old father had ventured out without his yellow star to witness the scene:

We had to stand in formation. The Nazis had surrounded the square with machine guns and small artillery. We were forbidden to sit, to leave the formation, to shade ourselves from the sun with a newspaper, to wear sunglasses, to light a cigarette or to motion to a friend. The Nazi soldiers and sailors observed us and hit us on the head, arms and elsewhere. Then they forced us to perform gymnastics, to crawl through the dust, to roll over and jump like frogs and more. This was all accompanied by shouts, curses and whippings. That day I saw how great man's inhumanity could be . . .[xxiv]

By the time I emerged from Molho, harrowed by my prolonged exposure to such horrifyingly recent history, the bright spring day had clouded over. The wind blowing up from the sea was cold and wet, and the Via Egnatia empty of all but a few pedestrians. The forlorn scene matched my mood so well that it was a while before I realized that the road had been cordoned off for a Good Friday procession. Listening to a doleful drumbeat, I waited for the first column of slow-marching policemen to draw level. Behind them hundreds of Boy and Girl Scouts shivered in their shorts and shirt-sleeves. Next came orderly columns of navy personnel, male and female, followed by a phalanx of priests bearing a weighty-looking wooden cross on their shoulders, their robes billowing out behind them in the wind. Soldiers in camouflage, with their guns at their sides, and a group of prominent townspeople tightly buttoned into suits and coats followed, ahead of yet another group of Orthodox churchmen, resplendent in the silver and purple robes reserved for mourning the Crucifixion of Christ. Behind them trundled a float decked with flowers. The heavy sweet scent of carnations mingled with the perfume of incense and lingered in the damp air.

The impatient hooting of car horns and roaring of motorbikes resumed. The sun came out again and a nearby market teemed with people making last-minute purchases for the Easter holiday. Stallholders were slashing their prices on whole lambs. Giant straw-berries and bunches of spring onions were going cheap. Thinking ahead to the long train journey to Istanbul the next day, I invested in some dried figs, a paper bag of oranges and a plastic bottle of water.

~

'A one-way ticket to Konstantinopoli, please.'

The Byzantine chant and puffs of incense smoke issuing from a little candlelit church to the right of the ticket hall had reminded me, just in time, that many Greeks are still mourning the fall of Constantinople to the Turks in 1453 and do not like to hear their ancient capital referred to by its Turkish name.

Standing on the station platform enjoying the early morning sunshine on my face, I scanned an English edition of a Greek newspaper, pausing only to study some senior Orthodox churchmen's comments on the meaning of Easter. Archbishop Anastasios of Albania had yoked his freedom and love creed to a more overtly political message for the occasion. Condemning 'economic globalis-ation' for resulting in 'the majority being crushed and exploited', he was proposing 'an ecumenical brotherhood, based on freedom, mutual respect and love, as they flow from the Cross and life-giving tomb of our risen Lord'.[xxv] The train pulled in and I climbed aboard. I was sorry to be leaving Thessaloniki but I could not linger as I had in Bari. That very evening I was planning to attend the glorious Easter night service at Istanbul's Orthodox Ecumenical Patriarchate, the last living relic of the Byzantine Empire in what had been the largest and most civilized Christian metropolis in the world between the fifth and fifteenth centuries.

The comfortably air-conditioned train hummed through Thessaloniki's eastern suburbs towards the grey-green mountains north of the city. With the glittering blue sea visible on the right and the mountains, fields of velvety new wheat and brilliantly whitewashed little churches on the left, we sped on east and my thoughts strayed back to Bohemond. Still on his best pilgrim's behaviour in that early spring of 1097, he had not inflicted his army on Thessaloniki but skirted the northern edge of the city, thereby sparing it a ransacking and perhaps its Jews their first pogrom. Like me he was hurrying towards Constantinople, but he had more pressing reasons than celebrating Easter for making haste.

Bohemond knew that other Crusading lords had already reached Constantinople and were jockeying for position and power as guests of Emperor Alexius before launching themselves into the territory of the Infidel Turk. The first to arrive had been Count Hugh, youngest son of the French king, harbouring ideas far above his station about the degree of respect his personage merited. Taking ship from Bari before Bohemond, he had sent an absurd message to Alexius demanding that he meet him at Dyrrachium: 'Know, Emperor, that I am the King of Kings, the greatest of all beneath the heavens. It is my will that you should meet me on my arrival and receive me with the pomp and ceremony due to my noble birth.'[xxvi]

Wise Alexius had known just how to handle the silly pup. Showering him with honours and gifts he cleverly concealed the simple truth that he was holding Count Hugh prisoner. In no time at all he had neutralized any threat Hugh represented by extracting from him an oath of loyalty, common practice in feudal Western Christendom but unknown in the east. After promising to return all conquered territories once owned by Byzantium to Alexius, just as Pope Urban had also insisted, Count Hugh was free to enjoy the best of Byzantine hospitality while he waited for other armies to turn up.

Next to arrive was a large force led by the Duke Godfrey de Bouillon and his two younger brothers, one of whom, Baldwin, was travelling with his wife and family. A handsome blond giant of no great brain but some piety – except where Pope Gregory and Jews were concerned – Duke Godfrey had led his expedition down through central Europe and, like the People's Crusaders and the German anti-Semites, experienced delays while in Hungary. The Hungarian king, understandably deeply suspicious of hordes of *milites Christi* since Peter the Hermit and the Germans had passed through, insisted on taking Baldwin and his family hostage. Their safe release was conditional upon their fellow Crusaders' good behaviour while crossing his realm. The army marched on without ugly incident, over the Danube into Byzantine territory to Belgrade which was still a deserted wasteland thanks to the attentions of the People's Crusaders five months earlier. Tightly supervised by Byzantine soldiers, it reached the northern shore of the Sea of Marmara without major mishap. But there, within two days' march of Constantinople, the Crusaders disgraced themselves by pillaging the surrounding countryside for a week.

At last sufficient discipline was restored for the army to resume its march to the capital, where Emperor Alexius awaited Duke Godfrey, planning to buy his oath of loyalty with another bout of generous gift-giving. Alexius despatched the preposterous but biddable Count Hugh to Godfrey with instructions to convince him that an oath of fealty to a Byzantine emperor was a small price to pay for a successful Crusade. But Godfrey was not persuaded. Some of his soldiers had met up with a few remnants from Peter the Hermit's expedition who were blaming their abject performance on Greek treachery. Godfrey was also reluctant to contradict an existing oath of loyalty he had sworn to Henry IV, and wanted to wait and see what other Crusading lords would do.

Alexius signalled his irritation at the delay by cutting off supplies to his guests. Safely reunited with his brothers after his few weeks' sojourn at the Hungarian king's pleasure, Baldwin retaliated by letting his part of the army loose in the Constantinople suburbs. The flow of supplies was rapidly resumed. By March, Duke Godfrey had still not come to heel. Alexius was dreading the arrival of yet more Crusaders in his capital and his patience was exhausted. Supplies to Godfrey's force were not stopped but gradually reduced. First there was no fodder for their horses, then no fish and finally no bread. The Crusaders resumed their raiding in the villages around the city and eventually fell foul of the imperial police. Count Baldwin boldly set an ambush and took sixty police captive, which provoked Duke Godfrey into going one better. He attacked Constantinople itself, at the gate nearest the imperial palace.

It was a solemn Maundy Thursday. The Byzantines were horrified by Godfrey's aggression, convinced that the Crusaders had not only taken leave of their Christian senses but at last revealed their true intentions: to conquer the golden city just as Robert Guiscard had dreamed of doing fifteen years earlier. But Alexius, anxious to avoid shedding the blood of fellow Christians three days before the holiest festival of the year, forbade any immediate armed response. 'He sat firmly on the imperial throne,' wrote his daughter, 'gazing cheerfully on them [his generals], encouraging and inspiring the hearts of all with confidence.'[xxvii] And the next day, Good Friday, he sent a message to Duke Godfrey. It said: ' "Have reverence . . . for God on this day was sacrificed for us all, refusing neither the Cross, nor the Nails, nor the Spear – proper instruments of punishment for evildoers – to save us. If you must fight, we too shall be ready, but after the day of the Saviour's resurrection." '[xxviii]

The shameful affair ended with Alexius having to unleash the full force of his army for which the Crusaders were no match at all. Duke Godfrey conceded defeat and on Easter Sunday took the required oath of allegiance. In return he was treated to a magnificent banquet and gigantic gifts of gold before being shipped with his army to a holding camp on the other side of the Bosphorus. Another horde of barbarian Crusaders was at the gates.

These latest arrivals were even less disciplined than Duke God-frey's force and led by minor lords whose names have not survived. After some strong-arming they were also compelled to swear oaths of loyalty but one of them committed a disgusting faux pas by seating himself on the emperor's throne just before the ceremony. Even Count Baldwin was outraged and told the man, ' "You ought never to have done such a thing, especially after promising to be the emperor's liege man. Roman* Emperors don't let their subjects sit with them. That's the custom here . . ." ' The offender replied with a few muttered words: ' "What a peasant! He [Alexius] sits alone while generals like these stand around him!" '.[xxix] In the ritualized splendour of that Byzantine court this Norman was feeling insecure. He must have been missing the old *familiaritas*, the atmos-phere of egalitarian informality typical of the northern kingdoms of western Europe, of Icelandic Althings and the court of Otto III. Alexius had his interpreter translate the man's surly response and, once the ceremony was over, called him to his side to ask his name and origins. The man declared himself a 'pure Frank' and bragged of his prowess in single combat. Wise Alexius advised the boastful oaf not to go looking for a fight with any Turk. ' "I know the enemy's methods. I've had long experience of the Turk," '[xxx] he warned him.

Alexius was about to come face to face with his deadliest foe for the first time since that October day fifteen years before when he had had to flee the Dyrrachium battlefield with his 'bright red hair straggling in front of his eyes',[xxxi] but he had calmly determined to manage Bohemond as he had done the others. Disarming him with a surfeit of generosity and hospitality, he would extract from him an oath of allegiance and then ship him and his army across the Bosphorus into Asia before the next crowd of hooligan Crusaders descended like a plague on the city. However, the luxury lodgings

---

* The Byzantines, the Eastern Romans of the ancient Roman Empire, called themselves the Greek word for Romans – *Romaioi*.

he carefully arranged for Bohemond were safely away from the imperial palace, on the opposite side of the Golden Horn and outside the city walls.

Bohemond arrived in Constantinople four days after Easter, on 9 April 1097. He had left the bulk of his army under the command of his nephew Tancred to celebrate the Easter weekend in a verdant valley off the main Via Egnatia. Anna Comnena, inspired by fond memories of what was surely a teenage love-hate crush on the handsome Bohemond, provides us with an unforgettable account of the Italian Norman's sojourn in her home city. She writes that Alexius received him the moment he arrived with a smile, a polite enquiry about his journey and some flattering references to the courage he had displayed in Dyrrachium back in 1082.

' "I was indeed your enemy and foe then," ' replied Bohemond, ' "but now I come of my own free will as Your Majesty's friend." 'xxxii

Judging that Bohemond would be prepared to take the all-important oath, Alexius dismissed him: ' "You are tired now from your journey. Go away and rest. Tomorrow we can discuss matters of common interest." 'xxxiii

At his lodgings in the famous monastery of St Cosmas and St Damian Bohemond found a sumptuous dinner laid for him, but immediately cooks appeared bearing platters of raw meat. They told him that if he did not wish to eat any of the food on the table he was welcome to have some more prepared to his liking. Alexius had astutely reckoned that Bohemond was bound to fear poisoning, and he was right. Bohemond did not touch a morsel of the feast set before him, not even with the tips of his fingers. Instead, he shared it all out among his followers. Anna Comnena is scathing: 'It looked as if he was doing them a favour, but that was mere pretence: in reality, if one considers the matter rightly, he was mixing them a cup of death. There was no attempt to hide his treachery, for it was his habit to treat servants with utter indifference.'xxxiv

The next day Bohemond casually asked his followers how they were feeling. 'Very well,' they all replied. He then took the oath Alexius required of him and duly received his magnificent reward:

Alexius had had the floor of a whole room in the palace so thickly carpeted with precious objects, rich cloths and gold and silver that 'it was impossible for anyone to walk in it'.ˣˣˣᵛ Bohemond was suitably amazed and accepted the gifts but almost immediately afterwards decided that the emperor was bribing him and refused the rich booty. Then, watching the servants packing it all away, he changed his mind again. The poorest of the Crusading lords, he needed the money. Guiscard would never have bungled like this. I could picture the old *Terror Mundi* graciously accepting the treasure, but immediately and very ostentatiously upstaging Alexius by redistributing it all to Constantinople's poor for the sake of his Lord Jesus Christ.

Bohemond was desperate to erase the past and forge so close a friendship with Alexius that the Byzantine emperor would entrust the supreme leadership of the Crusade to him. For all the famous Norman's military skill and leadership potential, Alexius could not have been further from obliging him, but he kept him sweet and guessing with the words, ' "The time for that is not yet ripe, but with your energy and loyalty it will not be long before you have even that honour." 'ˣˣˣᵛⁱ After giving Bohemond and his captains a briefing on Turkish military tactics, he sent him and his army across the Bosphorus to join the others and turned his attention to yet another wave of Crusaders, led by Count Raymond of Toulouse.

If anyone could rightfully claim the supreme leadership of the Crusade, it was Count Raymond, Pope Urban's first lay recruit to the venture. But the pope had been careful to keep the entire enterprise under his own spiritual direction, and Count Raymond had had to content himself with the honour of having Urban's representative, Bishop Adhemar of Puy, in his entourage. This latest group of lamentably undisciplined and poorly equipped Crusaders, from south-west France, had struggled down what is now the Slovenian and Croatian coast of the Adriatic as far as Dyrrachium, where they had picked up the Via Egnatia and turned east. In one of many skirmishes with the Byzantine soldiers policing their progress, Bishop Adhemar had been accidentally wounded. Leaving him to convalesce in Thessaloniki, Count Raymond's expedition had pushed on towards Constantinople, growing more and more unruly. Discipline had completely broken down by the time Count Raymond hurried on ahead alone, just as Bohemond had done.

News of a battle and his army's defeat by Byzantine soldiers reached Count Raymond when he was on his way to his first audience with Emperor Alexius and it only exacerbated his bad mood. The elderly Count, veteran of many wars against the Muslims in Spain, was tired after his difficult journey, disturbed by a rumour that Alexius was about to put Bohemond in charge of the Crusade and missing his friend Bishop Adhemar who would have counselled him about the wisdom of giving his oath of allegiance to a Byzantine emperor. Refusing to swear anything, he told Alexius that he considered only God to be his lord. Alexius respected his transparent honesty and piety, and the two men were soon brought closer by their shared distrust of Bohemond. According to Anna Comnena, Count Raymond told her father, ' "It will be a miracle if he [Bohemond] keeps his sworn word." 'xxxvii He also informed Alexius that if he, Raymond of Toulouse, could not be supreme commander of the Crusade, he would not mind serving in a united army of Eastern and Western Christians under the emperor's own command. But Alexius regretted that the perilous state of his empire did not permit him the luxury of a pilgrimage to Jerusalem. The count eventually swore a modified oath and was shipped across to Asia like the rest.

The last Crusader army to arrive in Constantinople was composed of Normans and Flemings. Depleted by a shameful rate of desertion while it lingered overlong in Norman southern Italy and by a disastrous shipwrecking in the Adriatic, this army was relatively well behaved. One of its leaders was Count Stephen of Blois, who was married to William the Conqueror's daughter, Adele. A devoted family man, Count Stephen had not fancied the idea of spending years far-faring to Jerusalem and back, but Adele had ordered him on his way. His letters home to her are some of the best historical sources about the expedition. The Emperor Alexius' customary

largesse astounded Count Stephen. 'Your father, my love,' he wrote
to his wife, 'made many gifts, but he was almost nothing compared to this man.'[xxxviii] Alexius invited Count Stephen to send one
of his sons to complete his education at the Byzantine court. 'Verily,
my beloved,' Count Stephen told his Adele, 'his Imperial Highness
has very often urged, and urges, that we commend one of our sons
to him.'[xxxix]

My train pulled into a little station. I was ordered off, out of
the air-conditioned cool into hot midday sunshine beating down on
a cracked platform. My Crusaders had already reached Constantinople and been ferried safely across the Bosphorus while I was forced
to suffer twinges of *Accidie* at this tiny frontier post, waiting for my
visa to Turkey. At last a scruffily uniformed Turk beckoned me into
a dusty office.

'You are English? Ten pounds.'

My passport was stamped and my ten-pound note dropped into
an empty drawer of a battered wooden desk.

~

Not many of us climbed back on board that holiday Easter Saturday
express to Istanbul. I counted five American backpackers, a ponytailed youth who might have been Italian and a stout elderly man
wearing very thick black shades clipped to his spectacles.

'I am Corleone Kalashnikov!' declared the latter, squeezing into
my compartment, one hand extended for shaking, the other tucked
inside his jacket as if nursing a gun. Grinning lopsidedly, he removed
his hand from his jacket and the shades from his spectacles to wink
a big blue eye at me in the sort of piratical manner Guiscard or his
son might have employed when plotting one of their dastardly
adventures. Slinging his satchel on the seat opposite me, he rubbed
his hands together gleefully and explained in heavily Scandinavian-
accented English, 'I like to have my international joke. Everyone
knows about the Mafia and guns, don't they? My real name is
Sigvard Sternberg.'

'Are you, by any chance, an Icelander?' I hazarded a wild hope. The idea of far-faring towards Constantinople with one of Thorvald's descendants was very appealing, but any Scandinavian would have satisfied me on account of their historical connection with the Byzantine capital through the Varangian Guard.

'Why should you think I'm from Iceland? I'm a Swedish Jew.' I could not help laughing at such an unlikely and yet, as far as my eleventh-century saga was concerned, entirely suitable identity. Sigvard very quickly grasped the point of my project, mentioned his love of Viking history and began regaling me with highlighted excerpts from his own life-saga.

In the 1950s he had left Sweden to study violin at the Moscow conservatory. Much like his Swedish Viking forebears on the Varangian route from the Baltic to the Black Sea, he had travelled up and down Russia, in his case making music and quaffing vodka. Like Arni Bergmann, Sigvard had married a Russian. Although the marriage had failed, he had never lost his love of her country and still spoke fluent Russian.

'Sometimes I pretend – just for a joke – that I am from the Russian Mafia. Corleone Kalashnikov is a good name, don't you think, for a Mafia man?'

He was reminding me of Anya, who had fantasized about dressing up as a Turkish drug-smuggler to tease the Swiss border guards. For years Sigvard had played his violin in provincial Swedish orchestras. Remarried and divorced again, he remained cheerfully convinced that he was watched over by a good angel.

'Always an angel helps me . . .' he asserted, with another of his cartoon winks.

'You're sounding rather Christian.'

'No! Judaism has angels too. Look at your Old Testament! But anyway I believe in angels because they are part of nature. I am not an observant Jew. Nature is my religion, my only religion.'

'You're a naturist.'

'Ho! Ho!' he laughed, and winked, but immediately turned serious again. 'No. I've arrived at my beliefs through logic. Jesus

Christ must have been a prophet because no one can be the son of God. Or even the daughter,' he added with a gallant nod in my direction. 'We don't know what God is, only that he is everywhere. What else is everywhere? Nature! So Nature must be God!'

'Not an expression of God, or his creation?'

'No. I *love* this God Nature. When I retire from working I have a dream to go back to my homeland and find an apartment in a small village near a lake and woods. I will swim every day, cut wood for my fire and hunt for berries and mushrooms . . .'

'You don't live in your homeland now?'

'No, no. For tax reasons I'm living in Thessaloniki for a year or two, teaching some students the violin. The rest of the time I swim in the sea and play with the children of Albanian immigrants who live in my block. They call me Mister Kalashnikov and I buy them ice creams . . .'

'You're not enjoying it there much?' I asked, gently probing beneath his surface bonhomie.

'No actually, not very much. That's why I'm taking this little holiday to Istanbul.'

He frowned and gazed out of the window at the red light bulb sun setting over a flat, scrubby plain. There was something on his mind, so I waited.

'You know what?' he said suddenly. 'This European Union is not going to work. It was good when it began, to stop another world war between France and Germany and make a united front against Soviet expansion. But, believe me, after what I have experienced in Greece, I know it's not going to work! The people in Brussels don't understand how people think in a country like Greece. Every-thing in that country is behind the back, under the table, around the corner, not logical or straightforward or easy.'

I was hearing the voice of every Norseman raised against what Otto III had once valued so highly as the Greek *subtilitas* that could erase his Saxon *rusticitas*. I remembered Emperor Alexius' subtly underhand management of Bohemond's first cooked dinner in Con-

stantinople, and how the pejorative adjective 'byzantine' has come
to denote precisely the quality that Sigvard was describing.

'Sweden should not be in this kind of EU,' continued Sigvard.
'We can keep some things in common, human rights and traffic
regulations, for example, but a closer union should only be made of
people with the same mentality and culture, then we will all understand each other and business will go well. No one will feel oppressed
then and no culture will be sacrificed so that everything from
Stockholm to Athens, from Warsaw to Lisbon, looks and feels and
tastes the same, and only the weather is different. Sweden could
easily make a small union with the rest of Scandinavia and with
England . . .'

'You think there could be many different mini-unions?'

'Yes, Greece could be connected with other Mediterranean
countries like Italy and Spain, or perhaps with the rest of the
Balkans. Germany and central Europe and maybe Poland could be
another group, and France could go with Holland and Belgium.
And all these unions could overlap into neighbouring unions on
some points if it was convenient.'

He was excited by his vision and I was beginning to warm to
it, not least because if it were ever to be implemented, the political
map of Europe would look much as it had done in the early eleventh
century. There would be King Canute's Danish commonwealth
recreated, including England. Germany could be the largest compo-
nent of a reborn Holy Roman Empire such as Otto III had ruled
over, perhaps excluding the city which had broken his heart and
health, but including central Europe and maybe even the rich lands
of northern Italy which had belonged to the pious and warlike
Countess Matilda . . .

'But what kind of union would Russia or Turkey, for example,
fit into?' I asked, as excited by geopolitics as Pope Urban had been
when dreaming up the First Crusade.

At that moment our compartment door slid open and in stepped
the ponytailed youth who might have been Italian. It transpired

that Sigvard and he were already well acquainted, having shared a compartment on the journey from Thessaloniki to the border.

'Victoria, this is my friend Eray. He is a tour guide from Istanbul,' said Sigvard, giving the young man's nose a welcoming tweak and shooting me another of his winks.

We shared the last of my figs and oranges, and continued the conversation.

'I don't know if Turkey will ever be able to join the EU,'* said Eray glumly. 'Most people still want to go in but we've got forty per cent inflation – it's about 1,250,000 Turkish lira to the dollar right now – and there's still the problem with the Kurds, and our coalition government includes members of the fascist party, the Grey Wolves. Anyway, Greece will never let us join. You know they still think Istanbul is their Constantinople? On the whole, people think that the real problem is that Europe doesn't want us in its EU because we're Muslims.'

'How strange! Europe sees the problem quite differently, as being all about human rights,' I replied. 'That the Turkish army is not under civilian control, that people are tortured in Turkish prisons, the Kurdish problem . . .'

Eray shrugged, and frowned at the window. As the train chugged into the night-time suburbs of Istanbul at last, I asked him why the Turkish fascist party called itself the Grey Wolves.

'Oh, it's all to do with the folk story about how the Turks first started settling on the Anatolian plain in about the year 1000. Every child knows it – I hope I can remember right. Let's see, there was once a big grey wolf who came out of a hole in a mountain somewhere far to the east of Turkey, somewhere like Uzbekistan or Kazakhstan. One day a Turkish child who had often seen the wolf decided to follow it back into the mountain. "Where's that wolf from and where is he going?" the boy said to himself, following the animal through a tunnel for a long time. At last he saw the light

---

* Turkey first applied for EU membership in 1987. Greece, Spain and Portugal were accepted. Poland, Hungary, the Czech Republic, Estonia, Latvia, Slovenia and Cyprus will enter before Turkey.

on the other side of the mountain, so he turned round and went back to his village to tell everyone about it. The tunnel was made big enough for men to pass through and off they went until they reached the land with green grass, trees and waterfalls in eastern Turkey. That's it.'

If the boy had not been brave enough to follow the grey wolf through the tunnel, I reasoned, the Turks would not have begun filtering into Asia Minor at the turn of the last millennium, Byzantium would not have lost the heartland of its empire at the battle of Manzikert in 1071, and Emperor Alexius would never have felt constrained to ask Pope Urban to send him a few *milites* to help defend Eastern Christendom. The Crusades might never have happened! But this was going too far. Sooner or later the First Crusade was bound to happen. Western Christendom was in a confidently expansive mood after the dark terrors of the tenth century and the earlier Middle Ages, and Pope Gregory had already planted the seed of Crusade in his failed expedition of 1074.

Istanbul, with its domes and minarets, ancient walls and Byzantine churches lit up, its sports courts floodlit and the uncurtained windows of apartment blocks all glowing with gold or blueish fluorescent light, looked thrillingly glamorous. I could easily imagine how in their eagerness to sample its super-civilized attractions, the Crusaders had forgotten their manners. The night breeze wafting through the compartment's open window was warm and smelt slightly of sea and rotting refuse. And suddenly, there in the gaps between the buildings, was the Bosphorus, opening into the Sea of Marmara, a fairy-lit pleasure boat relieving its silken blackness.

It was almost eleven o'clock; the train was two hours behind schedule. I had precisely an hour in which to reach the patriarchate for the midnight Easter service, and we had not even arrived yet.

~

Long before the turning off to the Ecumenical Patriarchate from the busy dual carriageway running around the Golden Horn, the line of parked tour buses – most of them with Greek number plates – had already begun. Police cars' flashing blue and red lights decorated the entrance to the narrow cobbled street leading up to the headquarters of the two hundred and seventieth patriarch of Constantinople.

Beneath its high protective walls and a loyally fluttering Turkish flag was a heaving, close-packed crowd of Orthodox Greeks (the tiny and ever-dwindling local community* as well as tourists) leavened with a few Orthodox Romanians and even Russians. All of them were dressed in their best and carrying candles. As I made for the entrance and a flight of steep steps, a screeching fight erupted. Two young Russians in miniskirts and dangerously sharp high heels came stumbling down towards me swearing back over their shoulders, nursing their scratched arms. People hissed as they passed. Almost lifted off my feet, I was carried on up the stairs and through the narrow doorway, up some more steps to the courtyard. Further progress was impossible. Behind me, two long-haired young men with the faintly musty smell and sweetly fervent look of novice Orthodox monks agreed that there were not as many people as the year before.

It struck me that there would have been plenty of room for us all in the old heart of the city, in the great cathedral of the Divine Wisdom which the Byzantine Emperor Justinian had built in the sixth century. Regretting the shrinking of golden Byzantium to these cramped quarters, I gave up all hope of bumping into my friend Grand Archdeacon Tarasios, a suave Greek-American from San Antonio in Texas, and the patriarch's right-hand man. I likewise despaired of reaching the little patriarchate church on the opposite side of the courtyard. Craning my neck for a glimpse of it, I was shocked to see it lit as bright as day for television cameras. The special attraction of attending the Orthodox Easter service here in the ancient home of Eastern Christianity is to witness the dispelling

* In 1900 the descendants of Byzantine Greeks in Istanbul numbered around 250,000. The Greek–Turkish hostilities of the twentieth century meant that by 1990 there were only around 5,000.

of the blackness caused by Christ's death on the Cross by a light miraculously kindled every year in Jerusalem's Church of the Holy Sepulchre and carefully transported all the way here by aeroplane and police car.

The appearance of that single flicker in the gloom and its spreading, from candle to candle through the crowds until it illuminates every face and corner, is an exhilarating sight. I had hoped it would be conducive to contemplating the mystery of the Resurrection, as *Frère* Émile back at Taizé had recommended. Disappointed, and wondering at the force of a faith which kept people standing out there in a suddenly chilly wind blowing down the Bosphorus, waiting for the long service to begin, I struggled down the steep stairs again and through the crowd to catch a taxi back to my hotel.

~

Easter Sunday morning was bright and warm again. Rustled by a light breeze, the lime trees lining the avenue leading to the sixth-century Byzantine-built Ayia Sophia were a shimmer of translucent green. The tourists queuing for tickets to enter the museum that had been the architectural wonder of the Christian world for nine hundred years were all wearing shorts and T-shirts.

By adding minarets and replacing most of the mosaics and icons with a series of heavy round plaques bearing the names of Allah and his caliphs, the Turks turned what had been 'The Great Church' into a mosque, before abandoning it in the last century for use as a museum. Daylight filtering meagrely through high dirty windows gave the gigantic open interior the forlorn air of a once grand, now obsolete Victorian railway station. I did not linger down there, struggling to picture the service which Cardinal Humbert and his friends had disgracefully interrupted on that July afternoon in 1054 to set in train the almost thousand-year schism between the Churches. Nor did I waste any time searching for traces of the gold-cloth factory which their arch-enemy, the ferocious Patriarch Michael Kerollarios, had illegally set up for his own profit in the cathedral crypt. There were two things high up in the building that interested me more.

Climbing the long stone stairway to the gallery, I walked around it, peering not down at the church and the heads of the milling crowds but very closely at centuries-worth of graffiti on the ancient greying marble sills between the arches. I was looking for a famous Viking graffito dating back to a century before the arrival of those Varangians which the first Christian king of Kievan Rus had presented to Byzantium. While fantasizing about happening across the name 'Thorvald' etched on the marble, I was almost as delighted to discover two scratched series of concentric squares. It was exactly the same sort of game which the bored Roman soldiers who had marked one of the marble slabs used to make Charlemagne's throne in Aachen had played. There were plenty of scratchings which might have been Viking runes but looked more like Greek letters. At last I found what I was looking for, carefully conserved under a pane of glass. A single name, long ago deciphered as 'Halvdan', was legible.

When we met for dinner later that evening I would tell my new Swedish Jewish acquaintance where to find it. On the train he had listened eagerly to all that I had been able to teach him about his Scandinavian forefathers' Varangian connection with Constantinople. I had amused him with the information that, rather like the pre-Norman conquest Anglo-Saxons, Varangians were frequently 'boiling with unrighteous fury and carried along in a riot of drunkenness'.[xl] I had told him how graciously Thorvald the Far-farer had been received by the Byzantine emperor and how, returning home from a stint in the Varangian Guard in the early eleventh century, another Icelander named Bolli Bollason had grown so accustomed to fine living in Constantinople that 'he would wear no clothes except those made of fine stuff or velvet and all his weapons were inlaid with gold', and how his countrywomen 'did nothing but gape at the splendid adornment of Bolli and his companions'.[xli]

The Byzantines had developed a set of useful guidelines for dealing with their warlike northern *Gastarbeiter*:

Foreigners . . . you should not promote to high rank nor entrust with great office of state . . . If foreigners serve [only] for clothing and bread, be assured that they will serve you loyally and whole-heartedly, looking only to the bounty of your hands for trifling sums of money and for bread . . . [None] of the above-mentioned emperors of blessed memory promoted a Frank or a Varangian to the rank of *patricius*.[xlii]

No Varangian was permitted to marry into the Byzantine royal family, a prohibition which never stopped the Varangians telling stories as tall as any Icelander's about how a Norwegian prince, serving incognito in the emperor's elite guard, had managed to have an affair with a niece of the Empress Zoe, the same Zoe Otto III had died too soon to marry back in 1002.

The Empress Zoe was on my mind because, featured in one of the few Byzantine mosaics which the Turks had not troubled to destroy when turning the church into a mosque, she was my second reason for visiting Ayia Sophia. Surrounded by a crowd of appreciative tourists, she was not hard to find. Against a glittering gold background, she is depicted with a magnificently blue-robed Christ seated on a rich throne, and her third husband, Emperor Constantine IX. Zoe and Constantine are clothed in pearl-studded garments of intricate pattern and rich colour but Constantine's rosy cheeks and beard look a little out of keeping with the rest of the mosaic. My guidebook helpfully explained that the original face filling that space had been that of her first or second husband; Constantine's was a later substitution. Zoe's face is a little faded and some of the tesserae around her jowls are missing. Her head is graciously inclined towards Christ but her rosebud mouth looks set to blow a raspberry.

I spent a long while there, contemplating the mosaic and the bizarre turns Zoe's life had taken after she learned of Otto's death and sailed back home from Bari. A Byzantine chronicler as excellent as Anna Comnena, a gossipy courtier called Michael Psellus, wrote a good deal about the woman who was so cruelly robbed of a chance to play her part in keeping Christendom united back in the early eleventh century.

Zoe was already fifty when she was married for the first time to an emperor already in his seventies and so ignorant of female biology that he could not understand why she did not conceive. In a desperate attempt to please him and cheat nature, Zoe resorted to every remedy she could obtain. The sceptical Psellus tells us that she began 'fastening little pebbles to her body, hanging charms about her, wearing chains, decking herself out with the rest of the nonsense'.[xliii] The aged emperor soon lost his appetite for conjugal relations, but not so Zoe. Her eye alighted on an epileptic young courtier called Michael who quickly understood that his career would depend on acting as besotted with her as she was with him. The emperor grew suspicious enough to have young Michael swear an oath on some relics to the effect that he had never touched Zoe, but Michael blithely perjured himself. Zoe was recklessly flagrant in her enjoyment of this late love and lust: 'In the eyes of all she clung to him and offered him her kisses, boasting that she had more than once had her joy of him.'[xliv] Soon, she was plotting to make him emperor.

The pair started poisoning her old husband. Soon the emperor's hair was falling out and his face was 'no more pleasant to look upon than that of men three days dead in their tombs'.[xlv] He was finished off by drowning in his swimming pool. Zoe assumed control of the empire and declared young Michael her emperor, but she was to be horribly disappointed. Michael never touched her again and banished her to the *gynaeconitis*, the palace women's quarters. A powerful spiritual father had made him ashamed of his wicked manoeuvring for power.

Bitterly repenting of his sins and his perjury, Michael began to spend much of his time in Thessaloniki praying at the tomb of St Dimitri, in the crypt of the basilica church whose Maundy Thursday service I had attended. He also built the Monastery of St Cosmas and St Damian where Alexius would lodge Bohemond some forty years later. Psellus waxes lyrical over its beauties, which were as bewitching as those of Abbot Desiderius' new church at Monte Cassino. As fervently pious as a St Nilus or St Romuald, Michael began consorting with poor hermits and beggars. Often, says Psellus, he 'put his face to the festering sores on their bodies, then – even more amazing – embraced them, folded them in his arms, tended them, bathed and waited on them, as though he was a slave and they his masters'.[xlvi] He also built a refuge for the prostitutes whom he sought to convert into nuns. In 1041, on the very day he had himself tonsured a monk at his new monastery, he died and was buried there.

A nephew of Michael's whom Zoe had obligingly adopted came to the throne next, and banished his benefactress to a monastery on a prison island in the Sea of Marmara. Not long afterwards, she was restored by popular demand and returned to the palace still wearing her nun's habit. Her younger sister Theodora was then retrieved from the monastery to which Zoe had sent her and the two of them ruled together for a year. In order to recreate the flavour of what Constantinople was like during that 'transformation of a *gynaeconitis* into an emperor's council chamber',[xlvii] Psellus pauses to provide his readers with a fascinating psychological sketch of Zoe, a woman remarkably like the young Otto. Her mood swings reminded Psellus of 'sea-waves, now lifting a ship on high and then again plunging it down to the depths'.[xlviii] Like her dead fiancé Otto and her second husband Michael, she was exceptionally God-fearing. We learn that 'there was no moment when the name of God was not on her lips'.[xlix] Psellus blames her and her sister for ruining the empire's fortunes with their frivolous generosity, fortunes which Alexius had great difficulty restoring in the 1080s. Most poignant of all, she was just as deliciously beautiful as Otto. At the age of sixty-two her hair was still golden and 'no part of her skin was wrinkled, but all smooth and taut, and no furrows anywhere'.[l]

Zoe soon got rid of her sister and seized complete power for herself, but she needed a man at her side to help her hold onto it. Constantine IX, with his 'singularly attractive smile',[li] was her third and last husband. Although well preserved, Zoe had finally lost all interest in sex and so did not mind when her consort flaunted his young mistress before her. In her dotage she spent all her time developing new fragrances and skin creams in a room that 'was no more impressive than the workshops in the market where the artisans and blacksmiths toil'.[lii] When she died in 1050, three years before Cardinal Humbert and his friends came to call on her husband, Zoe was seventy.

I left Ayia Sophia feeling heartily sorry that no Byzantine chronicler had penetrated the court of any Western Christian ruler, let alone the army of a First Crusader lord. For a start, another Michael Psellus would have told us more exactly what Theophano, Otto III, his Granny Adelheid, the saints Nilus and Adalbert, Pope Leo, Cardinal Humbert, Pope Gregory, Henry IV, his mother Agnes, Countess Matilda, Peter Damiani, Abbot Desiderius and Pope Urban had looked like. It seemed to me that Psellus and Anna Comnena had refined the art of saga-writing some seven hundred years before the appearance of the English novel and a good century before the Icelanders got around to putting quill to parchment. From a Psellus we would have learned of every ruler's last peccadillo. We would have been fully informed about any amorous adventures Otto III had had before he died; the matter of Pope Gregory's *obscoeni negotii* with Countess Matilda would not be shrouded in mystery; and we would know more precisely how Henry IV had misspent his youth and mistreated his two wives.

Corleone Kalashnikov and I misspent our Easter Sunday evening in an elegant little restaurant in the heart of the tourist-filled Sultanahmet district of the city. Ordering bottles of wine and plates of fresh fish, we settled in for a festive night's entertainment courtesy of a pair of excellent Turkish musicians, one of them a violinist. Staring fixedly at the fiddler's fingerwork, Sigvard could hardly contain his excitement. As soon as it was over, he was on his feet, shaking the violinist's hand, introducing himself by his favourite pseudonym, guffawing fit to burst and happening to mention that he was a professional violinist. The Turks smiled serenely and politely refused Sigvard's invitation to sit down with us and share another bottle of wine. In that case, replied Sigvard, could he perhaps borrow the violin for a moment? The violinist handed over his instrument but blanched as Sigvard busily set to work to retune it, tightening every string, loosening, re-tightening, one ear cocked for sound. A party of four Germans at one table and four Britons at another interrupted their conversations to watch his preparations.

The noise he produced for his opening piece was disappointing, his next effort was a oompah German number to which the Germans clapped along appreciatively but his third had even the Britons roaring for an encore. Standing up and positioning the violin face-up between his knees, he held both ends of the bow in his hands and bent over the instrument. Dragging the bow to and fro across it, he managed somehow to produce a simple catchy tune, a procedure which necessarily entailed shunting his ample rump back and forth in a hilariously lewd fashion. His audience wept with merriment.

'It's just a stupid party trick,' he said with one of his winks and a humble shrug, sitting back down to a crescendo of clapping.

Only then did I notice the two musicians, standing at the back of the restaurant by the kitchen door. Their faces wore expressions as disdainful and disgusted as any Byzantine's might have done at witnessing the drunken antics of the Varangians at play or the First Crusaders on the rampage. A young waiter approached Sigvard to defuse the tension with a dazzlingly sweet smile and a request: 'Can you play something by Vivaldi? Vivaldi is my favourite composer!' Sigvard obliged, then handed the instrument back to its owner. By the time the Turkish duo had delighted the German table with a rousing rendition of 'Kalinka', the cultural rift was more or less healed.

The following morning Sigvard and I explored the area of the city across the Golden Horn, opposite the Ecumenical Patriarchate. I knew the Monastery of St Cosmas and St Damian where Byzantines had received free medical treatment and Bohemond stayed no longer existed, but I wanted to see what had replaced it. Sigvard accompanied me because the district had for a long time been the city's Jewish quarter. We found a locked up synagogue and an equally closed Orthodox church, and wandered past a naval base with a barrier in front of it and through back streets full of little workshops producing parts for cars and domestic appliances. At the top of a hill we paused to admire the view across the Golden Horn towards the patriarchate. When we parted it was so that I could keep my appointment with Grand Archdeacon Tarasios at his office there.

He received me in a room as full as a film star's hotel suite of baskets of flower arrangements, boxes of chocolates and bowls of fruit and sweets. They were all Easter gifts from friends, he explained. Seated in comfortable chairs on opposite sides of a bowl containing Hershey kisses and Turkish M&Ms, we chatted easily. In his lazy Texan drawl he opined that Turkish–Greek relations had rarely been so good, and announced that the patriarch was all in favour of Turkey's entry into the European Union.

'Bartolomaios thinks that Europe should not just be a Christian club. He reckons there's room in there for Islam too. OK, Islam is not always very civilized but tell me, who are we to cast the first stone?'

With my Crusaders in mind, I laughed in hearty agreement and we passed on to Christian matters. He startled me with a bold assertion: 'You could say that Orthodoxy is one of the world's best-kept secrets. We Orthodox believe that this third millennium will be ours in the same way that the second belonged to Rome.'

Today's patriarch of Constantinople might not have the care of more than three thousand souls in the city his predecessors had presided over beside the emperors, but if Archbishop Atanasios of Albania was anything to go by, the Orthodox might just be right. Father Tarasios continued: 'Of course, we know there's a way to go before we see that happening. We have to admit that at the moment there are more good Catholic and Protestant Christians than good Orthodox. They package the faith better—'

'But you Orthodox have the treasure of all those monasteries,' I interrupted him enthusiastically.

'Sure we do. But some of those places are hotbeds of fanatical fundamentalism . . .'

'The tradition of spiritual fatherhood by monks also seems to me a very good one,' I said, watching the grand archdeacon as he leant back in his chair, pensively unwrapping a Hershey kiss.

'Correct. But there's another danger: the guru cult syndrome. You get control freaks taking on that kind of role, or you get guys who try to tackle psychiatric cases, or others who just don't do the job.'

I went on trying to boost his flagging morale by telling him my thesis that the Western Christian Church had taken some dangerous wrong turnings way back in the eleventh century.

'I'm very interested to hear that you have come to that con-clusion,' he said, his dark eyes lighting up. 'The papacy is too authoritarian. Too much power and autonomy has been taken away from the Catholic bishops. Did you know that our patriarch cannot even cross the Golden Horn to visit that church on the other side without the local bishop's say-so. How about that!'

Restored by this happy comparison, the grand archdeacon reached for a glossy coffee table book and began to tell me about a trip that he and the patriarch had recently made to what had been, until Robert Guiscard's conquest of Bari in 1071, Byzantine southern Italy, or Magna Graecia.

'Look right here,' he said, flipping the book open at a beautiful photograph of a church. 'Hasn't that gotta be Byzantine! All that Byzantine culture's making a comeback there. Catholics are begin-ning to give our churches back. You're never gonna believe it but there are guys there in some of the tiny villages who still speak a dialect of Greek!'

'Ooooh!' I gasped, bitterly regretting that I had missed this phenomenon.

'What I want you to see is that the 1054 schism line between Eastern and Western Christianity is not as straight as you think. Those people there feel their Byzantine past.'

Excitedly contemplating the spiritual reconquest of southern

Italy after a thousand years, I thanked the grand archdeacon and made for the patriarchate church next door. From a previous visit I recalled that it contained – among a great many other precious relics – a substantial part of the post against which Christ was flagellated before his Crucifixion. The pretty little church was empty, cool and quiet except for a single bedraggled-looking woman in a headscarf and long skirt who was making a round of the church, prostrating herself before every icon and sniffing loudly. Approaching me she began to sob and then to speak very fast in Russian. As far as I could make out through her tears, she was a poor pilgrim on her way overland to Jerusalem. Her meagre funds had run out. Worse still, neither the Syrians nor the Jordanians would issue her with a visa except via their embassies in Moscow, but she did not want to retrace her steps, her pilgrimage unaccomplished. Impressed by the medievally faithful spirit in which she seemed to be going about her far-faring, I made a donation towards her expenses. Still sobbing, she grabbed my hand and kissed it.

Back in the Sultanahmet district I was concentrating so hard on the Russian pilgrim and the recreation of Magna Graecia, that I was deaf to the blandishments of carpet sellers attempting to lure me into their emporia. At last, one of them managed to prick my conscience with a sharp barb.

'Excuse me, can I ask you one question? You don't talk to me? Why? Why do you come to Turkey if you don't want to talk to Turkish people?'

But of course I wanted to talk to Turkish people as well as recall eleventh-century Greek Byzantium! I was leaving town the next day to travel halfway across the country along the route the Crusaders had taken to ancient Antioch. The journey, by bus, would take me the best part of a week. How could I avoid talking to Turkish people?

~

Shivering with a cold I had caught by standing too long in the chilly breeze blowing up from the Bosphorus to the Ecumenical Patriarchate on Easter night, I made my way to Istanbul's long-distance coach station the next day. Boarding a bus, I chose a sunny window seat, blew my nose and fell fast asleep.

I had been looking forward to crossing the glamorous new sus-pension bridge over the Bosphorus to Asian Turkey, but when I woke we were in a line of vehicles waiting to board a ferry across the Sea of Marmara to a point on the far side near the camp which Alexius had had built for his English Varangians and then requisitioned for use by Peter the Hermit's Crusaders. The woman in the seat in front was offering me a rich tea biscuit, and it was a golden late afternoon. On deck, perched in the sunshine on top of a lifeboat box, watching boys peddling fancily wrapped sweets, sunglasses, cold drinks and lottery tickets to my fellow passengers, I felt as relieved as I had on reaching the Bodensee after a couple of days on the autobahn.

The ferry's slow progress across the smooth water was soothing after the din and bustle of Istanbul and I was also happy to be on my own again. Corleone Kalashnikov had been good but demanding company, and the evening before had been equally taxing. Still stung by the bitter complaint of the carpet seller, I had decided to pay a visit to a Turkish acquaintance at his shop on the other side of the city. A young international antiques dealer with a special love of Byzantine and Russian objects, Çem had looked more pros-perous but sounded less happy than when I had last seen him.

'Tiffs! Tiffs!' he had huffed and puffed, throwing his corpulent form into a pretty little armchair, pouring me a glass of chilled white wine and insisting I sample some of the canapés he had bought in my honour from the shop next door. 'Every Turk is a genetic tiff! Look at this,' he said, opening a crumpled newspaper. 'This government has spent 960 million dollars on cars for itself – they're all tiffs!'

'Oh! You mean thieves!'

'Yes, tiffs. Turks used to care about friendship; there was time to talk, to love, to help each other. Now it's only money. Look, this is my last telephone bill – 667,800,000 Turkish lira. How can I pay that? Tiffs! And we think we should go into Europe immediately? It'll take us another ten years, minimum. And now, with this crisis, who knows? Look here, a crazy thing,' he said, reading another headline in his paper. 'A seventy-eight-year-old man has murdered his two grandchildren because of this economic crisis!'

'And how's your business doing?' I had asked tentatively, glancing around the shop's imperial red walls which were hung with sepia-tinted photographs of the slaughtered Russian royal family.

'Pah! This country's finished now and I have no love in my life. I'm selling everything and emigrating to America,' he answered, throwing his newspaper aside. 'But I could come with you instead. Where are you going?'

'All the way to Antakya by bus, via places like Iznik, Konya, Kayseri and Gaziantep,' I said. 'I'm leaving tomorrow Çem.'

'But there are direct buses to Antakya. They take only eighteen hours.'

'I know, but I have to go the way the First Crusaders went. It took them about three months; it'll take me about a week.'

'No problem. I can come,' he had persisted, his eyes lighting up behind their glasses.

'It's a kind thought, but no.'

'You shouldn't travel alone! There are tiffs and . . . other things,' he went on, reminding me of the fussy German I had encountered on the S-bahn to Hamburg's main railway station.

'I managed in Albania. You don't need to worry.'

'Albania . . .? OK.' He had sighed, deflated and a little sad.

I recalled Taizé's lesson about the value of community and companionship. Should I be spurning Çem's gallant advances, I wondered. We might keep each other company, I thought, but quickly decided that I preferred my own.

Accidie and loneliness were devils waiting to pounce on a lone traveller but I was fairly handy at fighting them off. Generally I revelled in the knowledge that, for days and weeks at a time, no one I knew was certain where I was or what I was doing. The reverse side of the coin – the sad fact that no one anywhere relied on or needed me enough to have to know – had seemed a fair price to pay for this freedom. My father's near-fatal illness had changed that. I had liked being needed by my family so urgently that I had had to cut my journey in half. I was now calling London every other day.

As the ferry slowed down for the approach to the opposite shore and the sun prepared to set over low, spring-green hills, I was feeling as nervously excited to be setting out across Turkey as I had been about boarding that rickety old bus south from Tirana on my way to see Archbishop Anastasios. I guessed that the Crusaders had been feeling much the same in the late spring of 1097.

The almost empty bus bowled along narrow, potholed country roads, the now setting sun radiating a deepening orange light through its back windows and up its linoleum centre aisle. Out of the window I spied olive groves and orchards in pink and white blossom and guessed we must be nearing my destination when, through the trees and beyond a fringe of reeds, I glimpsed a gleaming lake. At its far end would be Iznik, the city which the Romans and Byzantines had called Nicaea. The road narrowed and we were delayed behind first a donkey-drawn cart and then a small red tractor. Duke Godfrey had judged this road to Nicaea equally ill-suited to heavy traffic, indeed dangerously vulnerable to attack. He was well aware that the People's Crusade had met its end on it the previous autumn, and signs of that wholesale carnage – the grisly mountain of bones Anna Comnena described – were still visible five months later. He despatched three thousand of his Crusaders, equipped with axes and swords, to widen the route over a mountain and signpost it for those who followed with wooden and metal crosses.

A well fortified Roman city with four gates, straight roads, six thousand metres of walls and two hundred and forty stout turrets,

Nicaea had been seized from the Byzantines by the Seljuk Turks*
who, by the 1090s, had loosely united the Muslim Middle East,
including Jerusalem itself, under their control. The Crusaders knew
little of this but they had heard of Nicaea because, back in AD325,
'powerful men of the Church' had gathered for a council there and
'established customs',[liii] notably the text of the Nicene Creed. Even
if the city was still populated with Byzantine Christians, they hated
to think of such a holy place in the hands of a people 'worshipping
the prodigies of heathendom'.[liv] Anyway, they had determined that
further progress east across the Anatolian plain would be impossible
unless they captured this stronghold, so perfectly protected by its
lake and surrounding mountains.

The seventeen-year-old sultan, Kilij Arslan, had heard rumours
of a new plague of *Franj*† heading for his territories but, recalling
how quickly and easily he had destroyed the People's Crusade, had
paid them little heed. Although he did reinforce his garrison at
Nicaea to allay the fears of his heavily pregnant wife, he remained
far to the east, quelling a rebellion. It was not until May 1097 when
the Crusaders arrived before the walls of Nicaea and set about
building 'a lofty war engine'[lv] and towers – a skill at which
Bohemond excelled – that a messenger reached him with the appalling news that this second wave of *Franj* looked nothing like the
raggle-taggle first one. These invaders were trained and properly
equipped, not a pathetically bedraggled mob accompanied by carts
loaded with their worldly possessions. And there were sixty thousand
of them, including some seven thousand mounted *milites*. Out of
the depths of Anatolia, Kilij Arslan hurried back west and tried
to break through the Crusaders' southern flank, which old Count
Raymond and Bishop Adhemar were holding. On 21 May, 1097,
battle was joined. 'Stout lances were shattered as they hit home

---

* The Seljuks were probably originally Christian or Jewish. A son of the clan's founder
was named Israel, later Turkicized to Arslan.
† *Franj* – Franks, the name given to any western and northern Europeans by Byzantines,
Turks and Arabs. The Arabs use it to this day, especially for the French.

hard, chests were ripped loudly open and poured out rivers of blood, and heads were cut off and flew like apples shaken from a tree.'[lvi]

By sunset Kilij Arslan was instructing Nicaea's Turkish garrison to save itself as best it could and retreating back east into the mountains. The triumphant Crusaders marched back to their camp under the city walls with gory Turks' heads impaled on the tips of their spears.

But they soon discovered that their blockade of the city was not effective, supplies were easily reaching the besieged by boat across the lake. The Crusaders turned to Alexius for help and he, glad of a chance to remind them how much they needed him, had a large part of his navy transported overland by bull-power from the Sea of Marmara onto the lake. The Turks were horrified; 'they grew weak with a fear of death, but the more they groaned and wept the more our own men were pleased and gave thanks to the Lord',[lvii] wrote a chronicler in Bohemond's army. No more supplies got through and this powerful proof that the Crusaders could count on Byzantine support broke the Turks' morale.

The Crusaders had planned their final assault on the city for 19 June, but on the morning of that day woke to find that the Turks had quietly surrendered – to Alexius. Byzantine troops were inside the city, blue and gold Byzantine banners fluttering over the city walls and everything in perfect order. Alexius was delighted. Nicaea had been spared a sacking and his Byzantine subjects were safe. He penned a happy note in lamentable Latin to the monks at Monte Cassino, presenting them with a precious 'epiloricum, adorned on the back with glittering gold'[lviii] and assuring them that he was taking good care of their fellow Western Christians.

The Crusading lords felt outmanoeuvred, and the rank and file cheated of their few days' pillaging. The Crusaders were only permitted to enter the liberated city in small groups under the tight supervision of Byzantine police. The emperor's civilized treatment of various Turkish nobles and the young sultana and her new baby son also bewildered the Western Christians. Recalling the People's Crusaders' allegations of Greek treachery, many read fresh grounds for mistrust into the clemency Alexius showed towards his Infidel prisoners.

Nothing looked as black and white, as Muslim and Christian, as it had done at home. The Byzantines were proving too subtle for the Crusaders, too inclined to avoid a good clean fight, and they were obviously not as irreconcilably opposed to the Muslims as the Crusaders had been led to believe. There were even Turks in the Byzantine army. The confusion extended to the Crusaders themselves. A French nun from St Mary of Trier who had joined Peter the Hermit's horde, been captured by a Turk on the dangerous road to Nicaea and then taken to live in that city, threw herself on the mercy of the Crusading lords when they arrived half a year later, complaining of having been raped. Recognizing her at once, a German count took her under his wing and saw to it that she was prescribed the right penance. But it transpired that her Turkish rapist loved her so much, he declared himself willing to become a Christian for her sake. Abandoning her penance and her vows, the nun eloped with him.

The bus passed one of the old Roman gates of the city and proceeded down a straight tree-lined avenue, past a mosque through the open door of which I could see the rounded backs of the crouching faithful. Next came the low-lying little Byzantine church where the Council of Nicaea had taken place, landscaped and tastefully floodlit, with a bus marked 'Stuttgart Bible Tours' parked in front of it. We lumbered on into narrower back streets, inching our way around dozens of little red tractors and trailers, neatly parked like family cars outside one- or two-storey houses. My growing impression of a small town entirely inhabited by fruit farmers was soon reinforced: disembarking, I set off down the main shopping street in search of aspirin to find that any shop resembling a chemist's sold only insecticides and fertilizers.

Very early the following morning I checked out of my hotel. For all the place's fancy mother-of-pearl-encrusted light switches, there had been no hot water and a horribly damp bed had exacerbated my cold. About a hundred yards away was a purple *pensiyon*

with a welcoming neon sign. There my anxious enquiry about hot
water received a cheery answer from a young hotelier. 'Relax, Max!
Twenty-four hours a day hot water!' he declared. After insisting that
I join him and a posse of departing Japanese backpackers for their
valedictory group photograph, he confided, 'For me, you know, the
most important thing in life is my friends.' Then he led me all
the way up to his roof terrace to show me his water heater. 'You
see? This clock here is set to twenty-four hours a day. OK? I am
Ali. Your name, my friend? Victoria? You will have a tea with me
now, Victoria.'

I wanted a shower but did as I was told, and we chatted.
When I explained to him how I came to be travelling alone across
Turkey, he broke open a fresh pack of cigarettes, lit one, exhaled
pensively and began: 'You want to know why the Crusaders – we
call them *haçli*, which means people with the cross – came to
Anatolia? To kill not Muslims, but Orthodox. The Byzantines suffered most from those first *haçli*.' He was probably right, at least as
far as ordinary Byzantines were concerned. For all their waxing
power, the Turks were still nomads at the end of the eleventh
century and utterly unsentimental at losing a city like Nicaea, while
the Byzantines' ancient civilization was concentrated in cities, and
plundering cities was what the Crusaders liked best.

Ali and I discussed Europe. He was as sure as Eray, the tourist
guide I had met on the train from Thessaloniki, that Turkey was
being kept waiting outside the gates of Europe – a little like Henry
IV in the snow before Canossa, it occurred to me – on account of
its religious identity. 'Any Muslim country in the European Union?
No!' he pointed out, before admitting that he was not himself one
hundred per cent in favour of Turkey joining the EU. Ali had
learned from his backpacker 'friends' that a process of homogenization was under way in Europe. He was worried that if Turkey
joined, there would be nothing left to attract visitors to his country.

'Now we have a nice bazaar economy – little shops, little *pensiyon*, little towns and villages. If Turkey goes into the EU, a German,

333

or a Swissman will come and make a big Western hotel here in Iznik. No job for Ali! It will be like your *haçli* coming again!'

I told him that I must have a shower before visiting the little Byzantine church of St Sophia, which had been built a couple of decades before the Crusaders arrived to besiege the city.

'Oh, yes, many of my friends like to visit that church, but not long ago some Christian missionaries came to make their propaganda there. The police chief came to me, very angry. He said, "Ali, these people are from your *pensiyon*. Are you Christian now?" "No, no," I told him. "I'm a humanist." But I had big problems. No more Christian propaganda here!'

In the bright morning sunshine the little church looked less glamorous than it had the evening before but more touchingly real. There were tufts of weed sprouting from cracks in its pretty Byzantine bricks and stonework, and under the un-ruined section of its roof sparrows as confidently noisy as the birds at Taizé were flying about. What had once been a richly tiled floor was roughly cropped grass speckled with daisies. Only one fragment of intricate mosaic remained, carefully protected by a sheet of glass. A modern historian of medieval Monte Cassino has identified the link between it and fragments of mosaic from the floor of Abbot Desiderius' basilica church. The abbot's Byzantine workmen had honed their artistry here, hundreds of miles away across the Balkans in an ancient Roman city surrounded by mountains and a lake, before reproducing the same design on top of a high limestone mountain in southern Italy and later in Salerno's *duomo*.

I savoured that thought awhile, and then another. St Nicholas of Myra and Bari had been one among the three hundred or so 'powerful men of the Church' attending the fourth-century Council of Nicaea, convened to formulate the Nicene Creed. That Creed had laid down that the third person of the Trinity, the Holy Spirit, 'proceeded' from God the Father. It was not until five hundred years later, in the ninth century, when Charlemagne high-handedly inserted the famous *Filioque* clause making the Holy Spirit proceed from God the Son as well as God the Father, that the first hairline crack in Christendom appeared. I remembered Arni Bergmann chuckling over his novel, telling me how he had imagined his Thorvald attending an eleventh-century church council and brilliantly solving this still thorny issue by likening the persons of the Holy Trinity to the various parts of an apple tree. Arni's Thorvald had maintained that the Holy Spirit proceeded from the Father and the Son only to the extent that an apple proceeds from a tree and a branch. An ingenious solution, but one too reliant on the sort of casuistry that Western Christian scholastic theologians became so adept at to appeal to the Byzantines. The matter still divides Catholic from Orthodox; to this day Orthodox Christians recite the original Nicene Creed.

I set off to walk around the edge of the town and found the long glittering lake much as it must have been when Alexius' ships were unharnessed from the bulls and launched upon its waters. The mountains were as high and protectively encircling as they had been when Kilij Arslan fled back into them to escape his Crusader pursuers. Parts of the stout walls the Crusaders had been so eager to storm were still visible, many feet thick and thatched with thick clumps of weeds. But I was interested to note that just inside those walls, in the backyards of houses as half built as the ones I had noticed in Albania, were towers of freshly fashioned fruit crates. Modern Iznik was a one-industry town of the kind that has become rare in western Europe. Enchanted by the place and by Ali's hospitality, I stayed two more nights and shook off my cold before setting out again.

∽

A week after the fall of Nicaea the Crusaders were on their way again too, in high spirits, to judge by the blithely optimistic missive Count Stephen sent home to his Adèle: 'I tell you, my beloved, that in five weeks we will reach Jerusalem from Nicaea, the city so often mentioned, unless Antioch [modern Antakya] resists us.

335

Farewell.'^{lix} It was the summer of 1097. Jerusalem was still two years away.

Fearful of not finding adequate food supplies, the Crusaders decided to divide their army in two for the next leg of the journey. Bohemond would set out first at the head of a contingent comprising all the French and Italian Normans, the Flemish, Stephen of Blois and a posse of Byzantines as guides. The second expedition would be led by old Count Raymond with Bishop Adhemar, Duke Godfrey and silly Count Hugh. It would comprise all the southern and eastern French.

The first army had been marching east for three days when, at dawn on the fourth, Sultan Kilij Arslan swooped down from a mountain towards Bohemond's still sleepy cohorts with an army he had easily collected in the east by spreading terrifying tales of the *Franj*. High up above the Crusaders on the mountain, he had noticed how completely their bodies and even their horses were protected by armour. An Arab chronicler described the enemy his sultan viewed on that hot July morning as 'virtual fortresses'.^{lx} Bohemond kept his head in the crisis. Gathering his *milites* together, he had just enough time to deliver a stirring speech, order the expedition's women to ferry water supplies up to the front line and send a messenger back down the road to tell Count Raymond to hurry up and join him. The Turks' 'war-like battle cry, in the horrible tones of their language'^{lxi} was already audible.

Bohemond led forty of his men into battle. Only one, the same oaf (Anna Comnena calls him 'that crazy idiot'^{lxii}) who had dared to sit on Alexius' throne back in Constantinople, disobeyed his orders by abandoning the battle line. They were soon on the defensive, blinded and confused by the Turkish mounted archers who rushed forward in a wave, shot their arrows and fell back to make way for another wave. It was sweltering and midday before Count Raymond showed up with the other half of the Crusading army. The Sultan was shocked. He had thought that in Bohemond's force he was facing the full strength of his enemy. Reinforced, the Crusaders were soon back on the offensive, and Kilij Arslan's shock turned to panic when he spotted yet another army of Crusaders on the hills behind him. It was some southern French *milites*, led by Bishop Adhemar. The prelate's clever diversionary tactic probably won the day. Once again the boy sultan was forced to flee back to the mountains, abandoning his tent and all his treasure. Flushed with success, the Crusaders rested for two days there at Dorylaeum.

Historians seem to agree that Dorylaeum was very near the modern Turkish town of Eskişehir, so I caught a bus there. The way was steeply winding, through green mountains adorned with a pretty blur of red poppies and tiny yellow flowers. Wherever possible the land had been turned over to fruit farming. Women in headscarves and baggy Turkish trousers hoed the earth between the trees. While the bus radio played jauntily wailing country and eastern, I surveyed places Sultan Kilij Arslan might have chosen for ambushing his foes and steep gorges from which his archers could have fired their ruinous rains of arrows. Approaching the outskirts of Eskişehir we passed a forest of unfinished high-rise blocks. Some landscaping had been attempted but weeds were already pushing through the paving stones. Where a flock of sheep grazed the long grass were some once fancy, now broken, park lights.

The bus pulled into an *otogar* as large as an airport. For the hour or so before my next bus left, I sat in a departure lounge like the lobby of a luxury hotel, surrounded by deep leatherette armchairs, polished parquet flooring and handsome brass ashtrays. On the other side of the electric glass doors in front of me were the buses, swooping in and out of their bays, loading and unloading their passengers. Travelling long-distance by Turkish bus was proving unexpectedly enjoyable. I liked the gigantic Mercedes coaches painted pretty lilacs, greens, oranges and yellows and emblazoned with names like ŞAMPIYON and ELEGANT, and I loved the debonair way the drivers' assistants hung out of their doors by one arm as their vehicles backed and turned before setting off. The bus that would transport me on over the Anatolian plain was a lemon-yellow beauty with a badly cracked windscreen.

On board, I was politely ushered into a front seat and offered a plastic beaker of water, Coke or tea and some biscuits. Seconds later, the smiling assistant was back, brandishing a bottle of yellow cologne which he splashed into my cupped hands. I watched the driver, a man as luxuriantly whiskered as the latter-day *gothi* I had met in Reykjavik, cupping his much larger hands for about a third of the bottle. He rubbed the fragrant liquid all over his forearms, neck and face, and into the tips of his moustache. Some worry beads and a bright bouquet of fabric flowers dangled prettily from his driving mirror, an embroidered doily graced his dashboard and his radio played more jaunty wailing. I felt as if I had been very hospitably received in someone's private home. On the road, gazing out ahead at the sandy, grey-brown flatness of the Anatolian plain all around, I rejoiced in all the technological advances the West had made in the second millennium; I was not having to travel as the Crusaders had done.

It was high summer when the Crusaders left Dorylaeum. Dressed as 'virtual fortresses' in all their armour, they suffered so terribly from thirst and hunger that women camp followers were giving birth and abandoning their new-borns. The Turks had cleverly smashed all the Byzantine water cisterns along the road. Food was in short supply because the Turks had also taken care to ravage the countryside they passed through on their retreat east. The Western Christians chewed thorn twigs. Worse still, for fear of Turkish raids, the greater part of the army had been advised by its Byzantine guides to take a very long route through territory more or less held by fellow Christian Armenians, who could be relied upon to supply them without a fight. But the Crusaders' horses were beginning to drop dead. One eloquent chronicler sketched a picture of the gradual and ghastly reversal of the natural order that happened as the famished soldier pilgrims and their animals blundered on across Anatolia towards their Lord's Holy Sepulchre: 'There most of our cavalry ceased to exist, because [thereafter] many of these became foot soldiers. For want of horses, our men used oxen . . . and, because of the very great need, goats, sheep and dogs served as beasts of burden.'[lxiii]

Accidie must have been a constant irritant. Was it all worth it? As they marched on, the ordinary Crusaders' resentment of the Byzantine guides and suspicions about the value of their advice grew. A month and a half after leaving Dorylaeum, they reached Iconium, modern Konya, which although nominally in Turkish hands for the past thirteen years, was temporarily and conveniently deserted in that late summer of 1097. The bounteous fertility of the surrounding area was a godsend, especially for old Count Raymond, who seemed about to expire, and Duke Godfrey, who needed to convalesce after a hunting accident.

I saw no signs of bounteous fertility as my bus approached Konya in the spring of 2001, on the evening of the same day I had left Nicaea. But, after five and a half hours of grey-brown sand speckled with thorn bushes or sheep and snow-capped Taurus mountains, I was glad to be approaching anywhere at all. The bus deposited me at another luxurious out-of-town *otogar* from where, with the help of a young college student, I caught a crowded *dolmuş* minibus into town. A diffident sort, the boy confided that he was hauling a large bag of his dirty washing home for his mother to do. He missed his family, he told me as we passed acres and acres of new or half-built high-rise blocks painted the same colours as the buses – candy pink, peppermint green, orange, lilac and yellow.

'Why so many blocks?' I asked him, feeling sorry that the twenty-first-century descendants of so nimbly nomadic a people as the Seljuk Turks had had to settle down to life in such places.

'If the authorities don't build blocks like these, people will start building their own, everywhere, with no planning,' he explained. I imagined tents, like Sultan Kilij Arslan's.

For the next three days I fell into a restful routine of sitting on buses with my paperback copy of the first volume of Sir Steven Runciman's *History of the Crusades* open on my lap, selecting my next destination according to the map provided in the middle of the book, accepting whatever refreshments I was offered and anointing my hands in cologne. At the regular stops, I got out to drink tea and admire the thoroughness with which the drivers' assistants hosed down their vehicles. Kayseri, the main city on the Crusaders' horrendously long detour north, was about to hold local elections. A poster showed a grinning moustachioed man pointing to a computer-generated image of an idealized new city centre. If that candidate had his way, the city – chaotically incoherent as a series of discarded theatre sets in spite of its wealth of ancient monuments – would become a pristinely ordered heaven of underpasses, multi-storey car parks, spotless pavements, gleaming glass high-rises and uniform people in tidy business suits. Kayseri would resemble Reims or Aachen railway stations. As a non-resident of the city, I far preferred the shocking sight of fish flip-flopping about on the wet pavement in front of a fishmonger's or the odd rusty *dolmuş* clanking past at high speed. I liked the dusty old men squatting on their haunches spitting sunflower-seed husks, the packs of youths in T-shirts and baseball caps and the pale young women looking strangely Edwardian in their veils and elegantly cut full-length coats.

The Crusaders seem to have fallen into their own hideous routine of miserable suffering leavened by bursts of ferocious fighting, for they could not avoid the occasional encounter with the Turks and Bohemond relished a skirmish. Their great trek across the southern rim of the Anatolian plain, their horribly lengthy march north into the Anti-Taurus mountains to Kayseri, or Caesarea as they would have called it, stretched on into autumn. By early October they were at last heading south again towards Antioch, but the weather had turned foul and the mountain road was almost impassable. They lost more men on that inhumanly arduous stretch of the journey than they did in any skirmish. Many of the remaining horses slipped over precipices, as did whole lines of baggage-laden goats, sheep and dogs. Exhausted by climbing, the knights tried to sell their heavier weapons to anyone with a lighter load. The more horrible the way became, the more superstitious the Crusaders – among them six French visionaries – grew. God must not be provoked into sending them any further adversity, they thought. When a Cluniac monk who had joined the Crusade 'not out of devotion but from levity'lxiv was discovered with a woman, he was whipped around the camp. There was much talk of expelling all women from the Crusade. As they struggled on – hungry, depleted and exhausted – towards Antioch, the thirty thousand or so remaining Crusaders attributed their survival to a miracle rather than to any wise advice from their Byzantine guides. 'We are few in comparison to the pagans. Truly God fights for us,'lxv was their verdict. A comet, shooting across the heavens sporting a tail shaped like a sword, cheered them on their way.

A view of the gigantic city of Gaziantep, which did not exist in the autumn of 1097, floating like a mirage over the flat plain, its high-rises as colourful as a mountain of children's toys, cheered me on my way. After Gaziantep the scenery changed for the better. We raced past green meadows and woods, along short stretches of new motorway raised on stilts like the ones bestriding the Alps, into long new tunnels and out again into deepening pink twilight. Mountains, as romantically hazy as nineteenth-century watercolours, lay ahead. As darkness fell, the bus turned off the motorway onto a road with a line of date palms down its middle, into the Middle East. At the time, I was not aware that this lovely, fertile Hatay region had indeed been a part of the Middle East, the property of neighbouring Syria, until as recently as 1939. In that year France and Britain, determined to prevent Turkey joining Nazi Germany in any forthcoming world conflict, bribed her into neutrality by giving her the region.* Signing away a valuable slice of another people's country was possible because France, citing its Crusader connection to the region, had been ruling Syria as a protectorate since the end of World War One. Syria and Lebanon remained French protectorates until 1946.

~

---

* Turkey remained neutral throughout the war and afterwards until 1952, when it joined NATO.

The First Crusaders felt at least as piously proprietorial about Antioch as they had about the birthplace of the Nicene Creed. The very word 'Christian' had been coined in Antioch and St Peter himself had set up the first bishopric in the city, once the third largest in the Roman Empire. The soldier pilgrims felt they had to recapture this 'land of God and of Christians which the blessed Peter the Apostle long since converted to the worship of Christ by his teaching'.[lxvi]

It would not be easy. Indeed, it would prove harder than anything else they had yet attempted. Built on the banks of the River Orontes, on a plain and three high mountains, Antioch's stout walls were twice as long as Nicaea's and had almost twice as many turrets. The city's glory days were already in the past but it remained an impressive sight. Market gardens, orchards, villas perched up in the foothills of the mountains, rich souks, a good river flowing through it and a gigantic citadel all made it a highly attractive but fiendishly daunting prospect. Antioch had no lake like Nicaea but the Crusaders would find it impossible to mount an effective blockade by surrounding the city because the land to the south was wildly inhospitable.

The emir of Antioch, the elderly Yaghi-Siyan, could rejoice in this fact, in his plentiful stores of honey, grain and oil, and in the sturdy fortifications with which Byzantium had endowed the city before surrendering it twelve years earlier. But he was less confident about the loyalty of his mostly Byzantine Christian subjects. Suspecting they might collaborate with their fellow Christian Crusaders, he sent every able-bodied Byzantine male outside the gates of the city to dig defensive trenches one day and then refused to let them back in again. ' "Antioch is yours," ' he assured them soothingly, ' "but you will have to leave it to me until I see what happens between us and the *Franj*." ' ' "Who will protect our wives and children?" ' they pleaded. ' "I shall look after them for you," '[lxvii] he promised, promptly throwing the Patriarch John into prison and stabling his horses in the cave church where St Peter had preached. The expulsion of his Christians left Yaghi-Siyan with less than a third the number of *milites* the Crusaders could still boast. And his worries did not end there. Desperate pleas to join him in a jihad against the approaching *Franj*, transmitted via one of his sons to the neighbouring emirs of Aleppo, Damascus and Mosul, had failed to meet with speedy or selfless responses.

Islam's conquering energy had abated in the half-millennium since the death of Mohammed and the Crusaders' greatest stroke of good fortune was to be arriving in the Middle East at a time when petty rivalries and quarrels between princelings almost as numerous as the warlords of Burgundy or southern Italy were rife. Amin Maalouf, the Lebanese historian and novelist, has dolefully noted: 'in Syria in the eleventh century, jihad was no more than a slogan brandished by princes in distress. No emir would rush to another's aid unless he had some personal interest in doing so. Only then would he contemplate the invocation of great principles.'[lxviii]

The Seljuks had been losing ground to the Fatimid dynasty of caliphs who had conquered Egypt and were eyeing southern Palestine and Jerusalem by the end of 1097. For the time being the Shi'te Muslim Fatimids, Arabs rather than Turks, could see no advantage in waging a joint jihad with Sunni Muslim Seljuks.

Yaghi-Siyan suffered the Crusaders' seizure of a supply train of cattle, sheep and grain and then their approach to the very walls of his city. For a whole two weeks he did nothing. The Crusaders likewise decided on a waiting game. Count Raymond had been all for boldly taking Antioch by storm, a strategy which might have succeeded given the emir's shortage of manpower, but he was overruled. Bohemond favoured a long, patient siege. The object of Anna Comnena's fascinated hatred calculated that, given enough time, he could probably find someone inside the city walls who was as willing to do a quietly advantageous deal with him as the Turkish garrison at Nicaea had done with Emperor Alexius. A jealous rival of the old emir, a greedy watchman or a stray Byzantine Christian could surely be persuaded to betray Yaghi-Siyan by opening a gate of the city. Envious of Duke Godfrey's brother Baldwin, who had recently abandoned the expedition to establish a Crusader state in

Armenian-held territory around Edessa,* Bohemond was determined to win Antioch for himself, and he needed time to manoeuvre. He was in luck. Most of the Crusaders, exhausted by their trek and daunted by the walls of Antioch, were happy to follow his lead, to wait and rest, and hope that Alexius would come to their assistance again with some of his new-fangled siege engines.

The siege was not very effective and intelligence useful to both sides flowed in and out of the city. The Byzantine Christians whom the emir had exiled attached themselves to the Crusaders' camp but kept in touch with their families and friends inside Antioch. They communicated with Arab Christians in the city, many of whom secretly suspected that life under *Franj* rule would be worse than it was under the Turks, and kept the emir well supplied with accounts of the enemy's strategic dithering and plunging morale.

When the Crusaders had arrived at Antioch in the autumn of 1097 after more than a year on the road, food had been plentiful and good. They had gorged themselves and not thought to lay in stores for the winter. Thirteen Genoese ships arriving at the nearby port of St Symeon with more supplies and reinforcements in October had contributed to the dangerously false sense of security. Before very long they were forced to wander further and further afield on foraging expeditions, risking murderous attacks from bands of Turks.

As winter drew on and cold torrential rain turned their camp into an eleventh-century Ypres, the Crusaders suffered terribly, although Count Stephen of Blois was still managing to sound cheerily inconsequential in his letters home to Adèle. 'What some say, that in all Syria one can scarcely endure the heat of the sun, is false, for among them it is like our western winter.'[lxix] He boasted to his wife about all the loot he had acquired: 'You may know for a fact, my beloved, that I now have twice as much of gold, and silver, and other riches.'[lxx] There was, of course, plenty more to say

---

* Baldwin set up the first Crusader state at Edessa, which lasted until 1154. Today the city is called Sanliurfa, or simply Urfa, in honour of its ancient beginnings as Assyrian and Hittite Urfa.

but he protested that he could not begin to tell her 'all that my heart holds, dearest'. He merely asked her to 'do well and make excellent arrangements for your land, and treat your children and your vassals with honour, as befits you, for you will surely see me as soon as I can possibly come. Farewell.'[lxxi] Poor Count Stephen's wistful references to the customs of his happy hearth and homeland sound touchingly like the sort of sentiments young men expressed in letters home from the trenches on the western front nine hundred years later, letters filled with anything but evocations of the muddy, bloody horror they were experiencing.

Count Stephen was silent on the subject of a frightening new force within the Crusading army. Known as the Tafurs* this army within an army was composed of thousands of *lumpen* camp followers who had been reduced to a state of shaggy savagery by the rigours of the journey through Asia Minor. They lived off grass and roots. On foot and armed with clubs, knives and catapults, they would rush into skirmishes and battles in as enraged and animal a state as the pair of Icelandic berserk brothers with whom Thorvald and Bishop Frederick had had to contend a century earlier. The Turks described them as 'no Franks, but living devils'.[lxxii] They were ecstatically pious devotees of people like Peter the Hermit who had joined the Crusade after his own failed venture, and were utterly convinced that they would be the ones to capture Jerusalem: ' "The poorest shall take it [Jerusalem]: this is a sign to show clearly that the Lord God does not care for presumptuous or faithless men." '[lxxiii] Led by their own 'king', a déclassé Norman *miles*, the Tafurs recognized no other authority. When Yaghi-Siyan complained of their behaviour to the Crusading lords, he was simply informed: ' "All of us together cannot tame King Tafur." '[lxxiv]

By December 1097 one in every seven Crusaders was dying of hunger and the entire expedition could boast only seven hundred horses. Some aid in the form of wine and food trickled in from nearby Cyprus, courtesy of the exiled Patriarch Symeon of Jerusalem

* The derivation of the word is obscure but it seems to have meant vagabond.

with whom Bishop Adhemar had tactfully made friendly contact. The news that Muslim Yaghi-Siyan was torturing his brother patriarch, John of Antioch, by putting the old man in a cage and hanging him over the city walls, doubtless made Patriarch Symeon more inclined to help the Western Christians. But Cyprus could not feed a whole army. Morale plunged so low in January 1098 that although the Crusaders were at last within reach of their goal some deserted. Peter the Hermit tried but failed to get away, only managing to escape punishment because he was so beloved of the Tafurs. The Crusade's chief Byzantine guide, Taticius, politely excused himself by leaving for Cyprus in search of more supplies.

As energetic as ever, Bohemond seized this chance to blacken the name of Byzantium. Was not Taticius' desertion a further example of the Byzantine treachery they had experienced back in Nicaea? Did such a people deserve to have Antioch restored to them as Pope Urban had ordered? Surely not. So saying, he spread a rumour that, since he was so sorely missed back home in Norman southern Italy, he might himself be forced to abandon the holy enterprise. The noxious Norman's fellow lords easily guessed what he was about, but Bohemond was the best military leader the Crusade had and the army begged him not to go. Next, Bohemond began dropping hints that the lordship of Antioch would be fitting payment for his sacrifice.

~

Fitting payment indeed.

On a breezily bright morning in late spring the modern Antakya I had seen nothing of the night before looked as charming as Bari. Just behind my hotel was the city's maze-like souk, where I went in search of some breakfast. A man spinning a hot metal disc on which he was cooking a wispy pasta he called angel hair, invited me to taste some. I passed sacks bursting with luminous-coloured spices, bright plastic buckets of olives, slabs of halva, stalls piled high with hair clips and brushes, mountains of shoes, curtains of hanging

animal carcasses and trays of sticky sweetmeats sprinkled with pistachio. At last I selected some gooey macaroons and a thimbleful
of viscous Turkish coffee, before walking on up through the city
past houses painted washed-out shades of peppermint, blue and
violet, in the vague direction of St Peter's cave church.

The narrow, steep stone alleyways amplified the sounds of a
television and of someone practising on a recorder. From the open
windows of a school came the raucous rhythmic chanting of
children. A faint smell of drains mingled with the scent of baking
bread. A woman out sweeping the stone step of her Ottoman-era
house with its overhanging wooden upper storey smiled and
beckoned me into a courtyard shaded by a single large lemon tree
for another coffee. We had a short mimed discussion about hair dye.
Outside again, a little girl carrying a thick pile of fresh flat round
bread, gave me one and accepted a macaroon in return.

The state-run museum of St Peter's church, where Yaghi-Siyan
had stabled his horses during the Crusaders' siege of Antioch, was
still closed, but a caretaker let me in. The cave church with its
late Crusader façade was dank inside, its rough floor stamped with
fragments of mosaic. In a corner was a stack of red plastic chairs
and a rubbish bin and on one of its pillars a notice bearing the
relevant quotation from the Acts of the Apostles. 'For a whole year
they [some Apostles] met in the church and taught a large number
of people, and it was in Antioch that the disciples were first called
Christians.'[lxxv]

The notice also informed me that the church had looked like
this after 1098 until the Crusader colonialists were forced out of
Antioch by the Turks a hundred and seventy years later. In 1856 it
had 'come into the possession' of the French consul in nearby
Aleppo, who presented it to the Vatican as a gift. The pope of the
day, Pius IX (he of the smug-faced marble statue in Rome's Santa
Maria Maggiore), had ordered its façade restored and entrusted it
to the care of some Italian friars he had sent to the city. The Turkish
state had then appropriated it. On a visit here a century later, Pope

Paul VI ruled that any pilgrims to this church earned themselves a plenary indulgence.

The caretaker was tapping me on the shoulder, miming drinking something and indicating that I should follow him. Seating me comfortably outside his booth, he brought me a glass of hot milk, almost straight from the cow to judge by its smell and viscosity. I was trying to mask its taste by alternating sips with puffs on a cigarette when the museum's security guard arrived for work. A fine figure of a Turk in his navy-blue uniform, he had neatly cut hair and very white teeth. Moments later we had cut a deal which involved his abandoning his post. For a paltry ten dollars he would drive me some twenty kilometres out of town to the ruined Byzantine monastery of St Symeon, wait while I did my sightseeing and then drive me all the way back again. 'But your job here?' I mimed in bewildered curiosity. A shrug and a dazzling smile were all the answer I received as he opened the passenger door of a battered yellow Lada for me. I wished I could tell him how much I appreciated his spontaneous offer and admired his profligate way with time, how I had travelled the length of western Europe and encountered precious little gratuitous kindness. In my notebook I scribbled emotionally: 'We westerners don't need Turkish carpets, ruins or beaches. We need their kindness and their willingness to spend time on us.'

St Symeon's monastery was much older than the Crusades. Its heyday was in the sixth century when St Symeon the Younger followed the saintly fashion of his time by spending twenty-five years of his life perched on a high stone pillar, contemplating God and railing against the immorality of the Antiochians. By the eleventh century the mountain-top monastery had become a vast and sprawling complex of churches and pilgrims' hostels, a favourite stop on any pilgrim's way south down the coast towards Jerusalem. The nearby port of St Symeon, where the Genoese ships bringing supplies and reinforcements had docked in the late autumn of 1097, also handled some of the eleventh-century pilgrim traffic. My handsome Turkish driver knew nothing of all this Byzantine history.

In fact, he had never visited the spot before, so we had some difficulty finding the unmarked turning off the main road up into the mountains. The Lada did not take kindly to the rough track across land as green and pleasant with olive and fruit trees as any I had seen on my travels.

Happy as a schoolboy playing truant, my companion was delighted by the pale grey ruins with their nooks and crannies and old walls to clamber over. While I stood in the middle of what had once been the monastery's central courtyard, by the stump of Saint Symeon the Younger's pillar, trying to imagine what it must have looked like to pilgrims struggling over the mountains inland from the coast and wondering if the hundreds of monks here had spared the Crusaders any of their food supplies, he capered about daring me to follow him up high on the walls, shouting and beckoning me over to enjoy a view or a particularly vertiginous drop. After standing side by side for a while enjoying the stiff breeze and the view over the lower green mountains towards the shining sea, we returned to the car. It did not start. From under the bonnet, my driver drew a plastic bag containing a loo roll. While fastidiously wiping his hands with a couple of sheets of it, he shook his head at the engine and, with one of his shining smiles, gave me to understand that such a thing had never happened before. Sitting in the driving seat turning the dud ignition, I cursed my recklessness. The place was utterly remote and my companion a stranger. Together we rolled the car back down the mountain track and at last it coughed into life again. I had had nothing to fear. Soon we were bowling back towards town and I was at leisure to return to my mini-saga of the siege of Antioch.

In March 1098 another fleet of ships, this time manned by Englishmen and led by Edgar Atheling, a disappointed claimant of the English throne,* sailed into the port of St Symeon. Aboard were some Italian pilgrims but also just what the Crusaders had

---

* Edgar Atheling had been forced to make way for William the Conqueror. In 1086 William had allowed him to emigrate to Norman south Italy with 200 *milites*.

been waiting for – some Byzantine siege engines, courtesy of Alexius. Count Raymond and Bohemond, each so distrustful of the other by now that they chaperoned each other everywhere, set off for the coast to collect the treasure and to try and recruit some fresh Crusaders. The Turks fell on the expedition, but the Crusaders got the better of them in the most serious skirmish of the siege. Count Stephen of Blois wrote a bragging letter home to Adèle, all about his part in the killing of 'thirty emirs, that is, princes and three hundred other noble Turkish knights, not to mention other Turks and pagans'.[lxxvi]

Spring was coming and food supplies improved, but the siege dragged on and, at last, the neighbouring emirs were gathering their armies to come to the relief of Antioch. Karbuqa, the powerful ruler of Mosul, was on his way. The Crusading lords sent an urgent message to Alexius, who was busy reclaiming Byzantine territories in western Asia Minor. The gist of it must have been: Did His Imperial Highness want his Antioch back, or not? If he did, he should know that, without a large army of fresh troops which only he could muster, the Crusaders were in mortal danger of finding themselves sandwiched between the Muslims in the city and the Muslims coming to its relief.

The outlook was so hopeless it provoked a fresh wave of desertions. Count Stephen of Blois's sudden departure was generally attributed to cowardice and poor health.* On his long way back home across Anatolia he encountered Alexius, who was heading south in response to the Crusaders' SOS. Along with a crowd of other deserters, Count Stephen inadvertently succeeded in putting the emperor off continuing on his way to rescue the Crusade by painting an unrelievedly grim picture of conditions at the siege. Bohemond's luck was in again, his way to the lordship of Antioch clear at last. Alexius was not en route to claim his city and, better still, Karbuqa had been delayed. Riled by Count Baldwin's new state

* Adèle was furious, and forced him to go on the Second Crusade.

at Edessa, the emir of Mosul had stopped off to besiege the count in his citadel there.

Bohemond used the breathing space to cement his friendship with an Armenian convert to Islam, an armourer named Firouz who hated Yaghi-Siyan for putting a stop to his black marketeering in cuirasses. Offering Firouz an attractive package of riches and safety guarantees, Bohemond requested his help with opening a gate of the city. Firouz agreed and 'hope now began to lift Bohemond's spirit greatly, and while he waited to enter the city his handsome face shone with inward pleasure'.[lxxvii] The moment had come to show his hand. Gathering his fellow Crusading lords for a meeting, he reminded them of the 'deadly weariness for which there is no known remedy'[lxxviii] that had settled on them all, high and low, in the nine months they had spent besieging the city. He suggested that they all think hard about ways to force Yaghi-Siyan into sub-mission, and then begged to be allowed to offer his own solution: ' "It seems to me right," ' he began, ' "if someone, whether by force, or in secret, or by bribery, manages to gain entrance, that everyone categorically agree to grant him rule over the city." '[lxxix]

The Crusading lords heartily disagreed with Bohemond of course, but Karbuqa was almost upon them and none of them had a better idea. Another meeting was called and a face-saving compromise reached. It was decided that if Alexius failed to arrive in time to help the Crusaders recapture the city and Bohemond 'by some trick'[lxxx] managed to force an entrance before Karbuqa's arrival, then Alexius could not reasonably expect Bohemond to hand Antioch back to him as previously agreed. Off Bohemond went to Firouz, to boast about 'how opportunity smiles in the working out of these matters'.[lxxxi] There was no time to be lost, he told his accomplice. Firouz advised Bohemond to throw Yaghi-Siyan off their scent by having his Crusaders sally out at night as if on their way to a routine skirmish but then double back suddenly to approach the city where he, Firouz, would be waiting to let them in. All one night the Crusaders marched, and 'before dawn offered its first rays, they stood before the towers over which the blessed traitor vigilantly stood watch'.[lxxxii] In Arab history, Firouz is not 'blessed' of course, but 'accursed'.[lxxxiii]

The plan worked and soon the Crusaders were pouring into Antioch:

> Wailing and shrieking filled the city; while throngs pressed through the narrow streets, the brutal, bloody shouts of the victors, eager to kill, resounded. As they recalled the sufferings they had endured during the siege, they thought that the blows that they were giving could not match the starvations, more bitter than death, that they had suffered.[lxxxiv]

There was hideous confusion in Antioch's streets. Many of the Crusaders had long since stopped shaving and grown shaggy beards, which meant they could easily mistake one another for the enemy. Bishop Adhemar had tried to guard against Crusader slaughtering Crusader by ordering them all to shave and wear silver crosses prominently displayed about their persons, but to little avail. When it was all over Bohemond and his fellow lords reported back to Pope Urban. Any Icelandic Viking would have understood the talk of revenge.

> We all wish and desire that it be made known to you how, by the compassion of God and by His most manifest assistance, Antioch has been captured by us, and how the Turks, who had hurled many insults at our Lord Jesus Christ, have been captured and killed; how we, pilgrims of Jesus Christ, on our way to Jerusalem, have avenged the wrong against Most High God.[lxxxv]

Only three days after the fall of Antioch, Karbuqa of Mosul arrived and the former besiegers of the city became the besieged.

～

Almost a thousand years after the Crusaders occupied Antioch, there are only two Western European Christians living in Antakya, one an Italian priest from somewhere near Canossa, the other a German member of an inter-faith dialogue group with links to Taizé. I encountered them both on my second day in town.

Padre Domenico was receiving a tour group of middle-aged Italian pilgrims when I found my way to his church and its pretty interior courtyard decorated with geraniums and orange trees. A trimly elegant figure in pale grey trousers and a jumper which matched his silver hair, he darted about here and there, distributing leaflets about the history of his church, offering his guests coffee, marshalling them all and me for a group photograph taken with his new digital camera and finally escorting them back to their hotel. On his return he bade me welcome. I explained my business and he sighed at my tentatively phrased conclusion that the aggressively fundamentalist Western Church had been behind heinous crimes against Byzantine Christians, Jews and Muslims in the eleventh century.

'Look, Pope Urban did not know exactly what was happening; most of the Crusaders only came for adventure,' he said.

Much like *Frère* Émile back at Taizé, he begged me to refrain from raking over the past again and instead look to the future. 'You and I are not responsible for what happened in that time, are we? We are responsible for taking decisions today! You know, a few years ago a very large group of Christians, mostly evangelicals from America, came here on their way to Jerusalem with the aim of apologizing for what the Crusaders did a thousand years ago. I told them that they were only bringing confusion.'

Instead of drawing him into an argument about how we in the West can afford to forget our past but our victims cannot because they are still suffering the ill-effects of it; instead of pointing out that we could help to heal the present by acknowledging past wrongs, I changed the subject. The same icebreaker question I had posed to sad-eyed Don Faustino back at Monte Cassino occurred to me.

'*Padre*, could you please tell me what a plenary indulgence is?'

'It is not easy to explain,' he began, measuring me with a penetrating look. 'The Church is the instrument which transmits the pardon of God . . .' He spoke for five minutes or so in terms I found incomprehensible and then clicked his tongue impatiently. 'You don't like this plenary indulgence, do you? Well, honestly, neither do I. The important thing is that a person should make a dramatic turn towards God, a true conversion. Last year, the jubilee 2000, I organized for Christians here to win a plenary indulgence, but it was not too easy for them. They had to go to confession and fast and walk all the way to the church of St Peter.'

We spoke about the size of his congregation.

'Christians here – Catholic and Orthodox – are few and getting fewer thanks to emigration but I do not despair. Young people are coming to my church because I do my services in Turkish. Many of the city's Orthodox Christians also come because they can't understand the ancient Aramaic in their own.'

'The Orthodox must be jealous of you,' I said. Early that morning I had dropped in at Antioch's Orthodox church, a handsome gift of the Orthodox Russians in the nineteenth century, and found six elderly Syrians droning through their liturgy while a bowed old priest wafted wisps of incense smoke over them. When it was finished, one of the old men had eyed me suspiciously and told me in the French he must have learned when Antioch still belonged to Syria and France was the protecting power, that if I was a Catholic I belonged with *Padre* Domenico.

'Relations between us are not so bad.' *Padre* Domenico laughed again. 'I always insist that the babies of Orthodox families are baptized in the Orthodox church.'

Padre Domenico believed in Christian ecumenism and was one of the many western European Catholic clergy who felt that the promise of the Second Vatican Council, that spring-time of the Church in the early 1960s, had been betrayed. I got the distinct impression that he deeply regretted the more authoritarian route Pope John Paul II had taken. When I asked him if he would be travelling down the coast for the Pope's visit to Damascus in a couple of weeks' time, he told me shortly, 'Probably not.'

'You're not too keen on this pope, are you?'

'It's the end of his pontificate – as difficult as landing a plane,' he answered with a smile. 'I can say one thing. He should not have appointed an Italian bishop to Turkey, only a Turk.' He paused a moment, before continuing, 'Something has to change. We need a new idea of a pope, and the division between the Christian Churches is ridiculous!'

I liked *Padre* Domenico so much that when he invited me to stay for one of his youth services, I immediately accepted. 'I am so inspired by the example of the first Christian Church here. You will see!' he said happily.

Twenty young people and I sat on a circle of chairs around the edge of a room, waiting for him to make his entrance. The friendly boy on my right, who informed me that both his parents were Orthodox Christians, had a pair of bongo drums between his knees. Beside him was another youth tuning a guitar. Everyone sang lustily and well, and a very beautiful young woman – as fashionably dressed in tight black jumper and trousers as either Anya in Konstanz, Marta at Canossa's *corteo* or the girl on the bus from Tirana – performed the readings with feeling and understanding. One by one, without being asked, the young people raised their hands in prayer and spoke about what they had just heard. Then *Padre* Domenico's reading whisked me all the way back to the year before and bright mornings with the Gospels in Taizé's meal tent.

' "Just as day was breaking, Jesus stood on the beach; yet the disciples did not know that it was Jesus. Jesus said to them "Children, have you any fish?" They answered him "No." He said to them, "Cast the net on the right side of the boat, and you will find some." So they cast it, and now they were not able to haul it in, for the quantity of fish . . ." 'lxxxvi

I vividly recalled *Frère* Hanyol's knees buckling under the mimed weight of a net bursting with a hundred and fifty-three different sorts of fish. We gave each other the kiss instead of the hand-shake sign of peace and Holy Communion was taken. I felt sure that Archbishop Anastasios would have approved of it all.

The service over, I thanked *Padre* Domenico and told him how much I had been reminded of my week at Taizé. A hint of a grimace flickered across his face, 'Taizé? Well, if you like Taizé you should stay for the next service too. A German woman, Barbara, will have a service of Taizé songs. Young Muslims as well as Christians usually attend.'

I concluded from his sudden chilliness that Antakya's only two Western Christians were not at peace with one another, that Barbara's ecumenical spirit must be more inclusive than *Padre* Domenico's. A tall, strong woman dressed in jeans and a safari waistcoat, she was already busy setting up her music stands and distributing Taizé songbooks. Soon she was efficiently instructing me to read various passages of the Bible at certain points in the service. Some of the young people from the first service had remained for hers, but sat cross-legged on the carpet instead of on the chairs. Others arrived. But without the Taizé monks' descants the songs were not as moving, and the ten minutes of silent contemplation was broken by the infinitely more poignant wail of a nearby muezzin. I was relieved when it was over.

We all repaired for coffee and snacks to Barbara's home, built for a nineteenth-century Antiochian merchant but tastefully restored and refurbished with every modern convenience including dimmer switches. It was as instantly covetable as the yellow house set in vineyards that I had seen on my walk near Taizé. Its wide interior courtyard was planted with citrus trees; the floor of a long workroom was covered with coconut matting, its walls hung with book shelves and musical instruments. The kitchen, all stone but with its original carved wooden fixtures, was a triumph of discreet modernity.

The next day I found myself in another tastefully modernized kitchen, this time with marble work surfaces and a view of a rose garden through French windows. I was lunching with *Padre* Domenico off spaghetti carbonara, breaded chicken, fresh green salad and a heavy red wine, all served by his Arab Christian housekeeper, Zeineb. She, her husband and her three small children were the priest's adopted family. I listened to him tease her about her diet, and tell her four-year-old that she was not going anywhere with him that afternoon until she had brushed her hair. After lunch he insisted on showing me Zeineb's twins snoozing in their basket. He could not have been prouder of them if they had been his own. I wondered if he knew about the eleventh-century Church's campaign against married priests; if he had come to resent his lot.

Alongside his home, work and surrogate family concerns, *Padre* Domenico also had property interests. Like Barbara, he had recognized the beauty and value of the city's Ottoman-era stone and wood houses with their shady interior courtyards. He took me on a quick tour of his properties which formed an expanding cluster around his church. First, there were the two houses he had had renovated with five thousand Deutschmarks given him by some German Catholics.

'Zeineb and her family live here, another Christian family in the other,' he explained.

'Don't the Turks get jealous,' I asked, 'with the nicest houses in the city going to Christians?'

He neatly sidestepped the question. 'Well, I couldn't let my housekeeper and her three children go on living in one room, could I? That wouldn't be very Christian, would it?'

Next door, through a beautiful carved stone doorway into a courtyard littered with stones and noisy with masons at work, was a house once owned by someone *Padre* Domenico described as a 'fanatical Muslim and nationalist' who had sworn never to sell his house to a Christian. 'He was forced to go back on his word,' said the priest with a delighted giggle. In the case of another house of similar size and beauty with the same elaborately coffered wooden ceiling, two brothers had fallen out so badly they had been unable to share the house and decided on a quick sale.

'It was too good an opportunity to miss, you see,' insisted *Padre* Domenico, 'but my superiors back in Rome were asking me, "Are you crazy? Are you going to buy up all the old houses in Antakya?" They were only convinced it was a good idea when I told them that the whole thing, with the restoration, would only cost . . . Let me see, in English pounds . . . What's the exchange rate of the pound to the Deutschmark? OK, about fifteen thousand pounds.'

∿

How to calculate the exchange rate for a Crusader's Byzantine besant, a solidus or a denarius? No matter. The chroniclers simply meant us to understand that while the captured city of Antioch was under siege from Karbuqa and his ally emirs, food was once again in desperately short supply:

> a little loaf of bread sold for a besant. Of wine I won't speak. They sold and ate horse and ass flesh; they also sold a cock for fifteen solidi, an egg for two solidi, and a nut for a denarius. Thus everything was very dear. They cooked and ate the leaves of the fig tree, grape vine, and thistle, and of all trees, so tremendous was their hunger. Others cooked the dry hides of horses, camels, asses, cattle and buffaloes . . .[lxxxvii]

One hungry *miles* spent a 'remarkable amount of money'[lxxxviii] on a camel's foot, which rendered him so listless he was scarcely able to sit on his horse. Bishop Adhemar tried to organize emergency relief for poorer pilgrims, but many of the Crusaders grumbled that Count Stephen of Blois had done the right thing by deserting the Crusade and were not remotely surprised when one of Bohemond's brothers-in-law absconded. Unaware that Stephen of Blois was responsible for putting Alexius off, the Crusaders could not forgive the emperor's continued absence.

If the horrible trek across Asia Minor had been conducive to miraculous visions and portents, how much more so was this second, apparently hopeless, siege of Antioch. In early June 1098, a slovenly and notoriously venal peasant Crusader from Provence found his way to Count Raymond's lodging with a marvellous tale about receiving frequent visits from St Andrew. Peter Bartholomew claimed that on each occasion Christ's Apostle had commanded him to go to Antioch's church of St Peter and dig up the lance which had been used by the Roman soldiers to pierce Christ's side while he was hanging on the cross, and St Andrew had grown increasingly irritated at the idle sot's refusal to obey him. Five times he had ignored his holy instructions, before finally plucking up the courage to come and see the count about the matter. The Crusading lords were divided in their response. Bohemond pooh-poohed the affair saying, ' "Beautifully was it contrived that St Andrew should appear to a man who, I hear, frequents taverns, roams the streets, is a friend to vanities and ingrained with folly! The holy apostle chose a fine person to whom to disclose the secret of heaven!" 'lxxxix Bishop Adhemar was equally suspicious, but for another reason. He found it distinctly odd that St Andrew should also have happened to complain to Peter Bartholomew about his, Adhemar's, preaching skills. Count Raymond, however, believed the peasant and organized a ceremonial dig at the described spot in the church of St Peter. After a whole day's fruitless rummaging, Peter Bartholomew, dressed only in a shirt, leapt into the trench alone and reappeared with an iron rod.

The discovery of the Holy Lance was just the powerful boost to morale the Crusade needed, equivalent to the timely invention of a tank or fighter plane, of a bouncing or nuclear bomb. A few days later St Andrew was back again, telling Peter Bartholomew that the Crusaders should go on a five-day fast and then march out of the city to attack the Turks. Victory would be theirs but, he had added sternly, there must be no pillaging of the enemy's tents.

Bohemond had already decided on the same bold course of action. News that Karbuqa's camp was riven with rivalries and stricken by an epidemic of desertions had greatly cheered him, and a tentative peace mission, headed by Peter the Hermit, had already failed. To Peter's offer of lenient treatment by the Crusading lords if they would convert en masse to Christianity, Karbuqa and his allies had simply replied: ' "We think you are mad to come from the ends of the earth, threatening with all your might to drive us from our homes, when you have insufficient supplies, too few arms, and too few men. Not only do we refuse to accept the name of Christians, but we spit upon it in disgust." 'xc

On 28 June 1098, divided into six armies, the half-starved Crusaders left the city, 'walking so slowly that not even a weak old woman would have asked for a slower pace'.xci Churchmen, armed with crosses and dressed in their full ceremonials, marched with them, 'eager to aid the soldiers with their tearful prayers, themselves awaiting the gift of martyrdom, if they should happen to be cut down'.xcii One of them carried the Holy Lance. Battle was joined, the Crusaders spurred on by a miraculous sighting of a band of white-clad knights led by St George. The Emir of Damascus led the retreat, causing the rest of the enemy camp to break up in panic. Karbuqa himself fled the field.

Bohemond must have been half out of his mind with joy, for he despatched to Alexius 'a whole cargo of noses and thumbs sliced from the Saracens'.xciii He also sent Karbuqa's fabulous tent – large enough to hold two thousand and constructed like a town with towers, walls and ramparts hung with silken cloths – home to the Cathedral of St Nicholas in Bari. The euphoria of victory was short-lived however because the tricky question of the lordship of Antioch remained undecided. Bohemond wanted it for himself; good Count Raymond insisted on returning it to Alexius.

A typhus epidemic carried off Bishop Adhemar in August. Inconsolable apparently, Bohemond vowed to carry the prelate's corpse on his shoulders all the way to Jerusalem. The bishop's demise robbed the Crusade of any respectability. No one else could claim the authority of Pope Urban. No one else had managed to keep his sights fixed on the higher purpose of the expedition and the vital importance of not exacerbating already bad relations with the Eastern Christians. Old Count Raymond had been fairly disin-terested in his conduct thus far, but he was sixty years old and poorly. No one felt fit or confident enough to march straight on down the coast to Jerusalem. Bohemond, who stepped into the power vacuum, sent a missive to Pope Urban, betraying not only his doubts as to how to proceed, but also his deep and dangerous hatred for his Orthodox Christian brothers.

> What therefore seems more proper in all the world than that you, who are father and head of the Christian religion, should come to the original and chief city where the Christian name was used, and bring to a conclusion on your own behalf the war which is yours? For we have beaten the Turks and the heathen, but we do not know how to defeat the heretics, the Greeks and the Armenians and Syrian Jacobites . . .[xciv]

Pope Urban must have wrung his hands in dismay on receiving this letter and felt towards Bohemond much as Guiscard had done some fifteen years earlier on learning that he had bungled the conquest of Constantinople. One of Urban's main motives for launching the Crusade had been the mending of fences with Eastern Christendom after all the damage wrought by Cardinal Humbert and then Pope Gregory. Bohemond was achieving quite the reverse. And there could be no question of Urban struggling out to Antioch, even by boat; he was too old and sick. But he desperately wanted to limit the damage the Crusaders were doing to the cause of the united Church. Convening a council, he invited as many Orthodox prelates as possible to Bari to discuss the thorny old question of the *Filioque*. It is remarkable that there are no Byzantine sources which refer to this meeting held in the crypt of St Nicholas' cathedral, perhaps because no patriarch troubled to attend it. Saint Anselm's efforts to reconcile the Byzantines to the idea of Western Christendom using the *Filioque* in the Creed fell on deaf ears. News of the Crusaders' behaviour on Byzantine territory was all the argument they needed to convince them of the non-negotiable superiority of their own ways.

Back in Antioch, the disreputable Peter Bartholomew was still being treated to regular visions of St Andrew. In one, the recently deceased Bishop Adhemar appeared beside the Apostle, abjectly apologizing for his earlier scepticism. In another St Andrew voiced his support for Bohemond's lordship of Antioch. More controversially, he commanded the Crusaders to appoint their own patriarch of the city in place of the Orthodox incumbent, John. St Andrew was also strongly of the opinion that the Crusaders should waste no more time but forge on south to their goal.

This was easier said than done as Count Raymond and Bohemond were still locked in a deadly argument over Antioch's future. The rank and file Crusaders finally forced the issue by threatening to burn down the city and march on towards Jerusalem alone. After an unspeakably miserable fifteen months in Antioch they had had enough of the place and only wanted to reach the holy city, win their plenary indulgences and a little loot, and go home. Bohemond and Count Raymond hastily divided the city between them and, leaving their rival garrisons to enforce the status quo, started south towards the town of Ma'arra where they imagined they could find food.

Ma'arat al-Numan, as it is today, lies across a modern border, in northern Syria. The distance I had travelled physically and mentally – via pogroms, battles, privations and sieges – since arriving in Thessaloniki two weeks before had left me drained of any energy to continue. Anyway, I wanted to reassure myself that my father was getting better and I had no Syrian visa. Colourful Gaziantep had an airport and a flight to Heathrow via Istanbul.

~

Round and round the plane went, sunshine slowly flooding the cabin, then shade. Sunshine, shade, sunshine, shade. The Austrian Airlines pilot's voice sounded weary.

'You have probably noticed that we have been in a holding pattern for the past fifteen minutes. Damascus Airport is closed due to the arrival of the Holy Father's aeroplane . . .'

I relaxed. The pope was on schedule, having survived his visit to Athens where he had been forced to apologize for centuries-old

injuries the Western Church had inflicted on Eastern Christendom.*
At last, everything was working out fine.

My father had made excellent progress, and I had not been
anticipating any trouble with my Syrian visa. But the previous
afternoon I had arrived at the Syrian consulate in Belgrave Square
to collect my passport only to learn that I had not been granted a
visa. My description of myself as a 'writer', who might not be trusted
to report favourably on what I saw in Syria, was to blame.

'But I'm not a journalist; I'm writing about history, eleventh-
century history!' I pleaded. It was no use. Authorization of any
writer's visa had to come from Damascus and took two weeks.

'But I have a seat on a plane tomorrow!' I told the flustered-
looking official, who shrugged his shoulders dolefully. 'If only you
hadn't written "writer" . . .' he said, shaking his head.

'What should I have written? Nurse? Acrobat? You wanted me
to lie? I am shocked that Syria can treat a guest so badly!' I
remonstrated furiously, deliberately aiming at the soft target of Arab
pride in their hospitality.

But when this too was answered by a sad shrug, I plucked
another weapon from my arsenal. Covering my face with my hands,
I began to sob as if my heart might break. The official was upset
and shouted into his telephone, but still the answer was no. For
almost two hours I laid determined siege to the poor man, crying
and pleading, crying and crying. Every time my tears seemed about
to dry up, I complained some more until the injustice of my treatment struck me afresh and I was ready to launch a fresh assault
with more tears and louder wails. I had never before had occasion
to behave in such an abandoned fashion.

'There is nothing I can do. You must leave now,' said the
distraught official at last. 'The embassy is closing. You will have to
leave by the main entrance.'

But something about his repeated angry telephone calls and the

---

* The sacking of Constantinople in 1204 during the Fourth Crusade was top of the
list.

way he had suffered me to remain there for so long, weeping and wailing, led me to suspect that the battle was not lost. As I made my slow, lamenting way down the entrance hall towards the front door, a handsome diplomat descended from on high. Leaning over a banister, he demanded to know what all the noise was about.

'Sir, sir! I'm sure *you* can help me! Please!' I wailed up at him.

One ear graciously cocked towards me, he listened to my woe. Within minutes he had bounded back upstairs with my passport, stamped it, scribbled on it and returned it to me, modestly insisting that it had been no trouble at all. 'But by giving you this visa I am taking personal responsibility for you. You should know that if you write anything damaging to Syria I will be the one to suffer,' he warned me, with a menacing flash of his dark eyes. So pleased was I with my visa, so mightily relieved that I would reach Damascus in time for the pope's visit, that I accepted a restoring cup of tea and, seated in a comfortable armchair, engaged in a few minutes' chat with the diplomat. No, no, of course not. I had no intention whatsoever of visiting Israel, I lied, realizing with a shock that the Syrians and Lebanese would be suspicious and even angry if they knew I was heading on south, to Jerusalem.

I had emerged feeling emotionally drained but only very slightly less well-disposed towards Syria than I had been before. Any amount of cruel manipulation, maddening red tape and hints of emotional blackmail paled beside the bestial behaviour of the Crusaders in Ma'arra.

After three days' march south the Crusaders had reached the town, which they had been led to believe was plentifully supplied with food. They were unaware of the place's nobler reputation as the birthplace of the blind poet, Abu' l'-Ala, who had died forty years before their arrival, having once wearily noted:

> The inhabitants of the earth are of two sorts:
> Those with brains, but no religion,
> And those with religion, but no brains.[xcv]

Abu' l'-Ala had perfectly understood long before anyone in Western Christendom, before even the fierce monk Hildebrand had risen to power as the fundamentalist Pope Gregory, that mankind's reasoning faculty and natural yearning for freedom were impossible to reconcile with the undemocratic dictates of any supreme but unseen God represented by an all-powerful priesthood. Alive today, he would have clearly seen that fundamentalist religion and open societies do not mix.

The Crusaders' two direct assaults on Ma'arra failed. For two weeks they besieged it instead, maddened by continuing food shortages and the chore of roaming the surrounding countryside in search of wood to build siege engines. The Arab inhabitants of the region shook with terror as they spied on Tafurs huddled around their campfires stripping the bones of any stray Saracen they had managed to snare. At last, Count Raymond's great wooden castle on wheels gained a first group of Crusaders entrance into the city. Bohemond, determined not to let Raymond outdo him, let the ten thousand or so Arab inhabitants of Ma'arra know that they could expect merciful treatment from him if only they would surrender. That night the fighting died down, but the following morning the entire Crusading army descended on the city, burning houses and massacring everyone in sight.

Bohemond's guarantees of safety counted for less than nothing. After the horrors they had suffered and perpetrated at Antioch, the Crusaders were out of control. The Tafurs surpassed themselves at Ma'arra: 'In Ma'arra our troops boiled pagan adults in cooking pots; they impaled children on spits and devoured them grilled,'[xcvi] wrote one Crusader chronicler, while another exclaimed that this time the Tafurs had gone too far: 'Not only did our troops not shrink from eating dead Turks and Saracens; they also ate dogs!'[xcvii] In an official report to Pope Urban the following year, the Crusading lords did their best to account for the atrocities by saying that 'a terrible famine racked the army in Ma'arra and placed it in cruel necessity of feeding itself upon the bodies of the Saracens'.[xcviii] Sounding genuinely bewildered, the Lebanese Arab author of *The Crusades*

Through Arab Eyes casts himself back nine hundred years and writes, 'Were they [the Crusaders] cannibals out of necessity? Or out of fanaticism? It all seems unreal, and yet the evidence is overwhelming . . .'[xcix] He notes that twentieth-century historians of the Crusades play down the grisly phenomenon, 'perhaps in the interests of the West's "civilising mission"?'[c] but that Arab epics are sprinkled with references to the cannibal *Franj*.

From Ma'arra the Crusaders continued south, but without Bohemond who abandoned the Crusade to return to Antioch and secure his lordship of the city. It was January 1099 and Count Raymond – barefoot, as befitted a pilgrim – had been granted the leadership of the expedition, a position only disputed by the ambitious Duke Godfrey. With a mere thousand *milites* and five thousand foot soldiers left, Count Raymond decided that the army was too weak to take the string of fortresses along the coast road and that they must reach Jerusalem and their dear Lord's tomb before there were too few of them left to fight for it. So they remained inland where they encountered local emirs too horrified by news of the capture of Antioch and Ma'arra to offer any resistance. Instead, they made the Crusaders welcome. If only the *Franj* would spare the locals the grosser manifestations of their culture, they were welcome to as much food, as many pack animals, horses and expert guides as their barbarous hearts desired. The Crusaders' morale picked up again. Plentiful loot was theirs for the asking.

On the hot afternoon I arrived in the Syrian capital, another large influx of *Franj* – namely Pope John Paul II, his Vatican retinue and a small army of Western press – was meeting with a similarly courteous welcome because their advent suited Syria very well. The pope had arrived here in Damascus to gladden the hearts of the Christian minority and to reach out a shaky hand to Muslims, but also as a humble pilgrim to the city Apostle Paul had preached in after being converted to Christianity in a blinding flash of light. Syria was enjoying a rare chance to display itself in front of Western television cameras and boost her reputation as a haven of religious tolerance in the Middle East. Her handsome young president, Bashar

Assad, was also skilfully exploiting the occasion for opportunities to complain about Israel's treatment of the Palestinians.

Damascus had been swept clean, its road markings repainted, its colourful crowds replaced by lines of bored young soldiers in dark mustard uniforms guarding any street the pope was scheduled to use. That warm evening, I wandered for miles until it was dark, through the new Damascus with its nondescript modern blocks and smart Western boutiques, and on, into the old Damascus of the French mandate and its gracious municipal buildings, palm-lined avenues, parks (infested by patrols of soldiers) and more blocks of large apartments, their windows lit by chandeliers. At last I came to the ancient walled city containing Ottoman-era houses like Antakya's, a gigantic covered souk, churches and the fabulous Umayyad mosque which the Pope would be visiting the next day.

By nine o'clock I was happily and thoroughly lost. The high black hill on which Cain had murdered his brother Abel was twinkling with dots of light, and I was unable to flag down a taxi back to my hotel because it was rush hour. Cars, driven by veiled women impatiently honking their horns and sporting pictures of the handsome young president and his deceased father in their back windows, tore past me. Taxis, their red- or blue-lit interiors packed with entire families, hurtled by, narrowly avoiding collisions with slow, shark-finned automobiles of the 1950s. The ambience was more thrillingly exotic than anything I had seen on my journey but the street lighting was too dim to read my map by. At last, someone kindly directed me into a nearby restaurant where an Irish teacher of English sat at supper with one of his Syrian students.

They invited me to share their platter of chips, their *fuul* (bean paste flavoured with lemon and garlic) and mint tea. As a Palestinian waiter bustled around finding me a chair and another plate of *fuul*, Richard, the teacher, a connoisseur of Arab culture and a fluent Arabic-speaker, dispensed some advice.

'Just remember, never mention having once been a journalist, and under no circumstances tell anyone you're going to Jerusalem. Don't ever say you have no religion – no one understands that –

but bear in mind that religion is a sensitive subject. About seventy per cent of the population is Sunni Muslim, but the members of two minorities – Christians and Alawite Muslims,* who are hardly Muslims at all actually – run the place. They were the people the French found they could do business with between the world wars, and they're still the top dogs. By the way, he's an Alawite,' said Richard, pointing at his student friend.

'Sorry, I didn't catch your name,' I said to the youth.

'You can call me the "First Lieutenant",' he answered me, with a charmingly modest smile.

'Work out for yourself what he is.' Richard chuckled, tearing himself a strip of bread to mop up his *fuul*.

But I could see why they were friends. The First Lieutenant was excellent company. Learned, witty and apparently utterly disenchanted with life as a secret policeman, he had recently fallen violently foul of his superior officer by questioning the man's right to banish him on a tour of duty to the Golan Heights.† He was looking for a way out, perhaps a period of study in America, for his true interests were intellectual.

'By the time I was nine I knew all Shakespeare,' he said, helping himself to more chips, 'and I have read Nieztsche's *Thus Spake Zarathustra* five times.'

'Why did you become a policeman in the first place then?' I asked him. 'Didn't you say your father was a judge?'

'He wanted me to have the power to control other people and, of course, the bribes are good, but I don't want these things.'

However, the First Lieutenant was unable to conceal his delight when, as we were walking back through the dark streets, past the city's law courts, a uniformed policeman saluted him respectfully. He thought he would attend the pope's service the next morning, if he could get up in time. 'It's not every day that a celebrity like

---

* The Alawite sect was founded at the end of the tenth century. They have no prayer houses and concentrate on the spirituality of Islam.

† The Golan Heights were a part of Syria until Israel annexed them in the 1967 war. Syria has not accepted the loss but Israel has built settlements in the area.

the pope comes to visit Syria,' he said proudly. Richard would 'definitely not' be there.

~

By five thirty the next morning I was in a taxi passing through impossibly clean streets lined with yawning soldiers on my way to the city's football stadium. I had discovered that although Pope John Paul – the name translates into Arabic as *Baba Johanna Boulos* – would not arrive at the venue until ten, I should get there early if I wanted a good seat.

Walking around the back of the stands, I fell in with an excited family party of three sisters, all wearing white and yellow baseball caps and T-shirts printed with a portrait of a youthful pope. From one of them, a young teacher of French who introduced herself as Melody, I learned that they had travelled all night by bus from a town in the far east of the country near the Iraqi border. Seated on folding chairs not too far from the front, we pooled our food supplies, snoozed on each other's shoulders and strolled around. Just as in Rome, mighty screens had been erected to relay close-ups of the pope's movements. Opposite the canopied rostrum where he would sit, at the back of the stadium, were two outsize portraits, of President Assad and his late father.

By eight fifteen the sun had come out. Melody produced an English-language textbook and requested my help with mastering the pronunciation of an absurdly enthusiastic conversation:

A: Did you work at home last night?
B: Yes, I washed the dishes and cleaned the house.
A: Did you do anything else?
B: Yes, I listened to the radio for a while.
A: Did you have a good time last night?
B: Yes, I had a wonderful time.
A: You'll probably have fun tomorrow too.
B: I'm sure I'll have an excellent time.

A warm-up session began. A voice over a powerful megaphone instructed the thousands of Syrian Christians gathering there to chant: 'Jo-han-na Bou-los!' (three claps) 'Wel-come!' (two claps). The flag-waving started, and the loud cheering and naming of contingents of Christians from all over the country. Slowly the heads of Syria's multiple Christian churches gathered on the podium in the shade of their red canopy. Aided by Melody's binoculars, I saw that the black-robed senior churchmen were sporting a splendid variety of hats. One wore a close-fitting black bonnet with silver spangles, another a plain black alchemist's hood. His neighbour had a bright red one with a wide black brim, the man in front of him a little onion dome, and behind him was a pointed black Klu Klux Klan affair. There were mitres of every size, some plain, some embroidered with pearls or gold. This ecclesiastical Ascot was, in fact, a gathering of all 'the heretics, the Greeks, and the Armenians and Syrian Jacobites' whom Bohemond had complained of not being able to defeat in his letter to Pope Urban after the capture of Antioch. Some of these ancient Eastern Churches had recognized the supremacy of the pope in the intervening nine hundred years, but there were many Orthodox attending the mass out of politeness or under duress. The night before, the First Lieutenant had explained to me that most Orthodox were far from happy about John Paul's visit, but the Orthodox patriarch himself was a close friend of the young president. Syria's religious leaders are firmly under secular control and the government does not countenance religious fundamentalism. Love of Syria and her presidential dynasty are the designated channels for that sort of passion.

Two noisy helicopters circled overhead. The mighty wind they stirred up flicked the baseball caps off people's heads and ruined the hairdos of the foreign diplomats' wives seated in the reserved front rows. The sun beat down and, just as I had back in Rome, I envied the churchmen their shady canopy. When the first footage of the pope, skimming down the avenue towards the stadium in his pope-mobile between lines of motionless soldiers, appeared on the giant screen, everyone climbed onto their chairs for a better view. I was as moved by the sight as I had been in Rome. At last, the white dot of his skullcap appeared up on the podium.

The old man expressed his deep joy at finding himself among so many Orthodox.

'The things that unite us are stronger than the things that drive us apart!' he claimed. 'This occasion is a symbol of our reunion!'

Syria's church–state relations and the president's exploitation of the pope's visit as an occasion to remind the world of Israeli infamy counted for nothing in that stadium. The pope, intent on going down in history as the man who healed the rift between East and West Christendom after almost a thousand years of schism, was happy just to be here. Like Pope Urban with his Council of Bari in 1098, he was hoping to undo the grievous damage wrought by the First Crusaders. It had been in Antioch, at Bohemond's instigation, that the first practical division of the Churches had been made manifest. By 1100, Bohemond's Crusader state of Antioch boasted two patriarchs, one Latin, one Greek. Jerusalem would soon follow that lead.

By midday I was bored, sunburnt and keen to leave. Melody was surprised and sure that soldiers or policemen would bar my exit, but thankfully she was wrong.

Later that afternoon, I stood at my hotel's reception desk, peering past the heads of the hotelier and his brother at the blurred television screen behind them. There was the immaculately white-robed pope, surrounded by bustling bearded Muslim clerics, in the Umayyad mosque that had once been a Byzantine basilica and still had the mosaics to prove it. John Paul's idea of conducting a joint service with the grand mufti had been politely rejected but the occasion was quite historic enough. No pope had ever set foot in a mosque before. I watched him sit down slowly and suffer his shoes to be exchanged for a pair of kitten-heeled white slippers trimmed with gold. Rising again with the aid of a stick, he ventured bravely out across a vast dark sea of richly patterned carpets towards the central shrine of Christ's cousin, John the Baptist. A grand marble edifice housing the saint's severed head, the monument was luridly illuminated by green strip lighting but still a powerful illustration of how the world's three great monotheistic faiths are links in the same chain, like generations of a single family. For Jews, John the Baptist is one of them. For Christians of East and West he is Christ the Saviour's messenger and forerunner. For Muslims he and his cousin and Mohammed are God's prophets.

'For all the times that Muslims and Christians have offended one another, we need to seek forgiveness,' said the pope, so bowed and shaky that he seemed to be bearing the accumulated burden of every one of those offences on his shoulders. I wondered how *Padre* Domenico back in Antioch could doubt the wisdom of striving to mend the past before building the future.

The next day the Umayyad mosque looked even bigger than it had on television. The small screen had not communicated its atmosphere either. That bright spring morning it was light, airy and palpably peaceful. Scattered here and there on the carpets were dozens of sleeping men. Some had curled up against pillars, their shoes and bags neatly ranged beside them. Some lay on their sides, with their heads resting on their hands. Some were spreadeagled on their backs and snoring, utterly at home in God's house. In my notebook I jotted down, 'hospitable Allah, hospitable Muslims'. The First Lieutenant later furnished me with a more prosaic explanation: 'Those men were all sleeping there like that because, for a change, the carpets were smelling good. According to my information they were cleaned in honour of the pope's visit.'

Richard had led us into the old city, to a popular restaurant in a glass-covered courtyard with a musically splashing fountain in its centre. All around us were young Syrians – male and female – enjoying *fuul* and chips, and leisurely apple- or cinnamon-scented smokes on the establishment's narghiles. The First Lieutenant was in high spirits and so eager to tell me about other goings-on in the mosque that he temporarily lost his excellent grip on the English language.

'Sometimes, when someone goes into the mosque, to a shrink—'

'You'll find he means a shrine,' Richard stage-whispered.

'Yes, when someone goes to a shrine, they lie down with a string tied to one finger because they hope to see a willy—'

'A willy?' asked Richard.

'Yes – you know Richard – a willy. It is our word for a holy man. They are waiting for a vision of a saint . . .'

The point of the tale was lost. The First Lieutenant blushed, bashful as a school boy, and we toasted my onward journey.

I would like to have spent longer in Damascus. The place had delighted me more than Antioch or Thessaloniki, more even than Bari. I felt sure that, as deliciously, refreshingly un-homogenized as any Westerner could wish, Syria's capital would have appealed to Arni Bergmann and the scientist-musician on the train from Ancona to Rome. Along with the sleeping men in the mosque and the ubiquitous portraits of the panda-eyed young president, I would remember a van wafting a minty fragrance from a mound of the fresh herb in its trailer and a sweating baker slapping rounds of fresh dough onto the sides of an open clay oven. I had liked my local juice bar, as overflowing with fruits as a Garden of Eden, and I had loved a child wearing a brown school uniform with military epaulettes, shouting at me, 'Are you happy in our city?'

I had been more than happy in Damascus but my Crusaders had not even stopped here, and there was somewhere else I had to see before I could journey on, across the border into Lebanon.

~

Richard had strongly recommended that I sample Aleppo's famous Baron Hotel – as Agatha Christie, Lawrence of Arabia and Kemal Ataturk had – but I was not much attracted to faded vestiges of the colonial era and my Crusaders had not been there either. Instead, I was heading only about a hundred miles north of Damascus to one of Syria's best-loved tourist attractions, the Crusader castle of Hosn al-Akrad, better known by its old Crusader name of Crac des Chevaliers.

The Crusaders had decided that the fortress, perched on top of its mountain, with commanding views over the hills and plain for miles around, was worth capturing not for any strategic reason but simply because they were famished as usual and the herdsmen of the region had prudently driven all their livestock inside it for safekeeping. Instead of repelling the foreigners, the wily Arabs – alerted to *Franj* ways by now – opened the castle gates and drove out herds of animals. The hungry soldier-pilgrims fell upon this bait and, in the process, dispersed all over the surrounding countryside. They were quite unable to group in time to fend off the Arabs' sudden attack and Count Raymond himself was almost captured. The following day the Crusaders sheepishly launched a more orderly assault on the fortress, only to find it utterly deserted but filled with food and loot. For three weeks they camped there, gorging themselves on their plentiful provisions, celebrating the holy Feast of the Purification and receiving embassies from local emirs interested in striking mutually advantageous deals with Count Raymond.

On a bus not as luxurious as the Turkish ones I had sampled but which did boast a video screen, I travelled out into a moon-desert landscape. Rain poured from a dark grey sky. When it stopped and the blood-red setting sun broke through again the hills turned from biscuit-beige to rose-pink and a rainbow appeared. Raindrops on the bus windows shone iridescent as pearls. Most of my fellow passengers were too transfixed by a World War Two romance set somewhere in snowy Scandinavia to notice this home-made natural drama. The next film was another domestic production. Its opening shot was of a chain gang of young Arab prisoners hard at work, their muscular shoulders shiny with sweat, digging a ditch in a golden desert. Next the screen filled with countless pairs of marching jackboots. The camera panned up to reveal that their owners' helmets were emblazoned with an outsize white Star of David. When the Jews raised their guns and fired, the Arab prisoners toppled backwards into the ditch. Out of nowhere a yellow bulldozer appeared to fill in the mass grave.

The point could not have been more clearly made: viewed through Arab eyes, the persecuted Jews of Christian Europe have become the persecuting Nazis of the Middle East. Today's Israel, founded by western-European-educated Jews, is as alien and unwanted a phenomenon as any of the Latin Crusader states. I was remembering the First Lieutenant's laborious explanation of a mystifying clumsy Arab pun.

'The Arabic word for Crusaders – literally "the people with the cross" – is *Al-saleebin*. The word is almost the same as *Al-mohtalin*, which means "the Occupier", which is Israel, of course.'

A minibus upholstered from floor to ceiling in soiled crimson damask transported me on the last leg of my journey, from Homs where I had spent the night, up the mountain to Crac des Chevaliers. The way was vertiginously steep and nerve-rackingly narrow – along a winding potholed road through tiny villages of half-built houses parading their satellite dishes like flags. The splendid views across neatly terraced hills, green at this time of year, reminded me of Burgundy. Small wonder the predominantly French First Crusaders had lingered three weeks here in January 1099 and that later Crusaders troubled to rebuild and expand the fortress to accommodate four thousand soldiers, a church, stables, a courtyard, dining halls, cellars and sleeping quarters. The *Franj* had held out here for almost two hundred years.

Outside the castle's main entrance was a line of tour buses, which suggested to me that visitors did not spend the night up here. I could see no hotel. The minibus driver was about to insist that I get out when I noticed a young man brooding darkly under a pine tree by the side of the road. He was Ahmed, he said, and his family happened to own a brand new hotel with magnificent views of the castle. Hopping aboard the minibus, he directed the driver on, along the crest of the slope and round to the neighbouring one, a few hundred yards away. There was his hotel, clinging to the mountainside like a poor man's miniature Monte Cassino.

An enthusiastic young man with a bodybuilder's physique, neat beard and a grin like that of a comic-book Saladin, Ahmed showed me round an establishment that was barely furnished and very poorly maintained. There were piles of rubbish in dark corners, empty plastic water bottles behind doors, chipped plaster and flaking paint-work. My room had ugly strip lighting but its own balcony with the best possible view of the Crac. I was admiring it, and the long green grass shimmering in the cooling breeze and glinting sunshine when Ahmed announced, 'Now we must walk to the ministry.'

'What ministry? Where?' I asked, imagining a local government office or police station at which I was legally obliged to register my presence in the area.

'I can show you . . . Look,' he said, taking my hand and leading me to the far edge of the balcony. 'Can you see the cross on top of the church?'

'Oh, you mean monastery, not ministry!'

'Yes, Greek monastery. Very beautiful!'

'But I need to see the castle . . .'

'Now is not a good time. It is closing soon. Tomorrow I will take you.'

I was tired and as hungry as a Crusader but I loved Orthodox monasteries, so, minutes later, Ahmed and I were tramping down the mountain together, through the high grass, across stony terraces and along an overgrown path. The lashing of thorns and nettles was uncomfortable but much worse was the way Ahmed insisted on presenting me with little bunches of wild flowers and seizing every opportunity to take my hand. On a narrow grassy knoll we stopped for a rest. There my discomfort turned to alarm and my alarm to fear. Ahmed's eagerness to show me a local house of God had thinly disguised quite another order of eagerness, for *obscoeni negotii*.

'I like to be with Western women,' he began. 'Everybody in the village knows that I must be with a Western woman, and all Western women like me. I think Western men are no good for their women because they work with computers all day so they are not strong, real men,' he continued, inviting me to squeeze his biceps. He then mimed a Western male, slumped flabby and narrow-shouldered in front of a computer screen. 'Me, I can do sex for one hour and a woman can have three, four, five climaxes!' he boasted. 'But I always use a condom. Then the woman is safe and I am safe!' So saying, he produced from his wallet a sample of the aforementioned article. Matter-of-factly spreading his knees, he mimed the task of putting it on.

'Ahmed, I don't want to talk about sex all the time. Let's go on,' I said curtly. I had jumped to my feet and set off again determinedly in the direction of the monastery. He followed.

'OK! OK! I only wanted you to know that it is possible with me if you want it. I have done sex with many Australian women, and English also. Last year an American woman called Samantha came here and we did so much sex–'

'Enough, Ahmed!' I interrupted him.

' – but Samantha was not good,' he continued regardless. 'She did not love me. I loved her. I waited and waited for her. Western women have no heart. They only take what they want . . .' Where had I heard that same sour note of resentment before? In Istanbul, from the carpet seller who had asked me why I had come to Turkey if I did not want to talk to Turkish people.

Ahmed was giving me to understand that the twenty-first-century heirs of the Crusaders in these parts were not savage Tafurs and bedraggled *milites* with the fire of fanatical faith in their eyes and nothing in their bellies, but shockingly emancipated Western women with 'Come hither' in their eyes and lust in their bellies. They were a dangerously attractive enemy intent not on war but sex with no strings attached. Generations of medieval Crusaders, as fascinated by the Arabs' undeniably richer civilization as many Arabs are by the West today, would also focus on sexual licentiousness as a means of demonizing their adversaries. Viewing my present discomfort through the zoom lens of history proved soothing.

'Ahmed, I'm very sorry your heart is broken, but please, no more about sex,' I begged him.

'What's the problem? Western television is only about sex – sex, only sex!' he repeated, gallantly thrashing aside the nettles for me. I tried a different line of defence.

'How old are you Ahmed? Twenty-five? I'm almost old enough to be your mother, so just leave the subject of sex alone, will you?'

'But you are young! My uncle is twenty-five like me and he is married to an Australian woman who is fifty-seven! She likes to do sex twenty-four hours a day, every day. An Arab man can do sex with a woman who is fifty, sixty, seventy years old. No problem!'

'Ahmed, that's enough! No, I don't want to hold your hand!'

'Why are you angry with me when I try to be nice with you?'

For a while he pouted and made sheep's eyes and complained that I had hurt his feelings, just like Samantha had. I wished he would revert to his old *idée fixe*. But by the time we reached the monastery the truth was sinking in at last: Orthodox monasteries and Crusader castles would always, for ever and ever, excite me more than any offer of sex with him.

Although I had not eaten all day I refused an invitation to dine with him back at the hotel. Instead, imprisoning myself in my bedroom, I snacked on a last handful of raisins I had bought in Damascus. But as Ahmed was serving me my breakfast the next morning it became clear that he had not forgotten his promise to show me around the castle. My face must have registered dismay because he seized my hand, gazed into my eyes and said, 'You are still angry with me? Don't worry! Today we will have a good time together.'

Today? I could not endure an entire day in his company.

'Ahmed, let's go to the castle together now, but after that I need to travel to Lebanon. You could advise me about getting a taxi to the border . . .'

'No problem. I will arrange everything and go with you to Lebanon. I have family in Tripoli.'

'No, thank you. I want to go alone,' I said bluntly, wondering if the unemployed and landless younger sons of Norman families who had gone to seek their fortunes in Guiscard's southern Italy or later on the Crusade had been quite as aimless and frustrated as my companion.

The Crac was vast. 'Three hectares,' muttered a surly Ahmed.

It was teeming with tourists, foreign and Syrian. We toured the stables, the storerooms and the ruined chapel with its Crusader Gothic arches. A faded Latin inscription, 'YOU MAY ENJOY GRACE, WISDOM AND BEAUTY, BUT BEWARE OF PRIDE WHICH ALONE MAY TARNISH ALL THE REST,' recalled Archbishop Anastasios's wise words about the many evils of egoism. We had just wandered out of the chapel when Ahmed pointed into a dark corner and said, 'That is where my family used to live.'

Grudgingly he explained that before the French had come to govern Syria in the 1920s, his great-grandparents and grandparents had resided, along with twenty other family groups and all their livestock, here inside the ruins of the Crac. He gave me to understand that the place had functioned like a self-contained village. Each family had had its designated area – the larger families occupying the entire banqueting hall or chapel for example, the bachelors in the narrow alcoves built into the castle walls, and smaller families like his in an ante-room or the corner of a storeroom. Every group had had its own tent and cooking fire, and the livestock had lived in the stables. The wily Arab herdsmen who had tricked the Crusaders when they came calling in early 1099 had inhabited the original castle in precisely the same fashion, I guessed.

During their mandate, the French archaeologists who arrived to marvel at Crac des Chevaliers high-handedly decided that it was a 'monument to France'[ci] which must be preserved for posterity. The inhabitants of the great fortress were paid some money and evicted from their home. As far as I could make out, Ahmed's great grandfather who had had a profitable camel dealership, had then bought much of the land around the castle. Hence the tourist restaurant run by Ahmed's brother, the holiday home behind the castle which belonged to his uncle and aunt and the gimcrack hotel with the perfect view where I had spent the night.

As we walked back there to collect my luggage and call a taxi, Ahmed trailed a few steps behind me, brooding, so I was free to note that I felt as disappointed by the absence of shepherds and camel dealers at the Crac as I had been by the absence of monks at Reichenau and Cluny.

The Lebanese border was about twenty kilometres away, south-west over the mountains towards the coast. We – Ahmed, myself and the taxi driver – drove past clusters of fancy white villas. They were the retirement homes, Ahmed told me, of Syrian *Gastarbeiter* who had made their fortunes in Saudi Arabia, Kuwait or America. The heat haze hanging over the landscape was doing a better job of hiding the valley below than Ahmed's show of lovelorn misery was of hiding his sexual frustration. I was missing my Crusaders, and especially Bohemond.

Bohemond had ventured out of Antioch, concerned not to miss the chance of further gains, but soon retreated back there again, thereby forfeiting a starring role in the capture of Jerusalem. He had his city and he had never cared very much about Jerusalem and his plenary indulgence. Count Raymond proved unable to resist the temptation to carve out his own principality on the coast, at Arqa, and delayed the expedition with another long siege. By the spring of 1099 the Shi'ite Fatimid Arabs of Egypt who now ruled Palestine in place of the Seljuk Turks had understood that they would prob-ably have to fight the *Franj*. Emperor Alexius had recently admitted to them that the Crusaders were way beyond his control and had broken all their oaths to him. The Fatimids tried to neutralize the approaching menace by making peace overtures, promising the Crusaders full access to the holy places in Palestine if they would abandon any idea of conquest. They seemed to be having as much difficulty imagining how the Crusaders could be both pious pilgrims and greedily violent invaders as we have today understanding how pious Muslims can be lethal suicide bombers.

The Crusading lords were unanimous in their rejection of the Arabs' decent offer, but the rank and file were restive and divided. Trouble had been provoked by St Andrew's resumption of his visits to Peter Bartholomew. The saint, flanked by St Peter and Christ himself, had ordered an immediate assault on the walls of Arqa. On hearing this, the Norman French had protested that the saint was blatantly favouring Count Raymond and his petty ambitions. They pronounced Peter Bartholomew a charlatan and his Holy Lance a fake. Raymond's southern French continued to insist that Peter was a saint and his discovery a true and precious relic. There, before the walls of Arqa, it was decided to put the matter to the test. Peter Bartholomew would be made to 'take nine steps hither and thither through the midst of a burning flaming'[cii] fire. If he emerged unscathed the Holy Lance was a relic; if not, it was junk. Dressed only in his shirt and breeches, Peter duly charged through the fire and was so horribly burnt that he almost collapsed back into the flames. He died twelve days later, claming he had met Christ in the fire. Count Raymond was badly discredited by the episode and Duke Godfrey's standing greatly improved.

At about the same time, in early April, a letter from Alexius reached the Crusaders. At last, he informed them, he was en route for Antioch and aiming to join the Crusade by the end of June. If they would wait for him he would be honoured to lead them to their final destination. But the Crusaders had grown accustomed to managing without him, especially since many of the local rulers were proving so obligingly disinclined to resist their advance. Anyway, most of the army detested anything to do with Byzantium and was keen to push onward. In mid-May a tearful Count Raymond gave in to Norman French pressure to abandon his siege of Arqa and with it his dream of winning his own Crusader state. The army hurried on, down the coast to the rich city of Tripoli, modern Lebanon's northernmost port, where I was planning to spend the night.

~

The border post was hellishly disordered.

Its muddy approaches were jammed with cars and gigantic lorries whose hot diesel fumes made the already hot fug of the afternoon unbreathable. After bidding a hasty farewell to Ahmed, I found a kindly-looking taxi driver with a raw, scarred face such as Peter

Bartholomew might have had if he had happened to survive his ordeal by fire. He offered me a bargain ride to Tripoli and, grabbing my passport, busied himself jumping queues to procure me my Lebanese visa.

'You have been to Syria,' said a sneering young Lebanese soldier while he stamped my passport, 'then you will love Lebanon.'

I had loved Syria and had great expectations of little Lebanon too, but the rainswept coast road to Tripoli was dismal. The dark sea was in turmoil and a high wind whipped the tops of the palm trees lining the road. On the narrow grey beach I spotted a squalid cluster of tents covered in plastic sheets badly secured by old car tyres, and guessed they must be the pitiful homes of Palestinian refugees. The dusty shops in the villages we sped through sold only car parts, advertised on rusting metal signs. Tripoli, when we reached it, looked about as appealing as Tirana – a broken-down town of crumbling apartment blocks dating back to the era of the French mandate with rusting iron balconies and rotting wooden shutters. In 1099 it had been rich enough to feed the entire Crusader army. Its short-sighted Sunni emir was apparently so keen to see the Shi'ite Fatimids driven out of Jerusalem he promised the Crusaders that if they won back the holy city he would become a Christian.

When at last the driver located the back-street hotel recommended by Ahmed, he demanded more than the price we had agreed and began to shout at me. I screamed back at him, gesticulating wildly, until he drove off, cursing. In a third-floor flat in one of those crumbling apartment blocks, in a room crammed with three beds and a table laid with a plastic cloth, a doily and a giant ashtray, I rested a while. Outside, the rain beat down on the balcony and dripped noisily from the door frame. From the other side of the lace-curtained bedroom door came the sounds of a football match in progress. The three men watching television in that main room were chain-smoking, to judge by the fumes curling up from under my door. I would have to battle through that room and out the other side if I wanted a shower. Immobilized by *Accidie*, I could not think of rising from the bed, let alone of going in search of another hotel.

I sought solace instead in the thought that eleventh-century pilgrims had often met with adversity on this last leg of the journey to Jerusalem. In 1056 a Bavarian bishop and a Norman abbot had so feared its rigours that they decided to sail down the coast instead. Another member of their party, a Norman monk, braved the land route but fell dangerously ill and, 'when at last he staggered from his bed he did not go another foot, but left the lands of the east and returned westward with all speed to Normandy'.[ciii]

The next morning the sun was shining again and Tripoli looking its best. A few steps from my hotel, where old women sold flowers in the main square, I spotted my taxi driver of the day before. We smiled at each other without rancour and I walked on down a main thoroughfare until I was hailed by a cheerful young man selling carpets and linoleum. Sitting there on the crowded pavement, sipping the cardamom-scented coffee he pressed on me, I listened to him tell me in heavily Canadian-accented English about the seven thousand members of his eight-hundred-year-old family, which was Muslim and based in a village somewhere up in the mountains behind us. His clan organized charitable works and I was welcome to stay in its guest house any time I liked, he said. He had spent five years in Canada where his relatives owned another large carpet shop.

'But my family is very strong and respected here,' he boasted. 'For example, no one who is not from my family can park right here outside this shop. Once a strange taxi came. Well . . . let's just say we had to take the guy to hospital to get some stitches. It was a good lesson to him!'

'But didn't he tell the police?'

'Police?' he queried vaguely, as if he barely recognized the word. 'No, no. Look, another example. When one of my uncles was killed by a member of another family, we took revenge. It was expected. Everyone here has a gun. Bang! Easy.'

The Muslim Lebanese sounded to me as violently clannish as

pre-Christian Icelanders or modern Albanians. But I knew that Lebanon's Christians – most of them followers of a fifth-century saint called St Maro – were just as famously warlike. During the civil war of the late twentieth century, Lebanon's Maronite militias had earned themselves grisly renown by slicing crosses into the flesh of their victims.

The Maronites had loved the Crusaders. Immediately after the capture of Jerusalem in July 1099 the Maronite patriarch had sent a congratulatory letter to the pope in Rome. In grateful recognition of this rare overture from an Eastern Christian Church, the Crusaders favoured the Maronites during the two hundred years they remained in the region, and by the end of the twelfth century the Maronites had repaid the compliment by recognizing papal supremacy.

Seven hundred years later the Maronites played another walk-on part in European history. In the early nineteenth century Europe's great powers were greedily eyeing the slow disintegration of the Ottoman Empire. Carefully eschewing the crude bellicosity of a conventional Crusade, they embarked on a more subtle invasion. They flooded the Holy Land, including modern Syria and Antioch, with Christian missionaries who built schools and hospitals and churches from which to spread the Gospel. By 1900 the *Encyclopaedia Britannica* was marvelling, 'Palestine is now covered with churches, monasteries, nunneries, hospices and hospitals and filled with clergy, monks, nuns and pilgrims as it has not been since the fall of the Latin [Crusader] kingdoms.'[civ]

The Muslim Ottomans were not blind to Christian expansionism. One Turkish governor complained that the French missionaries who teamed up with the Maronites were nothing but 'the Pope's light regular cavalry . . . who, under the garb of priests were, in fact, political agents and disturbers of the public peace.'[cv] When France received her Syrian mandate in 1920, her officials copied the Crusaders and the missionaries by favouring the Christian Maronites at the expense of the Muslims. France also championed the Maronites' plan to set up an independent Christian state.

Lebanon was duly created, with the Maronites in charge, and the mandate ended. By the 1970s the Maronites were no longer the majority within Lebanon but they did not want to relinquish their grip on power; nor did they fancy sharing their land with the mainly Muslim Palestinian refugees from Israel. Tacking Crusader crosses to their uniforms and hanging icons of St Maro from their rifle butts, they went to intermittent war with their Muslim neighbours for the next fifteen years, until 1990. Those Maronites who did not emigrate remain true to their beloved France to this day by giving their children French Christian names and often speaking French when *en famille*.

My friendly Muslim carpet dealer had disappeared to fetch me another coffee. When he returned his mood had changed.

'My plan now is to go back to Canada and never return here because I think there will be war again. You know how it's going now in Israel. I've just seen something on the television news in the coffee shop . . .'

He told me why it was that the state of play between the Israelis and the Palestinians – eight months of renewed and accelerating *intifada* – had a direct bearing on Lebanon. First, there were the hundreds of thousands of miserably restive Palestinian refugees in Lebanon to consider. Second, there were the thousands of Syrian troops stationed in Lebanon since the civil war to guarantee the peace whose presence was resented. Why? Because through these troops Syria backs Muslim fundamentalists in Lebanon who provoke flare-ups with the Israelis, trouble which most Lebanese and especially Maronites feel they can do without. The television news had just reported such a provocation.

~

A Maronite Christian called Émile drove me on down the coast road, past a number of Syrian army checkpoints, past all the McDonald's hamburger joints, casinos, nightclubs and gigantic resort hotels that Syria happily lacked, to Beirut. Émile was too young to have carved crosses in the flesh of any Muslim enemies but we chatted in French about how much he hated the Syrian army's continued occupation of his country.

In the sprawling concrete outskirts of Beirut I changed taxis and asked to be taken to a nice hotel in the centre of town. The driver shook his head uncomprehendingly. Of course. The centre of Beirut had been a battlefield for fifteen years, its smart hotels pocked with bullet holes, interiors gaping from shell blasts.

Many tons of rubble had had to be removed since the end of the civil war but now, on a small section of the gigantic area of levelled ground, a new Beirut seemed to be rising. I oohed and aahed over the elegant dark sandstone office blocks, most of them uninhabited and their ground-floor shop windows empty. Down a wide avenue lined with saplings I glimpsed a square and a bright new clock tower. An archaeological site had been cunningly landscaped into a multi-level park furnished with handsome wooden benches and a rockery. Between the buildings were pristine pavements and empty roads graced by flower beds, new rubbish bins, pretty street lamps, bollards and decoratively shining manhole covers. It was as neat as Aachen, as pretty as Parma, as elegant as Reims. A freshly painted skyscraper advertised itself as a Virgin Megastore, another as a Nike emporium, but neither was open for business. Pedestrian traffic lights winked on and off for no one to cross the roads. The oddest thing about the scene was not so much its lavish perfection or its eerie emptiness, but the absence of any signs of work in progress. Where were the legions of hard-hatted builders toiling away at erecting more of this beautiful new Beirut, I wondered. Later I would discover that the president of Lebanon, a fabulously wealthy businessman, had initiated this grand resurrection of the old Paris of the East, this quasi-Western playground of Arab oil sheikhs, in the hope of attracting back business lost during the civil war. But the money had run out. The region remains unstable and Lebanon's economy is in crisis.

My nice hotel room with its cable television and fluffy bathrobe was conveniently located in Christian east Beirut, up the road from the city's American University, where I planned to go in search of an eminent old history professor to whom someone back in Damascus had given me an introduction. But that business would have to wait until the following day, I decided, because CNN was featuring *Al-Naqba*, the fifty-third anniversary of the Palestinians' 'catastrophe'. The day the creation of the Jewish state forced seven hundred thousand of them out of their homes and off their land was being marked by some four million Palestinian refugees and their descendants scattered in the Arab states bordering Israel.

Here in Lebanon, around Tripoli and south of Beirut, in the refugee camps around Tyre and Sidon, Palestinian children had dressed up as their great-grandparents, stumbling and bowed under the weight of their precious possessions and unbearable suffering, waving sticks and chanting, 'We will return!' In Israel, in the West Bank towns and the Gaza Strip there were mass demonstrations, sirens, three minutes of mournful silence and displays of the carefully preserved keys to the homes and hopes lost half a century ago. The almost five hundred Palestinians killed in the past eight months of this second *intifada* were being piously remembered.

For twenty minutes, while my bath water cooled, I sat on my bed watching Yasser Arafat, hunched over his script, with his thick black-rimmed spectacles on his nose and a fuzzy view of his beloved Jerusalem behind him. He was promising his people that vengeance and Jerusalem would soon be theirs. His tone was monotonously angry.

'Fifty-three years of pain, of being refugees inside and outside our country . . . The bullets, the tanks, the planes will not stop us . . . It's time to say to those aggressors "Stop it!" . . . Killing our people and our young children will not stop us . . . It's our country, our capital is Jerusalem whether they like it or not! To all of you today, wherever you are, outside or inside this Israeli siege, keep faith! Stay patient. Victory is coming. It's coming SOON!'

A reporter commented that the speech contained Arafat's most explicit support to date for the *intifada* that had flared up in September 2000, while I was back in southern Italy thinking about mischievous Guiscard and his Italian Normans. Now and again in the intervening period I had caught a news item, and there had been the Syrians' undisguised hatred of Israel and the video on the bus from Damascus to remind me of the Palestinians' plight. But it was high time I thought about the Palestinians – both Muslim and Christian – and the extent to which they have also been luckless casualties of that Christian fundamentalism born out of a yearning for peace and order thousands of miles away in western Europe almost a thousand years ago.

To do that I would have to recall not France's but Britain's role in the Middle East during the stealthy missionaries' crusade in the early nineteenth century. Britain had been keen to gain a foothold in the region, not least because she distrusted the way Orthodox Russia claimed the right to protect the Ottoman Empire's hundreds of thousands of Eastern Christians, while France safeguarded the Catholics. But who was Britain going to protect? There were no Anglicans or other Protestants in the Holy Land in the 1830s but there were a few thousand Jews. These, many pious Britons judged worthy of protection. An evangelical belief that Christ's much-desired second coming could not take place without the conversion of the Jews to Christianity was in vogue.

British missionaries had duly arrived in Ottoman-ruled Palestine in the late 1830s and set to work. A first Protestant church was built in Jerusalem and an Anglican bishop – a Jewish convert with six children – installed. He found the Jews politely impervious to his evangelizing, but the Arabs, whether Christian or Muslim, proved easier to woo with promises of free education. By 1899 the city had gained its Anglican St George's cathedral, built to look as much like the chapel of New College in Oxford as possible. This was not so very extraordinary. Soon there was the modern American Colony up the road and the Germans had their pretty little slice of Bavaria with its copy of Charlemagne's cathedral at Aachen. The Russians boasted a gigantic Tsarist compound built to accommodate the thousands of Russian Orthodox pilgrims who flocked to the holy city every spring. The French and Italians had the stewardship of the prime Christian holy places via their Franciscan friars, and a revived Latin patriarchate.

It was not until halfway through the First World War that Britain took the decisive lead in the race to win Jerusalem from the collapsing Ottoman Empire. Three people, one of them an enterprising Russian Jewish chemist and two of them top British politicians were responsible for this feat. The Russian Jew was Dr Chaim Weizmann, who devoted his life to the foundation of the Jewish homeland in Palestine. The British politicians were Prime Minister David Lloyd George and his foreign secretary, Arthur Balfour. On the face of it these last two had nothing whatsoever in common.

The first was a Welsh miner's son, the other a patrician Englishman, but they were both Protestants and steeped in the Old Testament prophets who forecast a return of the Jews to their ancient Zion. ' "I could tell you all the kings of Israel," ' Lloyd George once observed. ' "But I doubt whether I could have named half a dozen of the kings of England and no more of the kings of Wales." '[cvi] Lloyd George was convinced of Jewish influence over world affairs, not least in America, and judged it no bad idea to win the Jews' support by obliging them in the matter of their ancient homeland. British influence in Palestine would serve at the very least to keep the French out, he calculated. Furthermore, he owed Dr Weizmann a favour. In 1915 Weizmann had boosted the British war effort by applying his chemist's mind to manufacturing acetone, a vital ingredient in the cordite needed to keep the guns firing on the western front.

Foreign Secretary Arthur Balfour's approach to Zionism was more intellectual and romantic. Balfour was keenly conscious of how much Western civilization owed the Jews, and of how cruelly that debt had been repaid since the era of the Crusades. Dr Weizmann nourished in the Englishman a firm desire to do ' "something material to wash out an ancient stain upon our civilisation" '.[cvii] As early as 1906 he had charmed and impressed Balfour by explaining the Zionists' refusal to be fobbed off with a homeland in what is now Uganda. Would Balfour mind swapping London for Paris, Weizmann had asked him. When Balfour replied, ' "But Dr Weizmann, we have London," ' the Zionist had fired back immediately, ' "But we had Jerusalem when London was a marsh." 'cviii Dr Weizmann managed to reduce Balfour to tears with his fervour. Like Lloyd George, Balfour was also convinced of the Jews' importance in world affairs and judged Zionism to be 'of far profounder import than the desires and prejudices of the 700,000 Arabs who now inhabit that ancient land'.cix

The Balfour Declaration, contained in a letter to Britain's most prominent Jew, Lord Rothschild, was signed on 2 November 1917. It said:

> His Majesty's Government view with favour the establishment in Palestine of a national home for Jewish people and will use their best endeavours to facilitate this object, it being clearly understood that nothing shall be done which may prejudice the civil and religious rights of the existing non-Jewish communities in Palestine . . .cx

Although undoubtedly a gigantic boost to Dr Weizmann's ambitions, nothing about this document could be 'clearly understood'. Did a 'national home' mean the same as a Jewish state? If not, then what was a 'national home'? And who were the 'non-Jewish communities' if not the Arabs who outnumbered the Jews by a factor of ten, and who could easily be excused for thinking the British had promised them a 'national homeland' too in exchange for their help with fighting the Ottoman Turks?*

By means of this fatally vague document Britain carelessly double-booked a distant land, a land she was meddling in without good economic or strategic reason.

By the time of the Balfour Declaration the British, under, General Edmund Allenby, had embarked on their conquest of Pales-

---

* Ottoman Turkey was allied with Germany against Britain, France and Russia during the First World War.

tine from the Ottomans, and Jerusalem surrendered a month after its signing. When General Allenby dismounted from his horse to walk, like any humble pilgrim, through Jerusalem's Jaffa Gate it was proudly noted that his was only the second Western Christian army in history to have liberated the holy city; the first being the Crusaders' in 1099. The bells of Westminster abbey rang out for the first time in three years of war and a joyful 'Te Deum' was sung in the Vatican. So began the miserably pointless British League of Nations mandate in Palestine which lasted almost thirty years, until 1948. In that year the British, reviled and hated by both the Jews and the Arabs whose overlapping territorial claims they could never have hoped to satisfy, packed their bags and left.

The British pulled out on 14 May, the day the Jews declared the independent State of Israel, the day of the Palestinians' Al-Naqba. CNN was still flashing through crowd scenes in a final round-up of the different 2001 Al-Naqba demonstrations all over the Middle East.

Walking down the road towards the American University in Beirut (AUB) the next morning provided me with graphic evidence of the extent to which European influence in the Middle East has been replaced by that of the new Western superpower, America, in the past half-century. I passed shop windows displaying American newspapers and books about self-improvement and business management. Opposite the university, between an American ice-cream parlour and a Burger King outlet, workmen were putting the finishing touches to a new McDonald's. A throng of students in American casuals chattered in American English to each other or into their mobile phones. The university itself, a solidly handsome mid-nineteenth-century building erected by Protestant American missionaries,* would have graced any town in New England. Only the dazzling view of the sea in the distance, beyond a garden filled with palm trees and flowers which could not have survived in so

---

* AUB was known as the Syrian Protestant College until World War II.

northerly a climate, located it there on a promontory overlooking the eastern Mediterranean.

The august professor I had come in search of was not available but I soon found myself on the fourth floor of the main building, explaining my business to a history lecturer. Dr Seikaly was standing behind a desk piled high with teetering stacks of books, frowning and scratching his beard as if I had disturbed him in the act of searching for something. I stared beyond him at the view from his window of palm trees, shining sea and sky. At last, he looked up.

'Crusade, you say? I went to a school run by English priests where the reward for Sunday school attendance was to become a "Crusader". You got a badge in the shape of a shield, with a red cross on it. Imagine rewarding Arabs with Crusader badges! Then you became a "Knight" and were given a Bible, I think . . .'

'Did you get all your badges?' I asked him.

'Oh yes!' He laughed and motioned me to sit on the other side of his chaotically fortified desk. 'I didn't mind going to Sunday school. There were lots of girls to see.'

Dr Seikaly was a tall Palestinian in his mid-fifties, elegantly ironic and self-deprecating. It was not easy to get him talking about a life which he deemed too sad and commonplace for light conversation. His home had been in Haifa, in northern Palestine. The family had left, like so many others, with the keys to their house, just before the town fell to the Israelis in 1948.

'My father always chose the wrong thing,' he said with a light laugh. 'We fled to Egypt – a very exciting train journey for a little boy, of course – to Cairo because we had relatives who had grown rich there under the monarchy. But the monarchy fell in 1952. In effect, we were refugees again . . .'

But they had stayed on in Egypt and Dr Seikaly had attended first a French school and then the English school where he had gained his badges, before moving to Lebanon. That second move had been simple enough. Lebanon's Christian Maronites were still in power at the time and had no objection to admitting a Christian Palestinian like him. Dr Seikaly had studied at AUB and been sent for a year to the 'swinging London' of the early 1960s for further studies before returning to AUB and continuing to teach right through the civil war.

'You know, here at AUB, many of us went on teaching through the worst of the fighting. Now of course everything's different. Peace comes, values change. People want to forget the hard war years, all the sacrifices made by individuals . . .' He sighed, scratched his beard and paused as if too polite to go on and speak his heart instead of his mind.

'I have been lucky. I'm not imprisoned in the Gaza Strip or a refugee camp here. I've been able to work and have a family. You see, I warned you, mine is not such an exciting story. But still, I feel hopeless now about this country and this region, really hopeless! My children want to live in America. When I retire, when my wife gives up her work with the Palestinian refugees, then we will go there too . . .'

'What kind of history do you teach?' I asked him, hoping to spare him a further slide into melancholy.

'My favourite – I say my favourite, but it's heart-rending – is a course called Palestine, 1917 to 1948. It's very difficult because I do not understand myself everything that I'm trying to teach,' he said, leaning over his desk towards me, his tone suddenly stern and deadly serious. 'When you undertake to create a "national home" for a Jewish people who have been strewn all over the world since AD 70, what are you doing? What are you doing? Can you tell me why you British did this? There were no good strategic reasons and the age of empires was ending. So what was it? Can you tell me what it was? The old mentality of the imperialists and colonialists, people who thought they were doing God's work? But what kind of answer is this for such a tremendous tragedy? Let me tell you something. According to our Arabic sources General Allenby said something like "Now the Crusades are over" when he walked into Jerusalem in 1917 . . .'

Now there was no stemming the flow from Dr Seikaly's heart.

'There is such an antipathy towards the Arabs, towards Muslims in the West. The dice are always stacked against us before we even start! Think of the number of lives that have been destroyed here over the last fifty-three years. It's worse even than the Holocaust! I can tell you that it is a very shocking and terrible thing when your life is screwed from the very start . . .'

Once again I heard the same sour note of resentment against the West, and quailed. A Turkish carpet dealer, a Syrian playboy and now a Palestinian academic.

'My dear Victoria,' he said with a smile, returning to his old ironic courtesy, 'you will forgive me if I have little to say about the Crusades. As you can see, we have too much here and now to think about!'

Dr Seikaly's tone suggested that a thousand years' hindsight was a luxury only Westerners could afford.

~

Thanks to the local emirs falling over themselves to appease and aid their unwanted guests from the West, the Crusaders were having an easier time of it than I was. The nearer I approached to my goal the more the present seemed to be impinging on my serene contemplation of the distant past. In Beirut a simple promise not to pillage the vineyards and orchards surrounding the city had secured the Crusaders free passage and rich gifts. Unlike me, they had not had to worry about negotiating the closed border between Lebanon and Israel.

Way back in Poland, drinking Coke with me in Poznan station, Waldemar's friend Father Christopher had plucked a paper napkin from its holder to sketch me a rough map of the Holy Land. On it he had marked the position of the UN peacekeeping troops he had served with, there on that Lebanese–Israeli border, and then asked me how I planned to cross it. I had a journalist friend who knew the region well, I told him. He would give me an introduction to the UN press officer who might possibly be persuaded to ferry me across into Israel in a UN vehicle. Father Christopher had looked doubtful.

'I'll try anyway,' I had said airily. 'If not, I can always take a boat to Cyprus and then another one back to Israel. Eleventh-century pilgrims did a lot of toing and froing between Cyprus and Jerusalem.'

After my meeting with Dr Seikaly I had called the UN press officer, a Turk called Mr Goksel, and arranged to meet him at the UN base at Naqoura, at three the following afternoon. It would take less than a couple of hours to get there by taxi down the coast road.

Mohammed the taxi driver's hilarious over-friendliness prevented me from enjoying the passing scene of half-built high-rises, dusty plastic green houses and giant oil tankers in Sidon's port. I was hard at work inventing a solid family background for myself and struggling to understand his pidgin French. Yes, yes, I was a *Madame* with a husband and three children, aged eight, five and three, I told him. Yes, *Monsieur* was caring for them all in my absence. By the time we reached Tyre I had learned that when Mohammed said, 'Victoria, Arabic music – hello?' he meant 'Do you like Arabic music?' When he said, 'Victoria, Mohammed – hello McDonald's?' he was inviting me to a burger dinner. 'Beirut, Victoria – hello!' was a suggestion that I emigrate to Beirut.

There were a few French tourists in Tyre – known as Sour in Arabic – drawn by its ancient Phoenician ruins. In the town's narrow back streets, in small alcoves in the walls of some of the houses, were icons of long-bearded St Maro. Fresh fish glittered in the gloomy souk. Down by the harbour some fishermen were untangling their nets and munching their lunch. I sat under a parasol advertising Heineken, enjoying the brilliantly sunlit scene, a fresh orange juice and the breeze blowing off the sea. The First Crusaders had tarried a couple of days here, enjoying its rich amenities and waiting for Duke Godfrey's brother, Count Baldwin, to arrive from his statelet of Edessa to join them for the final push towards the holy city.

I was not exactly loving Lebanon but the prospect of travelling straight on into Israel was not appealing either. Dr Seikaly had mentioned that now might not be quite the right time to visit the land he had stopped dreaming of being able to call his home.

Another taxi took me on south towards Naquora and the UN base. On the way over hills with a view of the glittering sea far below, along a narrow road deserted by all but the UN's white four-wheel-drive vehicles, we passed a deserted checkpoint of old car tyres and mud bunkers, adorned with a yellow Hezbollah flag. Opposite the fortified twenty-two-year-old UN base a whole village of corrugated-metal shacks had sprung up to cater to the soldiers' trade. We passed a video shop, a launderette, a souvenir stall and a watch mender's before stopping at the base's main entrance set in a high concrete wall topped with barbed wire. A young blue-helmeted Pole, his pale legs spindly in a pair of very short shorts, smilingly admitted me.

Chain-smoking Mr Goksel freely admitted that he had come here for six months in 1979 'and stayed for twenty-two years' because he thrived on the adrenaline of living and working between two countries which, if not actively at war with each other any longer, were not at peace either. Telephones rang, sweating underlings hurried in and out and a fax machine spewed paper. The smoke-laden air around Mr Goksel seemed to crackle with nervous energy although, as far as I aware, the situation had been calm for a year. On the night of 24 May 2000, Israeli forces had, without any warning, pulled out of the area of Lebanon they had occupied for eighteen years.*

'That was the end of an era, the moment we'd all been waiting for I suppose. Now our force here will be reduced by almost a third,' said Mr Goksel, swivelling on his chair. 'But I can tell you some-thing. If you had taken the road from Tyre to here a year ago, you would have had to pass through at least ten UN checkpoints!'

---

* Israel invaded in 1982, during Lebanon's civil war, to fight the Palestinian PLO who controlled the area.

I asked him about the Hezbollah flag flying from the single deserted checkpoint I had seen.

'Pah! It's nothing,' he said. 'That used to be an Israeli post. The Hezbollah have put their flag there for show. Otherwise, there's no sign of them around here at the moment.'

I was forming the impression that Mr Goksel missed the old days, that he was already bored by cross-border disputes over water pipes. Everything he said seemed to confirm that the border was quiet enough for me to cross. I asked him if he could help me.

'No. Out of the question. Impossible. No one gets across the border except UN personnel,' he said, tidying the papers on his desk as if to show me that he had better things to do than talk to me. 'I don't care which Crusade you are writing about, if you are a journalist or not. I'm afraid I cannot help you.'

Not until my taxi driver took me further on, up into the scrubby hills inland from the UN base camp, to the Fijian UN battalion camp, did I begin to resent Mr Goksel's intransigence. Leading me to a wire-mesh fence, the driver pointed through it and said simply, 'Israel.' Below us lay an ordered plain, as neatly squared off in lush green fields as parts of Germany or France.

I turned my back on it and headed back to Beirut to catch a flight to Cyprus and find a boat to Israel.

~

Eight months of renewed *intifada* had crippled the Orthodox Christian pilgrim trade from Cyprus to the Holy Land. Like the *Bruarfoss*, the *Nissos Kypros* set sail with more crew than passengers aboard on that balmy violet evening.

At a white plastic table on the top deck, I sat alone, drinking a can of Coke and reading more about the eleventh-century Norman abbot and Bavarian bishop who, fearing the arduous overland journey from Antioch to Jerusalem, had made the same detour via Cyprus. No sooner had they arrived on the island, rejoiced in their discovery of a church dedicated to St Nicholas of Myra and entered it, than the abbot had collapsed. ' "My body is in great pain," ' he had gasped, ' "and it seems that I should turn my desires towards the heavenly rather than the earthly Jerusalem." 'cxi The bishop hurried off in search of comfortable lodgings for his friend, telling the abbot not to move. Wrapping himself in his cloak and curling up in front of the altar, his hands crossed over his breast and his head resting on a marble step, the poor Norman had closed his eyes and expired. On his return the bishop 'marvelled and was full of grief'.cxii He called all the pilgrims lodged in the inns thereabouts to pray for the repose of his friend's soul and bury him by the church door. When the pilgrims found the corpse too heavy to carry, it was a sure sign that the good abbot merited 'a worthier place'cxiii. One was found and thereafter 'fevers and other sicknesses were healed' by him.

I did not want to expire like poor old Abbot Thierry, but if there had been an honourable excuse for ending my journey in Cyprus I would happily have made it, because I was scared. I had not needed Dr Seikaly's kindly warning that now was 'perhaps not the best time to visit Jerusalem'. The news was bad and getting worse. That the *Nissos Kypros* was sailing to Israel at all was mildly reassuring.

By 6.30 the next hot morning we were docking at Haifa, a dappled vista of white buildings and dense greenery tumbling down from the soaring height of Mount Carmel. The harbour itself, built by immigrant Thessaloniki Jews after World War Two, was dominated by a mysterious white fortress about the size of Rome's St Peter's but longer and without a single window*. Two tiny black figures came marching out of another super-modern structure, down a gleaming white concrete walkway towards the quay. Nothing else moved.

In a back street a few minutes' walk from the port I found a hostel which advertised itself as run by the Sisters of the Rosary. The smiling Palestinian nun who opened the door to me and showed

---

* The largest granary in the Middle East

me upstairs to a clean, bare room explained that she and one other nun ran the hostel and a small kindergarten.

'Can you hear the children singing?' she asked me, clasping her hands together happily.

I could hear a lot of arrhythmic clapping, snatches of a disco hit about living in the happy nation and a tape recorder being switched on and off.

'I love that song – it's so happy,' she said. 'There are so many disasters these days! Only yesterday a family caused a forest fire by cooking some coffee for their picnic and a child died of the heat . . .'

'And the country is almost at war,' I added.

'Almost? For eight months now we have been at war,' she corrected me.

Sister Rita told me that the hostel had been built in 1880 and run by German nuns who had worked 'terribly hard' at caring for displaced Palestinians until they left in 1988, having 'run out of vocations'.

'You know the Germans made a colony here, just down the road. It's very beautiful and from there you can see the wonderful new garden created by the followers of the Baha'i religion.'

The single day I spent in Haifa turned out to be the most baffling of my entire journey. The German Colony which Sister Rita had mentioned consisted of a single long broad avenue with solid white houses and gardens set back from the road. Recently repackaged as a tourist attraction, its bizarre history was attractively set out on dark green boards placed at regular intervals along the avenue. In much the same spirit as the hermit enthusiasts of the eleventh century who had been inspired by St Romuald and Peter Damiani to forsake their homes and build ideal communities in the forests of western Europe, hundreds of Protestant Germans had arrived here in the Holy Land in 1868. In the belief that Christ's second coming was imminent and that Jerusalem would be liberated from the Ottoman Turks after the Crimean War, they had set about preparing for his coming by building themselves a new Jerusalem. Many of them hailed from Martin Luther's home town,

Württemburg. Mostly poor and uneducated, they had been almost as hopeful as the People's Crusaders of finding a land flowing with milk and honey. After a disappointing false start with agriculture, the Haifa Templars, as they were known, turned their hands to building a meeting house with crenellations like a Crusader castle, to inscribing Biblical mottoes in Gothic German script over their front doors, to running the city's first public transport service and building a steam-driven power station. By 1875 a Baedeker guide was noting that, 'a few years ago members of the Temple Society founded a colony here [in Haifa] which, against the background of Oriental filth, stands out as particularly orderly and clean . . .'cxiv

But the Templars' religious zeal was flagging by the outbreak of World War One, and a third of the community joined the Nazi Party of Palestine during World War Two. The British authorities deported many to Australia and evacuated the remainder when Israel declared independence in 1948. A Jewish historian of the Haifa Templars, whose essay I was reading in the new museum, astonishingly dismissed their Nazi sympathies and World War Two as 'a simple twist of fate'. The mildness of his tone puzzled me until I noted that sixteen German *länder* had funded the refurbishment of the Haifa Templars' meeting house as a museum. And there were further plans to expand it, install lifts and open a café.

The new Baha'i Gardens, laid out on a series of terraces cascading steeply down from Mount Carmel, were as pleasingly symmetrical as Versailles with their jewel-green lawns, blazes of golden flowers and white marble flight of steps. But I decided I would have nothing to do with them or with the faith that had inspired them because I had quite enough to think about untangling the histories of Jews, Muslims and Christians in Palestine. Instead, I sought sanctuary from the broiling midday heat in a new shopping mall at the other end of the German Colony, but before I could pass through its electronic doors into air-conditioned cool I had to suffer a thorough frisking. A spate of Palestinian suicide bombings meant heightened security in all public places.

But where were the Palestinians, or even the Israelis? I was surrounded by Russians. Every person I asked for directions and everyone around me on the train whisking me to the top of Mount Carmel spoke Russian. The collapse of the Soviet Union in 1991 had prompted a gigantic Russian Jewish exodus. Russians now account for more than a sixth of Israel's population and many of them live in Haifa. As I wandered back towards the hostel, I imagined that the addition of so many Russians to a democracy as fragile and compromised as Israel's might prove, to say the least, a mixed blessing. Routinely distrustful of the Muslim minorities of their old Soviet Union, the Russian Jews seemed likely to support the toughest measures against Israel's Palestinian Muslims.

But the greatest, most baffling surprise of the day awaited me back at the hostel. As the hair-dryer-hot breeze of the day cooled, I dragged a chair from the landing onto the balcony and sat there reading and admiring the sunset and a view of the floodlit granary. An elderly woman in a light summer dress but without any hair joined me for a moment, before suddenly clapping her hands to her head and rushing back inside again. I guessed she must be an Orthodox Jewess, mortified at having forgotten her wig. But what was an Orthodox Jewess doing in a Roman Catholic hostel run by Palestinian nuns? A few minutes later she reappeared crowned with a honey-brown coiffure. '*Excusez-moi, Madame, mais il fait si chaud!*' she panted, getting herself a chair, slipping off her shoes and fanning her face. We laughed, and then chatted in French about Haifa's many attractions.

Before long, her husband, who spoke English and was a Christian Palestinian like Sister Rita, joined us. Although his wife was indeed a Jewess, he explained, she was not Orthodox but had lost all her hair as a result of the chemotherapy she had undergone for cancer. They lived in America but were here in Haifa for her treatment. An Arab married to a Jewess, Toufee Farah was a rarity but had a background very much like Dr Seikaly's. Educated at an Anglican boarding school just east of Haifa, he had graduated from AUB some twenty years earlier than Dr Seikaly, in 1948, and then found himself unable to return home to Haifa.

'A group of us came illegally in the end,' he remembered, 'walking over the border at night with donkeys. But we were unlucky; the Israelis caught us and threw us in prison here for three days. After that it was three months in a concentration camp.'

'Oh, no!' I gasped in sympathy.

'Actually, it was fine for us there.' He laughed. 'We were living like kings, perfectly well treated because we were Christians. For the Muslim Palestinians it was different of course, but we Christians didn't want to leave that place!'

After that he had looked for work as a pharmacist in Haifa. He had been barred from parts of the city and had soon learned that he would not get a job if he mentioned he was an Arab, but he had been 'lucky, because Toufee is not a typically Arab name'. Dr Seikaly, whose first name was unmistakably Muslim, would not have fared so well. I observed to Toufee that he did not seem to feel nearly as resentful towards the Israelis as most Palestinians.

'I know. When I talk to Arabs I have to be careful what I say because they think I am a traitor. I think I would have stayed more of an Arab if I had fled like most Palestinians did,' he agreed, 'but you know, the Israelis have not done anything worse than any other people in history. Of course, it's medieval plundering and slaughtering by a different name, but where's the big surprise in that? We humans belong to the animal kingdom, don't we?'

Toufee had reached an understanding of the world by stripping mankind back to his barest beastly essentials, way back beyond even the Viking Icelanders. On and on he talked, about dog eating dog, about nature being cruel and only the fittest surviving. When he began outlining his vision of a truer form of democracy modelled on a colony of bees, his wife retired for the night. The light died. In the apartments across the road television screens flickered and a couple toiled away hoisting a sofa up to a first-floor balcony. The sweet smell of something frying filled the air. We were silent a moment and then he continued.

'I can imagine that perhaps in one hundred years, when the Israelis have conquered the whole of the Middle-East, they will feel safe and strong enough to turn round and say they're sorry for all the cruel things they've done. Just like the pope is now doing about the Crusades and the Jews, or the Americans about the Red Indians.'

Shocked by Toufee's cynicism I was nevertheless impressed by the amount of serious attention he had given to world affairs. It was not until I had bidden him goodnight and then replied to his tentative knock at my door that I understood. Toufee presented me with a copy of his privately published 350-page work, entitled *The Arab–Israeli Conflict*. A quotation on the flyleaf read, 'Both predators, beast and Man, kill their prey. The former attacks when hungry, the latter when full.' The blurb on the dust jacket identified him as a child of the British mandate: 'Born in 1925 to Protestant Palestine-Arab parents, I came to the world naked, innocent and clean of all nationalism, religion and culture. Brought up in a devout manner, I had mixed between Churches and States [and] could not figure out where I belonged: to the Anglican Church and loyalty to Great Britain? To the Palestinian Arab nationality?'[cxv]

That night I dreamed I was bald and imprisoned, along with a swarm of bees, in a place that was sometimes a Nazi concentration camp, sometimes the Haifa Templars' meeting house and sometimes a Romanesque church.

At breakfast the following morning I encountered a tall, smiling German called Andreas, a video artist working on a series about coexistence among different ethnic communities. To the distant background accompaniment of the kindergarten children clapping along to their tape, he told me that the Palestinians and Jews of Haifa got on 'pretty well'. He was sure of finding a couple here willing to participate in his project and equally sure it would be no trouble to give me a lift on down the coast to Caesarea after breakfast.

On the way we passed a turning off the motorway to Atlit, to a reconstruction of a prison camp established by the British in the

1940s to detain Jewish refugees, and later, Nazi concentration camp survivors. Neither Andreas nor I suggested we tour it.

~

Ancient Roman Caesarea, founded by King Herod twenty-two years before Christ was born, is Israel's largest archaeological site. It was here, in AD 66, that a Jewish community first rose up against the Roman Empire's heavy-handed rule, and set off a chain of events which climaxed in AD 70 with the Romans' destruction of the Jewish temple in Jerusalem and the Jews' dispersal over the face of the earth for almost two thousand years. At about the same time, St Peter christened a Roman centurion and St Paul was charged with heresy; it would be another two hundred or so years before Christianity became the official religion of the Roman Empire. By the time the Crusaders passed this way in May 1099 the city with its enlarged harbour and richly cultivated hinterland had been prospering under Arab rule for the previous four and a half centuries.

The Arabs of Caesarea must have heard rumours enough about the First Crusaders by the early summer of 1099 to fear them like the plague. The emir of Acre, whose lands the Crusaders had already passed through, sent a carrier pigeon with a warning to his counterpart in Caesarea. His note summed up the foreigners as a 'dog-like race . . . [a] stupid, contentious and undisciplined mob'[cxvi] and called for concerted Muslim resistance. Intercepted by one of the Crusaders' hawks, the pigeon and its cargo fell to earth by a bishop's tent. The Caesareans paid the price, quite literally, for the emir of Acre's indiscretion. When the Crusaders attacked they were astonished to discover that the Arabs had swallowed their money, 'not wanting the Franj to get any of their property'. A chronicler goes into wonderful detail: 'it sometimes happened, when one of our men hit one of the Arabs on his neck with his fist, that he spat ten or sixteen bezants out of his mouth'.[cxvii]

Unlike many of the Arabs whom the Crusaders had so far

encountered, some of Caesarea's older inhabitants would have recalled an earlier and pleasanter visitation from another large group of *Franj*. Thirty-five years before, in 1065, approximately seven thousand German pilgrims led by two archbishops, some bishops and nobles and the private chaplain of Henry IV's *paupera et peregrina* mother Agnes, had passed through Caesarea en route for Jerusalem. Convinced by a story that the final day of judgement had been set for Easter Day 1065, they were planning to be in their Lord's home city, as near to the Saviour as possible, when it happened.

Lampert of Hersfeld, the excellent chronicler of Canossa, tells us that the young and extraordinarily handsome Archbishop Gunther of Bamberg cut a far finer figure than any of the Crusading lords. Unarmed as befitted a pilgrim, he provoked wonder, awe and envy wherever he went on account of his magnificent clothes and dazzling array of gold and silver tableware. The Byzantines of luxurious Constantinople had assumed he must be the German Holy Roman emperor, disguised as an archbishop for reasons of security.

The German pilgrims reached Caesarea on Maundy Thursday 1065 and rejoiced in the knowledge that they were on schedule, only two days' journey north of their goal. But the most dangerous part of the way was yet to come. At three o'clock on Good Friday, on the road from Caesarea to Jerusalem, they suffered a surprise attack from Arab bandits intent on relieving them of their riches. Lampert reminds us that the German pilgrims were unarmed: 'The majority of Christians did not consider it compatible with their faith to use their fists in self-defence or to protect their mortal lives (dedicated to God at the start of their pilgrimage) by having recourse to earthly weapons. They were consequently laid low by the first onslaught . . .'[cxviii] Lampert writes that a great many of the pilgrims were stripped of all they had, 'from threads to boot-laces'.

But the raid had enraged the pilgrims and baser instincts prevailed. Retaliating with stones, they moved swiftly to occupy a tall stone farmhouse. Archbishop Gunther installed himself on its top floor to direct operations. A series of skirmishes ensued, with the pilgrims capturing swords and shields from their attackers and engaging in hand-to-hand combat. The Arabs, who outnumbered the combatants, decided to besiege the farmhouse fortress. By Easter Sunday afternoon the poor pilgrims were still holed up in their refuge, beating off constant attacks, horribly hungry and dog-tired. One of the pilgrim priests counselled surrender. He maintained that they had all sinned most grievously in seeking to deliver themselves by recourse to arms, and he pointed out that there was little to fear since the Arabs only wanted to rob them, not to kill them. The pilgrims hearkened to his wise words and the two sides parleyed. The Arab chieftain, along with seventeen of his henchmen, arrived at the fortress and climbed a ladder to speak to Archbishop Gunther, who abased himself before the Arab, begging him to take everything and anything he wanted. Lampert claims that the Arab was shockingly unmerciful. He informed Archbishop Gunther that he 'would first seize everything they had, then eat their flesh and drink their blood'.[cxix]

This response is far too reminiscent of the eating and drinking of Christ's flesh and blood in Holy Communion to ring true and might have been invented as a means of excusing the disgustingly unchristian violence with which Archbishop Gunther then assaulted the Arab chieftain. He 'struck him so forcefully in the face with his fist, that the dumbfounded Arab was felled by the blow'.[cxx] Other prelates and pilgrims then seized the Arab chieftain's henchmen and 'bound their hands so tightly behind their backs, that most of them had blood streaming from burst skin and from under their finger-nails'.[cxxi]

There ensued more skirmishing until, at last, news of the pilgrims' imminent rescue by another Arab chieftain at the head of a mighty army reached them. The bandits fled in terror and the rescuers arrived to escort the *Franj* on their way to Jerusalem. Surprised by this timely courtesy, the German pilgrims never could understand why 'one devil had driven out another; in other words, that one heathen should wish to prevent another from attacking Christians'.[cxxii] Locked inside their *milites* mindset with their black and white view of a world peopled by bad Muslims and good Christians, they were puzzled by a more tolerant civilization which protected the weak against the criminal, even if the weak happened to be strangers professing a different faith.

Thinking hard about this story, I wandered along the beach at Caesarea, past groups of archaeologists toiling away at the ancient Roman remains in the shade of makeshift black awnings. Only thirty years before Pope Urban proclaimed the first armed pilgrimage to liberate the holy places from the Infidel, these seven thousand German pilgrims had still had scruples about resorting to arms. What had occurred in those thirty years to effect such a change in Western Christendom? A good deal.

A year after the Great German Pilgrimage, as it became known, Hildebrand had championed William the Conqueror's attack on England despite the fact that the Normans would be attacking fellow Christians. When Hildebrand became the fundamentalist Pope Gregory VII in 1073 he had set about planning his Crusade with Countess Matilda and pursuing the campaigns against simony and nicolaitism with renewed vigour. Only four years later, he clashed with Henry IV at Canossa, claiming that pope and Church should dictate to emperor and empire. By the early 1080s his *milites sancti Petri* and Henry's troops were physically battling for control of Rome. Meanwhile, Robert Guiscard and Bohemond had received Gregory's blessing for their expedition to attack Eastern Christendom and take Constantinople. A decade after the deaths of Gregory and Guiscard Pope Urban had embarked on a kind of perestroika which, like Mikhail Gorbachev's, sought to modify the work of his predecessors while preserving its essence. But his pious hopes of repairing the East–West schism by sending Western Christian *milites* to Emperor Alexius' aid were destined to come to nothing amid the mistrust and slaughter by the First Crusaders of anyone who was not Western Christian – Jew, Eastern Christian or Muslim.

Caesarea's ancient stones and late Crusader ruins did not hold my attention for long. When a Palestinian, fishing from the old harbour wall, mistook my polite smiles for a promise of *obscoeni negotii* I fled to the site entrance, collected my luggage and caught a couple of buses inland to Ramleh.

The Crusaders had found the small town deserted by its terrified Muslim inhabitants; I found it bright and busy and equipped with a prestigious new bus station and shopping mall, where a security man frisked me. After an hour or so in that perilously enclosed public place I was relieved to catch another bus on to Lod, a town known as Lydda in Crusader times. Across the aisle from me an Israeli soldier was sprawled over two seats, sleeping with his mouth agape and his gun in his lap. In front of him sat two young women in army uniforms and fashionable sunglasses, guns bulging at their hips. The bus radio blared a news bulletin: *intifada . . . intifada . . .*

Perusing a newspaper I had bought at the bus station, I discovered that a number of significant historical events had taken place on this same day, 30 May. In 1096 a German bishop had offered his own home as a refuge to Jews fleeing the wrath of rampaging First Crusaders. A Prussian pogrom* had begun on 30 May 1762, and a Russian one exactly a hundred and forty-four years later, in 1906. The last transport of Jews had left Hungary for the Nazi death camps on 30 May 1944 and the same day in 1972 had seen the massacre of twenty-four Jews by Palestinians at Tel Aviv Airport, near the small town where I was headed. As the bus bowled around neat roundabouts and along quiet suburban streets lined with new white houses set in gardens, I mused that I had just read the briefest possible history of European Jewry: toleration mixed with persecution, followed by almost a millennium of worse persecution culminating in mass extermination, followed by the export of Europe's 'Jewish problem' to the Middle East and the ongoing war to establish a national home in a land inhabited by Arabs. It was painfully clear that since the early twentieth century the Palestinian Arabs have been paying for a millennium's worth of European anti-Semitism.

* State-sponsored persecution of Jews.

Nothing of great significance was happening in Lod on the afternoon of 30 May 2001. A poor sort of place, inhabited by Palestinian Arabs and non-European Jews, and blighted by the roar of jets flying in and out of Tel Aviv's Ben Gurion Airport, it looked sadly scruffy after Ramleh's bus station cum shopping mall and the neat suburbs I had just seen. Trundling my luggage behind me, I set off in search of St George's church, built on the site of the sixth-century Byzantine basilica which Ramleh's fleeing Muslims had defiantly burnt down ahead of the First Crusaders' advance. It was not hard to find, thanks to the red and white flag of St George flying from its steeple. Nearby were an abandoned building site, an unfinished road and some unidentifiable ruins with weeds sprouting between cracks in the stones. But the atmosphere of neglect was unexpectedly mitigated by a few empty plastic bags – pink, blue, green and white – caught up by a breeze, dancing.

A sign by the door of the locked church said: 'KINDLY SHOW RESPECT FOR THE SANCTITY OF THIS PLACE. REFRAIN FROM IMPROPER DRESS, FIRE-ARMS, FOOD AND SMOKING. ANIMALS NOT ALLOWED.'

Another sign invited me to apply at the Orthodox convent opposite if I desired to visit the church. The convent door was opened by a far-faring young Romanian Orthodox nun with luminously calm green eyes. Delighted to hear that I could speak some Romanian and had once visited her beautiful home convent near the Ukrainian border, she insisted that I enter and refresh myself with a glass of orange juice and a chocolate wafer biscuit before she showed me around the church.

She explained to me that the adjacent mosque, with which the church shares a wall, is also dedicated to St George, whom Arabs revere as Al-Khader, the Green One. A youthful spirit employed to rescue those in distress, Al-Khader flies around the world and is found every Friday praying in one or other of Islam's holiest sites. The Western Christian myth of St George and the dragon was not documented until the thirteenth century, so the First Crusaders would have revered St George as the Eastern Christian soldier saint, martyred in AD 303.

The nun's version of the church's history was more myth than history but wonderfully colourful.

'When Arabs came here in 1054,' she told me, 'they walked halfway up the church before St George appeared to them saying "Stop! Stop, or I'll kill you!" They stopped, and that is why half the building is a mosque and half a church.'

Could she show me St George's white marble tomb in the crypt, I asked her. No, she could not, because it was being renovated. The church was gloomily hung with dark oil paintings and icons. I wanted to talk to her.

'Sister, I'm interested in the First Crusaders who came here in 1099 . . .'

'Oh, them! They came in the sign of the cross but they just stole all the relics from the Eastern Christians here. Then they sent them all over Europe, to France and even to Bucharest!' she said, busily plucking used yellow candle-ends out of a stand and throwing them in a bin decorated with a Byzantine double-headed eagle.

'Why were the Crusaders so bad to the Orthodox, do you think?'

'They were jealous, of course, of everything that we had and of our ancient tradition.'

I was left in no doubt that in her view relations between the twin halves of Christendom had not altered, let alone improved, in the last nine hundred years.

The Crusaders had pressed on from Ramleh to Lydda, found the burnt-out church of St George and vowed to rebuild it as the cathedral of the first Western Christian diocese in Palestine. They immediately appointed a Norman priest its first bishop and installed him in nearby Ramleh with a small garrison to protect him.

In 1917, General Allenby would also choose Ramleh as his first base, and an old Crusader tower for his home. There he passed the odd evening with a young American pilgrim and aid worker, poring over sayings of the Old Testament prophets. Dizzy with the grandeur of the historical moment, the aid worker read two Arabic words into Allenby's name – *Allah*, God and *nebi*, prophet – and decided that Allenby himself was a prophet of God. Giddy with admiration for his hero he penned him a hymn of praise, sung to the tune of 'O *Tannenbaum*':

> And God has led thee on, O Knight
>   Allenby, O Allenby!
> In thy great battle for the Right,
>   Allenby, O Allenby!
> The Earth's free nations now will bring
> Their genius to its glorying
> And they who sat in darkness sing
> For e'er of thee, O Allenby![cxxiii]

The first view General Allenby's forces had of their golden prize, Jerusalem, was precisely the same as that of the Crusaders, from a low mountain to the north-west of the city. Heartened by an eclipse of the moon which seemed to them to presage the eclipse of the Islamic crescent, the Crusaders had marched all the warm summer night long to reach the top of the mountain at dawn on 7 June 1099. Duke Godfrey had been on the road for exactly three years. With tears of joy in their eyes they celebrated by renaming the place Mont de joie – Mountjoy.

Long before Allenby's forces attacked the place in late November 1917, Montjoy had reverted to its old Arabic name, Nebi Samwill – Prophet Samuel. The British found themselves trying to capture the tomb of the Old Testament prophet housed in a mosque there on the mountain-top from Turks who swarmed down the slopes to repel them, one of them close enough for a fastidious English sergeant to 'smell the garlic on his hot breath'.[cxxiv] When the battle was won there were five hundred Turks to bury, according to one of Allenby's officers. Major Gilbert was profoundly stirred by the distant view of Jerusalem, like 'some fairy-place imagined in a dream . . . suspended in the sky . . . a mirage seen in the desert'.[cxxv] Back came all his school-boy history. In the flickering flash of a cigarette lighter the peak of a fellow officer's helmet suddenly looked to him 'exactly like a [Crusader's] raised visor'.

By the time I reached Nebi Samwill and clambered up the narrow stairs to the roof of the mosque, the sun was starting to set. I felt nothing like as emotional as Major Gilbert, just weary as any pilgrim reaching their goal and glad of a breath of a breeze. From that height, away south across a few low hills, Jerusalem was no golden bejewelled city suspended in the sky, no fairy-place or desert mirage, but a blur of brownish heat haze fringed with the odd whitish high-rise. I did not dare ask the burly Israeli soldier up there on the roof with me to lend me his binoculars for a moment. He was using them himself, carefully scanning the countryside all around for signs of hostile Palestinian activity. His radio crackled urgently.

From that height the crude simplicity of the struggle for living space that has been raging in this tiny country for well over half a century was as clear as a computer-generated image of a medieval battlefield. Built in tight, tidy clusters on the tops of the surrounding hills, the new Jewish settlements of red-roofed white houses in a ring around Jerusalem, look like the ranks of a battle-ready army, securely occupying all the high ground. Below them, between the hills, lie the old Arab villages, ill-disciplined, straggling and coloured a greyish donkey-brown.

My Israeli taxi driver drove me along the road to Jerusalem, past the settlements and a couple of Israeli checkpoints.

~

It was only 5.00 a.m., but the sudden urgent din of the dawn chorus in the tree outside my bedroom window shocked me wide awake and brought me out onto my tiny wrought-iron balcony armed with a packet of cigarettes and a litre plastic bottle of water.

The air was still fresh and the rising sun painting Jerusalem's limestone a rosy hue. Now it looked like a fairy-place, or like a gigantic cluster of pink pearls inlaid with the natural darkness of cypress trees and the brilliance of pale minarets. A precious, perfect place, before the day's noise and clamour started.

It occurred to me that from up there on that balcony, in December 1917, I would have had a privileged view of General Allenby walking through the Jaffa Gate into the wide cobbled square near the Citadel of the Tower of David to promise the colourful assembly of churchmen of all faiths and sects that he had come to preserve the city's holy sites. Back in July 1099, I might have seen the single minor halfway honourable episode in the Crusaders' conquest of Jerusalem.

Realizing his city was lost by mid-afternoon on 14 July, the Fatimid governor of Jerusalem, Iftikhar ad-Dawla, had retreated to the Tower of David which he then offered to hand over to Count Raymond in exchange for immunity for himself and his bodyguards. Count Raymond had kept his word and seen that Iftikhar and his men were escorted safely out of the city. But then there had ensued the orgy of pillage and slaughter which Arabs and Jews have never forgotten. The fanaticism that the Western Christians exhibited here in Jerusalem in July 1099 would equal anything Mohammed's nomad Arabs had achieved in the name of *Allah* during their aggres-sively expansionist period three centuries earlier. After July 1099 the Arabs knew that to survive at all against an enemy as barbarously intolerant as the *Franj* they would have to re-acquire their old *jihad* mentality.

Until then the Crusaders had certainly worried the Arabs but they had only affected one small fragment of their vast domains. Iftikhar ad-Dawla had not panicked at their approach, but instead made routine preparations. Calmly ordering the walls to be reinforced and all storehouses filled with food, he had stuffed his towers full of hay and cotton bales the better to withstand the shock of any Crusader bombardment. He imagined that if need be he and his garrison could hold out until an army from Egypt came to their rescue.

Iftikhar had also taken the wise precaution of poisoning the water supplies outside the city. Camped before the walls, sweltering in the dust, the Crusaders found themselves having to travel six miles for water. They stitched together ox hides and buffalo skins for use as receptacles and, as one chronicler recalled, 'drank the water from these vessels although it stank,·and what with foul water and barley bread we suffered great distress and affliction every day'.[cxxvi] Within days of their arrival, the lords were quailing at the prospect of another long siege, quarrelling about what to do next and trailing up to the Mount of Olives to seek the advice of an old hermit. To their dismay, the holy man advised them to attack the city the very next day, assuring them they could not fail if they had faith in God. They had not built any siege engines and lacked enough ladders to scale the walls, but they decided to trust him. They had grown used to miracles.

The assault was duly launched, but although the Crusaders succeeded in piercing the outer defences of the northern walls, it was soon aborted for lack of ladders. In the barren parched hills around the city, wood with which to build more ladders and siege engines was desperately scarce. However, to the Crusaders' great relief, news reached them that a fleet of four English and two Genoese ships had put in at the port of Jaffa with a cargo of food, rope and the nuts and bolts required for the manufacture of siege engines. Furthermore, the ships' crews were persuaded to break up their ships and haul the wood overland to the Crusaders' camp. The miraculously timely arrival of these supplies was hugely cheering.

Still competing for leadership of the expedition, Duke Godfrey and Count Raymond each had gigantic towers on wheels con-structed. Both were fitted with catapults and then carefully covered with iron plates and animal hides hardened by soaking in vinegar. But Duke Godfrey's tower boasted a special feature: a golden statue of Christ set high on its upper storey. It is said that while the adults toiled over the siege engines, the hordes of Crusader children, many of them named after the Crusading lords, armed themselves with reed lances and shields woven from willow and passed the idle hours staging mock battles against the children of Jerusalem.

The heat grew intolerable and the lords quarrelled bitterly over what to do with Jerusalem – assuming they managed to take it. The rate of desertion accelerated as rumours reached the soldier-pilgrims that the army of the Fatimid sultan was on its way from Egypt. The anxious moment favoured the rise of yet another visionary. This one, another Peter, claimed to be communicating with the spirit of the man whose comparative integrity, wisdom and strength they were all missing, Bishop Adhemar of Puy. According to Peter, Bishop Adhemar wanted the Crusading lords to stop squabbling over their ambitions. Instead, they were to proclaim a fast and walk barefoot and bareheaded, banners waving, in a procession around the walls of the city. If they accomplished all this in a spirit of true repentance they could be sure of conquering the city within nine days.

The Crusaders – now numbering a mere 1,500 *milites* and 12,000 foot soldiers – followed Adhemar's instructions to the letter. For three days they observed a strict fast, and on 8 July began their formal procession around the city walls. Jeered at from the walls by the city's Muslim defenders, they felt like their Saviour on his cross being mocked by Roman soldiers, and paid the enemy no attention. When they reached the Mount of Olives, Peter the Hermit preached them a rousing sermon. Reinvigorated, the Christians laboured on, putting the finishing touches to the two great wooden towers on wheels, and, two days later, they were ready to roll them into place.

The sight of the gigantic wooden structures astonished the Fatimid garrison, who had not been aware of their construction. Two Arab sorceresses with three helpers were employed to stand on the city walls and rain down curses on the monsters. Miraculously, a catapult in one of the towers fired off a boulder and despatched all five women. Showers of stones and Greek fire* hampered the positioning of Duke Godfrey's tower against the north wall, and Count Raymond's on Mount Sion in the south-west. Count Raymond's tower was the first in place but Iftikhar himself was commanding that section. His defence was so ferocious that no

* A lethal Byzantine invention – flaming pitch and sulphur.

southern Frenchman could get a firm foothold on the wall. On the morning of the next day, 14 July, Duke Godfrey's tower was safely rammed into place. His soldiers set fire to some bales of cotton and straw which the defenders of the city had hung over the walls to act as a buffer. Luck was on the Crusaders' side for the wind blew the thick black smoke back across the city. It blinded the Arabs and threw them into confusion, giving some Flemish *milites* time to lay a footbridge from the tower to the wall. Duke Godfrey followed them onto the wall, no doubt recalling with satisfaction how, fifteen years earlier, he had led the capture of Rome's St Peter's from Pope Gregory. He ordered the opening of a gate and urged on the Crusaders swarming up the ladders into the city.

Terrified, the Muslim defenders fled to the south-east corner of the city, to the Haram al-Sharif,* where their magnificent gold-domed mosque the Qubbat al-Sakhra† stands. If the worst came to the very worst, they would mount their final defence in the nearby Al-Aqsa mosque. But Bohemond's nephew Tancred was close behind them, having already found time to plunder the Qubbat al-Sakhra of 'more than forty silver candelabra . . . a great silver lamp weighing forty-four Syrian pounds, as well as a hundred and fifty smaller silver candelabra and twenty gold ones, and a great deal more booty'.[cxxvii] As the Arabs hurtled into the Al-Aqsa mosque and raced for the roof, Tancred and his men were upon them, hacking to left and right. As greedy for gold as they had been back at Caesarea, they 'split open their [Arabs'] stomachs when they were dead, in order to get bezants out of their intestines, which when they were alive, they had gulped down their ill-fated gullets'.[cxxviii]

The bloodletting had only begun. As soon as Iftikhar had admitted defeat and struck his deal over the Tower of David with Count Raymond, a more general slaughter started and lasted the remainder of the afternoon, all night and on into the next day. The city's Jews had fled to their chief synagogue for sanctuary, just as

* The Noble Sanctuary, but also the Jews' Temple Mount, the site of the temple the Romans destroyed in AD 70.
† The Dome of the Rock, built AD 691.

the English Varangians had to the Church of St Michael outside Dyrrachium almost twenty years earlier, and, like the Varangians, they suffered mass incineration.

One gruesomely graphic description of Jerusalem after the massacre speaks for itself: 'Piles of heads, hands and feet were to be seen in the streets of the city. It was necessary to pick one's way over the bodies of men and horses . . . in the Temple and porch of Solomon [the Muslims' Haram al-Sharif] men rode in blood up to their knees and bridle reins . . .'[cxxix] The Crusaders themselves, 'dripping with blood from head to foot',[cxxx] were a still more abominable sight.

Once every Jew and Muslim in the city was dead and every house sacked, the Crusading lords made their way through the empty Christian quarter – Iftikhar had exiled all the city's Eastern Christians in case they collaborated with the Crusaders – to the Church of the Holy Sepulchre, which contained the tomb of their dear Lord, to give pious thanks to him for their great victory. They rejoiced in the knowledge that they had avenged the insult to his good name, retrieved his rightful property, and secured their seats in his feasting hall in the sky with plenary indulgences.

In effect, the Crusaders had reverted to the old Germanic mores Thorvald the Far-farer had grown up with at Stora Giljá and which he had jettisoned in favour of Christianity, the mores the *milites* had failed to marry with their Christianity until Pope Urban had obligingly initiated this first armed pilgrimage. In Jerusalem in 1099 there was no trace of that turn-the-other-cheek religion which Thorvald had had such trouble practising and which Otto III had never been able to forget.

Old Pope Urban II died on 29 June, a fortnight after the taking of the city but before news of it had reached him. If he had lived to hear he might have died of heartbreak anyway, for the Crusaders' great military victory entailed a far greater spiritual defeat which would haunt Western Christendom through the second millennium. He might have recognized that the eleventh-century reforming popes' efforts to tame the *milites* by co-opting them into the Church's project of building God's kingdom on earth had failed. Instead, the Church had been co-opted into building an earthly kingdom, the papal monarchy, by means of territorial conquest, greed and bloodshed. The sixteenth-century Reformation would split Western Christendom itself into warring sides. But Protestant missionaries would prove at least as active as Catholic ones in the nineteenth-century missionaries' crusade. The *milites* spirit still ruled.

More than eight hundred years of warring in God's name in western Europe itself has only halted since the end of World War Two. By ceasing to define the continent as Christian any more, by opening it up to mass immigration from beyond the boundaries of traditional Christendom and by the efforts of people like Jean Monnet and Robert Schuman, we have hard-headedly bound up our self-inflicted wounds with economic ties, with the work of men like *Frère* Roger and with laws guaranteeing human rights. Human rights legislation is something all the great Abrahamic religions can agree upon, and such laws conveniently obviate the duty to strive for the one thing that set the Christian faith apart from either Judaism or Islam – the turn-the-other-cheek ideal.

I was in a city whose Jewish and Muslim inhabitants were still – thanks to centuries of crusading of one kind or another by Western Christians (including Americans) – trapped in a cycle of revenge, and too insecure and aggrieved to cease their warring.

Lingering long on my balcony, watching the impromptu *corteo* in the cobbled square below, I extracted a crumb of comfort from the fact that Jerusalem was in no danger whatsoever of becoming homogenized. A wimpled nun in a long habit swept swiftly past the squatting, smoking Arab taxi drivers, shopping bag over her arm, but was overtaken by a small Jewish boy on a scooter. Side locks flying in the breeze, he sped on by, narrowly missing a long-bearded Orthodox monk shambling along in a faded blue cassock. A police van hurtled past, lights flashing, siren screaming.

~

'Which way to the Church of the Holy Sepulchre please?'

'Down there – first left, third right,' said the Arab waiter at the café next door to my hotel, pointing to his left down a dark narrow alley lined with still-closed souvenir shops.

Out of the narrow gloom of the third right I emerged into a large shaded courtyard. Only a nearby minaret was tall enough to bask in the radiant sunshine. I regretted having to plunge on down some steps in the corner of the courtyard – past pillars scored with a forest of pilgrims' crosses and stuffed with scraps of paper inscribed with the prayers of the faithful – into the chilly, dark depths of the Church of the Holy Sepulchre.

I wandered through chapels, along dark naves, down into damp dark caverns and up again past more dark chapels, alcoves and niches, all of them cluttered with the accumulated paraphernalia of centuries of Christian worship. Somewhere was Duke Godfrey's sword, but I did not know where and I did not much care. Dark icons, gleaming lamps, candlesticks, heavy drapes and altar cloths, statues and unidentifiable stones were all conspiring to convince me that I was touring the madder corners of the collective Christian mind, and I wanted no part of that fetishism. The amorphous forms of black-robed clergy praying or sleeping or watching from dark corners, the echoes of footsteps and the hum of distant chanting were paranoia-inducing. I missed the openness and light of the great mosque in Damascus, its fresh carpets and sleeping men, the welcome. At last I found a lighter, airier chapel where an Italian priest was celebrating mass alone, before rows of empty pews. I sat down and listened to his Latin drone, but the noises he made slurping wine from his chalice, snapping the stiff communion wafer and washing and wiping after his lonely meal were so embarrassingly loud that I fled before he was finished.

It seemed to me that the monks of the various Christian sects – Roman Catholics, Greek Orthodox, Armenian Orthodox, Syrian Orthodox, Copts and Ethiopians – inhabit this damp murky maze in much the same way as the shepherds and camel dealers once occupied Krac des Chevaliers, but with a good deal more acrimony.

The Church of the Holy Sepulchre has been at least as bitterly and minutely contested by Christians as any area of Europe in the past thousand years or any part of Israel in the past fifty. The pitched battle fought between Franciscan and Greek Orthodox monks on 4 November 1901 over which denomination should have the right to clean the bottom step of the staircase leading from the courtyard up to the Franciscan chapel is famous. In 1918 a Franciscan vividly described the engagement, which had left seventeen of his brothers badly injured:

> Greek monks of low character, with a mixture of assassins disguised as monks, made use of arms, whilst others from the terraces above hurled upon the victims a torrent of large stones held in readiness for the purpose. On the Greek terraces someone even saw several cases of petroleum standing ready, together with inflammable rags, which were to be thrown upon the Franciscans gasping in their blood . . .[cxxxi]

Writing within months of General Allenby's conquest of the Holy Land, the same author rejoiced that 'the warrior-descendants of the Crusaders had reoccupied the Holy City' and heartily hoped that by taking back 'what belongs to them'[cxxxii] they would surely put a stop to such scandals.

Anxious to learn what Christendom's holiest shrine might have to teach us all today about the peaceful and efficient running of multinational institutions including our new European Union, I left the church and went to the nearby headquarters of the Franciscan Order in St Francis Street. There I encountered Father Athanasius, a big, soft American with a shy smile and a tendency to blush. He ushered me into a bare, windowless room for a chat about something he called 'the status quo'.

In 1852 the Ottoman Turkish rulers of Palestine tried to put a stop to the Christians' incessant wrangling in the Church of the Holy Sepulchre by freezing the situation as it stood at that moment – the status quo. To this day the Greek and Armenian Orthodox, whose communities were favoured under Ottoman rule, and the Franciscans, who were powerfully backed by France and the Vatican, remain the great powers in the Church of the Holy Sepulchre. But during the past half-century the status quo has been further defined by the addition of hundreds of bi- and trilateral agreements regulating almost every detail of the Church – its structures, its contents, its maintenance and its use.

On the wooden table between us Father Athanasius unfurled a large plan of the place. Its careful colour-coding indicated which pillar, portal, altar and alcove, door, threshold and wall belonged to which Christian sect. Greek Orthodox pale blue predominated.

'Probably ninety per cent of all the rights in the church are defined by now,' Father Athanasius told me with one of his smiles, 'but there are still serious clashes, like who gets to put a candle in the Chapel of Angels, which is right here. A candle implies the need for a candlestick and that means property rights.'

I was trying not to laugh. He sensed my amusement and protested, 'It's no joke; it's a great historical responsibility. Everyone is guarding against creeping infringement. My job is to see that we Catholics don't lose any rights, and the other guys are all doing the same. Sometimes it's really very difficult. There are a couple of rooms the Copts have night services in – right here, between these two pillars – which badly need doing up, but the Copts are too poor to pay for it. Will they let the rest of us help them out? No, they won't, in case any of us uses the occasion to make a claim. Take the beat-up chapel of St Joseph of Arimathea and Nicodemus over there, just by your thumb. Why hasn't it been fixed up? Because while we and the Greeks recognize the Armenians' claim to it, the Syrian Orthodox who use the place on Sundays and during Holy Week don't. So nothing gets done. And right now there's a broken manhole cover – here – which the Armenians are claiming sole rights to repairing, although the Greeks and us border on their property at that point and so have a part share in it. But that's nothing compared to the fact that Christ's tomb badly needs renovating. That means really extensive negotiation because it's common property. It'll be decades before anything gets done there! I don't even want to think about it!'

'It doesn't sound very Christian . . .'

Father Athanasius blushed before admitting that what keeps him awake at night is not the grotesque impiety of fighting over repairs to Christ's tomb but the certain knowledge that the church is not safe for the hundreds of thousands of pilgrims who visit it every year.

'It needs fire escapes and all that stuff but we're never going to agree on how to do it. How does that look? That's unchristian!'

Father Athanasius was red in the face, distressed, so I changed the subject by asking him how he felt about the pope's recent abject apology to the Greek Orthodox for the Fourth Crusaders' sacking of Constantinople in 1204. I had already gained the impression that the Greek Orthodox were the Catholic Franciscans' most trouble-some adversaries in the Church of the Holy Sepulchre, so I was not surprised when he swiftly recovered himself and replied that he saw no need for any apology. Next I asked him where he imagined this second Palestinian *intifada* might lead Israel. He expected much more violence, he said, and finally, once both sides had lost too much to bear, formal partition of the country.

'There'll have to be a tribal solution – just like we've got here,' he concluded with a sigh, pointing to his plan of the church.

When I left Father Athanasius it was afternoon but Jerusalem was still early-morning empty. Where the souvenir sellers should have been touting their wares there was echoing gloom. A small boy, idly kicking at the closed metal doors of one of the stalls, produced a sound like a ricocheting gunshot. From an upper storey came the urgent tones of a radio news bulletin. Somewhere nearby, heard but unseen, thousands of Palestinians were flooding out of their mosques after Friday prayers, strong as a river about to break its banks.

Out in the open by the Jaffa Gate, the air was hot and hazy as gun smoke. At the hotel I discovered that the Arab shops in the city's Christian and Muslim quarters were closed for the day in mourning for a well-loved leader who had died of a heart attack in Egypt. His funeral procession would pass straight through the Muslim quarter from Damascus Gate to his honoured burial site on the Haram al-Sharif in a couple of hours' time. Trouble was expected, warned the Palestinian receptionist, adding with an oddly excited smile, 'I will be there. He was my cousin, so I must help to carry his coffin.'

In the pristine new Jewish quarter of the city, Orthodox Jews were dressing in their Sabbath best – some in pale satin dressing gowns, thick white stockings and fur hats – and heading down in the suffocating heat to pray at the ruined western wall of their second temple. By the dark entrance to the Plaza of the Western Wall I encountered a posse of heavily armed Israeli police. Their walkie-talkies crackled with static. A small radio blared another news bulletin. I was turned back.

In a basement café I listened to a couple of Austrian journalists quiz the Israeli girl making their coffees about 'the situation' and I read the *Jerusalem Post*. The Russian-Israeli minister in charge of authorizing new settlements in the Palestinians' West Bank was in no mood for compromise: 'Time is running out very quickly . . . We are in a war but we are not using all our might . . . We need to fight with all our strength . . .'[cxxxiii]

Barred from entering the Muslim quarter, I walked into the Jewish area again and sat down to rest on some steps by a street artist and her friend. The street artist told me that she believed God had given the Jews Israel and the Arabs Egypt, and that a big war was about to start after which the Messiah would come. I wandered on up into the Christian quarter again, where I was accosted by a Finnish born-again Christian with an Australian accent. He told me that he would have died in the previous Sunday's bomb in a post office in the new city if he had not suddenly decided to have a shave before going out.

'Are you a believer?' he asked me abruptly, a fanatical light in his pale blue eyes.

'A believer in what?' I asked him, irritated that in Jerusalem of all places on earth he should think it unnecessary to specify which kind of believer.

'I mean, do you believe that Christ died to save us?'

'No, but . . .' I began, wanting to explain that I did believe in God.

He scowled and waved me away like a bothersome fly, leaving me feeling shaken and scared.

Here in Jerusalem at long last, I was nevertheless being denied any grand sense of culmination, any satisfying feeling of fulfilment. Instead, everything around me was flying apart in fragments, like shrapnel from an exploding grenade. Past and present were not one nor even attractively complementary here, but locked in deadly opposition and eternally incompatible. If my long voyage through the heart of Western Christendom had done nothing to change my mind about the tragic shortcomings of organized religion, my experience of Jerusalem was leading me to suspect that the world has also never known anything as appallingly dangerous. Who could blame the God of the Jews, Christians and Muslims for turning his back on peoples who had made his city a charnel house? If God wanted to show humankind how disgracefully it had distorted and abused his message, what better means than this? Jerusalem was deeply shaming.

The Icelanders had told sagas to steady their sense of themselves in their hostile natural world. I sensed that everyone in this ancient city was numbing the same existential terror of finding themselves helplessly insignificant in a godless universe, by battling over leading roles in sagas apocalyptic enough to end all sagas, forever. Here was the egoism Archbishop Anastasios had warned me of, monstrous and omnipresent, lethal and repellent. It may be that the terrible lesson western Europe's eleventh century taught us but the second millennium has still failed to ram home is that man is a greater danger to himself than the hostile universe will ever be, and never more so than when motivated by blind belief in Judaism, Christianity, Islam, Communism, National Socialism or global capitalism, which are all faces of the opposite of love, egoism.

I am writing these last few lines six weeks after Islamic funda-mentalists flew two aeroplanes into the towers of New York's World Trade Center and thereby provoked the mighty technological revenge of the world's only superpower and a 'crusade' against ter-rorism which could occupy the Western world for the rest of the twenty-first century. Otto III, the boy-emperor who might have kept Christendom whole and united Europe, died two years after the start of the last millennium; it may be that, along with New York's twin towers, any hopes for this new millennium have crumbled even sooner.

Training my millennial binoculars on this new *Terror Mundi* I think I recognize the mindset of men madly, egoistically bent on starring in another apocalyptic saga. The strategies to which Islamic fundamentalists resort today are just as disastrously opposed to love as those of the reforming Western Church a thousand years ago. But I also detect that deeper terror of eleventh-century Western churchmen: fear born of desperate yearning for order and meaning. Order and meaning are fearfully hard to come by in this secularized, globalized modern world.

CHRONOLOGY

874	Vikings settle in Iceland.
910	Cluny founded in Burgundy.
911	Vikings settle in Normandy under Rollo.
955	Magyars defeated by Saxon Emperor Otto I at Lechfeld.
972	Last Saracen brigands chased out of Alps.
980	Saxon German Emperor Otto III born.
	Byzantine princess Zoe born.
986	Thorvald the Far-farer, first apostle to Iceland, outlawed by the Icelandic Althing.
988	Kievan Rus converts to Eastern (Byzantine) Christianity.
994	Odilo installed as abbot of Cluny.
996	Otto III crowned Holy Roman emperor.
997	Adalbert-Wojciech martyred by east Prussians.
999	Gerbert of Aurillac installed as Pope Sylvester II.
1000	Iceland and Norway convert to Western (Roman) Christianity.
	Poland and Hungary granted first archbishoprics.
	Saxon Emperor Otto III goes on pilgrimage to Poland and opens Charlemagne's tomb.
	Greenlanders discover north-east coast of America.
	Norman adventurer mercenaries arrive in southern Italy.
	Turkish tribes begin migration into Asia Minor across Caucasus mountains.
1002	Emperor Otto III dies aged 21.
1003	Pope Sylvester II dies.
1007	Peter Damiani born.
1016	Conquest of England by Danish King Canute.
1030s	Peace of God movement at its height.
1040s	Truce of God movement.
	Norman Robert Guiscard joins his elder half-brothers in southern Italy.
1046	German Holy Roman Emperor Henry III sacks three rival popes and installs first German pope.
1048	Bruno of Tour installed as Pope Leo IX.
1049	Reform of Roman Church launched at Reims.
	Hugh installed as abbot of Cluny.

1050   Death of Byzantine Empress Zoe.

1053   Pope Leo IX defeated by Normans of southern Italy at Civitate. First promise of plenary indulgences in return for fighting for Church.

1054   Death of Pope Leo IX.
        Schism between Churches of Rome and Byzantium.

1059   Papacy allies with Normans of southern Italy by Treaty of Melfi mediated by Abbot Desiderius of Monte Cassino.
        Pope Nicholas II decrees all future popes to be elected by cardinals instead of appointment by Holy Roman emperors.

1065   Bishop Gunther of Bamberg leads 7,000 German pilgrims on pilgrimage to Jerusalem.

1066   Norman conquest of England.
        German Henry IV succeeds to throne of Holy Roman Empire.

1071   Byzantines defeated by Seljuk Turks at battle of Manzikert, and start losing control of Asia Minor.
        Byzantines defeated by Robert Guiscard at Bari and ousted from southern Italy.
        Consecration of Abbot Desiderius' church at Monte Cassino.
        Alexius I Comnenus installed as Byzantine emperor.

1072   Death of Peter Damiani.

1073   Hildebrand installed as Pope Gregory VII.

1074   Pope Gregory VII's aborted crusade with Countess Matilda of Tuscany.

1075   Two hundred and fifty shiploads of English fugitives from Normans arrive in Constantinople.

1077   Pope Gregory VII asserts supremacy of papal authority over Emperor Henry IV at Canossa.

1081   Henry IV descends on Rome for another bout in his contest with Gregory VII.

1082   Robert Guiscard, his wife Sichelgaita and son Bohemond invade the Byzantine empire.

1084   Pope Gregory rescued by his south Italian Norman allies who sack and burn Rome.

1085   Pope Gregory VII dies in exile in Salerno.
        Robert Guiscard dies on Cephallonia.

1087   Relics of St Nicholas removed from Myra to Bari.

1088   Abbot Hugh begins building Cluny's third church.
        Pope Urban II installed as pope.

1089   Consecration of Bari's cathedral of St Nicholas by Pope Urban II.

1095   Urban II preaches First Crusade.

1096   Pogroms against German Jews by First Crusaders.

1097   First Crusaders reach Constantinople and then Antioch.

1098   Siege of Antioch.
        Pope Urban II summons Council of Bari in vain attempt to heal schism with Byzantine Church.

1099   First Crusaders conquer Jerusalem.
        Death of Pope Urban II.

NOTES

Part One

    i Hreinsson, Vithar, (ed.), *The Complete Sagas of Icelanders*, vols. 1–5, Reykjavik, Leifur Erikson, 1997, p. 358

   ii Ibid. p. 359

  iii Ibid. p.359

  iv Ibid. p. 360

   v Ibid. p. 362

  vi Ibid.

 vii Ibid. p. 363

viii Laxness, Halldor, *Under the Glacier*, tr. Magnus Magnusson, Reykjavik, Vaka-Helgafell hf., 1999, p. 129

  ix Hreinsson, p. 364

   x Ibid. p. 365

  xi Ibid.

 xii Ibid. p. 367

xiii Ibid.

xiv Ibid.

 xv Ibid. p. 73

xvi Magnusson, Magnus, *Iceland Saga*, London, The Bodley Head, 1987, p. 140

xvii Ibid. p. 142

xviii Strömbäck, Dag, *The Conversion of Iceland*, London, University College, 1997, p. 53

xix Tschan, Francis J. (tr.) *History of the Archbishops of Hamburg-Bremen*, New York, Columbia University Press, 1959, pp. 228–9

xx Scherman, Katharine, *Iceland: Daughter of Fire*, London, Gollancz, 1976, p. 217

xxi Ibid. p. 222

xxii Sharpe, Revd.John (tr.) *The History of the Kings of England by William of Malmesbury*, London, Longman, 1815, p. 321

xxiii Ibid. p. 320

xxiv France, John, (tr., ed.), *Rodolfus Glaber: The Five Books of the Histories*, Oxford, Clarendon Press, 1989, pp. 116–17

xxv Guldencrone, Baronne Diane de, *L'Italie Byzantine: étude sur le haut moyen-âge (400–1050)*, Paris, Ernest Leroux, 1914, p. 436. Quoted from Thietmar of Merseburg.

xxvi Davids, Adelbert, (ed.), *The Empress Theophano: Byzantium and the West at the turn of the first Millennium*, Cambridge, Cambridge University Press, 1995, p. 49

xxvii Niluse, Baron de, *La vie de Sainte Adelaide Impératrice, tiré de Saint Odilon*, Paris, 1847

xxviii Althoff, Gert, *Otto 111*, Darmstadt, Primnus Verlag, 1997, p. 48. Quoted from *Quedlinburg Annals*.

xxix Ibid p. 50. Quoted from *Quedlinburg Annals*.

xxx Althoff, p. 160

xxxi Lattin, Harriet Pratt, (tr.), *The Letters of Gerbert with his papal privileges as Sylvester II*, New York, Columbia University Press, 1961, p. 15

xxxii Ibid. p. 198

xxxiii Southern, R.W., p. 230

xxxiv Meie, Hans-Jurgen, *Weltkulturerbe Quedlinburg*, Goslar, Studio Volkar Schadach, 1998, p. 17

xxxv Duby, Georges, *The Age of Cathedrals: Art and Society 980–1420*, London, Croom Helm, 1981, p. 9

xxxvi Tschan, pp. 66–7

xxxvii Riant, Paul, *Expéditions et pèlerinages des Scandinaves en Terre Sainte au temps des Croisades*, Paris, 1865–7, p. 102

xxxviii Guldencrone, p. 483

xxxix Ibid. p. 27

xl Blazynski, George, *John Paul II: A Man from Krakow*, London, Weidenfeld & Nicolson, 1979, p. 5

xli Willey, David, *God's Politician*, London, Faber & Faber, 1993, p. 234. Quoted from *Centesimus Annus* encyclical.

xlii Zamoyski, Adam, *The Polish Way: A Thousand Year History of the Poles and their Culture*, London, John Murray, 1987, p. 13

xliii Althoff, p. 139. Quoted from the Anonymous Gaul.

xliv Ibid.

xlv Ibid. p. 141

xlvi Zamoyski, p. 13

xlvii Althoff, p. 139

xlviii Zamoyski, p. 13

xlix Willey, p. 5

l Matus, Thomas, *The Mystery of Romuald and the Five Brothers: stories from the Benedictines and Camaldolese*, Wheathampstead, Anthony Clarke Publishers, 1994, p. 99

li Ibid. p. 101

lii Ibid. p. 134

liii Ibid. p. 139

liv Frankfurter Allegemeine supplement, 27 April 2000, 'On the Bumpy Road to EU Enlargement'

lv Bury, J. (ed.), *Cambridge Medieval History, Vol. III*, Cambridge, Cambridge University Press, 1922, pp. 213–14

lvi Ibid., p. 214

lvii Matus, p. 110

lviii Lattin, p. 290

lix France, p. 79

lx Mayr-Harting, Henry, *Ottonian Book Illumination: An Historical Study, Part One: Themes*, London, Harvey Miller Publishers, 1991, p. 119

lxi Norwich, John Julius, *Byzantium: The Apogee*, London, Penguin, 1993, p. 259

lxii Brooke, Christopher, *Europe in the Central Middle Ages, 962–1154*, London, Longman, 2000, p. 219

lxiii Monnet, Jean, *Memoirs* Richard Mayne (tr.), London, Collins, 1978, p. 523

lxiv Lejeune, René, *Robert Schumann: père de l'Europe 1886–1963*, Paris, Fayard, 2000, p. 168

lxv Frankfurter Allegemeine supplement, 10 April 2000

lxvi Isaiah 66:13–14

lxvii Papadakis, Aristeides, *The Christian East and the Rise of the Papacy*, Crestwood, New York, St Vladimir's Seminary Press, 1994, p. 169

lxviii Evans, Joan, *Life in Medieval France*, London, Phaidon Press, 1925, p. 106

PART TWO

i Blum, Owen J.(tr.), *Peter Damiani Letters*, Washington, Catholic University of America Press, 1989, Vol. 11 p. 258

ii Nineham, Dennis, *Christianity Medieval and Modern: A Study in Religious Change*, London, SCM Press Ltd, 1993, p. 178. Taken from *Patrologia Latina* 320.

iii McNulty, Patricia (tr., ed.), *St Peter Damian: Selected Writings on the Spiritual Life*, London, Faber & Faber, 1959, p. 10

iv Head, Thomas and Landes, Richard (eds.), *The Peace of God: Social Violence and Religious Response in France around the Year 1000*, Ithaca and London, Cornell University Press, 1992, p. 301. Quoted from *Patrologia Latina* 143:1000.

v Martin, L'Abbé Eug., *Saint Leon IX 1002–1054*, Paris, Librairie Victor Lecoffre, Paris, 1904, p. 95

vi Ibid. p. 96

vii Pellus, Daniel, *Reims: a travers ses rues, places et monuments*, Roanne, Éditions Horvath, 1983, p. 81

viii Smith L. M, *Cluny in the Eleventh and Twelfth Centuries*, London, Philip Allan & Co. Ltd, 1930, p. 3

ix Leclercq, J., *The Spirituality of the Middle Ages*, London, Burns & Oates, 1968, p. 117. Quoted from Bruno of Querfurt.

x France, p. 199

xi Bergmann, Arni, *Thorvaldur Vithförli*, Rejkyavik, Mal og menning, 1994

xii Mathew, Arnold Harris, *The Life and Times of Hildebrand, Pope Gregory VII*, London, Francis Griffiths, 1910, p. 75

xiii Nineham, p. 189

xiv King, James, C. (tr.), *Reichenau and its Three Churches*, Allgau, Hannes Oefele Verlag, 1992, p. 5

xv Martindale, C., *The Household of God*, London, Burns, Oates & Washbourne, 1935, p. 13

xvi Ibid. p. 17

xvii King, p. 7

xviii Ibid.

xix Fuller, John G., *The Day of St Anthony's Fire*, London, Hutchinson, 1969, p. 95

xx Book of Revelations 9:5–6

xxi Head and Landes, pp. 47–8

xxii Ibid. pp. 189–93

xxiii Fennell, John, *A History of the Russian Church to 1448*, London, Longman, 1995, p. 105

xxiv Duby, Georges, *The Age of Cathedrals: Art and Society 980–1420*, London, Croom Helm, 1981, p. 65

xxv Niluse, p. 158

xxvi Duby, p. 43

xxvii Ibid.

xxviii Duby, Georges, *The Three Orders: Feudal Society Imagined*, Chicago, University of Chicago Press, 1980, p. 98

xxix Evans, Joan, *Monastic Life at Cluny 910–1157*, London, Oxford University Press, 1931, p. 22

xxx France, p. 197

xxxi Cowdrey, H. E. J., *The Cluniacs and Gregorian Reform*, Oxford, Clarendon Press, 1970, p. 144

xxxii Smith, L. M., *Cluny in the Eleventh and Twelfth Centuries*, London, Philip Allan & Co.Ltd, 1930, p. 213

xxxiii Ibid.

xxxiv Spink, Kathryn, *A Universal Heart: The Life and Vision of Brother Roger of Taizé*, London, Society for the Promotion of Christian Knowledge, 1986, p. 44

xxxv Ibid. p. 77

xxxvi Ibid. p. 78

xxxvii Clement, Olivier, *Taizé: A Meaning to Life*, Chicago, GIA Publications Inc., 1997, p. 33

xxxviii France, p. 177

xxxix Avagliano, Faustino (ed.), *L'Eta dell'Abate Desiderio III*, 1. Soria Arte e cultura, Montecassino, 1992, p. 131

xl Pardoe, Rosemary and Darroll, *The Female Pope: The Mystery of Pope Joan*, Wellingborough, Crucible, 1988, p. 56. Quoted from *Oriens Christianus*, M. Le Quien, 1745, III, cols. 430/1.

xli Cross, F. L. (ed.), *Oxford Dictionary of the Christian Church*, London, Oxford University Press, 1958

xlii Daniel-Rops, H., *Cathedral and Crusade*, London, J. M. Dent & Sons Ltd, 1957, p. 395

xliii France, p. 219

xliv Tyler, J. E., *The Alpine Passes: the Middle Ages, 962–1250*, Oxford, Basil Blackwell, 1930, p. 28

xlv Ibid.

xlvi Lampe, Karl, *Germany under the Salian and Hohenstaufen Emperors*, Ralph Bennett (tr.), Oxford, Basil Blackwell, 1973, p. 74

xlvii Cowdrey, H. E. J., (tr., ed.), *The Epistolae Vagantes of Pope Gregory VII*, Oxford, Clarendon Press, Oxford, 1972, pp. 11–13

xlviii Ibid.

xlix Mathew, p. 79

l Ibid.

li Cowdrey, H. E. J., *Popes, Monks and Crusaders*, London, The Hambledon Press, 1984, p. 32

lii Cowdrey, H. E. J., *Pope Gregory VII 1073–1085*, Oxford, Clarendon Press, 1998, p. 429

liii Cowdrey, H. E. J., *The Crusades and Latin Monasticism*, Aldershot, Variorum Press, 1999, p. 32

liv Cowdrey, 1972, p. 97

lv Smith, p. 53. Quoted from William of Malmesbury.

lvi Gilchrist, John, *Canon Law in the Age of Reform, 11th–12th Centuries*, Aldershot, Variorum Press, 1993, p. 25

lvii *Annals of Lampert of Hersfeld*, p. 373

lviii Huddy, Mary E., *Matilda, Countess of Tuscany*, London, John Long, 1905, p. 81

lix Weinfurter, Stefan, *The Salian Century: Main Currents in an Age of Transition*, Philadelphia, University of Pennsylvania Press, 1999, p. 146

lx Duffy, Eamon, *Saints and Sinners: A History of the Popes*, New Haven, Yale University Press, 1997, p. 96

lxi Brooke, Christopher, *Europe in the Central Middle Ages, 962–1154*, London, Longman, 2000, p. 348

lxii Fuhrmann, Horst, *Germany in the High Middle Ages, c.1050–1200*, Cambridge, Cambridge University Press, 1986, p. 58

lxiii Leyser, Karl, *Medieval Germany and its Neighbours 900–1250*, London, The Hambledon Press, 1982, p. 138

lxiv Ibid. p. 9

lxv Lampert of Hersfeld, p. 121

lxvi Ibid. pp. 397–404

lxvii Heer, Friedrich, *The Holy Roman Empire*, London, Weidenfeld & Nicolson, 1968, p. 58

lxviii Mathew, p. 1

lxix Giovannini, A., Golinelli, P. and Piva, P., *L'Abbazia di San Benedetto Po*, Verona, Cierre Edizioni, 1997

lxx Huddy, p. 21

lxxi Lampert of Hersfeld, pp. 397–404

lxxii Ibid.

lxxiii Ibid.

lxxiv Cowdrey, 1998, p. 156

lxxv Blum, Vol. III, p. 200

lxxvi Ibid. Vol. III, p. 110

lxxvii Ibid. Vol. II, pp. 6–16

lxxviii Smith, p. 47

lxxix Blum, Vol. I, pp. 27–8

lxxx Ibid. Vol. II, p. 336

lxxxi Evans, p. 126

lxxxii Blum, Vol. III, p. 158

lxxxiii Leyser, Henrietta, *Hermits and the New Monasticism: A Study of Religious Communities in Western Europe 1000–1150*, London, Macmillan, 1984, p. 15

lxxxiv Ibid. p. 1

lxxxv Moore, R. I., *The Origins of European Dissent*, Toronto, University of Toronto Press, 1994, p. 51

lxxxvi Lawrence, C. H., *Medieval Monasticism: Forms of Religious Life in Western Europe in the Middle Ages*, London, Longman, 1984, p. 128

lxxxvii Taylor, Henry Osborn, *The Medieval Mind*, London, Macmillan & Co. Ltd, 1925, Vol. I, p. 393

lxxxviii Leyser, p. 31

lxxxix Taylor, p. 390

xc Ibid. p. 391

xci Southern, R. W., *Western Society and the Church in the Middle Ages*, London, Pelican, 1970, p. 136

xcii Blum, Vol. II, p. 232

xciii Davic, R. H. C., *A History of Medieval Europe: from Constantine to St Louis*, London, Longman, Green & Co., 1957, p. 235

xciv Sharpe, p. 257

xcv Ibid.

xcvi Cornwell, John, *Hitler's Pope*: London, Penguin, 1999, p. 11. Quoted from the *Syllabus of Errors*.

xcvii Kung, Hans, *The Catholic Church: A Short History*, London, Weidenfeld & Nicolson, 2001, p. 201

xcviii Gatto, Ludovico, *Storia di Roma nel Medioevo*, Rome, Newton & Compton Editori, 1999, p. 317

xcix Burman, Edward, *From Emperor to Emperor: Italy before the Renaissance*, London, Constable, 1991, p. 123

c Sharpe, p. 336

ci Norwich, John Julius, *The Normans in the South 1016–1130*, Harlow, Longman, 1967, p. 77

cii Sewter, E. R. A., (tr.), *The Alexiad of Anna Comnena*, London, Penguin, 1969, p. 54

ciii Ibid.

civ Norwich, p. 92

cv Ibid. p. 97

cvi Ibid.

cvii Ibid. p. 128

cviii Bloch, Herbert, *Monte Cassino in the Middle Ages*, Vol. I, Rome, Edizioni di Storia I Leterratura, 1986, pp. 10–11

cvix Newton, Francis, *The Scriptorium and Library of Montecassino 1058–1105*, Cambridge, Cambridge University Press, 1999, p. 236

cx Ibid. p. 128

cxi Sewter, pp. 63–4

cxii Green, Colonel J. H., *Cassino 1944, (Before, during and after)*, Cassino, Editore Lamberti, 1989, p. 46

cxiii Bloch, p. 67

cxiv Ibid.

cxv Ibid. p. 72

cxvi Ibid.

cxvii Ibid. p. 45

cxviii Carucci, Arturo, *San Gregorio VII e Salerno*, Naples, Instituto Anselmi, Naples, 1984, p. 85

cxix Ibid. p. 87

cxx Cowdrey, 1998, p. 680

cxxi Carucci, p. 90

cxxii Mathieu, Marguerite (ed.), *La geste de Robert Guiscard: Guillaume de Pouille*, Palermo, Istituto Siciliano di Studi Bizantini e Neoellenici, 1961, p. 251

cxxiii Norwich, 1967, p. 243

cxxiv Mathieu, p. 253

cxxv Douglas, Norman, *Old Calabria*, London, Picador, 1994, p. 56

cxxvi Cioffari, P. Gerardo, *Saint Nicholas*, Bari, Centro Studi Nicolaiani, 1994, p. 55

cxxvii Ibid. p. 58

cxxviii Ibid. p. 60

cxxix Ibid. p. 64

cxxx Shiels, W. J., (ed.), *Monks, Hermits and the Ascetic Tradition*, Oxford, Basil Blackwell, 1985, p. 87

cxxxi Bloch, Marc, *La Société Féodale:la formation des liens de dépendance*, Paris, 1949, p. 62

cxxxii Sewter, p. 66

cxxxiii Brooke, p. 305

cxxxiv Ibid. p. 138

cxxxv Deuve, Jean, *L'épopée des Normands d'Italie*, Conde-sur-Noireau, Charles Colet Éditions, 1995, p. 54

cxxxvi Sewter, p. 147

cxxxvii Ibid. p. 148

cxxxviii Ibid. p. 149

cxxxix Ibid. p. 150

cxl Ibid. p. 171

cxli Ibid.

cxlii Ibid. p. 188

cxliii Heon, E., *Les Normands d'Italie: Robert Guiscard*, Coutances, 1866, p. 27

cxliv Pettifer, James, *Blue Guide: Albania*, London, A&C Black, 1996, pp. 83–4

cxlv Praschniker, Camillo, *Muzakhia und Malakastra*, Vienna, Archeologische Untersuchungen in Mittelalbanien, 1920, p. 136

PART THREE

i Sewter, p. 308

ii Ibid.

iii Riley-Smith, Jonathan, *The First Crusade and the Idea of Crusading*, London, Athlone Press, 1986, p. 36

iv Riley-Smith, Jonathan, *The First Crusades 1095–1131*, Cambridge, Cambridge University Press, 1997, p. 70

v Krey, August (ed.), *The First Crusade*, Princeton, Princeton University Press, 1926, p. 46

vi Ibid. p. 41

vii Evans, Joan, *Life in Medieval France*, London, Phaidon Press, 1925, p. 83

viii Sewter, p. 312

ix Riley-Smith, p. 81

x Krey, p. 62

xi Sewter, p. 317

xii Morris, Rosemary, *Monks and Laymen in Byzantium, 843–1118*, Cambridge, Cambridge University Press 1995, p. 271

xiii Chazan, Robert, *European Jewry and the First Crusade*, Berkeley, University of California Press, 1987, p. 57

xiv Ibid.

xv Ibid. p. 102

xvi Ibid. p. 69

xvii Ibid. p. 107

xviii Ibid. p. 112

xix Ibid. p. 107

xx Krey, p. 52

xxi Nehama, J., *Histoire des Israélites de Salonique*, Vol. I, Salonica (Thessaloniki), Librairie Molho, 1935, p. 79

xxii Communauté Israelite de Thessalonique, *In Memoriam: Homage aux victimes juives des Nazis en Grèce*, Thessaloniki, 1988, pp. 253–4

xxiii Matkovski, Alexander, *A History of the Jews in Macedonia*, Skopje, Macedonian Review Editions, 1982, p. 186

xxiv Ibid.

xxv *Kathimerini*, April 13–16, 2001

xxvi Sewter, p. 315

xxvii Ibid. p. 320

xxviii Ibid.

xxix Ibid. p. 325

xxx Ibid. p. 326

xxxi Ibid. p. 149

xxxii Ibid. p. 327

xxxiii Ibid.

xxxiv Ibid.

xxxv Ibid. p. 328

xxxvi Ibid.p. 329

xxxvii Ibid.p. 330

xxxviii Runciman, Steven, *A History of the Crusades: 1. The First Crusade and the Foundation of the Kingdom of Jerusalem*, London, Penguin, 1951, p. 168

xxxix Krey, p. 100

xl Dudley, L. H. (ed.), *Custom Is King: Essays Presented to R. R. Marett*, London, Hutchinson's, 1936

xli Blondal, Sigfus, *The Varangians of Byzantium*, Cambridge, Cambridge University Press, 1978, p. 207

xlii Obolensky, Dimitri, *The Byzantine Commonwealth: Eastern Europe, 500–1453*, New York, St Vladimir's Seminary Press, 1974, pp. 304–5

xliii Sewter, E. R. A., (tr.), *Fourteen Byzantine Rulers: The Chronographia of Michael Psellus*, London, Penguin, 1966, p. 65

xliv Ibid. p. 76

xlv Ibid. p. 81

xlvi Ibid. p. 107

xlvii Ibid. p. 155

xlviii Ibid. p. 157

xlix Ibid. p. 186

l Ibid. p. 158

li Ibid. p. 221

lii Ibid. p. 186

liii Grocock, C. W., and Siberry, E. (tr., ed.), *De Via Hierosolymitana of Gilo of Paris*, Oxford, Clavendon Press, 1997, p. 71

liv Ibid.

lv Ibid.

lvi Ibid. p. 79

lvii Levine, Robert, (tr.), *Guibert de Nogent: The Deeds of God through the Franks*, Woodbridge, The Boydell Press, 1997, p. 64

lviii Krey, p. 111

lix Ibid. p. 109

lx Maalouf, Amin, *The Crusades through Arab Eyes*, New York, Schocken Books, 1984, p. 16

lxi Ibid.

lxii Sewter, p. 341

lxiii Krey, p. 119

lxiv Ibid. p. 36

lxv Riley-Smith, 1986, p. 91

lxvi Daniel, Norman, *The Arabs and Medieval Europe*, London, Longman, 1975, p. 119

lxvii Gabrieli, Francesco,(tr., ed.), *Arab Historians on the Crusades*, New York, Dorset Press, 1989, p. 5

lxviii Maalouf, p. 21

lxix Krey, p. 156

lxx Ibid. p. 131

lxxi Ibid.

lxxii Cohn, Norman, *The Pursuit of the Millennium: Revolutionary Millenarians and Mystical Anarchists of the Middle Ages*, London, Pimlico, 1993, p. 66

lxxiii Ibid. p. 66

lxxiv Ibid. p. 67

lxxv Acts 11:26

lxxvi Krey, p. 157

lxxvii Levine, p. 90

lxxviii Ibid.

lxxix Ibid. p. 91

lxxx Ibid.

lxxxi Ibid.

lxxxii Ibid. p. 92

lxxxiii Maalouf, p. 32

lxxxiv Levine, p. 93

lxxxv Krey, p. 160

lxxxvi John 21:4–8

lxxxvii Krey, p. 171

lxxxviii Levine, p. 109

lxxxix Krey, p. 239

xc Levine, p. 108

xci Ibid. p. 109

xcii Ibid.

xciii Robinson, I. S., *The Papacy 1073–1198: Continuity and Innovation*, Cambridge, Cambridge University Press, 1990, p. 333

xciv Papadakis, Aristeides, *The Christian East and the Rise of the Papacy*, Crestwood, New York, St Vladimir's Seminary Press, 1994, p. 92

xcv Maalouf, p. 37

xcvi Ibid. p. 39

xcvii Ibid. p. 40

xcviii Ibid. p. 39

xcix Ibid. pp. 40–1

c Ibid. p. 270

ci Beattie, Andrew and Pepper, Timothy, *Syria: The Rough Guide*, London, The Rough Guides, 1998, p. 154

cii Krey, p. 241

ciii Ibid.

civ Kreutz, Andrej, *Vatican Policy on the Palestinian-Israeli Conflict: The Struggle for the Holy Land*, New York, Greenwood Press, 1990, p. 30

cv Randal, Jonathan, *The Tragedy of Lebanon: Christian Warlords, Israeli Adventurers and American Bunglers*, London, Chatto & Windus, 1983, p. 41

cvi Segev, Tom, *One Palestine Complete: Jews and Arabs under the British Mandate*, London, Abacus, 2001, p. 36

cvii Tuchman, Barbara, *The Bible and the Sword*, New York, Ballantine Press, 1984, p. 316

cviii Ibid. p. 40

cix Segev, p. 45

cx Tuchman, p. 339

cxi Chibnall, Marjorie (tr., ed.), *The Ecclesiastical History of Orderic Vitalis*, Vol. III, Oxford, Clarendon Press, 1969, p. 71

cxii Ibid. p. 73

cxiii Ibid.

cxiv Carmel, Alex, 'Between the Mountain and the Sea', Haifa City Museum, 2000

cxv Farah, Toufee, *The Arab-Israeli Conflict*, Woodbridge, New Jersey, Ken & Scatter Publications, 1998

cxvi Holam, Kenneth and Hohlfelder, Robert, *King Herod's Dream*, New York, W.W. Norton & Co., 1988–90, p. 218

cxvii Daniel, Norman, *The Arabs and Medieval Europe*, London, Longman, 1975, p. 135

cxviii Lampert of Hersfeld, pp. 97–103

cxix Ibid.

cxx Ibid.

cxxi Ibid.

cxxii Ibid.

cxxiii Finley, John, *A Pilgrim in Palestine after its Deliverance*, London, Chapman & Hall, 1919, p. 29

cxxiv Gilbert, Vivian, *The Romance of the Last Crusade: with Allenby to Jerusalem*, New York, William B. Feakins Inc., 1923, p. 129

cxxv Ibid. p. 127

cxxvi Peters, F. E. *Jerusalem: the Holy City in the Eyes of Chroniclers, Visitors, Pilgrims and Prophets from the days of Abraham to the Beginnings of Modern Times*, Princeton, University of Princeton, 1985, p. 284

cxxvii Gabrieli, p. 11

cxxviii Daniel, p. 135

cxxix Peters, p. 285

cxxx   Benvenisti, Meron, *The Crusades in the Holy Land*, Jerusalem, Israel
        Universities Press, 1970, p. 38
cxxxi   Baldi, Paschal, *The Question of the Holy Places*, Jerusalem, Franciscan Press,
        1955, p. 90
cxxxii Ibid. p. 98
cxxxiv *Jerusalem Post*, 1 June 2001, Interview with Natan Sharansky

BIBLIOGRAPHY

Adalsteinsson, Jon Hnefill, *Under the Cloak*, Uppsala, Sweden, Almqvist & Wiksell
    International, 1978
Allibone, Finch, *In Pursuit of the Robber Baron*, Luton, Lennard Publishing, 1988
Althoff, Gert, *Otto III*, Darmstadt, Primus Verlag, 1997
Armstrong, Karen, *Holy War*, London, Macmillan, 1988
Arnold, Benjamin, *Medieval Germany, 500–1300: A Political Interpretation*, London,
    Macmillan, 1997
Arquillière, H. X., *Saint Grégoire VII: Essai sur sa conception du pouvoir pontifical*,
    Paris, 1934
Attwater, Donald, *Saints of the East*, London, Harvill Press, 1963
Auden, W.H. and MacNeice, Louis, *Letters from Iceland*, London, Faber & Faber,
    1937
Avagliano, Faustino, *L'eta dell'abate Desiderio III: I Storia Arte e Cultura*, Montecassino,
    1992
Barber, Richard, *The Knight and Chivalry*, London, Longman, 1970
– *The Penguin Guide to Medieval Europe*, London, Penguin, 1984
Barraclough, Geoffrey, *The Medieval Papacy*, London, Thames & Hudson, 1968
– *The crucible of Europe: the ninth and tenth Centuries in European history*, London,
    Thames & Hudson 1976
– (ed.), *Eastern and Western Europe in the Middle Ages*, London, Thames & Hudson,
    1970
Bartlett, Robert, *The Making of Europe: Conquest, Colonization and Cultural Change
    950–1350*, London, Penguin, 1993
Beckwith, John, *Early Medieval Art: Carolingian, Ottonian, Romanesque*, London,
    Thames & Hudson, 1964
Benedikt, S. Benedikz, *The Varangians of Byzantium: An Aspect of Byzantine Military
    History*, tr., ed. Sigfus Blondal, Cambridge, Cambridge University Press, 1978
Benvenisti, Meron, *The Crusades in the Holy Land*, Jerusalem, Israel Universities
    Press, 1970
Bernhardt, John W., *Itinerant Kingship and Royal Monasteries in Early Medieval
    Germany*, Cambridge University Press, Cambridge, 1993

Birch, Debra, *Pilgrimage to Rome in the Middle Ages: Continuity and Change*, Woodbridge, The Boydell Press, 1998

Blazynski, George, *John Paul II: A Man from Krakow*, London, Weidenfeld & Nicolson, 1979

Bloch, Herbert, *Monte Cassino in the Middle Ages*, Vol. I, Rome, Edizione di Storia e Letteratura, 1986

Bloch, Marc, *Feudal Society*, London, Routledge & Kegan Paul, 1961

Bohner, J.F., *Regesta Imperii: Die Regesten des Kaiserreiches 980(983)–1000*, Koln BohlansNachf./Gratz, 1956

Bolgar, R.R., *The Classical Heritage and its Beneficiaries*, Cambridge, Cambridge University Press, 1954

Brico, Rex, *Taizé: Brother Roger and his Community*, London, Collins, 1978

Brinkley, Douglas and Hackett, Clifford (eds.), *Jean Monnet: The Path to European Unity*, London, Macmillan, 1991

Brittain Bouchard, Constance, *Sword, Miter and Cloister: Nobility and the Church in Burgundy 980–1198*, Ithaca, Cornell University Press, 1987

Brooke, Christopher, *Europe in the Central Middle Ages 962–1154*, London, Longman, 2000

Brooke, Rosalind and Christopher, *Popular Religion in the Middle Ages: Western Europe 1000–1300*, London, Thames & Hudson, 1984

Bunemann, Richard, *Robert Guiskard: Ein Normanne Erobert Suditalien 1015–1085*, Koln, Bohlau Verlag, 1995

Burman, Edward, *From Emperor to Emperor: Italy before the Renaissance*, London, Constable, 1991

Bury, J. (ed.), *Cambridge Medieval History*, Vol. III, Cambridge, Cambridge University Press, 1922

Byock, Jesse L., *Medieval Iceland: Society, Sagas, and Power*, Berkeley, University of California Press, 1988

Carucci, Arturo, *San Gregorio VII e Salerno*, Naples, Istituto Anselmi, 1984

Champillon-Figeac, M. (tr.), *La Chronique de Robert Viscart, par Aimé, moine de Mont Cassin*, Paris, Jules Renouard, 1835

Chazan, Robert, *European Jewry and the First Crusade*, Berkeley, University of California Press, Berkeley, 1987

– *In the year 1096: The First Crusade and the Jews*, Philadelphia, The Jewish Publication Society, 1996

Chibnall, Majorie (tr., ed.), *The Ecclesiastical History of Orderic Vitalis*, Vol. III, Oxford, Clarendon Press, 1969

Clément, Olivier, *Taize: A Meaning to Life*, Chicago, GIA Publications Inc., 1997

Cohn, Norman, *The Pursuit of the Millennium: Revolutionary Millenarians and Mystical Anarchists of the Middle Ages*, London, Pimlico, 1993

Congar, Cardinal Yves, *Église et papauté*, Paris, Les Éditions du Cerf, 1994

Cornwell, John, *Hitler's Pope: the Secret History of Pius XII*, London, Penguin, 1999

Cotterill, H. B., *Medieval Italy during 1000 years (305–1313)*, London, George G. Harrap & Co., 1915

Cowdrey, H. E. J., *The Cluniacs and Gregorian Reform*, Oxford, Clarendon Press, 1970

– *Popes, Monks and Crusaders*, London, Hambledon, 1984

- *The Crusades and Latin Monasticism*, Aldershot, Variorum Press, 1999
- *Pope Gregory VII 1073–1085*, Oxford, Clarendon Press, 1998
- *The Age of Abbot Desiderius*, Oxford, Clarendon Press, 1983
Daniel-Rops, H., *The Church in the Dark Ages*, London, J. M. Dent & Sons Ltd, 1959
- *Cathedral and Crusade*, London, J. M. Dent & Sons Ltd, 1957
Dasent, George Webbe, *The Story of Burnt Njal*, Edinburgh, 1861
Davids, Adelbert (ed.), *The Empress Theophano: Byzantium and the West at the turn of the First Millennium*, Cambridge, Cambridge University Press, 1995
Davies, J.G., *Pilgrimage Yesterday and Today: Why? Where? How?* London, SCM Press, 1988
Davies, Norman, *Europe: A History*, Oxford, Oxford University Press, 1996
Davis, R. H. C., *The Normans and their Myth*, Thames & Hudson, London, 1976
- *A History of Medieval Europe: from Constantine to St Louis*, London, Longman, Green & Co., 1957
de Nilinse, Baron, *Odilo: La vie de Sainte Adelaide Impératrice*, Paris, Societé de Saint Victor, 1847
Deuve, Jean, *L'épopée des Normands d'Italie*, Conde-sur-Noireau, Charles Colet Éditions, 1995
Douglas, David, *The Norman Achievement*, London, Collins/Fontana, 1972
Duby, Georges, *The Age of Cathedrals: Art and Society 980–1420*, London, Croom Helm, 1981
- *L'an mil: Europe au Moyen Age*, Paris, Flammarion, 1984
- *The Three Orders: Feudal Society Imagined*, Chicago, University of Chicago Press, 1980
Duchêne, Francois, *Jean Monnet: the First Statesman of Interdependence*, New York, W. W. Norton & Co., 1994
Duffy, Eamonn, *Saints and Sinners: A History of the Popes*, New Haven, Yale University Press, 1997
Dvornik, Francis, *The Kiev State and its Relations with Western Europe*, Transactions of the Royal Historical Society, 4th series, Vol. XXIX, 1947
- *The Making of Central and Eastern Europe*, London, The Polish London, 1949
- *Byzance et la primauté Romaine*, Paris, Les Éditions du Cerf, 1964
Eco, Umberto, *Art and Beauty in the Middle Ages*, New Haven, Yale University Press, 1986
Edwards, W. A., *Medieval Scrap-heap*, London, Rivingtons, 1930
Erdmann, Carl, *The Origin of the Idea of Crusade*, Princeton, Princeton University Press, 1977
Evans, Joan, *Monastic Life at Cluny 910–1157*, London, Oxford University Press, 1931
- *Life in Medieval France*, London, Phaidon Press, 1925
Eyck, Frank, *Religion and Politics in German History: from the beginnings to the French Revolution*, London, Macmillan, 1998
Farrugia, Edward and Gargano, Innocenzo (eds.), *Every Monastery is a Mission*, Verruchio, Pazzini Editore, 1999
Fleckenstein, Josef, *Early Medieval Germany*, Amsterdam, North Holland Publishing Company, 1978

Fletcher, Richard, *The Conversion of Europe: From Paganism to Christianity*, London, HarperCollins, 1997

France, John (tr., ed.), *Rodolfus Glaber: The Five Books of the Histories*, Oxford, Clarendon Press, 1989

Frey, August C. (ed.), *The First Crusade:the Accounts of Eye-witnesses and Participants*, Princeton, Princeton University Press, 1921

Fuhrmann, Horst, *Germany in the High Middle Ages c. 1050–1200*, Cambridge, Cambridge University Press, 1986

Fuller, John G., *The Day of St Anthony's Fire*, London, Hutchinson, 1969

Gabrieli, Francesco (tr., ed.), *Arab Historians on the Crusades*, New York, Dorset Press, 1989

Gatto, Ludovico, *Storia di Roma nel Medioevo*, Rome, Newton & Compton Editori, 1999

Geary, Patrick, *Furta Sacra*, Princeton, University of Princeton Press, 1978

Gelsinger, Bruce E., *Icelandic enterprise: commerce and economy in the Middle Ages*, Columbia, South Carolina, University of South Carolina Press, 1981

Gilchrist, John, *Canon Law in the Age of Reform, 11th-12th Centuries*, Aldershot, Variorum Press, 1993

Giovannini, A., Golinelli, P. and Piva P., *L'abbazia di San Benedetto Po*, Verona, Cierre Edizioni, 1997

Gislason, Gylf, *The Problem of Being an Icelander: Past, Present and Future*, Reykjavik, 1973

Gjerset, Knut, *History of Iceland*, London, George Allen & Unwin Ltd, 1922

Grindea, Meron (ed.), *Jerusalem: The Holy City in Literature*, London, Kahn & Averill, 1981

Gilbert, Major Vivian, *The Romance of the Last Crusade: with Allenby to Jerusalem*, New York, William B. Feakin Inc., 1923

Giscard d'Estaing, Valéry, *Jean Monnet*, Fondation Jean Monnet pour l'Europe Centre de Recherches Européennes, Lausanne, 1989

Guldencrone, Baronne Diane de, *L'Italie Byzantine: étude sur le haut moyen-âge (400–1050)*, Paris, Ernest Leroux, 1914

Graham-Campbell, James, *The Viking World*, London, Weidenfeld & Nicolson, 1989

Gurevich, A. J., *Categories of Medieval Culture*, London, Routledge, Kegan & Paul, 1985

Halecki, Oscar, *Millennium of Europe*, Notre Dame, Indiana, University of Notre Dame Press, 1963

Hapgood, David and Richardson, David, *Monte Cassino*, London, Angus & Robertson Publishers, 1984.

Hastrup, Kirsten, *Culture and History in Medieval Iceland: An anthropological analysis of structure and change*, Oxford, Clarendon Press, 1985

Hay, Denys, *Europe: the Emergence of an Idea*, New York, Harper Row, 1957

Hayward, Fernand, *History of the Popes*, New York, E. P. Dutton & Co. Inc., 1931

Head, Thomas and Landes, Richard, (eds.), *The Peace of God: Social Violence and Religious Response in France around the Year 1000*, Ithaca and London, Cornell University Press, 1992

Hebblethwaite, Peter, *The Next Pope: History in the Making*, London, HarperCollins, 2000

Heer, Friedrich, *The Intellectual History of Europe*, London, Weidenfeld & Nicolson, 1966

– *The Holy Roman Empire*, London, Weidenfeld & Nicolson, 1968

– *God's First Love: Christians and Jews over Two Thousand Years*, London, Weidenfeld & Nicolson, 1970

Heon, E., *Les Normands d'Italie: Robert Guiscard*, Coutances, 1866

Hertzstein, Robert E. (ed.), *The Holy Roman Empire in the Middle Ages: Universal State or German Catastrophe*, Boston, D. C. Heath and Company, 1966

Hetherington, Paul, *Medieval Rome: a Portrait of the City and its Life*, London, The Rubicon Press, 1994

Heverkamp, Alfred, *Medieval Germany 1056–1273*, Oxford, Oxford University Press, 1988

Hollander, Lee M., *The Skalds*, Princeton, Princeton University Press, 1945

Hood, John C. F., *Icelandic Church Saga*, London, Society for Promoting Christian Knowledge, London, 1946

Holmes, George (ed.), *The Oxford Illustrated History of Medieval Europe*, Oxford, Oxford University Press, 1988

Honan, William H., *Treasure Hunt: A New York Times Reporter Tracks the Quedlinburg Hoard*, New York, Forum International Publishing Corp., 1997

Hreinsson, Vithar (ed.), *The Complete Sagas of Icelanders*, Vols. 1–5, Reykjavik, Leifur Eriksson, 1997

Huddy, Mary E., *Matilda, Countess of Tuscany*, London, John Long, 1905

Hunt, Noreen, *Cluny under St Hugh 1049–1109*, London, Edward Arnold Publishers Ltd, 1967

– (ed.), *Cluniac Monasticism in the Central Middle Ages*, London, Macmillan, 1971

James, Harold, *A German Identity: 1770 to the Present Day*, London, Phoenix Press, 2000

Jockle, Clemens, *Encyclopedia of Saints*, London, Parkgate Books, 1997

John Paul II, His Holiness, *Crossing the Threshold of Hope*, London, Jonathan Cape, 1994,

Jones, Gwyn, *The Vikings*, Oxford, Oxford University Press, 1968

Joranson, E., 'The Great German Pilgrimage of 1064–65', *The Crusades and Other Historical Essays*, L.J. Paetow (ed.), New York, F.S. Crofts & Co., 1928

Karlsson, Gunnar, *Iceland's 1100 Years: History of a Marginal Society*, London, Hurst & Company, 2000

Kedar, Benjamin Z., *Crusade and Mission: European Approaches towards the Moslems*, Princeton, Princeton University Press, 1984

Keen, Maurice, *The Pelican History of Medieval Europe*, London, Penguin, 1969

Kloczowski, Jerzy, *A History of Polish Christianity*, Cambridge, Cambridge University Press, 2000

Knowles, David, *The Evolution of Medieval Thought*, London, Longman, 1962

Knowles, David and Obolensky, Dmitri, *The Christian Centuries, Vol.2 The Middle Ages*, London, Darton, Longman & Todd, 1969

Küng, Hans, *Christianity: its Essence and History*, London, SCM Press Ltd, 1995

– *The Catholic Church: A Short History*, London, Weidenfeld & Nicolson, 2001

Lacey, Robert and Danziger, Danny, *The Year 1000*, London, Little, Brown, 1999

Lacroix, Paul, *Religion and Military Life in the Middle Ages and in the period of the Renaissance*, London, 1874

Lampe, Karl, *Germany under the Salian and Hohenstaufen Emperors*, Oxford, Basil Blackwell, 1973

Lapidge, Michael (ed.), *The Blackwell Encyclopedia of Anglo-Saxon England*, Oxford, Blackwell, 1999

Lattin, Harriet Pratt (tr.), *The Letters of Gerbert with his papal privileges as Sylvester II*, New York, Columbia University Press, 1961

Lawrence, C. H., *Medieval Monasticism: Forms of Religious Life in Western Europe in the Middle Ages*, London, Longman, 1984

Laxness, Halldor, *Under the Glacier*, tr. Magnus Magnusson, Reykjavik, Vaka-Helgafell hf., 1999

Leclercq, J., *Saint Pierre Damien Hermite*, Rome, Editori di Storia e Letteratura, 1960

Leclercq, J., Vandenbroucke F. and Bouyer, L., *The Spirituality of the Middle Ages*, London, Burns & Oates, 1968

Leighton, Albert C., *Transport and Communication in Early Medieval Europe*: AD 500–1100, Devon, David & Charles, 1972

Lejeune, René, *Robert Schuman: père de l'Europe, 1886–1963*, Paris, Fayard, 2000

Lemp, Michel de and Laslier, Roger, *Trésors de la Bibliotheque Municipale de Reims*, Reims, 1978

Levine, Robert (tr.), *Guibert de Nogent: The Deeds of God through the Franks*, Woodbridge, The Boydell Press, 1997

Leyser, Karl, *The Ascent of Latin Europe: An Inaugural Lecture Given before the University of Oxford*, Oxford, Clarendon Press, 1986

– *Communications and Power in Medieval Europe: The Gregorian Revolution and Beyond*, London, The Hambledon Press, 1994

– *Rule and Conflict in Early Medieval Society: Ottonian Saxony*, London, Edward Arnold, 1979

Leyser, Henrietta, *Hermits and the New Monasticism: A Study of Religious Communities in Western Europe 1000–1150*, London, Macmillan, 1984

Ludlow, James M., *The Age of the Crusades*, New York, The Christian Literature Company, 1896

Maalouf, Amin, *The Crusades through Arab Eyes*, New York, Schocken Books, 1984

MacCulloch, J.A., *Medieval Faith and Fable*, London, George G. Harrap & Co. Ltd, 1932

MacDonald, A.J., *Hildebrand: A Life of Gregory VII*, London, Methuen & Co., 1932

McGuire, Patrick, *Friendship and Community: the Monastic Experience 350–1250*, Cistercian Publications Inc., Kalamazoo, Michigan, 1988

McNulty, Patricia (tr., ed.), *St Peter Damian: Selected Writings on the Spiritual Life*, London, Faber & Faber, 1959

Magnusson, Magnus, *Iceland Saga*, London, The Bodley Head, 1987

Man, John, *Atlas of the year 1000*, London, Penguin, 1999

Martin, l'Abbé Eug., *Saint Leon IX 1002–1054*, Paris, Librairie Victor Lecoffre, 1904

Martindale, C., *The Household of God*, London, Burns Oates & Washbourne, 1935

Mathew, Arnold Harris, *The Life and Times of Hildebrand, Pope Gregory VII*, London, Francis Griffiths, 1910

Mathieu, Marguerite (ed.), *La geste de Robert Guiscard, Guillaume de Pouille*, Palermo, Instituto Siciliano di Studi Bizantino e Neoellenici, 1961

Matkovski, Alexander, *A History of the Jews in Macedonia*, Skopje, Macedonian Review Editions, 1982

Matus, Thomas, *The Mystery of Romuald and the Five Brothers: Stories from the Benedictines and Camaldolese*, Wheathampstead, Anthony Clarke Publishers, 1994

Mayr-Harting, Henry, *Ottonian Book Illumination*, London, Harvey Miller Publishers, 1991

Mazower, Mark, *Hitler's Greece*, New Haven, Yale University Press, 1993

Meie, Hans-Jürgen, *Weltkulturerbe Quedlinburg*, Goslar, Studio Volker Schadach, 1998

Ménager, L.R., *Les fondations monastiques de Robert Guiscard, Duc de Pouille et de Calabre*, Tubingen, Quellen und Forschingen aus Italienischen Archiven und Bibliotheken, band 39, Max Niemayer Verlag, 1959

Mills, Ludo J. R., *Angelic Monks and Earthly Men: Monasticism and its Meaning to Medieval Society*, Woodbridge, The Boydell Press, 1992

Monnet, Jean, *Memoirs*, Richard Mayne (tr.), London, Collins, 1978

Moore, R.I., *The Origins of European Dissent*, Toronto, University of Toronto Press, 1994

– *The First European Revolution*, Oxford, Basil Blackwell, 2000

Morrall, John B., *The Medieval Imprint*, London, A. C. Watts & Co., 1967

Morris, Colin, *The Papal Monarchy: the Western Church from 1050 to 1250*, Oxford, Clarendon Press, 1989

Morton, H. V., *A Traveller in Southern Italy*, London, Methuen, 1983

Nehama, J., *Histoire des Israelites de Salonique: La communauté Romaniote – les Sefardis et leur dispersion*, Salonica, (Thessaloniki), Librairie Molho, 1935.

Newton, Francis, *The Scriptorium and Library of Montecassino, 1058–1105*, Cambridge, Cambridge University Press, 1999

Nineham, Dennis, *Christianity Medieval and Modern: A Study in Religious Change*, London, SCM Press Ltd, 1993

Norwich, John Julius, *The Normans in the South 1016–1130*, Harlow, Longman, 1967

– *Byzantium: The Apogee*, London, Penguin, 1993

Oakley, Francis, *The Crucial Centuries: The Medieval Experience*, London, Terra Nova Editions, 1979

Oldenberg, Zoe, *The Crusades*, London, Weidenfeld & Nicolson, 1998

Olleris, A., *Vie de Gerbert: premier pape francais sous le nom de Silvestre II*, Clermont-Ferrand, 1867

Oppenheimer, Sir Francis, *Frankish Themes and Problems*, London, Faber & Faber, 1952

Papadakis, Aristeides, *The Christian East and the Rise of the Papacy*, Crestwood, New York, St Vladimir's Seminary Press, 1994.

Pardoe, Rosemary and Darroll, *The Female Pope: The Mystery of Pope Joan*, Wellingborough, Crucible, 1988

Pellus, Daniel, *Reims: a travers ses rues, places et monuments*, Roanne, Éditions Horvath, 1983

Pertz, Georgius Heinricius, *Scriptores Rerum Germanicarum*, Hanover, Impensis Bibliopolii Hahniani, 1865

Peters, F. E., *Jerusalem: the Holy City in the Eyes of Chroniclers, Visitors, Pilgrims and Prophets from the Days of Abraham to the Beginnings of Modern Times*, Princeton, Princeton University Press, 1985

Phillips, Jonathan (ed.), *The First Crusade: Origins and Impact*, Manchester, Manchester University Press, 1997

Pognon, Edmond (ed.), *L'an mil*, Paris, Gallimard, 1947

Powell, John, (ed.), *Chronology of European History*, Vol. 1, Chicago, Fitzroy Dearborn Publishers, 1997

Pulsiano, Phillip (ed.), *Medieval Scandinavia: an Encyclopedia*, New York, Garland Publishing Inc., 1993

Ranke-Heinemann, Uta, *Eunuchs for Heaven: The Catholic Church and Sexuality*, London, Andre Deutsch, 1988

Reuter, Timothy, *Germany in the Early Middle Ages, c.800–1056*, London, Longman, 1991

Riant, Paul, *Expéditions et pèlerinages des Scandinaves en Terre Sainte au temps des Croisades*, Paris, 1865–9

Riche, Pierre, *Gerbert d'Aurillac: Le pape de l'an mil*, Paris, Fayard 1987

Rietbergen, Peter, *Europe: A Cultural History*, London, Routledge, 1998

Robinson, I. S., *Authority and Resistance in the Investiture Contest*, Manchester, Manchester University Press, 1978

– *The Papacy, 1073–1198: Continuity and Innovation*, Cambridge, Cambridge University Press, 1990

Rochemaure, Duc de la Salle de, *Gerbert Silvestre II: le savant, le faiseur de rois, le pontife*, Rome, Imprimerie Editrice Romana, 1914

Rosenwein, Barbara H., *Rhinoceros Bound: Cluny in the Tenth Century*, Pennsylvania, University of Pennsylvania Press, 1982

Riley-Smith, Jonathan, *The First Crusade and the Idea of Crusading*, London, Athlone Press, 1986

– *The First Crusade, 1095–1131*, Cambridge, Cambridge University Press, 1997

– *The Oxford History of the Crusades*, Oxford, Oxford University Press, 1999

Riley-Smith, Louise and Jonathan, *The Crusades: Idea and Reality 1095–1274*, London, Edward Arnold, 1981

Runciman, Steven, *A History of the Crusades:1. The First Crusade and the Foundation of the Kingdom of Jerusalem*, London, Penguin, 1991

– *The Eastern Schism*, Oxford, Clarendon Press, 1955

Russell, Frederick H., *The Just War in the Middle Ages*, Cambridge, Cambridge University Press, 1975

Santunione, Giovanni, *Inseguendo un mito Matilde di Canossa*, Modena, Edizioni Il Fiorino, 1996

Sawyer, Peter and Birgit, *Medieval Scandinavia: from Conversion to Reformation*, Minneapolis, University of Minnesota Press, 1993

Scherman, Katharine, *Iceland: Daughter of Fire*, London, Gollancz, 1976

Scott, Martin, Medieval Europe, London, Longman, 1964

Setton, K. M. (ed.), A History of the Crusades, Philadelphia, University of Pennsylvania Press, 1955

Sharpe, Revd John (tr.), The History of the Kings of England by William of Malmesbury, London, Longman, 1815

Shepherd, Naomi, The Zealous Intruders: The Western Rediscovery of Palestine, London, Collins, 1987

Shiels, W. J. (ed.), The Church and War, Oxford, Basil Blackwell, 1983

– Monks, Hermits and the Ascetic Tradition, Oxford, Basil Blackwell, 1985

Short, Ernest, A History of Religious Architecture, New York, Norton & Company Inc., 1936

Smith, L. M., Cluny in the Eleventh and Twelfth Centuries, London, Philip Allan & Co. Ltd, 1930

Snigiel, Kazimierz, U Grobu Swietego Wojciecha, Gniezno, Tum, 1997

Southern, R. W., Western Views of Islam in the Middle Ages, Cambridge, Massachusetts, Harvard University Press, 1962

– The Making of the Middle Ages, London, Pimlico, 1993

– Western Society and the Church in the Middle Ages, London, Pelican, 1970

– Medieval Humanism and Other Studies, Oxford, Basil Blackwell, 1970

Sox, David, Relics and Shrines, London, George Allen & Unwin, 1985

Spink, Kathryn, A Universal Heart: The Life and Vision of Brother Roger of Taize, London, Society for the Promotion of Christian Knowledge, 1986

St John, Christopher, A Little Book of Polish Saints, London, Burns & Oates Ltd, 1910

Stourton, Edward, Absolute Truth: the Catholic Church in the World Today, London, Viking, 1998

Strömbäck, Dag, The Conversion of Iceland: A Survey, London, University College, 1997

Sumption, Jonathan, Pilgrimage: An Image of Medieval Religion, London, Faber, 1975

Taylor, Henry Osborn, The Medieval Mind, London, Macmillan & Co. Ltd, 1925

Tellenbach, Gerd, Church, State and Christian Society at the Time of the Investiture Contest, Oxford, Basil Blackwell, 1948

Trystram, Florence, Le coq et la louve: Gerbert et l'an mil, Paris, Flammarion, 1982

Tschan, Francis J., History of the Archbishops of Hamburg-Bremen, New York, Columbia University Press, 1959

Tyler, J. E., The Alpine Passes: the Middle Ages 962–1250, Oxford, Basil Blackwell, 1930

Uniker-Sebeok, Jean and Sebeok, Thomas A., Monastic Sign Languages, Berlin, Monton de Gruyter, 1987

Villari, Pasquale, Medieval Italy: from Charlemagne to Henry VII, London, T. Fisher Unwin, 1910

Vingtain, Dominique, L'Abbaye de Cluny: centre de l'Occident médieval, Paris, Éditions de patrimoine, 1998

Wagner, David L. (ed.), The Seven Liberal Arts in the Middle Ages, Bloomington, Indiana University Press, 1983

Watt, W. Montgomery, *The Influence of Islam on Medieval Europe*, Edinburgh, Edinburgh University Press, 1972

Weinfurter, Stefan, *The Salian Century: Main Currents in an Age of Transition*, Philadelphia, University of Pennsylvania Press, 1999

Whitney, J. P., *Hildebrandine Essays*, Cambridge, Cambridge University Press, 1932

Willey, David, *God's Politician*, London, Faber & Faber, 1993

Wills, Garry, *Papal Sin: Structures of Deceit*, New York, Doubleday, 2000

Wright, Thomas, *Early Travels in Palestine*, London, Henry G. Bohn, 1868

Yewdale, Ralph Bailey, *Bohemond I: Prince of Antioch*, Princeton, Princeton University Press, 1924

Zamoyski, Adam, *The Polish Way: A Thousand Year History of the Poles and their Culture*, London, John Murray, 1987

INDEX

451

Europe in
the year 1000